Open Source for Knowledge and Learning Management: Strategies Beyond Tools

Miltiadis Lytras
University of Patras, Greece

Ambjörn Naeve
KMR Group, Royal Institute of Technology, Sweden

IDEA GROUP PUBLISHING
Hershey • London • Melbourne • Singapore

Acquisition Editor:	Kristin Klinger
Senior Managing Editor:	Jennifer Neidig
Managing Editor:	Sara Reed
Assistant Managing Editor:	Sharon Berger
Development Editor:	Kristin Roth
Copy Editor:	Angela Thor
Typesetter:	Michael Brehm
Cover Design:	Lisa Tosheff
Printed at:	Integrated Book Technology

Published in the United States of America by
Idea Group Publishing (an imprint of Idea Group Inc.)
701 E. Chocolate Avenue
Hershey PA 17033
Tel: 717-533-8845
Fax: 717-533-8661
E-mail: cust@idea-group.com
Web site: http://www.idea-group.com

and in the United Kingdom by
Idea Group Publishing (an imprint of Idea Group Inc.)
3 Henrietta Street
Covent Garden
London WC2E 8LU
Tel: 44 20 7240 0856
Fax: 44 20 7379 0609
Web site: http://www.eurospanonline.com

Library of Congress Cataloging-in-Publication Data

Open source for knowledge and learning management : strategies beyond tools / Miltiadis Lytras and Ambjorn Naeve, editors.
p. cm.
Summary: "This book presents learning and knowledge management from a point of view where the basic tools and applications are provided by open source technologies. It explains an intense orientation to the critical issues of the open source paradigm: open source tools, applications, social networks, and knowledge sharing in open source communities"--Provided by publisher.
Includes bibliographical references and index.
ISBN 1-59904-117-0 (hardcover) -- ISBN 1-59904-118-9 (softcover) -- ISBN 1-59904-119-7 (ebook)
1. Knowledge management. 2. Organizational learning. 3. Open source intelligence. I. Lytras, Miltiadis D., 1973- II. Naeve, Ambjorn.
HD30.2.O64 2006
658.4'038--dc22

2006032169

British Cataloguing in Publication Data
A Cataloguing in Publication record for this book is available from the British Library.

To those who see beyond their local boundaries both in their egos and capacities and are inspiring a world of connecting souls full of light, peace, democracy and well being for all.

Open Source for Knowledge and Learning Management: Strategies Beyond Tools

Table of Contents

Foreword

This book provides an edited collection of original papers that examine how open source software (OSS) represents a new way to think about how organizations learn, or how they can support learning practices using the ways and means of OSS development. OSS, in many ways, is a revolutionary approach to the development of new IT applications, and thus, potentially a disruptive means for stimulating both organizational and IT innovation, as well as new ways and means for acquiring, representing, and operationalizing new forms of organizational knowledge. This book thus provides a refreshing look at the topic of organizational learning in terms of focal themes that include how OSS communities can support organizational development, how knowledge management systems and capabilities within organizations can benefit from or exploit OSS methods, and how government agencies and educational institutions can benefit from the adoption and assimilation of OSS applications, methods, and communities. We can consider each of these themes in turn, as well as some subthemes that arise across many chapters where these themes are found. Similarly, we can further reflect on what topics related to OSS and organizational learning are not addressed in these few chapters, and thus point to opportunities for further study in this area.

The first theme addresses how communities of interest or communities of practice arise to support the ongoing development and support of successful OSS systems, and how these communities then may expand to support user communities in different application areas. The chapter by Reinhardt and Hemetsberger examines how the KDE OSS project community ensures the ongoing success and continuous development of the multimillion lines of source code that constitute the K Development Environment through the continuous turnover and migration of apprentice contributors and expert software developers. The chapter by Demetriou, Koch, and

Neumann examines how the evolution of the OpenACS framework for developing community-oriented Web sites had to endure a history of organizational transformations and transitions as different commercial interests and investors sought to ensure (or exploit) its commercial success. The chapter by Francq examines how "social browsing" software designed to support knowledge sharing can be constructed from user contributed profiles of their areas of interest, which in turn can be assembled into communities of interest through this software. These three chapters collectively underscore how the ongoing development of OSS depends on the concomitant development of its developer-user community, and conversely, the development of this social community depends on the ongoing development, use, and support of the community of software components and artifacts that collectively form the OSS system within the community. OSS systems and communities can thus be recognized once again as socio-technical interaction networks that cannot be separated into social systems and technical systems whose ongoing development and evolution are independent (Scacchi, 2005).

The second theme examines the development of knowledge management systems and methods that are built with OSS components or built to encourage or exploit sharing and reuse of knowledge through OSS development practices. The chapter by Rech, Ras, and Decker describes the Riki system, which is intended to facilitate the sharing and reuse of knowledge that arises in traditional software engineering projects. The chapter by Hocht and Rech complements the preceding one by showing how the system they design for managing the knowledge artifacts that arise in agile software engineering projects must be human centered in order to enable effective software engineering knowledge sharing. In contrast, the chapter by Butler, Feller, Pope, and Murphy presents a case study that describes their effort to construct and deploy a portable knowledge asset development system that supports the open elicitation and capture of knowledge found in governmental and nongovernmental organizations in Ireland. Each of these three chapters thus stresses the role of the development of OSS systems as a core capability for enabling organizational learning and thus organizational transformation in different organizational settings.

The next theme examines how government agencies can benefit from the adoption and assimilation of OSS systems, methods, and communities. As noted previously, the chapter by Butler and associates examines the development of an OSS system targeted for adoption by government agencies within Ireland. The chapter by Gotze, Herning, Wernberg-Tougaard, and Schmitz provides a scheme for evaluating when and how government organizations should adopt OSS systems for use in providing public or administrative services. Similarly, the chapter by Castilho, Sunye, and associates outlines policies and strategies they have put into practice for encouraging the adoption and use of OSS tools they have developed, and brought together for use, within 2,100 public schools. Together, these chapters help to reveal that government organizations need to learn how to most effectively and efficiently adopt, deploy, use, and sustain OSS systems, and that the knowledge that must be learned and put into practice differs in many ways from that of traditional IT systems provided by commercial vendors or contractors that support government agencies.

The last theme found in this volume examines how educational institutions can benefit from policies that encourage and guide the adoption and assimilation of OSS applications, methods, and communities. This turns out to be perhaps the dominant theme, as it is the focus of four chapters. The chapter by Damiani, Mezey, Pumilia, and Tammaro (with other contributors) draws attention to the need for educational organizations to adopt an open source organizational model that encourages an open culture for education through knowledge sharing, interoperable learning support systems, and reusable educational system components whose quality can be continually assessed and readily assured. The chapter by Vuorikari and Sarnow examines policies that support initiatives of the European Schoolnet, focusing on the development and exchange of open learning resources. The chapter by Bouras and Nani examines similar issues and concerns in building and accessing learning resources and online courses for distance education. Finally, as noted previously, the chapter by Castilho, Sunye, and associates focuses attention on policies and strategies that support the adoption and deployment of OSS-based educational resources. Overall, much like the situation for government organizations, educational authorities and institutions both require and benefit from policies and strategies that help learn how to effectively to guide their own adoption and deployment of OSS-based educational resources.

Beyond these four major themes, two additional subthemes can be seen across many of the 13 chapters in this volume. These include the first subtheme, that the adoption, deployment, and use of OSS systems both requires and benefits from an understanding of the development practices, processes, and community dynamics found in different OSS projects (Scacchi, Feller, Fitzgerald, Hissam, & Lahkani, 2006). Adopting and using OSS systems seems to require that the people in an organization need to learn how the particular OSS systems they will use are developed, and how, as users, they may need to contribute to the project communities that are developing and sustaining the systems at hand. This need seems to differ in kind from that associated with IT systems provided as proprietary systems from commercial vendors, whereby users are not typically expected to be required to learn about how such systems were developed or why, though perhaps such involvement might prove beneficial. The second subtheme is that a growing number of OSS systems increasingly are expected to serve in the role as "social software"—that is, as software whose intended usage is to help people in different organizational settings to cooperate (share), coordinate (interoperate), or collaborate (work together with open or transparent learning resources). Both of these subthemes point to opportunities for further study into how OSS can support or facilitate organizational learning.

Finally, there are a number of topics that were not addressed in the 13 chapters in this volume. Of course, no single volume can be expected to be comprehensive or exhaustive, especially when the topic of the edited collection of chapters is new and unexplored, or when prior studies have appeared infrequently in different journals, conferences, or workshops. So by pointing to these additional topics, the intent is merely to help seed future research studies, thereby complementing and building on the contributions appearing in this first volume on OSS and organizational learning.

For example, what roles can (a) OSS development project communities, (b) OSS-based knowledge management systems, (c) social software, or (d) OSS development practices play in encouraging, facilitating, or inhibiting organizational learning? Similarly, how might OSS development practices, processes or community dynamics encourage, facilitate, or inhibit organizational learning in large corporations? How do large OSS project communities that are organized and governed by foundations (e.g., Apache, Mozilla, Eclipse, Gnome) learn how to improve both how they develop and how they support large software systems with globally decentralized, loosely coupled development teams? Next, how do different kinds of organizations learn from the patterns of success and failure in OSS development projects? (Here, it can be noted that the vast majority of OSS projects found in Web portals like SourceForge.net have less than two developers and have never released any software source code running or not. Thus though there are many success stories in the world of OSS development projects, there are many more incomplete or unsuccessful efforts that have so far garnered little research attention or publication). Last, what are the empirically grounded models or theories that account for OSS-based organizational learning, do they offer testable predictions or refutable hypotheses, and how do they compare to prior models/theories of organizational learning that do not assume a central role for OSS systems, development practices, processes, or project communities? As before, even this list of additional topics is by no means complete or exhaustive; instead, it is merely suggestive of the breadth, depth, and intellectual richness of the opportunities that lie ahead for further studies of open source software and organizational learning. Finally, as should be clear from the diversity of topics and application areas addressed in this volume, future studies will likely employ scholarly resources and methods drawn from multiple fields of study. Therefore, this volume constitutes the starting point for the studies that will follow and build from those presented here.

Walt Scacchi
Institute for Software Research
University of California, Irvine

References

Scacchi, W. (2005). Socio-technical interaction networks in free/open source software development processes. In S. T. Acuña & N. Juristo (Eds.), *Software process modeling* (pp.1-27). New York: Springer Science+Business Media Inc.

Scacchi, W., Feller, J., Fitzgerald, B., Hissam, S., & Lakhani, K. (2006). Understanding free/open source software development processes. *Software Process: Improvement and Practice*, *11*(2), 95-105.

* * *

A volume investigating the underlying mechanisms of open source organizations, and how learning and organizational practices are affected by adopting open source methods, is very timely. Open source is clearly more than just a method for building software. It would be interesting enough if it were just an innovative "mode of production" for the new artifact called software. But, as this volume investigates, the ideas behind open source software, those of intellectual property approaches that guarantee access and not exclusion, and the learning and application of knowledge at distributed nodes that are coordinated but not centrally controlled, point to even more revolutionary changes in the world. These open approaches to work and development contain more than just a perspective on how people could work freely together. They point to ways of realizing more of the creative human spirit and economic efficiencies simultaneously. The investigations into just what open source processes are, and how they can be effective in producing both products and organizational change, help us see this broader context of the open source and free software approaches.

The advent of widely accessible, easily approachable global communications, through the Internet and the Web, has driven the costs of collaboration and cooperation in the construction of software, and other knowledge artifacts, through the floor. It is not by chance that many of the early software contributions in this arena themselves contribute to making communication and collaboration easier, and hence help build the communities that are their very creators. All this has brought together communities of interest and practice that have been busy realizing value for themselves and others, and at the same time creating new ways of value-creation. Simply in the process of going about their business, they have created new ways of doing business. Understanding how this has happened is an urgent task; a task this book provides significant contributions to.

As more parts of the world become essentially digital, as models of pharmaceutical chemicals become central containers of our knowledge about those chemicals, for instance, or buckets of bits hold the movies and music we want to see and hear, or more and more of our education goes online and advanced education increasingly involves apprenticeships in partially or wholly online communities, more and more arenas of creativity and knowledge become open to the disruptive forces of open source thinking and methods. If effective drugs can result from open source efforts, as effective software has, then we should endeavor to understand, as quickly as we can how these methods can be applied in that industry.

The freedom to modify and redistribute these collective efforts, and the ability of individuals to choose where and how they contribute to a product are at the center of these new approaches. This is more than just a way of distributing work. It is an engine for creating intellectual property that can benefit organizations and the public alike. Learning how open source practices contribute to learning and how organizational evolution results from adopting such practices is a worthwhile theme for such a collection as this. The authors here make a welcome contribution to both our self-understanding and our future modes of working.

Joseph Hardin
Sakai Foundation
School of Information
University of Michigan

Preface

Very few trips in the process of evolution in information technology can be compared with the one of open source software. Millions of people worldwide are working collaboratively, exploiting each other's capacities and capabilities toward the achievement of significant milestones. Amazing networks of experts, knowledge communities, and multidisciplinary teams use innovative models of cooperation and collaboration and prove how knowledge and learning management can develop new unforeseen opportunities for sustainable development.

They develop excellent tools, applications, and solutions for diverse problems and needs, and they motivate more and more professionals and open minds to contribute to the enhancement of their developments. If you try to comment on this exciting community, then the first obvious conclusion is a single word: UNBELIEVABLE. Yes, it is really unbelievable how these people are "breaking" the rules of the commercial market, and how, without any financial compensation, they give their minds and souls for their "open software" project.

When we decided to edit this book, we knew from the beginning that this project would be a magnificent journey into the worlds of open knowledge and creative collaboration. It was not only because in the Knowledge Management Research Group, at the Royal Institute of Technology, (KMR Group, http://kmr.nada.kth.se) in the last years we have developed numerous open source-based tools for knowledge and learning management. It was mostly because the world of open source is full of brilliant ideas and shiny people who enjoy working for their tools and applications and sharing their knowledge and experiences. Traditionally, most studies on open source software have two alternative destinations and objectives. Either they discuss the success of open source structure and they try to transfer the findings (social networking, shared vision, shared mental models, etc.) to business settings, or they analyze the qualitative characteristics of open source software.

With more than 50 contributors, this edition is really amazing. A wide range of issues is discussed with a clear focus. We want to communicate that open source for knowledge and learning management sets a brand new context for value creation in education, government, business, academia, research, culture, health, and so forth. Living in tough days where competition is increasingly global, the joint efforts of open source communities provide an alternative route for solutions to well-known problems. From a knowledge society's point of view, the bridging of the gap between knowledge creation and use requires the deployment of numerous infrastructures and social networks. The "Society of Active Citizens" is not a political verbalism. From a technological adoption perspective, open source solutions to knowledge and learning management have a clear advantage. They demonstrate how effective the knowledge and learning management can be if there is proper inspiration and strategy.

Definitely, open source software, and especially open source applications for knowledge and learning management, gain more attention from day to day. This edited book has a clear strategy and vision. We decided from the beginning to develop a book for the various segments of society that are interested in open source software approaches and their contextualization for knowledge and learning management. In fact, we developed a book not for the few experts, but for the entire society, and we are really proud of this.

This book also has a strategic fit within the Knowledge and Learning Society Book series of IGI. We decided for the first 2 years of the Series to concentrate on the emerging technologies and paradigm shifts that are challenging the development of the infrastructures of the knowledge and learning society. In fact, three editions summarize this strategic objective.

- **Intelligent Learning Infrastructure for Knowledge Intensive Organizations:** A Semantic Web Perspective [more info: http://www.idea-group.com/books/details.asp?id=4925].
- **Open Source for Knowledge and Learning Management:** Strategies Beyond Tools.
- **Ubiquitous and Pervasive Knowledge and Learning Management:** Semantics, Social Networking and New Media to Their Full Potential [already in bookstores/finished in parallel with the current edition].

We do believe that these three editions cover the most fascinating aspects of knowledge and learning management nowadays, and therefore can act as reference editions. Open source is here to stay. Not just because it is at the top of the list of the research agenda for e-Europe and several similar political and government initiatives worldwide. But mostly because it demonstrates how collective intelligence can go beyond the capacities of isolated groups.

This edited book is about open source for knowledge and learning management. But, in fact, it is about realizing that when people are sharing the same visions and working together, then they can do great things.

Our vision goes a step further. We want a better world for all. And we are convinced that knowledge and learning is the TOTAL GLOBAL response to our competitive days.

We encourage you to be part of this exciting journey.

June 2006

Miltiadis D. Lytras

Ambjörn Naeve

Structure/Editing Strategy/Synopsis of the Book

When dealing with open source software, it is really of no sense to try to be exhaustive. Moreover, when you are trying to investigate the new insights of open source software and approaches to knowledge and learning management, then the mission becomes even more complex.

This is why, from the beginning, we knew that our book should be selective and focused. In fact, we decided to develop a book with characteristics that would help the reader to follow several different journeys through the contents. We also decided to open the book to big audiences. While we could pursue, through our excellent contacts and great network of collaborators, a publication aiming to promote the discipline, we decided that it would be most significant (from a value-adding perspective) to develop a reference book. And this is what we have done, with the support of great contributors: A reference book for open source for the knowledge and learning management community providing an excellent starting point for further studies on the topics.

Having already the experience of the edition of "Intelligent Learning for Knowledge Intensive Organizations: A Semantic Web perspective," and getting feedback from hundreds of researchers from all over the world, we decided to keep the same presentation strategy. We have tried, and we really think that we have succeeded, to develop a book that has three characteristics:

- It discusses the key issues of the relevant research agenda.
- It provides practical guidelines and presents several technologies.
- It has a teaching orientation.

The last characteristic is a novelty of our book. Several times editions like this one seem like a compilation of chapters, but without a clear orientation to the reader. This is why every edited chapter is accompanied by a number of additional resources that increase the impact for the reader.

In each chapter we follow a common didactic-learning approach:

- At the beginning of each chapter, the authors provide a section entitled *Inside Chapter*, which is an abstract-like short synopsis of their chapter.

At the end of each chapter there are some very interesting sections, where the reader can spend many creative hours. More specifically, the relevant sections are entitled:

- **Internet session:** In this section the authors present one or more Web sites, relevant to the discussed theme in each chapter. The short presentation of each Internet session is followed by the description of an *Interaction*, where the reader (student) is motivated to take a guided tour of the Web site and to complete an assignment.
- **Case study:** For each chapter, the contributors provide "realistic" descriptions of one case study, which the reader must consider in order to obtain strategic advice.
- **Useful links:** They refer to Web sites with content capable of exploiting the knowledge communicated in each chapter. We decided to provide these links in every chapter, even though we know that several of them will be broken in the future, since their synergy with the contents of the chapter can support the final learning outcome.
- **Further readings:** These refer to high-quality articles available both in Web and electronic libraries. We have evaluated these resources as of significant value, and we are sure that readers will find them significant.
- **Essays:** Under this section a number of titles for assignments are given. In the best case, essays could become working research papers. The general rule is that we provide three to six titles for essays, and in their abstract title, readers can find an excellent context of questioning.

The edited book consists of 13 chapters. We will try, in the next paragraphs, to give an overview of the contents, and also to explain the strategic fit of each chapter to our vision. In the Foreword, Professors Walt Scacchi and Joseph Hardin provide their personal understanding of the book, and highlights many uncovered themes. We are really grateful for, and honored by, their contributions.

Eirini Kalliamvakou, in *Open Source Software Basics: An Overview of a Revolutionary Research Context*, gives a nice introduction to the OSS context and presents several guidelines for further exploitation.

Christian Reinhardt and Andrea Hemetsberger in *Of Experts and Apprentices: Learning from the KDE Community*, provide the first significant insight for knowledge and learning management. Open source communities give manifestations on knowledge sharing, and expert support to peers and colleagues. According to their abstract:

Free and open source software (F/OSS) communities are self-organizing, social entities, which collaboratively create knowledge and innovate. Their fundamentally new approach of developing software challenges traditional principles of collaboration and learning. In contrast to well-organized and planned commercial projects, F/OSS development constitutes a continuous, iterative process of constant, incremental improvements made by various self-motivated contributors. Within such projects organizational structures emerge that enable a large number (i.e. hundreds or even thousands) of volunteers to commit themselves to freely chosen work, yet collaboratively realize a joint enterprise. The success of F/OSS communities genuinely depends on a constant flux of new members in order to ensure the sustainability. These aspirant members must be culturally integrated and taught in order to become expert members. This, in turn, increases complexity. Hence, these integration processes must be sophisticated, yet simple. Project coordination and new member integration, therefore, play a key role for the success of F/OSS communities. This is a challenging task, given that developers rarely meet face-to-face. New member integration takes place in online environments. It is their design and usage which are crucial for the success of such online efforts. The aim of this chapter is to discuss new member integration and learning, firstly in a theoretical manner by applying a 'communities of practice' perspective on F/OSS communities, and, secondly, by providing empirical evidence from the KDE project.

Organizations have much to learn from approaches like the ones described in the chapter by Reinhardt and Hemetsberger. The networked organization has to provide processes and systems that create a soft and hard infrastructure for the exploitation of knowledge wealth.

The *Luisa STREP* (Strategic Targeted Research Project) within EU/FP6, http://luisa.atosorigin.es/www (**L**earning Content Management System **U**sing **I**nnovative **S**emantic Web Services **A**rchitecture), where KMR (http://kmr.nada.kth.se) is a key partner, addresses the development of a reference semantic architecture for the major challenges in the search, interchange, and delivery of learning objects in a service-oriented context. From another point of view, it would be extremely challenging to exploit how semantic social networking with mobile and wireless networks expand the borders of communication. In our edited book *Ubiquitous and Pervasive Knowledge and Learning Management: Semantics, Social Networking and New Media to Their Full Potential* edited book, these topics are analyzed further.

Jörg Rech, Eric Ras and Björn Decker in *Riki: A System for Knowledge Transfer and Reuse in Software Engineering Projects*, elaborate further on the same context. Their chapter gives an overview of the reuse of knowledge and so-called learning components in software engineering projects, and raises several requirements one should keep in mind when building such systems to support knowledge transfer and reuse

Many software organizations have a reputation for producing expensive, low-quality software systems. This results from the inherent complexity of software itself, as well as from the chaotic organization of developers building these systems. Therefore, the authors set a stage for software development based on social software for knowledge and learning management to support reuse in software engineering, as well as knowledge sharing in and between projects. In the RISE (Reuse in Software Engineering) project, they worked with several German SMEs to develop a system for the reuse of software engineering products such as requirement documents. The methodology and technology developed in the RISE project makes it possible to share knowledge in the form of software artifacts, experiences, or best practices based on pedagogic approaches.

Rech, Ras and Decker are developing a new edited book entitled, *Emerging Technologies for Semantic Work Environments: Techniques, Methods, and Applications*, which we recommend to you.

Christian Höcht and Jörg Rech in *Human-Centered Design of a Semantically Enabled Knowledge Management System for Agile Software Engineering* provide an interesting methodology, which was developed during a German research project, and which enables and supports the design of knowledge sharing platforms, such as WIKIs, based on pedagogic standards and engineering techniques. Developing human-centered systems is considered by the authors as a challenge that addresses a wide area of expertise—computer scientists as well as social scientists. These experts have to work closely together in order to build intelligent systems to support agile software development.

Human-centered knowledge and learning management is also a key challenge. In a recent interview with the president of the Association for Information Systems, Michael Myers, he stated that "The field of IS has always been about RELATION-

SHIPS, not things in themselves" (interview available at http://www.srcf.ucam.org/~mpp26/miltos/MyersPDF.pdf). From this point of view, human-centered design requires a multifold analysis of parameters that justify a personalized approach to the management of tacit and explicit knowledge and learning.

Tom Butler, Joseph Feller, Andrew Pope and Ciaran Murphy in *Making Knowledge Management Systems Open: A Case Study of the Role of Open Source Software* give an excellent example on how open source can be the basis for open KM systems.

Their chapter presents an action research-based case study of the development of pKADS (portable knowledge asset development system), an open source, desktop-based knowledge management (KM) tool, implemented in Java and targeted at government and nongovernment organizations. pKADS was a collaborative project involving Business Information Systems, University College Cork, Ireland and the United Nations Population Fund (UNFPA), and it was funded by the government of Ireland. Development of the application took just 3 months, using an agile development approach and some reuse of existing open source code. The chapter discusses the background of the pKADS project and prior UNFPA KM efforts, the technical and conceptual architectures of the pKADS application, the roles played by open source components and open data standards, the rationale for releasing pKADS as open source software, and the subsequent results. Future research, in the form of developing open source, Intranet/Internet-based KM tools for the Government of Ireland—eGovernment Knowledge Platform (eGovKP) is also briefly discussed.

Christian Wernberg-Tougaard, Patrice-Emmanuel Schmitz, Kristoffer Herning, and John Gøtzeand in *Evaluating Open Source in Government: Methodological Considerations in Strategizing the Use of Open Source in the Public Sector* promote further the discussion of the previous chapter and concentrate on public sector and government's exploitation of F/OSS.

The use of free and open source software (F/OSS) in the public sector has been accelerating over the last 10 years. The benefits seem to be obvious: No licensing costs, unlimited flexibility, vendor independence, a support community, and so forth. But as with everything else in life, a successful implementation of F/OSS in government is not as simple as it might look initially. The implementation of F/OSS should build on a solid evaluation of core business criteria in all their complexity. The authors analyze the evaluation considerations that government bodies should undertake before deciding between F/OSS and traditional software (SW), including the way knowledge networks and communities of practice work, total cost of ownership, and core functional requirements. The chapter presents a methodology conceptualizing this process in a comprehensive framework, focusing on the interaction between the strategic and business process level and the SW/infrastructure level. The chapter aims at presenting a framework enabling IT-strategists and management from the "business side" of public sector institutions to evaluate F/OSS vs. traditional SW in tight cooperation with the IT-side of the organization.

Ernesto Damiani, Paul G. Mezey, Paolo M. Pumilia and Anna Maria Tammaro, in *Open Culture for Education and Research Environment*, discuss a key aspect of open source in the context of knowledge and learning management for research and education. (Have a look also at their great event in OSS 2006 – Workshop on Preserving Quality in an Open Environment, http://openculture.org/como-2006.)

More specifically in their chapter, emphasis is placed on the open source organizational model, highlighting some of the key elements of the open culture: knowledge sharing technologies, interoperability, reusability, and quality assurance. Some contemporary theoretical and technological issues that are becoming of paramount importance for building a cross-disciplinary research and knowledge-sharing environment are outlined, pointing out those cultural changes implied by the increasing adoption of the ICT. In the unprecedented abundance of information sources that can be reached through the Internet, the growing need for reliability will not be met without a major change of scholars', teachers', and learners' attitudes to foster enhanced trusted relationships.

Riina Vuorikari and Karl Sarnow, in *European National Educational School Authorities' Actions Regarding Open Content and Open Source Software in Education*, provide a reference chapter for all those interested in the policies and actions towards the deployment of FOSS at the European level.

Their chapter provides an overview of policies in the area of e-learning that 10 European countries, all members of European Schoolnet, have taken regarding open content and free and open source software (FOSS) to be used to support and enhance learning. Additionally, it elaborates on the European Schoolnet's initiatives to support open learning resource exchange in Europe. European Schoolnet (EUN, http://www.eun.org/portal/index.htm) promotes the use of information and communication technologies (ICT) in European schools acting as a gateway to national and regional educational authorities and school networks throughout Europe. A variety of actions have been initiated by a number of European educational authorities from analysis and feasibility studies to the development of educational software based on open source as well as open educational content.

Christos Bouras and Maria Nani, in *Using Open Source to Building and Accessing Learning Objects and Online Courses*, demonstrate how open source can be the basis for open LMSs. According to the authors, as e-learning continuously gains the interest of the scientific community, industry, and government, a wide variety of learning technology products have been incorporated into the market place. Advances in information and communication technologies are in favor of the incorporation of innovative services and functionalities in such systems, though content creation and delivery remain the two key factors in any e-learning system. Therefore, in this chapter, they present the design and implementation of a tool targeted at building and accessing learning objects and online courses through the Web.

This tool aims to facilitate instructors and trainers to easily develop accessible, reusable, and traceable learning content that can meet their distant students' needs for anytime and anyplace learning. Learners are able to access learning content in addition to consulting, at any time, reports on their interactions within a course, and get support by subject experts. Furthermore, all users can request to upgrade their role in the system and, thus, actively participate in the learning process. Special attention has been paid to the utilization of reliable and qualitative open source technologies and Web standards so that the proposed solution can form an easily accessible system.

Neophytos Demetriou, Stefan Koch, and Gustaf Neumann, in *The Development of the OpenACS Community*, present OpenACS, with its community, as a case study documenting the forces acting between commercial interests, securing investments, and technical development in a large open source project with a large proportion of commercial involvement. OpenACS is a high-level community framework designed for developing collaborative Internet sites. It started from a university project at MIT, got momentum from the ArsDigita Foundation, and split up into a commercial and an non-commercial version based on open source. OpenACS has proven its durability and utility by surviving the death of its parent company (ArsDigita) to grow into a vibrant grassroots collection of independent consultants and small companies implementing diverse and complex Web solutions around the globe for NPOs, philanthropy, and profit. A heritage from this history is a still dominant position of contributors with commercial interests that, in its intensity, is above the norm found in open source projects.

Pascal Francq, in *The GALILEI Platform: Social Browsing to Build Communities of Interests and Share Relevant Information and Expertise*, gives an excellent example on how social browsing can be a key theme of knowledge and learning management in organizational settings and in humanistic computing.

For a few years, social software has appeared on the Internet to challenge the problem of handling the mass of information available. In this chapter, Francq presents the GALILEI platform, using social browsing to build communities of interests where relevant information and expertise are shared. The users are described in terms of profiles, with each profile corresponding to one specific area of interest. While browsing, users' profiles are computed on the basis of both the content of the consulted documents and the relevance assessments from the profiles. These profiles are then grouped into communities, which allows documents of interest to be shared among members of the same community, and experts to be identified.

Marcos A. Castilho et al., in *Making Government Policies for Education Possible by Means of Open Source Technology: A Successful Case*, provide an interesting case. We really love this chapter because we prefer, instead of just verbalisms and big visions, to see things working in daily tough life.

In their chapter, they describe the products and services offered by the Department of Computer Science of the Federal University of Paraná within the scope of the Paraná Digital project. The department has designed laboratories with Internet access to 2,100 public schools of the state, with innovative technology, through an environment entirely based upon free software tools, centralized management as well as continuous maintenance, and betterment of the services offered. They place special emphasis on strategies, aiming at contributing to the adoption of such strategies in contexts relatively similar to theirs.

Finally, Marc Alier Forment, in *A Social Constructionist Approach to Learning Communities: Moodle*, discusses the influence of the main learning paradigms: conductism and constructivism. He comments also on the need to apply the OSS development model and licences to the creation of open content, to be collaboratively created in communities. The social reality of OSS communities that become learning communities is described by the principles of social constructionism; this paradigm has been applied in the creation of Moodle.org, a true learning community built around the OSS learning management system: Moodle. For sure, an excellent case study and a significant contribution to the book.

In the next section, there is a preface, developed by Professor Walt Scacchi, University of California, Irvine, CA, that highlights new destinations for studies on the organizational aspects of open source. We are really grateful and honored for his contribution.

Please find below a short list of FOSS applications developed in our Knowledge Management Research Group (KMR Group) in Royal Institute of Technology, Sweden (http://kmr.nada.kth.se).

We would be happy to build further collaborations for this enhancement.

Conzilla: A Concept Browser

Conzilla is a concept browser aiming to provide:

- An effective environment for collaborative knowledge management
- A flexible human-semantic interface for editing and presenting information on the machine-Semantic Web

Conzilla presents content in contexts through concepts. A concept is regarded as the boundary between its inside, which contains its content (components), and its outsides, which represent the different contexts in which the concept appears. A context is graphically represented in the form of a context-map. All elements in Conzilla can be equipped (annotated) with additional information (metadata). Typical content consists of Web pages, images, movies, references to books or geographical places, etc.

Right-clicking on a concept brings up a menu with three choices: Contexts, Content, and Information.

- Selecting Contexts opens a sub-menu, which lists all the other contexts where this concept appears.
- Selecting Content opens a window (to the right) where the content-components of the concept are listed. Pointing to a content-component brings up information about it, and double-clicking opens another window where the corresponding content is shown.
- Selecting Information brings up a window, which contains information (meta-data) about the concept, concept-relation or context under investigation.

The basic principles behind conceptual browsing have been developed by the KMR-group since 1997 under the lead of Ambjörn Naeve. Conzilla is developed under an open source license and provided at no cost. For more information see www.conzilla.org.

Collaborilla is a collaboration service within Conzilla, which will be released in early 2007. Collaborilla will enable the publication of different parts of collaboratively constructed context-maps from different sources. This will make it possible to:

- Reuse and extend concepts and concept-relations published by others; for example, students could refine "skeleton maps" published by teachers
- Create new context-maps that include existing concepts and concept-relations from other publishers
- Add content to others' concepts, concept-relations and context-maps, in order to examplify ideas from other publishers
- Add comments (metadata) on others' concepts, concept-relations and context-maps
- Perform agreement and disagreement management in the form of bottom-up conceptual calibration by building "conceptual bridges" between different context-maps—thereby agreeing, disagreeing, commenting on, or refining existing concepts and/or concepts-relations

SHAME: A Library for Editing and Presenting RDF

SHAME is a library that leverages editors, presentations, and query interfaces for resource-centric RDF metadata. The central idea of SHAME is to work with *Annotation Profiles,* which encompasses:

- How the metadata in RDF should be read and modified
- What input is allowed, for example, multiplicity and vocabularies to use
- Presentational aspects like order, grouping, labels, and so forth

These annotation profiles are then used to generate user interfaces for either editing, presentation, or querying purposes. The user interface may be realized in a Web setting (both a jsp and velocity version exists) or in a stand-alone application (a java/swing version exists).

SHAME is open source and has been developed by the KMR group since 2003, see the Web page for more information and a demo: http://kmr.nada.kth.se/shame.

SCAM: A Framework for Metadata-Intense Applications

SCAM, Standardized Contextualized Access to Metadata, is a framework that provides a basis upon which different metadata-intense applications can be built. The design of SCAM is derived mainly from the demands of applications, such as archives and personal portfolios, and consists of two major parts:

- A **repository** for Semantic Web metadata expressed in RDF. Access to metadata is controlled on the level of records (i.e., metadata around a central resource) and collections of records that are called contexts. There is also search functionality, which can be restricted to specific contexts if so preferred.
- A **middleware** simplifying the development of Web-based applications. The middleware builds upon the WebWorks controller, Velocity template language, and provides solutions for metadata navigation, presentation, and editing.

A wide variety of applications have been developed on top of SCAM ranging from personal digital portfolios to a search and browsable media library for TV programs.

SCAM is open source and developed as a joint effort where the KMR-group stands for the scientific and technical coordination. See the homepage for more details: http://scam.sourceforge.net/

Confolio: An Electronic Portfolio System

A Confolio system contains a number of electronic portfolios, where each portfolio functions as a personal information archive. Such an archive can contain:

- *Digital material*, such as documents, films, pictures, slides, and so forth
- *Information* and *opinions* about this *digital* material
- *Information* and *opinions* about *nondigital* material, such as persons, books, concepts, events, and so forth

The access to material, information, and/or opinions can be restricted to individuals and groups, which makes it easy to create protected areas for collaboration and knowledge sharing. Searching for material can either be performed over an individual portfolio or over an entire confolio system. Moreover, each confolio system can be plugged into a distributed (peer-to-peer) network, which enables search and exchange for information and opinions within a global publication network.

The Confolio system is developed on top of SCAM and SHAME, two frameworks for metadata management on the Semantic Web. These frameworks, and hence also Confolio, have focused on interoperability and standards from the start, in order to avoid “leaving the users behind” as technology evolves and new functionality is to be integrated into the work environment.

The Confolio system is open source and developed as a joint effort where the KMR-group stands for the scientific and technical coordination. See the homepage for more details, http://www.confolio.org.

Acknowledgments

We finalized this book, *Open Source for Knowledge and Learning Management: Strategies Beyond Tools*, in June 2006—Ambjörn in the beautiful archipelago of Stockholm and Miltiadis in Monemvassia, a lovely Greek village.

So the time has come for us to express our deepest appreciation and respect to the 39 contributors of this edition. Their knowledge, expertise and experience are evident in every line of this edition. It sounds typical, but it is the ultimate truth. Each edition is an outlet where the world of ideas seeks a fertile ground. And this ground is not self-admiring. It requires the interest and insights of people. Hence, our second deepest thank you goes to our readers in academia, industry, government and society in general.

We also thank the publishers and supporting staff during the various stages of the development and production of this book. In Idea Group Inc., we have found more than just publishers and excellent professionals. We have found great supporters of a shared vision to develop books/editions and knowledge for a highly demanding society. So to Mehdi, Jan, Kristin, and Meg, please accept our warmest compliments for your encouragement and inspiration. You prove to us every day that IGI is not only a high quality publishing organization, but also a community that cares for its people.

Last but not least we would like to thank by name a few colleagues that, in various ways, have motivated us to work towards our vision for the deployment of information technologies in our society. In our academic life, we have a clear motto. We want to make things happen, and due to our intrinsic motivation to be of good will and very optimistic people, we really love those who encourage others and who say "go on, we stand by you."

Miltiadis:

My warmest compliments and thanks go to Gottfried Vossen and Gerd Wagner who supported me in my vision to establish AIS SIG on Semantic Web and information systems. I also feel blessed to have Miguel-Angel Sicilia as a great friend and collaborator.

In my Greek academic world, my thinking has been deeply affected by professors Athanassios Tsakalidis (University of Patras) and Georgios Vassilacopoulos (University of Piraeus) to whom I express my heartfelt thank you.

My deepest appreciation and a great thank you also to Amit Sheth, who accepted my invitation to serve as editor-in-chief of the *International Journal on Semantic Web and Information Systems*. I learn every day from Amit that leading academics are hard working people, helping and encouraging others to follow their achievements.

I would like to thank especially Efstathia/Maria Pitsa (University of Cambridge), Maria Pitsa (University of Piraeus), Nikos Korfiatis (Copenhagen Business School), and Martin Papadatos (University of Cambridge) for the great support in all the recent initiatives.

And to Theodora, Dimitris, Hara, and Katerina, all my love is the best thank you for the colors you're giving my life. Sas agapo.

Ambjörn:

First, I want to express my gratitude to the PhD-students and programmers that have made my work as head of the Knowledge Management Research Group so effective and enjoyable: Matthias Palmér, Mikael Nilsson, Fredrik Paulsson, Henrik Eriksson, Jöran Stark, Jan Danils, Fredrik Enoksson and Hannes Ebner. Without their commitment to excellence, the KMR-group would not have managed to establish itself on the international research scene.

My very special thank you to Mia Lindegren, director of Uppsala Learning Lab, with which the KMR-group closely collaborates. Without the unwavering support of Mia, the KMR-group would not have existed in its present shape.

I also want to acknowledge my gratitude to Jan-Olof Eklundh, Yngve Sundblad and Nils Enlund at KTH. Over the years—and against all odds—they have provided "incubator environments" that have enabled the growth of the unacademic and controversial discipline of knowledge management at KTH.

My sincerest thank you to Janiche Opsahl, Agneta Sommansson and Krister Widell of the Swedish Educational Broadcasting company (UR). They have had the courage to apply some of the KMR open source tools in a sharp industrial setting, which has given us invaluable feedback and practical experience with knowledge management problems of the real world.

Moreover, I want to express my gratitude to the members of the PROLEARN network of excellence, who have been instrumental in establishing our collaboration with leading European actors in Technology Enhanced Learning and Knowledge Management. Prominent among them are: Wolfgang Nejdl, Peter Scott, Kevin Quick, Erik Duval, Martin Wolpers, Ralf Klamma, Amine Chatti, Katherine Maillet, Milos Kravcik, Marcus Specht, Daniel Burgos, Rob Koper, Alexander Karapidis, Gustaf Neumann, Bernd Simon, Fridolin Wild, Barbara Kieslinger, Margit Hofer, Borka Jerman-Blasic, Tomaz Klobucar, Constantin Makropolous, Vana Kamtsiou, Dimitra Pappa. Tapio Koskinen, Anna-Kaarina Kairamo and Pertti Yli-Luoma.

Finally, just like Miltiadis, I am grateful for the friendship and collaboration of Miguel-Angel Sicilia, who is constantly using his network to bring us into interesting proposals.

So, once more, the journey was full of exciting experiences and we are really grateful to all the people that stand by us.

Geja sou filaraki, we made it!

Chapter I

Open Source Software Basics: An Overview of a Revolutionary Research Context

Eirini Kalliamvakou, Athens University of Economics and Business, Greece

Abstract

The open source software (OSS) development area of research presents a fresh and generous domain for analysis and study. In line with this, it is important to have a high-level understanding of the "open source phenomenon" before being able to delve deeper into specific niches of research. OSS presents a rich picture and because of that, both academics and practitioners have shown intense interest in producing high-quality literature. This chapter provides an initial understanding of what OSS is and how it has come to be the exciting research platform that it is today, attracting attention from various sources. In addition, we take an overview of the research streams that have formed in recent years, and the basic findings of attempts made to transfer lessons from OSS to other research areas.

Open Source Software at a Glance

Open source software (OSS) has received growing attention in recent years from various perspectives. The thriving numbers behind OSS adoption and contribution have captured the attention of academic research that, in the past years, has been trying to decipher the phenomenon of OSS, its relation to already-conducted research, and its implications for new research opportunities.

OSS has a definition that focuses on specific characteristics that software has to serve in order to be labeled as "open source." The Open Source Initiative (OSI) is a nonprofit corporation dedicated to managing and promoting the OSS definition for the good of the community; thus, acting as the official organization behind OSS. Based on the OSS definition provided by OSI, any software that has the characteristics listed below is considered to be OSS, and vice versa:

- Free redistribution
- Access to source code
- Derived works allowed under the same license
- Integrity of the author's source code
- No discrimination against persons or groups
- No discrimination against fields of endeavor
- Distribution of license
- License must not be specific to a product
- License must not restrict other software
- License must be technology-neutral

The current OSS landscape presents a very interesting picture. Although the idea behind OSS dates back to the 1960s and the UNIX era in the 1980s, the official term of OSS was coined in 1998 and, at the same time, the OSI was created. Since then, the OSS movement has evolved at a very fast pace. Prime examples of successful OSS projects include operating systems (Linux, FreeBSD, OpenBSD, NetBSD), Web browsers (Firefox, Konqueror), graphical environments (KDE, Gnome), productivity applications (OpenOffice), programming languages and infrastructure (Apache, MySQL), and development tools (GNU toolchain, Eclipse). These widely accepted OSS endeavors show that, today, a wide range of OSS applications are available and they present a viable and robust alternative to proprietary software solutions.

In addition to the presence of prime examples in the OSS environment, the plethora of OSS projects is impressive. Project support sites are online environments that provide tools for listing and managing OSS projects while supplying information such as developer teams, maturity stage, latest versions, and so forth. Two of the biggest and most well-known support sites, *Sourceforge.net* and *Freshmeat,* have reported to have more than 125,000 and 40,000 listed projects in the summer of 2006, respectively. Although many of these projects are still in designing stages, these numbers reveal the dynamics behind OSS and its evolution/adoption. Furthermore, this striking progress of OSS provides an intricate motive for conducting research in such a context.

Open Source Software as a Research Context

Open source software is developed in a way different than proprietary software. Development is done inside communities of developers that work on code for their personal satisfaction or need. However, lately, a trend has formed inside large companies, that pay their employees to contribute to OSS projects, using this as a platform that enables them to affect the introduction of new software features so that the final OSS product is better aligned with the company's interests and needs. An open question remains as to how expanded this trend currently is, and whether the "paid volunteers" are involved in the process of developing OSS software primarily out of their own satisfaction or are assigned to it exclusively by their employers.

Independent of this fact, the community-oriented development leads to the efficient production of high-quality software available for use by anyone interested. This is an important element of OSS, the prime motivation for developers is not to "make software" as requested by clients or employers, but mainly to satisfy their own software needs, which cannot be fulfilled by vendor-supplied software. After the software is prototyped, it can be made public for anyone who wishes to use, modify, and redistribute.

OSS communities have significant similarities with professional software engineering teams utilized by software houses. However, these two organizational structures also portray critical differences that show that they stand quite far apart. It is important to note that since not all companies organize their software development efforts in the same mode, and also, there is a wide variety of organizational structures inside OSS projects, similarities and differences between them can be valid upon different occasions. The most basic differences are pictured in Table1.

Inside OSS communities, there are rules to be accepted and respected by both the developers and the users. Also, there is always some hierarchy of roles, although this hierarchy can take many forms, depending on the internal organization of each project and the profiles of its developers and owners. Through various case stud-

Table 1. Differences between OSS and proprietary software projects (Based on Crowston & Howison, 2005)

	OSS projects	**Proprietary software projects**
Release planning process	Own ideals about quality and features	Time-to-delivery pressure
Quality assurance	Developers do not have write access to the repository	Developers have write access to the repository
Leadership	Leaders are required to have proven competence via previous contributions	Project leadership is a hierarchical level where people are promoted by other than technical criteria
Tools and standards	Use of standardized tool chains (not modern modeling tools and techniques)	Each project may opt for another technology leading to different set of tools (code re-use between projects is limited)
Motivation of developers	Desire to learn and establish new skills (fun-to-code)	Typical task assignment by hierarchical superiors or salary incentives (not as efficient)
Roles of members	Members assume roles according to personal interests	Tasks are assigned

ies (Cox, 1998; Gacek et al., 2004; Moon & Sproull, 2000; Mockus, Fielding, & Herbsleb, et al., 2002; Moon & Sproull, 2000), a hypothesized model of OSS project structure is suggested. The model consists of concentric circles of persons that serve different roles within the project and have different responsibilities. At the center of this onion-like form, we find the team of core developers that contribute most of the code, and also have the role of overseeing the project's evolution and design. Core developers also review and check-in the patches submitted by co-developers that belong to the consecutive circle. In the next circle, we find active users of the project's product that do not write code but provide bug reports, testing of new releases, and also use-cases. Finally, in the outer circle (for which there is no specific border), we find the software's passive users that do not have an active presence in the project's mailing lists and forums. This onion-like structure is shown in Figure 1.

What is surprising and initially hard to explain in the case of OSS is *how it is possible to build software of top quality that, in many cases, outperforms the products of multimillion-dollar companies with a vast amount of resources*. The answer seems to lie beyond issues of money and resources and closer to self-organizing communities and networks between developers. The OSS phenomenon has brought forth a different perspective in the way software is created. New paradigms regarding technical,

Figure 1. The OSS onion-like model of organization (Crowston & Howison, 2005)

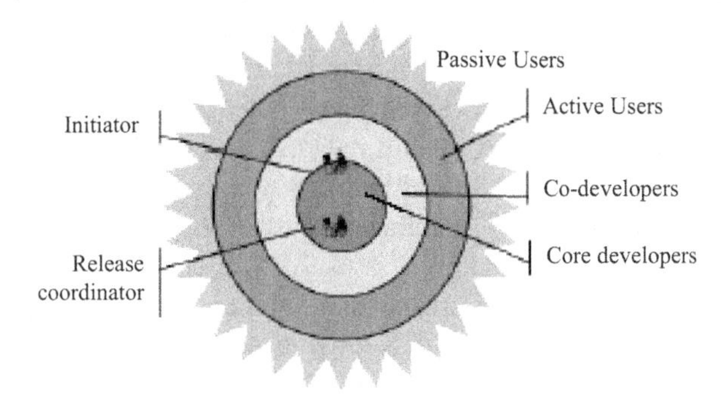

legal, team formation, and organization and knowledge dissemination issues have converted OSS development into an interesting and intriguing research topic. Although the majority of studies, at least at the beginning of the spread of OSS, were mostly concerned with the technical elements behind its success, some other aspects related to OSS soon presented interesting research questions. Hence, concepts like *community* and *social interaction* are currently under investigation and reveal their great importance when interpreting and understanding many questions.

Since OSS is presenting such an interesting research area with useful conclusions and implications also for other domains of research, it is important that a researcher has at least a brief overview of discussions and studies that have formed the OSS literature. In the next section, we will take a look of at a limited number of very influential studies that portray the multidisciplinary approach to OSS research and the intriguing results that it can provide. Through this approach, we will be able to gain a deeper understanding of the research context offered by OSS.

OSS Literature

As it is expected, the core of researchers of open source software, at the beginning, mostly consisted of software engineers with the basic aim to understand the processes associated with OSS development and get a global picture of it. However, as it is evident now, along with the technical aspects of OSS, also social, economic, organizational, and other issues form its rich picture. This is why in the last few years the "OSS phenomenon" has attracted the attention of not only software engineers, but also researchers from many other disciplines and backgrounds.

OSS became a matter of study in the late 1990s, although it can be traced back to the 1980s and even earlier (Salus, 2005). The first studies came from individuals actively involved in OSS development communities (rather than academic researchers) who published results regarding the OSS development processes and outcomes as well as its economic implications for the software development industry/scenery in general. Also, popular voices at that time were those of OSS advocates that discussed ethical and philosophical aspects of OSS (Stallman, 1999), although published later, is a good example). A third group of references regarded the use of applications, with little attention to the development process itself. Academic papers related to OSS began to appear around 2000 in workshops and in conferences and a little later in scientific journals and magazines. After extensive research on the literature on OSS development, we have found almost no significant references before 1998.

Early Works Try to Decipher the Development Process

The most widely-known, representative and influential text of that time is the well-known essay by Eric S. Raymond "The Cathedral and the Bazaar" (Raymond, 1998). Although the text is not supported by an empirical study of many projects (only the *Linux kernel* and *fetchmail* projects are discussed), "The Cathedral and the Bazaar" made an important contribution by establishing a metaphor. Traditional software development projects were modeled as cathedrals, where the development process is centralized and highly dependent on just a few persons whose roles are clearly defined. Release management follows a closed planning, user feedback is limited, and contributions by external developers are not fostered. In opposition to the cathedral we find the bazaar, where there is lack of planning (at least in the first stages of the project) and everything starts with the need of a developer and his/her ability to create software that meets that need. Developers publish often and users are regarded as co-developers under the bazaar model. Obviously, the bazaar model represents a more flexible and open way for the software development process that stands contrary to the cathedral model. It is important to note that the cathedral model should not be mistaken as representing only proprietary software; some OSS projects from the GNU project (such as the GNU Compiler Collection and the GNU Emacs editor) fall under the cathedral model of development although they are OSS.

Almost immediately after "The Cathedral and the Bazaar" was released (first through the Internet, later published), other authors started either to build on top of it or severely criticize it. One well-known follow-up came from Bezroukov (Bezroukov, 1997), who made a point saying that the bazaar development model is not some revolutionary phenomenon, but just a different form of "scientific community." Bezroukov considered Raymond's ideas as too simple to match reality, and proposed other models based on academic research that could better explain the phenomenon.

As far as development models for OSS are concerned, Vixie compared the classical waterfall model with the processes used in the production of OSS (Vixie, 1999). According to Vixie, the waterfall model is composed of a set of a complete and logical sequence of steps aiming at obtaining a final product, while the OSS development model relies on the absence of formal methods. Such methods prove unsatisfactory for programmers who voluntarily devote time to program. This lack of formality, Vixie argues, is compensated for by user feedback and by the introduction of software engineering methods (developers define a methodology to face a specific problem for which they are experienced enough). Therefore, it is obvious through Vixie's argument that no ad hoc development model exists for OSS; the methods and practices evolve with the project and usually show a tendency to formalization of tasks.

Identifying Research Streams in OSS

Although, as it is evident above, the early works in OSS literature were concerned with the development model of OSS, this picture quickly changed. This coincided with, and was the result of, the rapid expansion of OSS and its successful use and adoption by a growing mass of interested parties. This success needed both to be explained and also to investigate whether it could prove useful for other research areas (related or not to software engineering that was the principal environment for the birth of OSS). Therefore, the extensive review of literature for OSS led us to discover and reveal two main research streams that confirm these inherent needs. These two research streams can be visualized in Figure 2.

Applying OSS Research Conclusions to Other Domains

The first research stream uses the conclusions drawn from OSS case studies and the lessons learned via studying and investigating OSS, and tries to identify whether these successful lessons can be utilized in other contexts. One of the first concerns has been whether for-profit organizations could profit by adopting the seemingly effective practices of OSS. Seeing how the OSS development model proves to be successful (judging from the results it achieves). it would useful for organizations to follow similar models to make their own software development models more efficient. Several studies point that such a shift (from "traditional" to OSS model of development) can be achieved given that the organizations will be willing to change in terms of processes, internal organization, and philosophy.

Figure 2. Research streams in OSS literature

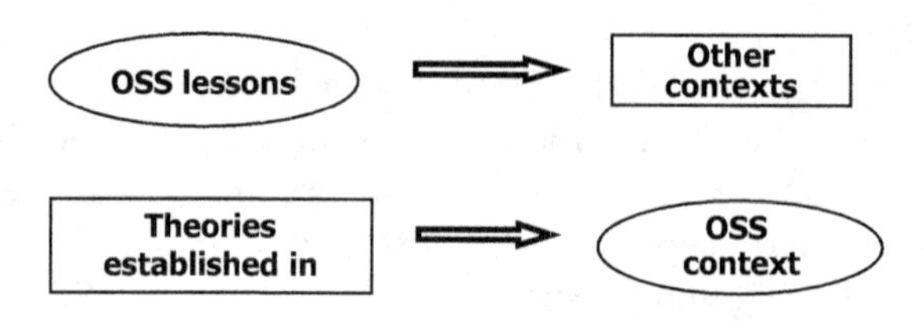

Sharma et al. (Sharma, Sugurmaran, & Rajagopalan, 2002) argued that the success of the OSS model is setting the stage for a structural change in the software industry, transforming it from manufacturing to a service industry. Therefore, they explored how for-profit organizations can foster an environment similar to OSS in order to reap its numerous advantages to manage their own software development efforts. After examining the OSS environment using a framework based on dimensions of structure, process, and culture (Galbraith, 1973; Miles & Snow, 1978; Robey, 1991) from organizational theory literature, Sharma et al. (2002) offered their own framework for creating hybrid-OSS communities inside organizations. Their proposed framework included properties of community building, community governance, and community infrastructure. It appears from this work that the ability of organizations to move to a hybrid-OSS environment will depend on:

1. The ability of management and workers to understand the OSS philosophy
2. The development of mutual trust between management and workers
3. The workers' perception of being involved in challenging and innovative projects
4. The motivation of workers to participate in such projects

The arguments of Sharma et al. (2002) concerning the internalization of OSS development model characteristics by organizations is also asserted by another study published a little earlier. In a technical report by the Software Engineering Institute of Carnegie Mellon University, it is stated that "industries, specifically those in the software-development business, are beginning to support the idea of development in the style of OSS." The report analyses several OSS case studies and provides useful conclusions, as well as a set of guidelines for organizations that consider adopting a model of development or internal structure similar to an OSS project.

The organizations' interest to incorporate the successful OSS mechanisms in their own practices was also discussed by Cook (2001), who described the motivators for those involved in OSS, and then defined the problems that need to be overcome for this incorporation to happen. OSS motivators, according to Cook, are the same factors that appear as contradictions between OSS and CSS (closed-source software). The different "organizational structure" (the benevolent dictatorship), the pool of resources, the level of talent, the motivations for contribution, and the fact that OSS is not attempting to redesign the wheel are the contradictions that are cited as separating OSS projects from commercial organizations. As a result, Cook proposes the features that can be imbibed from OSS environments to traditional organizations:

1. Interacting with customers in certain domains
2. Rewarding talent
3. Allowing individuals to register as potential contributors

Following the same line of thought, several studies have been concerned with whether the successful patterns of online and offline collaboration, team building, and coordination can be utilized in other contexts besides the OSS development environment, for example in organizations. Yamauchi, Yokozawa, Shinohara, and Ishida (2000), based on observation, interviews, and quantitative analysis of two OSS projects (FreeBSD Newconfig Project and GNU GCC Project), found evidence that suggests that spontaneous work coordinated afterward is effective, rational organizational culture helps achieve agreement among members, and communications media moderately support spontaneous work.

These findings could imply a new model of dispersed collaboration. Although the same argument is shared by other researchers as well, like Crowston and Howison (2005), Gallivan (2001) seems to counter this belief by proposing that trust and effective online collaboration of OSS developers is not a critical factor to a project's success, but that it is "various control mechanisms [that] can ensure the effective performance of autonomous agents who participate in virtual organizations" (OSS projects are viewed as virtual organizations by the author). However, Gallivan's study is not backed by empirical data to support this claim, but rather a content analysis of already published OSS case studies and the literature that they are based on.

The general effects of OSS on software engineering have been the subject of considerable analysis. Jorgensen (2001) studied the incremental software development model followed in the FreeBSD project where a stream of contributions goes into a single branch in the repository and is required to preserve the software in a working state. This is a process that creates a succession of development releases, akin to the practices of OSS that utilize frequent releases, but different from the commercial software development line of thought. This fact was also mentioned in "The Cathedral and the Bazaar," where the "release early, release often" (Raymond, 1998) principle of the bazaar model was discussed for its superiority and more effective results. This incremental model has had its effects on more and more commercial software development efforts that have incorporated it.

Scacchi (2002) described and analyzed four OSS development communities to understand the requirements for OSS development efforts, and how the development of these requirements differs from those traditional to software engineering and requirements engineering. He discovered eight kinds of *software informalisms* (software development processes that do not follow the typical route of software development companies) that play a critical role in the elicitation, analysis, specification, validation, and management of requirements for developing open source software systems. This enables considering a reformulation of the requirements engineering process, having a large effect on software engineering in general.

All studies presented in this section share the common characteristic of investigating the applicability of OSS principles and conclusions to other areas of research and practice. In the following section, we will review studies that belong to the second of the two research streams mentioned earlier.

Investigating how Other Disciplines Apply to the OSS Context

The second research stream is interested in almost the opposite approach. Here we see studies that build on theories established in various disciplines, and review their applicability in the context of OSS. The main disciplines accounting for the majority of the studies of this type are economics, sociology/psychology, software engineering, and network analysis.

Lerner and Tirole (2004) acknowledged the initial puzzlement that OSS causes to an economist. However, they argued that existing economic frameworks can explain OSS- related activities. In their study, they draw on labor and industrial organization literature to give alternative views to the OSS trend. Here, programmers are seen as incurring opportunity costs of time, and the long-term benefits of participating in OSS projects are shown. These long-term incentives are further empowered under three conditions: (a) the more visible the performance to the relevant audience, (b) the higher the impact of effort on performance, and (c) the more informative the performance about talent, for example, Holmström (1999). As a result, Lerner and Tirole conclude that there are economic incentives entangled in the OSS processes, although they are different from the incentives in software development companies and hence may not be directly recognizable.

In a study by Johnson (2002), OSS development is modeled as the private provision of a public good. Such models of public good provision have been studied by many researchers (Bergstrom, Blume, & Varian, 1986; Bliss & Nalebuff, 1984; Chamberlin, 1974; Palfrey & Rosenthal, 1984; Bergstrom, Blume, & Varian, 1986; Bliss &

Nalebuff, 1984) and are at the center of economic theory. Based on that, Johnson shows that the superior ability of the open source method to access the Internet talent pool, and to utilize more private information, provides an advantage over the closed source method in some situations. Nonetheless, free riding (which is a crucial problem when discussing public goods) implies that some valuable projects will not be produced, even when the community of developers becomes large.

Bitzer, Wolfram, and Schroder (2004) adapted a dynamic private-provision-of-public-goods model to reflect key aspects of the OSS phenomenon. In particular, instead of relying on extrinsic motives for programmers (e.g., signaling), his model was driven by intrinsic motives of OSS programmers, arguing that since programming software is associated with the risk of failure (e.g., in terms of the development of the software is not successful or the project does not become famous), extrinsic motives (signaling) are unable to explain the OSS phenomenon in full, and can rarely be linked to the motives of initiators of OSS projects. This approach, in a sense, challenges earlier views that analyzed the economic aspects of OSS based on extrinsic motives. According to Bitzer et al., the motives for a programmer to initiate a project are the mix of:

1. The need for a particular software solution
2. Fun or play
3. Gift culture, social standing

Motivation of OSS developers has been a recurrent theme for studies either from an economic (Torvalds & Diamond, 2001; Hars & Ou, 2002; Hertel, Nieder, & Herrmann, et al., 2003; Krishnamuturthy, 2002; Lakhani & Wolf, 2003) or a sociological/psychological perspective (Weber, 2004).

In discussing a framework for analyzing OSS, Feller and Fitzerald (2000) study and use two previous frameworks which that have been very influential in the IS field: Zachman's IS architecture (ISA) and Checkland's CATWOE framework from soft systems methodology (SSM). Furthermore, Lawrie and Gacek (2002) use basic software engineering principles and metrics to discuss dependability issues regarding OSS. There is a large number of studies discussing technical or evaluation issues in OSS that draw on the software engineering scientific area, but their technicality does not support our analysis, and thus they are not presented in this literature review.

Through this overview, it became evident that the area of OSS-related research spans a number of disciplines and contexts. Researchers of OSS today are not strictly software engineers, and issues of interest are not limited to development and engineering principles. A lot of different perspectives have been considered in order to explain OSS expansion and philosophy and, at the same time, a lot of different domains of research have stepped up with the desire to utilize all the successful practices that OSS development has to offer. It is a collective aim for the research and analysis of OSS development to continue, and for knowledge and best practices to be transferred to other areas as well.

Conclusion

The purpose of this chapter was really introductory. Many of the FOSS historical issues as well as research topics will be covered in detail in the next chapters, where special emphasis will be paid to the knowledge and learning management context. From this point of view, it is really exciting to reveal the mutual beneficial relationships of FOSS and knowledge and learning management and their linkages that support sustainable performance and development.

References

Bergstrom, T., Blume, L., & Varian, H. (1986). On the private provision of public goods. *Journal of Public Economics*, *29*, 25-49.

Bezroukov, N. (1997). A second look at the cathedral and the bazaar. *First Monday*, *4*(12). Retrieved on 20/11/2006 http://www.firstmonday.org/issues/issue4_12/bezroukov/index.html

Bitzer, J., Wolfram, S., & Schroder, P. H. J. (2004). *Intrinsic motivation in open source software development*. MIT Working Paper.

Bliss, C., & Nalebuff, B. (1984). Dragon-slaying and ballroom dancing: The private supply of a public good. *Journal of Public Economics*, *25*, 1-12.

Chamberlin, J. (1974). Provision of collective goods as a function of group size. *American Political Science Review*, *68*, 707-716.

Cook, J. E. (2001). Open source development: An Arthurian legend. In J. Feller, B. Fitzgerald, & A. van der Hoek (Eds.), *Making sense of the bazaar: Proceedings of the 1st Workshop on Open Source Software Engineering*. Retrieved May 19, 2006, from http://opensource.ucc.ie/icse2001/papers.htm

Cox, A. (1998). *Cathedrals, bazaars and the town council*. Retrieved March 22, 2004, from http://slashdot.org/features/98/10/13/1423253.shtml

Crowston, K., & Howison, J. (2005). The social structure of free and open source software development. *First Monday*, *10*(2). Retrieved on 20/11/2006 http://www.firstmonday.org/issues/issue10_2/crowston/index.html

Feller, J., & Fitzgerald, B. (2000). A framework analysis of the open source software development paradigm. In W. Orlikowski, P. Weill, S. Ang, & H. Krcmar (Eds.), *Proceedings of the 21st Annual International Conference on Information Systems* (pp. 58-69). Brisbane, Queensland, Australia.

Gacek, C., & Arief, B. (2004). The many meanings of open source. *IEEE software*, *21*(1), 34–40.

Galbraith, J. R. (1973). *Designing complex organizations*. Reading, MA: Addison-Wesley

Gallivan, M. J. (2001). Striking a balance between trust and control in a virtual organization: A content analysis of open source software case studies. *Information Systems Journal*, *11*(4), 277-304.

Hars, A., & Ou, S. (2002). Working for free? Motivations for participating in open-source projects. *International Journal of Electronic Commerce*, *6*(3), 25-39.

Hertel, G., Nieder, S., & Herrmann, S. (2003). Motivation of software developers in open source projects: An Internet-based survey of contributors to the Linux Kernel. *Research Policy* (Special Issue: Open Source Software Development), *32*(7), 1159-1177.

Homström, B. (1999). Managerial incentive problems: A dynamic presective. *Review of Economic Studies, 66*, 169-182.

Johnson, J.P. (2002). Economics of open source software: Private provision of a public good. *Journal of Economics & Management Strategy, 11*(4), 637-662.

Jørgensen, N. (2001). Putting it all in the trunk: Incremental software development in the FreeBSD open source project. *Information Systems Journal*, *11*(4), 321-336.

Krishnamurthy, S. (2002). Cave or community? An emprical examination of 100 mature open source projects. *First Monday*, *7*(6). Retrieved May 19, 2006, from http://www.firstmonday.org

Lakhani, K., Arim, R., & Wolf, R. G. (2003). *Why hackers do what they do: Understanding motivation effort in free/open source software projects*. MIT Sloan School of Management Working Paper, no. 4425-03.

Lawrie, T., & Gacek, C. (2002). Issues of dependability in open source software development. *ACM SIGSOFT Software Engineering Notes*, *27*(3), 34-37.

Lerner, J., & Tirole, J. (2004). *The economics of technology sharing: Open source and beyond.* NBER (Working Paper 10956).

Miles, R. E., & Snow, C. C. (1978). *Organizational strategy, structure, and process*. New York: McGraw-Hill.

Mockus, A., Fielding, R. T., & Herbsleb, J. D. (2002). Two case studies of open source software development: Apache and Mozilla. *ACM Transactions on Software Engineering and Methodology*, *11*(3), 309-346.

Moon, J. Y., & Sproull, L. (2000). Essence of distributed work: The case of Linux kernel. *First Monday*, *5*(11). Retrieved on 20/11/2006 http://www.firstmonday.org/issues/issue5_11/moon/index.html

Palfrey, T. R., & Rosenthal, H. (1984). Participation and the provision of discrete public goods: A strategic analysis. *Journal of Public Economics*, *24*, 171-193.

Pappas, J. (2001). *Economics of open source software.* Working Paper. Retrieved May 19, 2006, from http://opensource.mit.edu

Raymond, E. S. (1998). The cathedral and the bazaar. *First Monday*, *3*(3). Retrieved May 19, 2006, from http://www.firstmonday.org/issues/issue3_3/raymond/

Robey, D. (1991). *Designing organizations* (2nd ed.). Burr Ridge, IL: Irwin.

Salus, P. (2005). *The daemon, the gnu and the penguin.* (Published as a series of articles in Groklaw). Retrieved May 19, 2006, from http://www.groklaw.net/article.php?story=20050623114426823

Stallman, R. (1999). The GNU operating system and the free software movement. In C. DiBona, S. Ockman, & M. Stone (Eds.), *Open sources: Voices from the open source revolution.* Cambridge, MA: O'Reilly and Associates.

Scacchi, W. (2002). Understanding the requirements for developing open source software systems. *IEEE Proceedings - Software*, *48*(1), 24-39.

Sharma, S., Sugurmaran, V., & Rajagopalan, B. (2002). A framework for creating hybrid-open source software communities. *Information Systems Journal*, *12*(1), 7-25.

Torvalds, L., & Diamond, D. (2001). *Just for fun: The story of an accidental revolutionary*. HarperBusiness.

Vixie, P. (1999). Open source software engineering. In C. DiBona, S.Ockman, & M. Stone (Eds.), *Open sources: Voices from the open source revolution.* Cambridge, MA: O'Reilly and Associates.

Weber, S. (2004). *The success of open source.* Cambridge: Havard University Press.

Yamauchi, Y., Yokozawa, M., Shinohara, T., & Ishida, T. (2000). Collaboration with lean media: How open source software succeeds. In *Proceedings of the ACM Conference on Computer-Supported Work* (pp. 329-338).

Appendix I: Useful URLs

A free/open source research community (also provides a database of online papers)
http://opensource.mit.edu/

The Free Software Foundation
http://www.fsf.org/

Freshmeat
http://freshmeat.net/

Libresoft
http://libresoft.urjc.es/index

The Open Source Initiative (OSI)
http://www.opensource.org/

SourceForge.net
http://sourceforge.net/

Appendix II: Further Reading

DiBona, C., Ockman, S., & Stone, M. (1999). *Open sources: Voices from the open source revolution.* Sebastopol, CA: O'Reilly & Associates.

Glyn Moody, G. (1997). The greatest OS that (n)ever was. *Wired*, *5*(8). Retrieved from http://pauillac.inria.fr/~lang/hotlist/free/wired/linux.html

Raymond, E. S. (2003). *The art Of Unix programming*. Addison-Wesley.

Senyard, S., & Michlmayr, M. (2004). How to have a successful free software project. In *Proceedings of the 11th Asia-Pacific Software Engineering Conference,* Busan, Korea (pp. 84-91). IEEE Computer Society.

Chapter II

Of Experts and Apprentices: Learning from the KDE Community

Christian Reinhardt, University of Innsbruck School of Management, Austria
Andrea Hemetsberger, University of Innsbruck School of Management, Austria

Abstract

Free and open source software (F/OSS) communities are self-organizing, social entities that collaboratively create knowledge and innovate. Their fundamentally new approach of developing software challenges traditional principles of collaboration and learning. In contrast to well-organized and planned commercial projects, F/OSS development constitutes a continuous, iterative process of constant, incremental improvements made by various self-motivated contributors. Within such projects, organizational structures emerge that enable a large number (i.e., hundreds or even thousands) of volunteers to commit themselves to freely chosen work, yet collaboratively realize a joint enterprise.

The success of F/OSS communities genuinely depends on a constant flux of new members in order to ensure the sustainability. These aspirant members must be culturally integrated and taught, in order to become expert members. This, in turn, increases complexity. Hence, these integration processes must be sophisticated, yet simple. Project coordination and new member integration, therefore, play a key role for the success of F/OSS communities. This is a challenging task, given that developers rarely meet face-to-face. New member integration takes place in online environments. It is their design and usage that are crucial for the success of such online efforts. The aim of this chapter is to discuss new member integration and learning, firstly in a theoretical manner applying a "communities of practice" perspective on F/OSS communities, and secondly by providing empirical evidence from the KDE project.

Introduction

The free and open source software (F/OSS) collaboration and learning model has attracted considerable attention, mostly because its mere existence and the way it works contradicts existing theories and counteracts common business practices (Kuwabara, 2000; Lanzara & Morner, 2003; Lerner & Tirole; 2002, Thomke & von Hippel, 2002; von Hippel & von Krogh, 2003; Wayner, 2000). F/OSS communities are self-organizing social entities that collaboratively create knowledge and innovate (cf. also Hemetsberger & Reinhardt, 2006; Lee & Cole, 2003). Due to its globally distributed developer force and the possibility to collaborate on a large scale, F/OSS software projects enjoy extremely rapid code evolution and highest software quality (Cubranic & Booth, 1999). With products such as Linux, Apache, Perl, KDE, and Gnome desktop, to name a few, F/OSS development is also highly successful in an economic sense. Some authors even propose to apply the F/OSS approach to other industries, for instance in the automotive industry (Evans & Wolf, 2005), and learn from it as a best-practice example for successful online collaboration.

This fundamentally new approach in developing software challenges traditional principles of collaboration and learning (Ducheneaut, 2005; Mockuss, Fielding, & Herbsleb, 2000; Pal & Madanmohan, 2002) as a well-organized and planned endeavor. Instead, F/OSS software development constitutes a continuous, iterative process of constant, incremental improvements made by various contributors (Metiu & Kogut, 2001). Within such projects, organizational structures emerge that enable a large number (i.e., hundreds or even thousands) of volunteers to commit themselves to freely chosen work. All projects are located in arbitrary locations, and the volunteer contributors rarely or never meet face-to-face. F/OSS projects do not follow an explicitly predesigned project plan, schedule, or list of deliverables, but rather follow an evolutionary path of growth (Mockuss et al., 2000). "In a nutshell,

Figure 1. Chapter overview

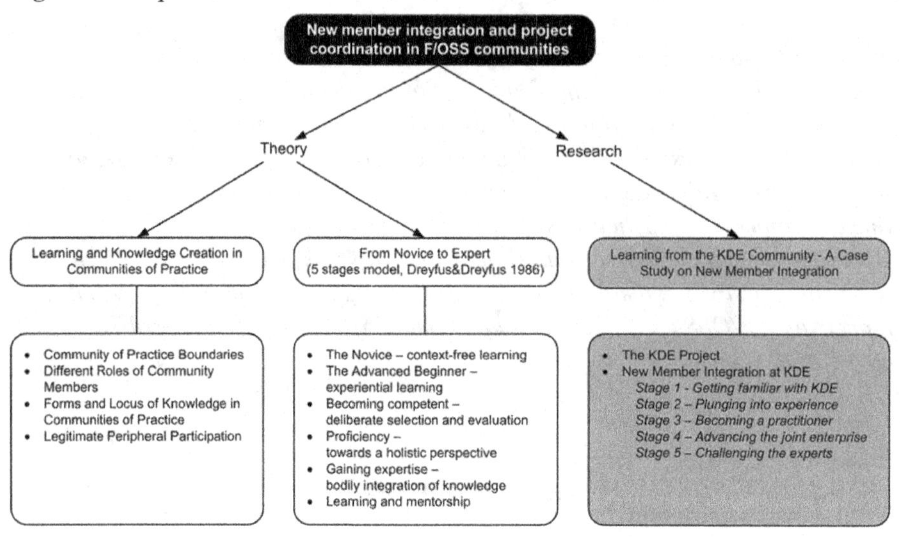

… open-source software projects are evolutionary systems based on dense interactions between humans and technical artifacts within an electronic media" (Lanzara & Morner, 2003).

Software development is a knowledge-intensive activity that often requires very high levels of domain knowledge, experience, and intensive learning by those contributing to it (von Krogh, Spaeth, & Lakhani, 2003). An assertion in much of the literature on F/OSS is that the success of a project in terms of producing the software relates to the growth in the size of the developer community (Moody, 2001; Raymond, 1999; Sawhney & Prandelli, 2000). Hence, the success of this innovative endeavor genuinely depends on a constant flux of new members in order to ensure the sustainability of F/OSS projects. These aspirant members must be culturally integrated and taught in order to become expert members. This, in turn, increases complexity. Hence, these integration processes must be sophisticated, yet simple. Furthermore, as successful projects mature, their technology grows more complex, and only a small number of people who have been actively involved from the beginning fully understand its architecture (von Krogh et al., 2003). Project coordination and new member integration, therefore, play a key role for the success of F/OSS communities. This is a challenging task, given that developers rarely meet face-to-face. New member integration takes place in online environments. It is their design and usage that are crucial for the success of such online efforts.

The aim of this chapter is to discuss new member integration and learning, firstly in a theoretical manner, and secondly by providing empirical evidence from the KDE project. To this end, we will first look at new member integration in F/OSS communities from a "communities of practice" perspective, and discuss its implications and drawbacks. In the following, theoretical conceptualizations are offered that set forth a deeper understanding of how aspirant members proceed from novices to experts. The KDE project community will serve as an example of how F/OSS communities of practice establish online environments that are supportive with respect to distinct learning stages of aspirant members. A discussion of the findings and a future outlook will be provided to conclude the chapter.

Learning and Knowledge Creation in Communities of Practice

F/OSS projects can be viewed as emergent social collectives with individuals working on similar problems. The community members self-organize to assist one other and share perspectives about their work practice, which results in learning and knowledge creation within the community (Hemetsberger, 2002). The "communities of practice" approach, a well-established concept from organization theory, has been applied by several researchers (Lee & Cole, 2003; Madanmohan & Navelkar, 2002; Tuomi, 2000; Zhang & Storck, 2001) to describe the organizational structures of F/OSS projects. The concept of community as a cultural learning platform occupies a prominent role within this approach:

Since the beginning of history, human beings have formed communities that share cultural practices reflecting their collective learning: from a tribe around a cave fire, to a medieval guild, to a group of nurses in a ward, to a street gang, to a community of engineers interested in brake design. (Wenger, 1998a)

Lave and Wenger (1990) have introduced this concept to address groups of people who are informally bound together by shared expertise and interest, and create knowledge. Communities of practice fulfill a number of functions with respect to the creation, accumulation, and diffusion of knowledge in organizations. As Wenger emphasizes, they are "living" nodes for the exchange and interpretation of information. Because of their shared understanding, they know what information to communicate and how to communicate in the most effective manner. Furthermore, community members work together on problems, discuss novel ideas, test new concepts, and gather information on new developments, both inside and outside the organization, thus helping to keep the organization at the forefront of a field.

Learning, knowing, and sharing knowledge, however, are not abstract processes undertaken for their own sake, but are rather part of belonging to the community and engaging in community practices. A community of practice exists because it produces a shared practice as members engage in a collective process of learning (cf. Wenger, 1998a, 1998b). Acting knowledgeable in communities of practice involves two components: the competence that the community has established over time (i.e., what it takes to act and be recognized as a competent member), and an ongoing *experience* of the world as a member in the context of a given community and beyond. Accordingly, learning is defined as interplay between social competence and personal experience. According to Wenger (Wenger, 1998a, 2000) a community of practice defines itself along three dimensions:

- **Joint enterprise:** To be competent is to understand what the enterprise is all about in order to be able to successfully contribute to it.
- **Mutual engagement:** Through interacting with one another, members build their community. They establish norms and relationships of mutuality that reflect these interactions. To be competent is to be able to engage with the community and be trusted as a partner in these interactions.
- **Shared repertoire:** Communities of practice have produced a shared repertoire of communal resources (vocabulary, routines, sensibilities, artifacts, tools, stories, styles, etc.). To be competent means having access to this repertoire and being able to use it appropriately.

Knowing that, the successful integration of new members must take into account that learning proceeds along two lines. It is task-related knowledge, on the one hand, that has to be transformed and passed on to aspirant community members. However, it is first and foremost a question of enculturation, of mutuality, and the adoption of a shared repertoire that enables new members to join the community.

Community of Practice Boundaries

Through a shared history of collective practice and consequent learning, the members establish the community's knowledge, which, by its very nature, creates boundaries. The collectively held knowledge fosters the emergence of the community's own identity as a single social collective that consequently shapes the identities of its members. Having a sense of identity is a crucial aspect of learning in organizations; it helps to sort out what is important and what to avoid, with whom to identify, in whom to trust, and with whom one should share knowledge (cf. Wenger, 1998a, 1998b).

However, communities of practice cannot be considered in isolation from the rest of the world, or understood independently of other practices. Members do not spend their entire time within one single community of practice. They also acquire knowledge outside of the community, possibly as part of another community of practice. Larger F/OSS projects, which consist of several subprojects, could be characterized as a network of communities of practice (cf. Tuomi, 2000). Consequently some members might act as brokers between communities. Wenger (1998a) even suggests that "... they can introduce elements of one practice into another." Added to which the interaction of members with community outsiders, such as users of an F/OSS product or companies commercially interested in a F/OSS project, might stimulate learning. According to Granovetter (1973), weak network ties between social entities might be an even superior source of innovation than the strong ties within, as they build bridges between more diverse knowledge, and thus foster innovative combination. Therefore, the learning potential of a community of practice presents itself as twofold: the knowledge that members develop at the core, and the knowledge created through interactions at the boundaries of the community. "The core is the center of expertise, radically new insights often arise at the boundary between communities" (Wenger, 1998a). Hence, community boundaries must be permeable, but still unambiguous in order to enable identity building.

Different Roles of Community Members

Members within a community of practice occupy different roles. Because of their different level of expertise, diverse motivation and specific specialization members take on different jobs in the practice of a community (cf. Hemetsberger & Pieters, 2001; Madanmohan & Navelkar, 2002; Zhang & Storck, 2001). Rather than being assigned to a particular role by someone else within the F/OSS community, members assume their roles according to their personal interest in the project. Previous research on F/OSS projects has found several different roles that members may occupy (Hemetsberger & Pieters, 2001; Ye & Kishida, 2003). The Project Leader is often the person who has initiated the project being responsible for its vision and overall direction. Core Members or Maintainers are responsible for guiding and coordinating the development of a F/OSS project. These Core members have been involved with the project for a long period of time and have made significant contributions to the development of the software. Developers regularly contribute new features and fix bugs. They are one of the major development forces of F/OSS systems. Peripheral Developers only occasionally contribute new functionality or bug fixes to the existing system. Bug reporters, readers, and passive users occupy roles at the boundaries of the community. They constitute a melting pot of potentially new members, aspirants, and advocates of a community.

Individuals, of course, transcend their roles towards a more advanced stage of expertise. It is exactly these role transformations that distinguish F/OSS project from other software projects, within which roles are normally fixed. It is also these role transformations from joining to contributing that are interesting to look at from the perspective of socialization and knowledge creation, because they bear the potential for learning and innovation. However, strong links have to be established between individual participants and the socio-technical network of a project in order to be able to fully exploit community knowledge.

Forms and Locus of Knowledge in Communities of Practice

With regard to task-related knowledge, much of the community's expertise is held by its expert members. Community experts retain specific task-related knowledge as "living" repositories. Their individual knowledge becomes interlinked within a spatial and technologic environment and consequently constitutes a transactive memory, that is "... the set of knowledge possessed by group members, coupled with an awareness of who knows what" (Faraj & Sproull, 2000:1556). Thus, metaknowledge about who is an expert in a particular field becomes an important knowledge component within a community of practice. "By knowing the location rather than the content of what is being stored, and by relying on one another to furnish necessary detail, team members can enhance their own memory stores and reduce their cognitive effort" (Faraj & Sproull, 2000:1556).

Beyond individual, task-related expertise, there also exists knowledge on a collective level. As members of the community of practice share background knowledge and participate in the give and take of collaborative and cooperative activities, they are actually negotiating meaning. Thus, they are building knowledge not only as individuals, but as a group (Maddux, Johnson, & Willis, 1997) that possesses a collective mind constituted by their culture (cf. Weick & Roberts, 1993). Culture cannot be attributed to any individual of the specific group, but only to the group as a comprehensive collective. This entails that "the more [members of a group] share those implicit, expert models that have been pushed to the unconscious, the less they need to communicate in order to secure cohesive action" (Stacey, 1993:177). Thus, collective knowledge in terms of shared norms and rules of a community lower the cost of communication, facilitate coordination, and influence the direction of search and learning (Kogut & Zander, 1996).

Legitimate Peripheral Participation

Apparently, knowledge about social norms and rules needs to be shared among members to facilitate learning and the creation of new knowledge. "Just because we do see the world in terms of what has already been given to us by our social background, we find ourselves creatively constructing sense out of what might otherwise be puzzling, incoherent experience" (McKinlay, Potter, & Wetherell,

1993:135). This does not mean, however, that only those who have already acquired the necessary knowledge are able to join a community of practice. In fact, there are processes that allow newcomers to move towards full participation in the socio-cultural practice of such a community. These processes are subsumed under the concept of "legitimate peripheral participation" (Lave & Wenger, 1990). Central to this concept is to regard learning not as being taught or instructed, that is, learning about practice, but to rather as becoming a practitioner (cf. Brown & Duguid, 1991); by participating, the learner observes the practice of the other members of the community. Newcomers first have to assimilate the norms and values of the community and analyze the activity of the experts before they are able and capable of contributing to the group. Furthermore, they have to build an identity for themselves, and become more visible to the core members of the group (Ducheneaut, 2005). In this first phase of integration, people can participate in different ways and to different degrees. "This permeable periphery creates many opportunities for learning, as outsiders and newcomers learn the practice in concrete terms, and core members gain new insights from contacts with less-engaged participants" (Wenger, 1998a). Newcomers may then take different roles in the status hierarchy of the community, depending on their level of expertise. These processes of partial and eventually full integration into the core of a community are of vital importance to the sustainability of a F/OSS project.

The processes by which new members join an existing F/OSS community and eventually become contributors have been analyzed by von Krogh et al. (2003) and Duchenaut (2005). Their findings suggest that newcomers proceed from initial stages of observation and peripheral monitoring of the development activity to reporting, active engagement, obtaining write access to the code, taking charge of small tasks, and finally, contributing work into the project's architecture. In communities of practice, learners develop much of their knowledge through direct observation of practice and face-to-face contact. The importance of creating the right context for learning and knowledge sharing has been emphasized by Nonaka and Takeucki (1995) and von Krogh et al. (2000) as the central knowledge enabler in organizations. Online communities, on the other hand, operate in a completely different context with regard to time and space. They therefore have to apply alternative, Web-technology-based ways of supporting and mentoring aspirant members that guide them on their way from novice to expert.

From Novice to Expert

Acquiring expertise is not a matter of learning facts. In order to become a skillful expert member of a community of practice, aspirant members have to engage in practice and experience (Benner, 2001). However, as an individual proceeds from novice to a more proficient learner, the manner of how learners acquire new knowledge tends to differ. Dreyfus and Dreyfus (1986) have illustrated the process of becoming an expert in a five-stage model (cf. also Baumgartner & Payr, 1999; Fink, 2000). This model is described in more detail.

The Novice: Context-Free Learning

Being a complete novice in a topic means that one is not able to build on previously acquired knowledge, obviously due to the lack of experience. Consequently, the first step is to realize what information is relevant for the guidance of intelligent action and how the different pieces of information can be distinguished from one other. Learning is context free; situational influences are not taken into consideration. Therefore, information should be presented to the novice in a general and context-free form, as he is not yet able to recognize any contextual interrelation. As the novice knows nothing about situational dynamics, he runs the risk of not being aware of those facts that underlie situational change. Hence, novices tend to over-generalize situations, relying too much on the constancy of information. Without any guidance, novice problem solvers tend to jump into problems, limit initial problem statements, and select first impression solutions without exploring problem situations. In this stage, it is most helpful to present to the learner relevant, declarative facts in a clearly defined, explicated form. Due to the lack of contextual knowledge, a novice can only stick to the rules and follow instructions step-by-step. At this stage, becoming knowledgeable relies very much on explicit forms of knowledge. Learning, at this stage, can be supported by giving clear advice, and offering explicit rules and guidelines for action. Furthermore, the information given should be entirely explicit. Given this, learners should refrain from diving into practice at this early stage, as this will likely lead to frustration and demotivation.

However, knowledge that can be expressed in words and numbers represents only the tip of the iceberg of the entire body of possible knowledge (Nonaka, 1994). Polanyi (1966:4) differentiates between directly codifiable "explicit knowledge" and "tacit knowledge," which lies far beyond this explicit level. A prime example of tacit knowledge is that of riding a bike: people who say they are able to ride a bike must, by definition, know which way to turn the handlebars to prevent a fall to the left or right. But if asked, most cannot answer which way to turn; thus, the knowledge to stay upright while riding a bike is obviously of tacit nature. Tacit knowledge is the most important source of innovation (von Krogh, Ichijo, & Nonaka, 2000). It is the type of knowledge that is typically held by experts through practice and experience; hence, it is tacit knowledge that novices lack in their first stages of learning. The main problem at the novice stage is the learner's uncertainty in the interpretation of the situation, action, and outcomes. This could lead to a paradoxical situation when one is learning something fundamentally new. Plato has illustrated this paradox in his dialogue with Meno:

Socrates is talking to Meno, who pretends to know what virtue is. And Socrates quickly shows him that he has not the faintest idea what virtue is, and Meno becomes absolutely furious, and he finally bursts out with this: "But how will you look for something when you don't in the least know what it is? How on earth are you going to set up something you don't know as the object of your search? To put it another way, how will you know that what you have found is the thing you didn't know?" (cf. Schön, 1987)

The only way out of this dilemma is to plunge into experience, even though this plunge may be full of loss until one gets to the place where he begins to understand what learning is all about (cf. Schön, 1987).

The Advanced Beginner: Experiential Learning

The advanced beginner starts using the abstract knowledge obtained as a novice and engages in his first personal experiences. By constant, repetitive application of context-free knowledge the learner elaborates situational, and more complex knowledge. Knowledge is no longer only of explicit nature, but through experiencing the environment, tacit knowledge also develops. When advanced beginners encounter a similar situation in the future, their experiences influence their course of action. It is important to note here that a simple transfer of tacit knowledge from a mentor to a learner is not possible. According to the constructivist learning theory, knowledge, which is to a certain extent context-specific and tacit, has to be recreated within the mind of a learner (cf. also Szulanski, Winter, & Cappetta, 2000). Hence, at this stage, the learner engages primarily in firsthand experience. Experience is required for any new knowledge creation. Similarly, Polanyi (1969:132) contends that "knowledge is an activity which would be better described as a process of knowing." Or as Maturana and Varela (1992) formulate it concisely: "All knowing is doing, and all doing is knowing."

The crucial cognitive process that links thoughts and action—consequently enabling learning and knowledge creation—is "reflection," that is, the evaluation of experiences and attribution of meaning. Reflection is highly dependent on past experiences and the respective knowledge structure stored in the brain. Schön (1987, 1982) has distinguished two forms of reflection that are relevant when learners engage in experience: reflection-in-action and reflection-on-action. Reflection-in-action refers to thinking about action while the action is still in progress. In Schön's model, coming to know is self-consciously active and inherently connected to the situation at hand. Reflection-in-action affects action as well as the construction of the environment. Weick (1979) refers to this simultaneousness of action and construction of the environment as "enactment." Thereby, he emphasizes the active role of the knowing subject in the creation of knowledge, which is in sharp contrast to models of passive learning and views of learning as a mere adaptation to the environment. An essential ingredient in reflection is surprise at one's spontaneous response to the unexpected, to behaviors and results that could not be predicted from the antecedent actions. Schön (1982) emphasizes that a good deal of reflection-in-action is, in fact, initiated by an experience of surprise. This leads us to engage in experimentation and test our new way of seeing the situation (Schön, 1987). This is also what is meant by improvisation.

To conclude, learners at this stage are no longer depending on explicit rules, but rather need tasks and opportunities to engage in practice and experimentation. At this stage, a variety of experiences should be offered; however, not without highlighting information and knowledge that may be important in order to master these first experiences.

Simultaneous thinking and acting is not imperative to the creation of knowledge. Action can also be interpreted with hindsight, making it possible to generate new knowledge after the action has been executed. The act of reflecting-on-action enables us to spend time exploring why we acted as we did, what was happening within the surrounding environment, and so on. In so doing, we develop sets of questions and ideas about our activities and practices; thus challenging our theories-in-use. Moreover, we might also "reconfigure" already acquired knowledge in an innovative way resulting in the creation of new knowledge (cf. Cook & Brown, 1999). This, of course, is only feasible when learners have already developed mental models and more elaborate theories about their field of expertise. They are on their way to becoming competent.

Becoming Competent: Deliberate Selection and Evaluation

A competent knower is aware of context-free and situational rules. In action, he is able to interpret the situation and evaluate the different factors affecting it. Therefore, he is able to pick out the most relevant elements of a situation and draw his attention towards them. Competent individuals organize these experiences into formal decision-making processes. They also construct conceptual models that aid them in their decision-making. Upon the evaluation of a situation, a competent person is able to formulate objectives and decide upon appropriate actions to be taken to achieve them. Therefore, learners are now also able to reflect on their actions taken and engage in reflection-on-action. Competence also gives rise to double-loop learning, in contrast with mere single-loop learning processes.

According to Argyris (1992), single-loop learning means that a mismatch of intention and outcome leads to a change in action. An illustrative example for single-loop learning comes from engineering: A thermostat is programmed to detect states of "too cold" or "too hot" and to correct the situation by turning the heat on or off. The underlying mental models governing the action are not reflected at all. But if the thermostat would ask itself questions such as why it was set at a certain level of heat (e.g., 30°C), or why it was programmed the way it was, it would then be a double-loop learner (cf. Argyris, 1992).

In order to achieve double-loop learning, attention must not only be directed towards the solution of a problem, but also to its construction. Consequently, reflection—beyond a mere interpretation of the consequences of action—demands the questioning of the variables that govern action. Thus, the theories-in-use that guide action in a specific way have to be revealed, evaluated, and revised if they are found to be inappropriate.

What tends to be problematic at this stage of competence is that the knowledge repertoire may still be too small to evaluate the situation in its full complexity. Thus, the evaluation of the situation could be misleading, as relevant factors or interrelations are not addressed. Competent people also tend to overestimate their own capabilities.

At this stage of the learning process, it is most obvious that learners are already self-sufficient learners. No explicit rules must be given, nor must they be provided with guided experience. However, clear objectives are of help. Moreover, due to a potential competence overestimation bias, they should be confronted with the strengths and weaknesses of their ideas and problem solutions. Help from experts who have developed more sophisticated problem solutions is also beneficial at this stage.

Proficiency: Towards a Holistic Perspective

Proficient individuals, who take the conceptualization one step further, seek to understand the overall situation. The distinctive characteristic of this stage is that the knower ceases to deconstruct situations into single factors, in favor of perceiving it in a more holistic way. Consequently, tacit knowledge is applied in two different ways: proximal and distal (Polanyi, 1958). Proximal tacit knowledge constitutes a subsidiary awareness on which the knowing subject can rely upon. Therefore, the individual is able to focus his awareness on a few decisive elements of the situation. Decisions are not only made by evaluating the situation, but by drawing attention to what is most urgent.

Individuals at this stage of learning form "mental models" that constitute "deeply held internal images of how the world works, images which limit us to familiar ways of thinking and acting" (Senge, 1994:174). These models are like lenses through which the knowing subject perceives the environment influencing his perception, cognition, and action (cf. Stacey, 1993). Furthermore, knowledge at this stage is so elaborate that cognitive capacity delimits its storage and retrieval in its full complexity. Previously acquired knowledge is stored in the mind as a holistic scheme and internalized below the level of awareness into the subconscious mind. Such "compressed experience" (cf. Weick, 1995) permits more efficient usage of the brain's limited capacity, and as more and more knowledge is stored and interlinked in the nonconscious mind, the brain's cognitive capability increases, finally resulting in expertise.

Gaining Expertise: Bodily Integration of Knowledge

On the ultimate stage of knowing, the skills still intuitive in the previous stage become bodily integrated and are therefore nonconscious. It would even appear that routine action does not demand any cognitive effort of the expert at all. Since experts have a plethora of experiences from which to draw upon, they are able to act on intuition; they are not limited by the rules. Experts are able to handle complex situations successfully. Experts are therefore also able to teach other individuals and offer them guidance. Thoughts and actions based on expertise depend largely on the quality of the applied mental models and their suggested direction of focal awareness towards the element of the situation that really matters. Proficient individuals, and especially experts, apply holistic mental models that are nonconscious. Most of their problem-solving strategies run so smoothly that experts cease to reflect their everyday doing. However, focusing exclusively on the solution of problems might lead to "skilled incompetence." Experts are prone to overlook subtle changes in the environment, therefore not raising doubt on their side. These changes may be severe, resulting in inappropriate actions of the expert (cf. Stacey, 1993). Only when decisions turn out to be incorrect does previously reflected knowledge come back into focal awareness. Similar to the stage of proficiency, skilled incompetence could result from intuitive action, and lead to incorrect decisions and inferior problem solutions due to a lack of double-loop learning. As a consequence, organizations are in need of individuals who constantly challenge their expert members and stimulate double-loop learning. Therefore, not only experts can become mentors for the less-experienced learners within a community of practice, but also those less-experienced learners can take a prominent role in the learning process of a community by preventing skilled incompetence.

Learning and Mentorship

Mentorship in F/OSS communities would be impossible if it would solely rest on the shoulders of a handful of experts. Community members who are already more advanced learners can support this process of becoming an expert by being a mentor to the newcomer. To act as a mentor does not require being an expert. "Experts may lack patience to guide a novice, and, from the novice's viewpoint, someone more proximate in experience may be a better teacher than the expert because the knowledge gap is not as great" (Swap, Leonard, Shields, & Abrams, 2001:101). For the learner, it is particularly the very first learning steps that are the most difficult, as he does not even know yet what questions to ask. Berends (2002) has introduced two terms for initiating a learning process, depending on who takes the first initiative. "Pulling" refers to requests from novices to more advanced learners. "When pulling one needs to know what information is relevant and who might be a possible informant" (Berends, 2002:9). In contrast to this, "pushing" means that the more advanced learner takes a proactive role and preselects what he or she considers as being important for the inexperienced learner. Billett (1994) suggests four different processes by which a mentor can support a novice:

- **Modeling:** This involves an advanced knower executing a task so that learners can observe and build a conceptual model of the processes required to accomplish tasks successfully.
- **Coaching:** As learners carry out activities, an advanced knower observes and monitors this behavior. By providing hints, feedback, clues, and tips, the learner is supported in achieving the desired outcome.
- **Scaffolding:** This support can take the form of providing the learners with opportunities to acquire knowledge that is within the scope of learners' ability. By executing the task themselves, the applied knowledge is no longer abstract, but gets related to the specific context and situation; thus, also involving the creation of tacit knowledge.
- **Fading:** This consists of gradual removal of support until learners are able to conduct the task autonomously and push some acquired knowledge to the unconscious mind.

As already stated, mentoring is not only positive for those who receive support, but also for the supporters. Because the advanced knower who supports the learner has to make his thinking explicit, he is forced to reflect consciously on his action (cf. Schön, 1987). Added to this, as newcomers do not rely on subconscious mental models, they may come up with different perspectives, and may even cause a rethinking of taken-for-granted assumptions. These are the ingredients for a successful learning environment. Although it is primarily a question of culture and communication processes that help organizations to foster double-loop learning, technology and its appropriate use can promote such a learning culture. The following case study will demonstrate how these processes can be successfully implemented in an online learning environment.

Learning from the KDE Community: A Case Study on New Member Integration

The KDE Project

KDE is one of the largest F/OSS projects to date. KDE is a desktop environment for UNIX workstations, similar to those found under the MacOS or Microsoft Windows. With the increasing popularity of UNIX, in particular its F/OSS variant Linux, the need for such a graphical user interface arose. In October 1996, Matthias Ettrich posted a message on an Internet newsgroup asking for help to create a desktop environment for Linux. Today, a vast number of developers constantly work on the creation of a visually attractive contemporary desktop environment with a consistent look and feel, standardized menus and toolbars, a centralized dialog driven configuration engine, and many other progressive features. More than 1,000 developers situated all over the world work and communicate via the Internet. Up to date, their collaboration has resulted in around 4 million lines of code. The core developer group consists of 35 programming experts whose responsibilities are predominately coding (http://www.kde.org/people/gallery.php) and deciding on KDE policies. Additionally, hundreds of volunteers support KDE, engaging in a variety of tasks such as graphic design, writing documentation, and translation.

During a 4-month period, the project community was thoroughly observed in order to gain a deep understanding of their activity. A research approach similar to Kozinets' netnography (Kozinets, 1998, 2002) and Glaser and Strauss' grounded theory (Glaser, 1978; Glaser & Strauss, 1967; Goulding, 2002) was chosen. During the observation phase, memos were written, and categories were developed, coded, and regularly discussed within the research team. A procedure of open, axial, and selective coding, as described by Goulding (2002), was applied. External open-source affiliates were included in discussions, and F/OSS conferences were visited in order to grasp the cultural background of the open-source movement.

The community operates a general Web site at http://www.kde.org. From there, links guide the interested visitor to numerous other Web sites maintained by the community. For coding-related content, the community provides the developers'

Web site (http://developer.kde.org), where all source code, tools, documentation, and other task-related content is stored. For work purposes, common groupware and workflow applications are used that help keep track of the current work status. Among these applications is a bug database where advanced users can report bugs. The subversion (SVN) application is possibly the most important tool for programmers who work simultaneously and must keep track of all the coding. Furthermore, comments on parts of the code can be integrated into the SVN, which aims to help others to understand the logic applied. A forum and newsgroups are dedicated more specifically to advanced users who exchange thoughts and discuss important topics related to KDE in an asynchronous manner. Internet relay chat (IRC) is also used as a synchronous tool for communication. The most important communication tools for developers are the numerous mailing lists in which developers reflect upon their work and discuss strategic issues. All workflow and communication is archived and open for all to read and follow.

New Member Integration at KDE

Stage 1. Getting Familiar With KDE

The first point of contact for aspirant members of the KDE community is the project's general Web site, http://www.kde.org/, which offers a great variety of information, such as what KDE actually is, the history of the development, future goals, success stories, the most important people involved in KDE, news, current announcements, and much more. Hypertext allows visitors to browse through the content according to their individual interests, supporting self-determined learning of people with diverse backgrounds and motivations. The information mainly provides organizational and institutional knowledge.

Following the link "Getting involved" leads to explicit information about the different possibilities for contribution to the project. Developers are invited to visit http://developer.kde.org/—the site that is dedicated exclusively to present and primarily future KDE developers. The main menu items are "Documentation," "Release schedules," "Get the source code," "Compile KDE," "Tools," "Bindings," "Join the team," and "Project policies." This conglomeration of detailed explicit descriptions and rules allows the newcomer to acquire task-related knowledge before engaging in coding. Browsing and digesting this information requires considerable effort.

Self-motivation is one of the most important principles of the KDE development model. Hence, this is also expected from anyone who wants to get involved with the community. The following brief excerpt, taken from the kde-devel-mailing list, provides an example for that mentality:

Hello Everyone,

I am totally new to KDevelop, please let me know what it is, when I saw it for the first time I found it as if it is for developing new applications for KDE ...

Please tell me how to start with KDevelop ... if I want to develop some Applications like what we do with visual basic on Windows platform then what is the best (Let me know whether I can do something with QT Designer for Developing Applications to run on Linux ...)

Anyone please help me in this regard ... I am very much interested to develop GUI applications for Linux ...

Thanks & Regards

In an answer, this poster received the following message:

Maybe you want to wait for Visual Basic for Linux? Perhaps it is available in about 50 years. Since you are new to Linux I can give you the astonishing advice to read the documents which come with your system or are available at http://www.kde.org/. I do not believe that someone here has the time to write the documentation especially for you.

I do not know where you come from. Perhaps you are used to Win systems. Obviously new users there get a short introduction to system and all software packages by Bill himself.

You can believe me that I do not expect this mail to help you, but I could not resist.

Sorry!

This answer gives the clear and explicit advice as to where newcomers are supposed to look for the first contact with the community—at the community's Web site. The harsh tone of the answer shows the disregard for not putting any efforts in solving one's own problems, before engaging in person-to-person interactivity with community members. Apart from the emphasis on self-sufficient learning, here the community also seeks to avoid distraction. The questions of novices are too basic to provoke much valuable reflection on developer's action; hence, they are of no use to the community. Furthermore, the same questions are repeatedly brought up by different newcomers over time, which allows for an efficient entry process by standardization. A sophisticated means to present explicit information to newcomers in a standardized manner are lists of frequently asked questions (FAQs). Neus (2001) has described the high value of FAQs for learners:

In contrast to practically all other forms of documented knowledge, the FAQ is structured not from the perspective of the 'knower', but is collaboratively created over time and structured from the perspective of the 'knowledge seeker'. It is therefore a much more efficient way of educating people and bringing them to a common level of understanding.

Stage 2. Plunging Into Experience

Central to the theory of communities of practice is that learning constitutes a process of becoming a practitioner. Therefore, it is necessary that aspirant members develop the ability to use the KDE developer tools quickly in order to create software. To support the advanced beginners' first steps, the community applies a scaffolding process by providing tutorials. In contrast to common documentation, which only provides an abstract description of how things work, tutorials are much more oriented towards the activity of using tools, and coding itself. Tutorials present exercises within the scope of learners' ability, together with a step-by-step guidance of how to master these exercises. Thus, they support prearranged experience combined with directed reflection-in-action. In order to enable experience as intended by the author of the tutorial, a suitable situation has to be ensured, and the situational factors have to be made comprehensible for the learner, for example, using exactly the same version of software tools. Coding is a well-suited task with respect to these requirements. Using the appropriate operating system and developer tools guarantees the suitable context. The execution of correct action must therefore result precisely in the proposed outcomes. In order to allow for a constant comparison of the outcomes of the learners exercise with the proposed solution, tutorials contain explicit visual information in the form of screenshots.

In addition to the deliberately prepared tutorials, aspirant developers also benefit from the openness prevailing in the KDE community. All previous communication is preserved in forums, newsgroups, and, in particular, archives of mailing lists. The archives are freely accessible for everyone who is interested. It is thus possible for a newcomer to retrace the history of the community as an observer:

Figure 2. Reflecting on social practice through observation

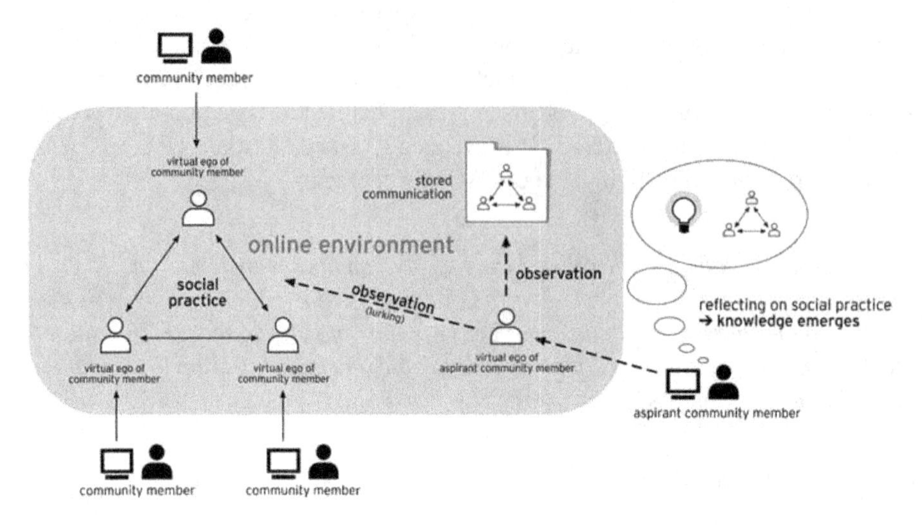

Recording [past interactions] in the form of electronically mediated communication provides a way to expand the participation of a particular individual in group processes without necessarily re-engaging each of the individuals to recapitulate their discussion for the benefit of new members. (Steinmueller, 2000)

Allowing the interested reader not only to glance at distillated explicated knowledge, but to follow the entire stream of communicative interaction, helps the reader to reexperience the social practice of the KDE community. Thus, archives of comprehensive and coherent past communication are not only repositories of explicit knowledge, but have the potential to convey tacit knowledge as well.

Moreover, it is also possible to observe the community's ongoing communication. The term "lurking" refers to the presence in cyberspace combined with observation of communication, but no active participation. The learning effect of lurking for the individual is the most likely reason why KDE allows everyone to observe the discourse going on in their mailing lists. Even the core developers' mailing list is open for observation, although active participation is restricted to those members who have qualified themselves by their expertise. If it is desired that average community members become experts they should have the possibility to observe what it means to behave like an expert. Beyond, every community member should have the possibility to comprehend the strategic decisions directing the further development of their joint enterprise.

Another mentionable aspect is that by observing social practice, the learning individual does not acquire tacit knowledge from another single individual; rather it acquires tacit knowledge from the community of practice, that is, a social collective.

The individuals engaged in the observed communication are not relevant because of "who they are" but because of the roles they take and the communicative behavior they show. The social tacit knowledge of a community of practice is predominately collective knowledge, not stored within any single individual's brain but within the entire community.

A very positive effect on learning is also realized by another form of openness, that of the source code. Reading the source code and the author's comments, which are written directly into the source, allow the reader to reexperience the process of coding. Changes of code are tracked in detail by a diff application in the SVN repository, using colors and tables that depict the changes made. This fosters learning according to the process that Billett (1994) has labeled "modeling."

Once a newcomer is familiar with the basic community's competence, the learning process takes places by legitimate peripheral participation in developing KDE source code. The possibilities for doing that are manifold. On http://www.kde.org/helping/, the following is suggested to newcomers:

If you are interesting in starting to program for KDE, think small. We've found that looking at all of KDE can be a bit overwhelming to people just starting out. We recommend doing one of the following:

- *Go to the bug database, find a random bug, fix it, and send a patch to the maintainer.*
- *Take a favorite KDE application and implement a missing feature that you really would like.*
- *Find a KDE 2.x application and port it to KDE 3.x.*
- *Find a favorite console or plain X applications and write a KDE shell for it.*
- *Check out the Jobs Board for an open job that you might like to do.*
- *Use your imagination! The possibilities are almost limitless.*

Stage 3. Becoming a Practitioner

As proposed by the KDE community, a good chance for new developers to actively contribute to a F/OSS project is fixing a bug. The specific way F/OSS projects handle bug fixing is reported to be one of the main advantages of their development model. The decisive factor is that the realization of a bug and the consequent correction are split within the community. In a study on the Linux kernel development project, Lee and Cole (2003) report that the demarcating difference of the F/OSS development model, compared to commercial software development, lies within the overcoming of geographical and time constraints, which enables an unequally larger number of people to participate. Also Raymond (1999) points out that the increased number of people who participate in the software development process is one of the main advantages of the F/OSS model. He refers to this specific characteristic as "Linus' Law": "Given enough eyeballs, all bugs are shallow" (Raymond, 1999:9). This statement refers to two consequences of an increased amount of people involved in the software improvement process. Firstly, a large group of advanced users testing the software helps to find problems quickly. Secondly, within a large group of developers, it is easier to find someone who already knows, or is willing to learn, how to fix it. The voluntary assignment to bug fixing fosters self-determined learning.

The bug database is the tool that enables even advanced users to report a bug in such a way that developers get the information they need in order to be able to fix the bug. Under the Web address http://bugs.kde.org/ bug, reporters find a standardized entry form to report bugs in great detail, accompanying with situational facts like, for example, the computer environment in which the malicious software was tested. This allows developers to reflect on the problem in a double-loop manner. To successfully fix a bug, it is not only necessary to realize a malfunction in the software, but first and foremost to construct the problem correctly; something that could not be expected to be done by users. In order to keep bug reporting efficient, all bug reports are tracked within the bug database. Thus, users are urged to first search the database for already existing reports before posting a new one. If the same problem has already been reported, it is possible to extend the report with further details by attaching comments.

Bug reports do not provide explicit guidelines to solutions, but induce learning suitable on the level of a competent learner by confronting them with problems and ideas. Nevertheless, bugs are delimited problems modularized from the overall problem of developing a comprehensive software tool. In that phase, when developers are still developing their competence, the overall picture on the software tool is not needed. For them, fixing a bug can be classified as a scaffolding process. The more advanced developers who have the big picture in mind are the maintainers who are responsible for a specific software tool. They evaluate the solution to a bug—in F/OSS jargon a "patch"—before it is integrated in the source code of the software tool. If a maintainer judges the suggested solution as not suitable for the overall source code, he rejects the patch. However, rejections are argued and accompanied by explicit explanations of the shortcomings that have led to the rejection. A developer, who has reached an acceptable level of competence, is granted an account to the SVN code repository. From this time on, the developer is allowed to integrate patches to the source code on his own. Granting write access to the repository marks an important transient phase from the role of an advanced beginner to a role of a competent programmer. Hence, it is also accompanied by a strong social symbolism and pride on the side of the competent learner.

The depth of knowledge, even among competent KDE developers, is unequally distributed. As a result of specialization, which is inevitable to reach the stage of ultimate expertise, developers are masters of different knowledge areas. Furthermore, even within specific knowledge areas, the level of knowledge differs, as not all developers are equally talented or have invested the same effort in learning. As a consequence, developers frequently come to a point where their own knowledge is insufficient for completing their work. However, as a member of the KDE community, members have access to the knowledge of others. Accessing others' knowledge in an online community bears the advantage that it is not necessary to "know who" (cf. Ernst & Lundvall, 1997) is in charge of the information needed. In cyberspace, it is only necessary to "know where" to get in contact with the people who know. However, it is necessary to know exactly where to pose a question in order to get the most reliable answer. Exchange relationships develop between an individual and the network as a whole, rather than between individuals (Faraj & Sproull, 2000).

In order to enable a match between knowledge seeking and providing, community members use a variety of synchronous and asynchronous communication tools. Not all tools that provide the possibility for person-to-person interactivity are used by developers in the same way. Forums or newsgroups are predominantly inhabited by users and not by developers. This might be due to the fact these tools are pull technology. Developer questions are frequently very specific, and it is very unlikely that the knowledgeable specialist would deliberately log in and reply. However, users and advanced beginners frequently meet in these places, therefore making the chance of matching requests and answers much higher. A further opportunity for developers to get in contact is the IRC channel #kde-devel. In this channel, knowledge seeking was observed, although the greater part of communication was socio-emotional in nature.

Mailing lists are the main tool for KDE developers to communicate with each other and engage in reflection. Before KDE developers post a question to a mailing list, however, they are requested to search the archives. If one has subscribed to the appropriate list, he can be certain that all experts of a specific domain are reached, even without their active engagement. As mailing lists are push technology, subscribers get forwarded all messages sent to the list. Hence, the chance to achieve a match of requests and answers is much higher in mailing lists.

Because all communication is stored in the archives, cyberspace also constitutes the long-term memory of the community. In the KDE archives, community members may find solutions to problems that have been previously discovered and documented (cf. also Steinmueller, 2000). Hence, the need for redundant communication is reduced.

Stage 4. Advancing the Joint Enterprise

Developing for F/OSS projects must be a challenging and joyful task in order to continuously attract a large pool of developers who are willing to spend their spare time without financial remuneration. Thus, the KDE community has realized that it is not a viable approach to present a blueprint for a project—no matter how brilliant it may be—and then ask developers to slave away without room for creativity and opportunity to actualize their own ideas in consideration of their own programming skills and development perspectives. With regard to the strong culture for self-assignment of tasks prevailing in F/OSS projects, proficient developers are required. Those who push forward the entire project have to be able to balance their individual motivations with the overall need of the joint enterprise. As a consequence, it is essential to have a functioning implementation of the whole source code readily available at all times, even if it is not perfect and complete. Modularization of tasks is definitely useful for the actual challenge of writing code, but developers must also have the possibility to review the comprehensive state of the entire source code at all times in order to be able to select the most urgent and appropriate task in which to apply themselves.

Of utmost importance for the proficient and expert developers is to find an agreement on the objectives and the advancement of their joint enterprise. This requires a continuous and ongoing discourse on the direction of further developments. In order for a developer to be able to follow the discussion, it is essential that he develops a shared perspective about the problems. The formulation of a problem is the basis for any conceptualization of a possible solution and genuinely depends on the mental construction of the situation. The way we see the world will influence all further thoughts. Thus, developers have to approach the world in a similar way in order to achieve mutuality in communication. A shared perspective is an essential prerequisite to achieve understanding in collaborative conceptualization. The more congruent the individual perspectives are, the better a developer can follow the other's line of arguments, even if they build to a large extent on tacit knowledge and are therefore poorly expressible through language.

Developers present their ideas, for example, for a new application or feature within an existing one, and ask others to comment on them. Upon such initial messages, lively interactive conversations occur, with comments supporting and further elaborating on the idea, presenting a different perspective towards the problem and so, perhaps, suggesting a different approach, or pointing towards flaws or even errors in the presentation. Thus, the conversation evolves around the construction of the problem itself. Knowledge creation, then, occurs in a double-loop manner. The dynamic process of such interaction is not foreseeable, and sometimes ideas emerge that none of the developers has had before engaging in the conversation. Such conversations are the origin of innovation. The following interaction is taken from a mailing list conversation and supports such a viewpoint:

... I'm just hawking around a few ideas with intentional questions to move into other fields, so that it can provoke a few thoughts and questions about directions :)

Another participant replied:

And this is the great thing about mailing lists. Had we not had the long threads we had (the IRS started to collect taxes on the word "had" just about now), this idea would have never come up, and we'd be at a loss. This cross-pollination of ideas is one of the things I love the most about open source.

Coding solutions for well-defined problems is not the radical innovative act in software development. It is rather the problem definition and subsequent conceptualization of a solution that are the sources of innovation. However, problems are not out there in the world waiting to be detected and solved, they are actively constructed by the community members. Innovative knowledge creation happens when double-loop learning is achieved. The findings of Raymond support this perspective: "Often, the most striking and innovative solutions come from realizing that your concept of the problem was wrong" (Raymond, 1999:13). Involving more people in the problem construction also results in an increase of different perspectives. Increased input of new ideas and higher awareness for flaws is the consequence of parallel reflection on the collaboratively created meaning. The arguments put forward have to be clear and justifiable. In the case of no consent, the community can challenge those arguments and put forward counterarguments (cf. also Dafermos, 2001). As a consequence, the process of problem construction is a more thorough and innovative one.

Problem and idea-related discourse occurs predominately in mailing lists that support communication in a way that puts more emphasis on the content of communication than on the people who communicate. When a message is posted, it is not clear beforehand who will respond. The addressee is the entire group of participants of the mailing list. Whoever feels the need to reply is free to do so. A reply on the reply, however, could be given by the author of the initial message, but also by someone else. Thus, communicative interactions can emerge involving a variety of different contributors. The dynamic communication process is only loosely coupled to the authors of messages. And also those mailing list participants who do not actively communicate participate cognitively in that they individually reflect on the ongoing discourse. "Each individual contributes to and then selectively takes from the text to further his own thinking, thus both socially and cognitively constructing meaning" (Lapadat, 2002).

An important characteristic of mailing lists is that person-to-person interactivity is asynchronous. First of all, it would be impossible for KDE developers, who are located all over the globe, and who have jobs and lives beside their work for KDE, to find designated times when all could gather together, for instance, in an IRC channel. From a knowledge creation perspective, asynchronous communication provides a valuable additional benefit. Engaging in face-to-face communication only allows for reflection-in-action; one has to think and talk simultaneously.

There is usually no time to reflect on one's own statement, because in synchronous interactive communication, the communication partner takes turn immediately and thus requires attention. As a result, unconscious mental models are hardly ever reflected and questioned. Furthermore, the time to reflect on the statements of others is usually quite limited in synchronous communication. In contrast, asynchronous communication provides the necessary time for deep reflection.

The possibility to create meaningful interaction is enhanced by the fact that communication is exclusively based on text. The KDE mailing list does not allow for direct inclusion of graphics or any content other than text. Only links that are directing to other resources may be added. Developers occasionally make use of this possibility, particularly for presenting screenshots. As mailing lists can also be regarded as push technology, all participants are actively involved in the entire communication process, and have the possibility to contribute while it is still in progress. This is an important feature if the whole group wants to gain from the continuous participation of every single developer.

Stage 5. Challenging the Experts

Interestingly, although communication gains from the participation of more developers and their different perspectives they contribute, KDE limits the access to the core developers' list, kde-core-devel. Reading the list is open to everyone, but the possibility to post a message is only granted to a limited number of developers who have qualified themselves by their high-grade contributions and their engagement for KDE. The crucial factor is the advanced level of communication within the core developers' list. Participating in discourse on strategic issues requires a considerable amount of experience and knowledge from participants. This restriction can be seen in analogy to Habermas' theory of communicative behavior as an approach towards an "ideal speech situation" (Habermas, 1981).

Nevertheless, non-core developers can also subscribe to the core developers' mailing list and observe the ongoing discourse. This allows them to reflect on the ongoing discourse in order to understand strategic decisions for the KDE project. Beyond that, they have numerous other possibilities to comment on the KDE strategy. The announcement of the fourth generation of the KDE project illustrates this. After months of discourse among core developers in their mailing lists, they published the idea behind KDE 4. Members of the core group issued announcements in their personal Web logs, on the community's Web log "KDE Dot News" (http://dot.kde.org/) and on several online magazines dedicated to F/OSS, for example, NewsForge. Upon these announcements, lively discussions were begun by hundreds of commenters to those publications. KDE 4 was also a major issue on the KDE community's annual conference, where numerous core developers faced discussions with other developers, power users, and the general public interested in KDE. KDE core developers got extensive feedback and challenges with regard to their strategic decision. By deliberately presenting their thoughts, ideas, and their future strategic perspectives, KDE experts force themselves to rethink their expert judgments. As skilled incompetence is a result of nonconscious expert judgments, opening up their thoughts and theories-in-use to the public, therefore, entails an important function for knowledge creation.

Discussion and Implications

Much of what has been demonstrated by F/OSS projects, and the KDE case, in particular, has been previously proposed by innumerable theorists and practitioners. However, many of the proposed success factors for knowledge creation are ultimately linked to two crucial factors that many organizations are lacking: self-determined learning and access to a global pool of interested, aspirant members. The KDE case vividly demonstrates the key role of new member integration for the sustainability of a community project. Although this is easy to comprehend, the implementation of appropriate processes and rules for integration is not at all easy. Project communities have to define rules and norms, roles, and facilities that offer opportunities for learning. They have to offer mentorship to those who are interested in contributing in order to help them on their way to becoming a competent member. However, and most importantly, they also have to prevent developers and core developers from distraction, as they constitute the community's most valuable source of innovation and new software development.

F/OSS communities try to solve these potential threats by a sophisticated balance of establishing different community roles for different tasks, with different rights and duties. On the other hand, these roles are ascribed to community members according to their individual stage of learning progress. Drawing on the work of Dreyfus and Dreyfus (1986), this chapter has illustrated these learning stages from novice to expert, and described how they are interlinked with the integration processes elaborated by the community. Web technology, applications and communication tools, in particular, provide the necessary technologic basis for the successful design of these processes. However, technology does not have to be overly sophisticated. On the contrary, it seems that the deliberate restriction to the use of simple and easy to use applications helps the learners to find their way through the overwhelming complexity and amount of knowledge and software that has been built by the community. To conclude, successful learning environments find a balance of member roles, e-learning tools, and a step-by step integration process.

In a first and very sensitive phase, aspirant members need rigid and clear guidance, however, without discouragement, and without distracting competent and expert members. It would be disastrous for the community if expert members would have to take over a mentoring role for thousands of interested learners. On the other hand, it is vital that aspirant members are supported. Explicit rules and clear guidance on easy-to-find Web sites in the form of FAQs, policy statements, and many other online documents help to manage the first stage of entry.

The second stage is characterized by enabling experience on the side of the learner. However, these first plunges into experience must, first of all, exactly simulate real-life programming in order to be of help in more advanced stages, but at the same time be presented in small, digestible pieces of work. With the help of tutorials, learners get immediate feedback to their efforts, as they can compare their outcomes with that of an expert. Even in this phase, person-to-machine interactivity is able to partly replace person-to-person contact. Furthermore, this stage is characterized by intensive observation of the community, of discourse, and code. By doing that, the advanced learner is able to reexperience task-related and social practice.

Knowing how a community functions is important before being able to actually participate and contribute. Thus, the next stage is dedicated to becoming a practitioner and eventually gaining full access to the source code. With entry into this stage, status and pride come into play. Herein an important role transition from the advanced beginner to the competent contributor takes place. This phase is characterized by legitimate peripheral participation, review, and feedback. It ultimately results in being granted write access to the source code repository and full integration into the community.

In the next two stages, although still learning stages, the roles between learners and mentors are reversed. Now proficient members and experts take the role of mentors for those who are less experienced and give valuable advice on requests in the mailing lists. Their archived discourse also provides a helpful source for learners who are searching the site for answers to their questions. However, those stages are also characterized by compressed experience and skilled incompetence. Therefore, continuous, ongoing reflection, in a double-loop manner, is crucial for the success of the community effort; F/OSS communities open up their work and their thoughts to the world in order to overcome these potential drawbacks. Openness, in every sense of the word, is crucial. New knowledge hardly emerges in frozen environments, but more easily springs out of diversity and a multitude of participants, which can only occur in loosely integrated systems where there is room for controversies and multiple views.

References

Argyris, C. (1992). *On organizational learning*. Oxford: Blackwell.

Baumgartner, P., & Payr, S. (1999). *Lernen mit Software*. Innsbruck: Studienverlag.

Benner, P. (2001). *From novice to expert - Excellence and power in clinical nursing practice*. New York: Prentice-Hall.

Berends, J. J. H. (2002, June 15). *Knowledge sharing and distributed cognition in industrial research*. Paper presented at the 3rd European Conference on Organizational Knowledge, Learning, and Capabilities, Athens, Greece.

Billett, S. (1994). Situating learning in the workplace - Having another look at apprenticeships. *Industrial and Commercial Training, 26*(11), 9-16.

Brown, J. S., & Duguid, P. (1991). Organizational learning and communities-of-practice: Toward a unified view of working, learning, and innovation. *Organization Science, 2*(1), 40-57.

Cook, S. D. N., & Brown, J. S. (1999). Bridging epistemologies: The generative dance between organizational knowledge and organizational knowing. *Organization Science, 10*(4), 381-400.

Cubranic, D., & Booth, K. S. (1999). Coordination in open-source software development. In *Proceedings of the 7th IEEE International Workshop on Enabling Technologies: Infrastructure for Collaborative Enterprises*.

Dafermos, G. N. (2001). Management and virtual decentralised networks: The Linux Project. *First Monday, 6*(11). Retrieved from http://www.firstmonday.org/issues/issues6_11/dafermos/

Dreyfus, H., & Dreyfus, S. (1986). *Mind over machine*. New York: The Free Press.

Ducheneaut, N. (2005). Socialization in an open source software community: A socio-technical analysis. *Computer Supported Cooperative Work (CSCW), 14*(4), 323-368.

Ernst, D., & Lundvall, B. A. (1997). *Information technology in the learning economy —Challenges for developing countries*. DRUID Working Paper No. 97-12. Retrieved June 2, 2002, from http://www.druid.dk/wp/pdf_files/97-12.pdf

Evans, P., & Wolf, B. (2005). Collaboration rules. *Harvard Business Review, 83*(7), 1-9.

Faraj, S., & Sproull, L. (2000). Coordinating expertise in software development teams. *Management Science, 46*(12), 1554-1568.

Fink, K. (2000). *Know-How-Management: Architektur für den Know-How-Transfer*. München: Oldenbourg.

Glaser, B. G. (1978). *Theoretical sensitivity*. Mail Valley, CA: Sociology Press.

Glaser, B. G., & Strauss, A. L. (1967). *The discovery of grounded theory*. New York: de Gruyter.

Goulding, C. (2002). *Grounded theory - A practical guide for management, business and market researchers*. London et al.: SAGE Publications.

Granovetter, M. (1973). The strength of weak ties. *American Journal of Sociology*, *78*, 1360-1380.

Habermas, J. (1981). *Theorie des Kommunikativen Handelns*. Frankfurt a. Main: Suhrkamp.

Hemetsberger, A. (2002). Fostering cooperation on the Internet: Social exchange processes in innovative virtual consumer communities. *Advances in Consumer Research*, *29,* (pp. 354-356).

Hemetsberger, A., & Pieters, R. (2001). *When consumers produce on the Internet: An inquiry into motivational sources of contribution to joint-innovation*. Paper presented at the Fourth International Research Seminar on Marketing Communications and Consumer Behavior, La Londe.

Hemetsberger, A., & Reinhardt, C. (2006). Learning and knowledge-building in open-source communities—A social-experiential approach. *Management Learning*, *37*(2), 187-214.

Kogut, B., & Zander, U. (1996). What firms do? Coordination, identity, and learning. *Organization Science*, *7*(5), 502-518.

Kozinets, R. V. (1998). On netnography: Initial reflections on consumer research investigations of cyberculture. *Advances in Consumer Research*, *25*, 366-371.

Kozinets, R. V. (2002). The field behind the screen: Using netnography for marketing research in online communities. *Journal of Marketing Research*, *39*(2), 61-72.

Kuwabara, K. (2000). Linux: A bazaar at the edge of chaos. *First Monday*, *5*(3). Retrieved November 2006 from http://www.firstmonday.org/issues/issues5_3/kuwabara/

Lanzara, G. F., & Morner, M. (2003). *The knowledge ecology of open-source projects*. Paper presented at the 19th European Group of Organization Studies (EGOS) Colloquium, Copenhagen.

Lapadat, J. C. (2002). Written interaction: A key component in online learning. *Journal of Computer Mediated Communication*, *7*(4). Retrieved November 2006 from http://jcmc.indiana.edu/vol7/issues4/lapadat.html

Lave, J., & Wenger, E. C. (1990). *Situated learning: Legitimate peripheral participation*. Palo Alto, CA: Institute for Research on Learning.

Lee, G. K., & Cole, R. E. (2003). The Linux kernel development: An evolutionary model of knowledge creation. *Organization Science 14*(6), 633-649.

Lerner, J., & Tirole, J. (2002). Some simple economics of open source. *Journal of Industrial Economics, 50*(2), 197-234.

Madanmohan, T. R., & Navelkar, S. (2002). *Roles and knowledge management in online technology communities: An ethnography study*. Indian Institute of Management-Bangalore, Digital. Retrieved June 24, 2002, from http://opensource.mit.edu/papers/madanmohan2.pdf

Maddux, C. D., Johnson, D. L., & Willis, J. W. (1997). *Educational computing: Learning with tomorrow's technologies*. Boston: Allyn & Bacon.

Maturana, H. R., & Varela, F. J. (1992). *The tree of knowledge: The biological roots of human understanding* (2nd and revised ed.). Boston: New Science Press.

McKinlay, A., Potter, J., & Wetherell, M. (1993). Discourse analysis and social representations. In G. M. Breakwell & D. V. Canter (Eds.), *Empirical approaches to social representations* (pp. 134-156). Oxford: Clarendon Press.

Metiu, A., & Kogut, B. (2001). *Distributed knowledge and the global organization of software development*. Knowledge@Wharton. Retrieved May 29, 2002, from http://knowledge.wharton.upenn.edu/PDFs/1003.pdf

Mockuss, A., Fielding, R. T., & Herbsleb, J. (2000). *A case study of open source software development: The Apache server*. Paper presented at the International Conference on Software Engineering, Limerick, Ireland.

Moody, G. (2001). *Rebel code: Inside Linux and the open source revolution*. New York: Perseus Press.

Neus, A. (2001). *Managing information quality in virtual communities of practice*. Retrieved July 3, 2002, from http://opensource.mit.edu/papers/neus.pdf

Nonaka, I. (1994). A dynamic theory of organizational knowledge creation. *Organization Science, 5*(1), 14-37.

Nonaka, I., & Takeuchi, H. (1995). *The knowledge-creating company*. New York: Oxford University Press.

Pal, N., & Madanmohan, T. R. (2002). *Competing on open source: Strategies and practise*. Indian Institute of Management, Bangalore. Retrieved June 24, 2002, from http://opensource.mit.edu/papers/madanmohan.pdf

Polanyi, M. (1958). *Personal knowledge—Toward a post-critical philosophy*. London: Routledge.

Polanyi, M. (1966). *The tacit dimension*. New York: Anchor Day Books.

Polanyi, M. (1969). *Knowing and being*. Chicago: University of Chicago Press.

Raymond, E. S. (1999). The cathedral and the bazaar. *First Monday*. Retrieved June 19, 2002, from http://firstmonday.org/issues/issue3_3/raymond

Sawhney, M., & Prandelli, E. (2000). Communities of creation: Managing distributed innovation in turbulent markets. *California Management Review, 42*(4), 24-35.

Schön, D. (1982). *The reflective practitioner - How professionals think in action*. New York: Basic Books.

Schön, D. (1987). *Educating the reflective practitioner*. Meeting of the American Educational Research Association. Retrieved May 30, 2002, from http://educ.queensu.ca/~ar/schon87.htm

Senge, P. M. (1994). *The fifth discipline*. New York et al.: Currency Doubleday.

Stacey, R. D. (1993). *Strategic management and organisational dynamics*. London: Pitman Publishing.

Steinmueller, W. E. (2000). Will new information and communication technologies improve the 'codification' of knowledge? *Science and Technology Policy Research, 9*(2), 361-376.

Swap, W., Leonard, D., Shields, M., & Abrams, L. (2001). Using mentoring and storytelling to transfer knowledge in the workplace. *Journal of Management Information Systems, 18*(1), 95-114.

Szulanski, G., Winter, S., & Cappetta, R. (2000). *Knowledge transfer within the firm: A replication perspective on stickiness*. Knowledge@Wharton. Retrieved May 31, 2002, from http://knowledge.wharton.upenn.edu/

Thomke, S., & von Hippel, E. (2002). Customers as innovators - A new way to create value. *Harvard Business Review, 80*(4), 74-81.

Tuomi, I. (2000). Learning from Linux: Internet, innovation, and the new economy. *Empirical and Descriptive Analysis of the Open Source Model*. Retrieved January 8, 2003, from http://www.jrc.es/~tuomiil/articles/LearningFromLinux.pdf

von Hippel, E., & von Krogh, G. (2003). Open source software and the private-collective innovation model. *Organization Science, 14*(2), 209-223.

von Krogh, G., Ichijo, G., & Nonaka, I. (2000). *Enabling knowledge creation*. New York: Oxford University Press.

von Krogh, G., Spaeth, S., & Lakhani, K. (2003). Community, joining, and specialization in open source software innovation: a case study. *Research Policy, 32*, 1217-1241.

Wayner, P. (2000). *Free for all: How Linux and the free software movement undercut the high-tech titans*. New York: Harper Business.

Weick, K. E. (1979). *The social psychology of organizing* (2nd ed.). Reading, MA: Addison-Wesley Publishing.

Weick, K. E. (1995). *Sensemaking in organizations*. Thousand Oaks, CA: Sage Publications.

Weick, K. E., & Roberts, K. H. (1993). Collective minds in organizations: Heedful interrelating on flight decks. *Administrative Science Quarterly*, *38*, 357-381.

Wenger, E. C. (1998a). Communities of practice: Learning as a social system. *Systems Thinker* (June).

Wenger, E. C. (1998b). *Communities of practice: Learning, meaning, and identity.* Cambridge: Cambridge University Press.

Wenger, E. C. (2000). Communities of practice and social learning systems. *Organization*, *7*(2), 225-246.

Ye, Y., & Kishida, K. (2003). *Toward an understanding of the motivation of open source software developers.* Paper presented at the International Conference on Software Engineering (ICSE2003), Portland, OR.

Zhang, W., & Storck, J. (2001). *Peripheral members in online communities.* Retrieved 3rd July 2002, from http://opensource.mit.edu/papers/zhang.pdf

Appendix I: Internet Session: Evaluating the Tools and Services Provided by Sourceforge.net

http://www.sourceforge.net/

Service listing to be found at:

http://sourceforge.net/docman/display_doc.php?docid=753&group_id=1

Interaction

Sourceforge.net is the world's largest F/OSS collaborative development repository currently hosting more than 100,000 F/OSS projects. Numerous communities use the opportunity to host their joint enterprise on sourceforge.net, utilizing the various tools and services provided by the OSTG ("Open Source Technology Group"). Take the service listing as your starting point and explore how the various tools and services are used by the developers and evaluate them in regard to their learning support according to Dreyfus & Dreyfus' five-stage model.

Appendix II: Case Study

Integrating Hi-Fi Freaks in the Development of High-Class Loudspeakers

As a product manager for loudspeakers at a highly specialized manufacturer, you have established a forum on your company's Web site a year ago. The primary intention to set up this forum was giving consumers the possibility to ask experts within your company questions on your products and give some firsthand feedback. But you realize that an ongoing, lively discourse emerged not only on your products, but rather on loudspeakers in general. Your employees appreciate the exchange with your customers. And among the visitors of your forum are other very knowledgeable hi-fi experts who do use your products but make modifications and are very selective with their whole hi-fi setup. They strive for the perfect audio experience. And so do a lot of other hi-fi freaks that regularly visit the forum to extend their knowledge by engaging in threads on various topics. People exchange their use experiences and share detailed technical background information, instructions for speaker modification, ideas for do-it-yourself experiments, and so forth.

The people on your forum not only talk about loudspeakers, but a lot of them also get their hands on the "production" of their perfect hi-fi setup. As you have read about F/OSS online communities and their ability to collaboratively create innovative products you ask yourself: "Would it be possible to integrate those involved people on our forum more systematically in the development of our high-class loudspeakers?"

(*To get a feeling for discussions among hi-fi freaks you can visit http://www.hifi-forum.net/*)

Questions

1. Your employees, consumers and other interested people meet on your forum. What are their possible motivations for contribution to the ongoing discourse? Can you identify different roles?
2. What kind of relationships could be established among the different actors within the online environment? What benefits could you potentially provide to other people (e.g., knowledge, sense of belonging to a community, advancements in products) and what benefits could different actors provide to you (e.g., information, work).

3. What kind of integration strategy could you set up for newcomers? Pay attention to the learning stages of Dreyfus and Dreyfus' five-stage model.
4. What advises for technologic interfaces design could you give?

Appendix III: Useful URLs

1. The KDE community Web site:
   http://www.kde.org/
2. The KDE news Web log 'KDE Dot News':
   http://dot.kde.org/
3. Other important F/OSS projects:
   Apache: **http://www.apache.org/**
   Linux: **http://www.kernel.org/**, **http://www.linux.org/**
   Mozilla: **http://www.mozilla.org/developer/**
   MySQL: **http://dev.mysql.com/**
   Perl: **http://www.perl.org/**
4. Sourceforge, The home of more than 100,000 F/OSS projects:
   http://www.sourceforge.net/
5. Com-Prac is a global forum on communities of practice:
   http://groups.yahoo.com/group/com-prac/
6. DMOZ: Open directory references to communities of practice:
   http://dmoz.org/Reference/Knowledge_Management/Knowledge_Flow/Communities_of_Practice/
7. First Monday special issue on open source:
   http://firstmonday.org/issues/special10_10/
8. Knowledge Garden, a public service of Community Intelligence Labs, provides further information on communities of practice:
   http://www.co-i-l.com/coil/knowledge-garden/cop/index.shtml
9. Opensource.MIT: Free and open source research community supported by MIT:
   http://opensource.mit.edu/

10. Slashdemocracy.org provides a collection of papers on communities of practice:

    http://slashdemocracy.org/cgi-bin/page.cgi?g=Knowledge_Management%2FCommunities_of_practice%2Findex.html

11. Dick Stenmark's extensive discussion on the concept of knowledge from a knowledge management perspective:

    http://www.informatik.gu.se/~dixi/km/index.html

Appendix IV: Further Readings

Brand, A. (n.d.). *Research on the KDE project to gain more insight in new forms of organization and collaboration.* Several of his publications can be found on the Web site of the Project Electronic Labour Markets (PELM): http://www.soz.uni-frankfurt.de/arbeitslehre/pelm/brand.html

Dreyfus, H., & Dreyfus, S. (n.d.). *From Socrates to expert systems: The limits and dangers of calculative rationality*. Presents their five-stage model with illustrative examples. Retrieved from http://ist-socrates.berkeley.edu/~hdreyfus/html/paper_socrates.html

Füller, J., Bartl, M., Mühlbacher, H., & Ernst, H. (2004). *Community based innovation – A method to utilize the innovative potential of online communities.* Paper presented at Hawaii International Conference on System Sciences, HICSS-37, Big Island. Retrieved from http://csdl2.computer.org/comp/proceedings/hicss/2004/2056/07/205670195c.pdf

Hemetsberger, A., & Reinhardt, C. (2006). Learning and knowledge-building in open-source communities—A social-experiential approach. *Management Learning*, forthcoming (pp. 354-356).

Himanen, P. (2001). *The hacker ethic—A radical approach to the philosophy of business*. New York: Random House.

Schön, D. (1987). *Educating the reflective practitioner.* Meeting of the American Educational Research Association, Washington, DC. Retrieved from http://educ.queensu.ca/~ar/schon87.htm

von Krogh, G., Spaeth, S., & Lakhani, K. (2003). Community, joining, and specialization in open source software innovation: A case study. *Research Policy*, *32*, 1217-1241.

Wenger, E. (n.d.). *A brief introduction to the community of practice theory*. Retrieved from http://www.ewenger.com/theory/index.htm

Wenger, E. C. (1998). *Communities of practice: Learning, meaning, and identity.* Cambridge: Cambridge University Press.

Possible Titles for Papers/Essays

- Designing an Effective E-Learning Environment to Support the Different Learning Stages of Volunteer, Employee, and Customer Innovators
- The Role of Corporate Culture in the Integration of External Partners for Cooperation in Innovation Processes
- Integrating Corporate Innovation Processes and Knowledge Creation Processes in Online Communities
- Toolkits for Individual Online Learning
- Toolkits for Collective Online Knowledge Creation

Chapter III

Riki: A System for Knowledge Transfer and Reuse in Software Engineering Projects

Jörg Rech, Fraunhofer Institute for Experimental Software Engineering (IESE), Germany
Eric Ras,Fraunhofer Institute for Experimental Software Engineering (IESE), Germany
Björn Decker, Fraunhofer Institute for Experimental Software Engineering (IESE), Germany

Abstract

Many software organizations have a reputation for producing expensive, low-quality software systems. This results from the inherent complexity of software itself as well as the chaotic organization of developers building these systems. Therefore, we set a stage for software development based on social software for knowledge and learning management to support reuse in software engineering as well as knowledge sharing in and between projects. In the RISE (Reuse in Software Engineering) project, we worked with several German SMEs to develop a system for the reuse of software engineering products such as requirement documents. The methodology and technology developed in the RISE project makes it possible to share knowledge in the form of software artifacts, experiences, or best practices based on pedagogic approaches. This chapter gives an overview of the reuse of knowledge and so-called Learning Components in software engineering projects and raises several requirements one should keep in mind when building such systems to support knowledge transfer and reuse.

Introduction

The software industry develops complex systems that often have a reputation of being expensive and of low quality. One approach for coping with the increasing complexity of these systems is software reuse—the sharing of knowledge about software products, processes, people, and projects in an organization.

But the poor and often nonexistent documentation of this knowledge inhibits easy recording, collection, management, comprehension, and transfer. The knowledge, for example, in the form of requirement descriptions, architectural information, design decisions, or debugging experiences, needs a systematic, minimally invasive, methodological, and technological basis to strengthen its reuse and transfer in software organizations.

Knowledge management (KM) and *learning management* (LM) seem to have the potential for building this basis if they are used in synergy. However, the relationships between these two promising fields have not been fully understood and harnessed yet. On the one hand, learning as the comprehension of knowledge is considered to be a fundamental part of KM, as employees must internalize shared knowledge before they can use it to perform a specific task. So far, research within KM has addressed learning mostly as part of knowledge sharing processes, and focused on specific forms of informal learning (e.g., learning in a community of practice) or on providing access to learning resources or experts. On the other hand, LM includes techniques to preprocess and formalize knowledge, and might also benefit from other KM approaches. Especially, those approaches that support technical and organizational aspects in an organization can be used in addition to professional e-learning systems.

In this intersection between KM and LM, the Wiki technology (cf. http://en.wikipedia.org/wiki/Wiki) promises to be a lightweight basis to capture, organize, and distribute knowledge that is produced and used in organizations. Wikis are Web-based knowledge repositories where every user can freely submit or retrieve knowledge.

The *RISE* (*Reuse In Software Engineering*) project was started to support software engineers via the reuse of didactically enriched software artifacts from all software development phases in SMEs (small and medium enterprises). As the basis for knowledge transfer, we have developed a reuse-oriented Wiki (Riki) with fast and liberal access to deposit, mature, and reuse experiences made in software projects. Our Riki was extended by search technologies using case-based reasoning technology and ontologies to provide a formal and consistent framework for the description of knowledge and experiences. Ontologies and templates enrich the Riki content with semantics that enable us to didactically augment the knowledge within the Riki with additional information and documented experiences.

The RISE system sketches our approach for software reuse and tackles several problems of traditional KM and LM in learning software organizations. We use *semiautomatic indexing of pages* to improve retrieval and enable the semiautomatic creation and evolution of ontologies from Wikis (i.e., Wikitologies). The *cooperative adaptation* of knowledge to community needs and the *didactic augmentation* of content and interface are targeted to improve the usability of lightweight KM applications in agile environments.

In this chapter, we give an overview of the methodology and technology developed in the RISE project to build the reuse-oriented Wiki framework named Riki. As depicted in Figure 1, we describe in the *Background* the relevant background about knowledge and learning management, as well as software engineering and Wikis. This is followed by *Problems and Challenges* containing the targeted problems and objectives examined in the RISE project.

Our main contribution for knowledge transfer and reuse in software engineering is summarized in *Semantic-Based Reuse in SE: The RISE Approach*, which contains both the methodology in *RIME: The RISE Methodology for Knowledge Transfer and Reuse* and the technology in *Riki: The Reuse-Oriented Wiki*. Furthermore, several best

Figure 1. Outline and structure of the following chapter

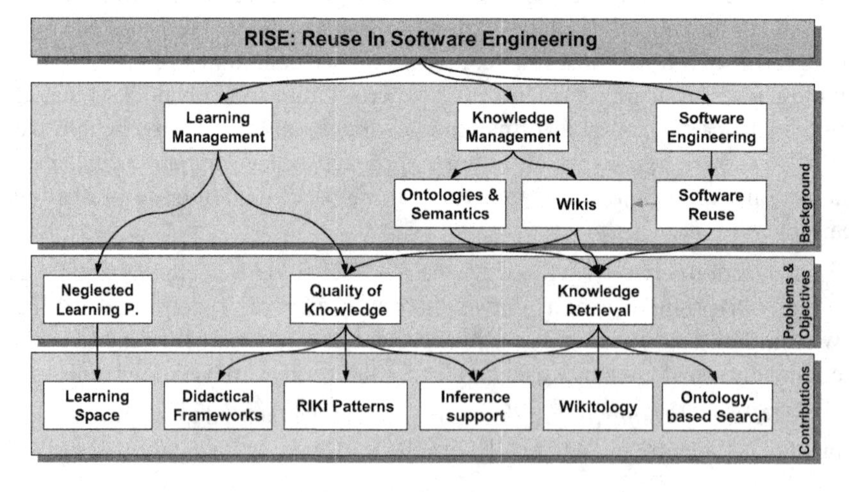

practices, Wiki patterns, and lessons learned gathered during the project are listed in *RISE in Retrospective*. Finally, we finish this chapter with our conclusions.

Background

This section is concerned with the background and related work in knowledge management with Wikis, problem-based and experiential e-learning in Wiki systems, and reuse for software development artifacts. It gives an overview of related Wikis for SE, for example TRAC, Snip Snap, and MASE.

Software Engineering and Reusable Knowledge

The discipline of *software engineering* (SE) was born in 1968 at the NATO conference in Garmisch-Partenkirchen, Germany (Naur & Randell, 1968; Simons, Parmee, & Coward, 2003). At the same conference, the methodical reuse of software components was motivated by Dough McIllroy (McIllroy, 1968) to improve the quality of large software systems by reusing small, high-quality components. The main concern of software engineering is the efficient and effective development of high-qualitative and very large software systems. The objective is to support software engineers to develop better software faster with tools and methods.

Software Reuse

The reuse of existing knowledge and experience is a fundamental practice in many sciences. Engineers often use existing components and apply established processes to construct complex systems. Without the reuse of well-proven components, methods, or tools, engineers have to rebuild and relearn these components, methods, or tools again and again.

Today, *reuse-oriented software engineering* covers the process of development and evolution of software systems by reusing existing software artifacts. The goal is to develop complex software systems in shorter periods of time or with higher quality by reusing proven, verified, and tested components from internal or external sources. Trough systematic reuse of these components and feedback about their application, their internal quality (e.g., reliability) is continuously improved. But reuse of components is only appropriate if the cost of retrieving and adapting the component is either less costly or results in higher quality than a redeveloped component.

Since the 1980s, the systematic reuse and management of experiences, knowledge, products, and processes was refined and named *Experience Factory* (EF) (Basili, Caldiera, & Rombach, 1994). This field, also known as *Experience Management* (Jedlitschka, Althoff, Decker, Hartkopf, Nick, & Rech, 2002), or *Learning Software Organization* (LSO) (Ruhe & Bomarius, 1999), researches methods and techniques for the management, elicitation, and adaptation of reusable artifacts from SE projects. The *Component Factory* (CF) as a specialization of the EF is concerned with the reuse of software artifacts (Basili, Caldiera, & Cantone, 1992) and builds the framework in which further analysis and retrieval techniques are embedded.

In the beginning, only the reuse of source code was the focus of reuse-oriented software engineering. Today, the comprehensive reuse of all software artifacts and experiences from the software development process is increasing in popularity (Basili & Rombach, 1991). Besides source code artifacts such as requirements, design document, test cases, process models, quality models, and best practices (e.g., design patterns) are used to support the development and evolution of software systems. These artifacts are collected during development or reengineering processes and typically stored in special artifact-specific repositories.

Software Engineering Experience and Knowledge

The terms knowledge, information, and experience are defined in multiple, more or less formal, and often contradictory ways. Models that define these terms and the processes that transit from one to another differentiate between tacit and implicit knowledge (Nonaka & Takeuchi, 1995) or between data, information, knowledge, ability, capability, and competence (North, 2002). There are positions such as by Stenmark (Stenmark, 2001) that consider the usage of the term "knowledge," for information stored in a computer, inappropriate. In this model, tacit knowledge can, in fact, exist only in the heads of people, and explicit knowledge is actually information. However, the terminology used in the theory and practice of knowledge-based systems (KBS) and knowledge-discovery in databases (KDD) considers knowledge to be information stored together with its context, and we follow this convention throughout this paper.

Types of Knowledge

More specifically, we base our view of knowledge on the model of the architecture of human knowledge developed by Anderson. He classified knowledge not according to its content, but according to its state in the person's long-term memory. Two types of knowledge were defined (Anderson, 1993; Gagné, Briggs, & Wager, 1988):

- **Declarative knowledge** consists of 'knowing about'—e.g., facts, impressions, lists, objects and procedures, and 'knowing that' certain principles hold. Declarative knowledge is based on concepts that are connected by a set of relations forming a network that models the memory of a person. For instance, declarative knowledge items in the domain of software engineering might be: a definition of 'test case,' a listing of defect types, a detailed explanation of key testing principles.
- **Procedural knowledge** consists of 'knowing how' to do something, that is, skills to construct, connect and use declarative knowledge. It contains the discrete steps or actions to be taken, and the available alternatives to perform a given task. For instance, procedural knowledge items in the domain of software engineering might be: a method for deriving test cases from requirements, a method for classifying defects choosing the right reading technique to perform an inspection.

Both declarative and procedural knowledge can be abstract or concrete. The knowledge can be connected to more or less concrete information that can be described technically, for example, by semantic networks. Nevertheless, knowledge about situations experienced or about evaluating facts or determining circumstances in given situations cannot be classified as declarative or procedural knowledge. Therefore, a third form of knowledge has extended the spectrum of knowledge in cognitive science (Enns, 1993) when Tennyson and Rasch (Tennyson & Rasch, 1988) defined contextual knowledge as another type of knowledge:

- **Contextual knowledge** consists of 'knowing when, where and why' to use or apply declarative or procedural knowledge. Contextual knowledge is created by reflecting on the usage of declarative and procedural knowledge in practice in different contexts. Contextual knowledge enables the individual to be aware of commonalities between situations, and of the appropriateness or applicability of principles or procedures in a new context.

In summary, three types of knowledge have been presented. Documented and stored experiences consist mainly of contextual knowledge. They originate, in most cases, from expert memories, and lack declarative basis background knowledge and detailed procedural knowledge, resulting in them being ineligible for learning purposes.

Furthermore, we identified the following *general artifacts* that are based on the six knowledge types from knowledge management (Mason, 2005):

- **Know-how:** Recorded information about how to do something. This can range from general *guidelines* about how to design a system to more specific and personal experiences about using a tool or software library.
- **Know-who:** Recorded information about a *person* (i.e., developer or maintainer). This can range from who designed a specific subsystem to who has knowledge about a customer.
- **Know-why:** Recorded *rationales* why something was done or decided. For example, why a design technique was applied or a defect had not been removed from the system.
- **Know-what:** Recorded information about the *status* of something (e.g., the current situation). This includes information about the current status of a project or system that was elicited from the project manager.
- **Know-where:** Recorded information about the *location* of something (esp. knowledge). This includes where an algorithm is implemented in the source code as well as information about where to find the project plan or a process description.
- **Know-when:** Recorded information about the *situation* (e.g., time or version) when something happens or a process is applied. This can range from when defects are introduced into the system to when the quality assurance process should be applied.
- **Know-if:** Recorded information about the *consequences* of an action. This can range from what happens if a defect is removed to the effects of applying a specific quality assurance technique.

Figure 2. Types and characteristics of knowledge

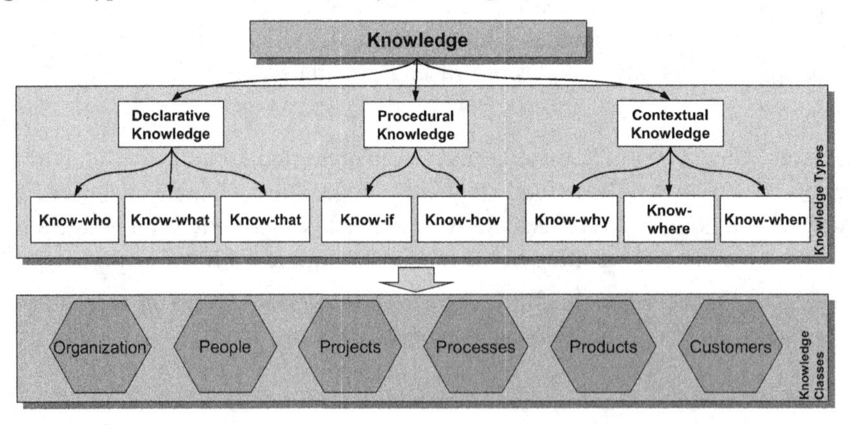

- **Know-that:** Recorded information about the *facts* of something. This can range from information about the characteristics of a quality defect to a model of the development process.

The interconnections between these knowledge types are depicted in Figure 2. The organizational elements at the bottom of the picture are classes of information that are typically existent in (software) organizations. In a KM system, knowledge, or more specifically the know-how, know-who, and so forth, about the organization, products, projects, people, processes, customers, as well as further knowledge (e.g., about a technology such as Java or EJB) is stored. We refer to this group as the OP4C model (Organization, People, Processes, Projects, Products, and Customers).

Software Engineering Artifacts

Software engineering is concerned with the planning, management, design, development, and implementation of large-scale, complex software systems. During these processes, several documents, architectures, ideas, and experiences are created or made. In software reuse, the umbrella term *artifact* is used to describe explicit knowledge objects that are considered for reuse, such as:

- **Methods and techniques** from phases such as project planning, requirements analysis, or programming that describe the know-how.
- **Patterns** about the analysis and structure of software systems (i.e., analysis and design patterns) or the management of processes (i.e., process patterns). In general, these represent knowledge that was created by the aggregation of single experiences, either by human expert judgement or by methodological approaches (Basili, Costa, Lindvall, Mendonca, Seaman, Tesoriero, et al., 2002).
- **Products** used in software projects such as project plans, product descriptions, demonstration installations, or presentation slides, as well as products produced and consumed in these projects, such as requirement documentations, architectures, software libraries, or source code.
- **Models** about the software quality (i.e., quality models) or the execution of processes (i.e., process or lifecycle models) that were used in projects and adapted to the organization and the individual needs of the project and its team.
- **Defects** found in a software system or in a project that reduce its functionality, maintainability, or other aspects like performance. Associated information of this artifact is, for example, their location, characteristics, and reactive or

preventive measures. If a specific type of defect is recorded over and over again, it might be summarized in a so-called antipattern.

- **Descriptions** of the organization, people, projects, processes, products, and customers (O4PC) as well as technologies (e.g., EJB and JBoss), development rules, interface style guides, corporate quality assurance guidelines, or the corporate identity style.

Knowledge Management and Learning Management

Knowledge as the fourth factor of production is one of the most important assets for any kind of organization, and for all areas of science. Unfortunately, today few experts who have acquired valuable experience through their day-to-day work share this knowledge with other people in the organization. For example, experiences about how to solve complex problems in software development, such as installation or optimization issues, are typically not shared with colleagues.

Knowledge Management

Knowledge management is concerned with methods and technologies to enable an organization to record, inspect, adapt, and share knowledge cooperatively on a large scale. Recording, elicitation, and adaptation of knowledge are the most critical tasks in knowledge management with respect to further reuse of knowledge. The lower the quality of the knowledge is that is recorded (e.g., due to missing context information), the more complex it gets to understand and apply the knowledge in a new context. The participation of colleagues such as managers, employees, or external experts helps to record knowledge from multiple points of view.

In the domain of software engineering, software development can be considered as a human-based, knowledge-intensive activity. Together with sound methods, techniques, and tools, the success of a software project and the software quality itself strongly depends on the knowledge and experience brought to the project by its developers. This fact led to the development and use of experience-based information systems (EbIS) for capturing, storing, and transferring experience (Nick, 2005). Experience management (EM) can be seen as a subfield of KM that aims at supporting the management and transfer of relevant experiences (Bergmann, 2002; Tautz, 2001). The software system used for managing, storing, retrieving, and disseminating these experiences is called an experience-based information system (EbIS) (Jedlitschka & Nick, 2003), which is based on the experience factory concept. Another type of system that is not based on the EF concept is lessons learned systems (LLS) (Weber, Aha, & Becerra-Fernandez, 2001). Amongst the definitions for lessons learned, the most complete definition, is:

A lesson learned is knowledge or understanding gained by experience. The experience may be positive, as in a successful test or mission, or negative, as in a mishap or failure. Successes are also considered sources of lessons learned. A lesson must be significant in that it has a real or assumed impact on operations; valid in that it is factually and technically correct; and applicable in that it identifies a specific design, process, or decision that reduces or eliminates the potential for failures and mishaps, or reinforces a positive result. (Secchi, Ciaschi, & Spence, 1999)

Learning Management

KM and learning management (LM) both serve the same purpose: facilitating learning and competence development of individuals, in projects, and in organizations. However, they follow two different perspectives. KM is related to an organizational perspective, because it addresses the lack of sharing knowledge among members of the organizations by encouraging individuals to make their knowledge explicit by creating knowledge elements, which can be stored in knowledge bases for later reuse or for participating in communities of practice. In contrast, e-learning emphasizes an individual perspective, as it focuses on the individual acquisition of new knowledge and the socio-technical means to support this internalization process. In the following two sections, expectations on learning content and related specifications and standards that address these expectations are presented.

Expectations on Today's Learning Content

Especially in industrial training settings, learning objectives mostly correspond to concrete, well-defined job-related skills, specific tasks to be done, or problems to be solved. Hence, the delivered learning material and learning approach must suit the current situation that the learner finds himself in. The situation changes over time while the learner is performing his work. Nevertheless, conventional learning systems leave no space for dynamic selection and sequencing of learning material. In addition, the expectations on e-learning content are high (cf. SCORM 2004 2nd Edition Overview page 1-22, http://www.adlnet.org/scorm/index.cfm):

- **Accessibility:** "the ability to locate and access instructional components from one remote location and deliver them to many other locations".
- **Adaptability:** "the ability to tailor instruction to individual and organizational needs".
- **Affordability:** "the ability to increase efficiency and productivity by reducing the time and costs involved in delivering instruction".

- **Durability:** "the ability to withstand technology evolution and changes without costly redesign, reconfiguration or recoding".
- **Interoperability:** "the ability to take instructional components developed in one location with one set of tools or platform and use them in another location with a different set of tools or platform".
- **Reusability:** "the flexibility to incorporate instructional components in multiple applications and contexts".

It is impossible to improve all aspects together. For example, in order to support high adaptability of learning content, more effort has to be spent on realizing adaptation mechanisms and preparing learning content so that it can be adapted to specific learning situations. This will decrease the reusability of the content and its interoperability with other learning management systems. Therefore, tradeoffs have to be made by focusing on the most important aspects for a given purpose. *Semantic-Based Reuse in SE: the RISE Approach* will elaborate on which aspects Riki will focus on. The requirement for content that fulfills these aims leads to the concept of cutting learning material into so-called learning objects with associated metadata. Since then, many standards and specifications have been developed to offer a strong fundament for learning content with the previously listed characteristics.

E-Learning Standards and Specifications

Numerous initiatives like AICC (the Aviation Industry CBT Committee), ADL (Advanced Distributed Learning), IEEE LTSC (the Learning Technology Standards Committee of the IEEE) and IMS Global Learning Consortium have made efforts to establish standards. For several years, a number of initiatives have agreed to cooperate in the field of standards. Among the many available standards and specifications, the ones most relevant for Riki are described in the following.

The LTSC has developed the Learning Object Metadata Standard (LOM). This standard will specify the syntax and semantics of learning object metadata, defined as the attributes required to fully/adequately describe a learning object. Learning objects are defined here as "any entity, digital or non-digital, which can be used, re-used or referenced during technology supported learning." A huge amount of specifications is being developed by the IMS consortium. Several of these specifications have been incorporated and, in some cases, been adapted by ADL to define the SCORM reference model. SCORM describes that technical framework by providing a harmonized set of guidelines, specifications, and standards based on the work of several distinct e-learning specifications and standards bodies. These specifications have one aspect in common: by separating the content from the structure and layout, they enable the author to develop different variants of learning material very efficiently, while relying on the same set of learning objects. *SCORM sequencing and navigation* provides techniques to sequence learning objects by means of learning activity trees, and the IMS Learning Design specification allows expressing more sophisticated pedagogical concepts by means of a more extensive role concept. However, they prescribe structures for expressing more or less generic instructional designs, and do not provide possibilities for adapting instructional design during run-time. Nevertheless, despite their limitations, Riki will especially make use of specific concepts within SCORM (such as *sharable content object*, *organization*, *manifest*, *learning activity tree*, etc.) and parts of sequencing and navigation. Especially the contextualization of knowledge and experience (i.e., embedding the information in a context) plays a crucial role in Riki. Part of the context description could be done, for example, according to the IMS Learner Information Package specification in order to describe the content owner, or other content related roles. The Dublin Core Metadata Initiative (DCMI) has developed the *Dublin Core Metadata Element Set* outside of the e-learning domain. DC defines a very simple set of metadata attributes that can be used for describing general resources. Since the content of a Riki should be annotated as unintrusively as possible, DC will be a starting point for describing RISE content.

Wikis and Semantics in Software Engineering

The Semantic Web initiative is concerned with the enrichment of information on the Internet through the use of exchangeable and machine-readable metadata. To structure the knowledge in a "mini"-Internet, as represented by a KM system such as a Wiki, we also planned to enrich the knowledge encoded on the Wiki pages with additional metadata. In the remainder of this section, we describe Wikis in general, followed by two overviews of Wikis for SE organizations and Wikis with integrated metadata support, which form the basis of our Riki system (i.e., semantic Wikis).

Wikis facilitate communication through a basic set of features, which allows the project team to coordinate their work in a flexible way. From the authors' point of view, these basic features are: *one place publishing*, meaning that there is only one version of a document available that is regarded as the current version; *simple and safe collaboration*, which refers to versioning and locking mechanisms that most Wikis provide; *easy linking*, meaning that documents within a Wiki can be linked by their title using a simple markup; *description on demand*, which means that links can be defined to pages that have not been created yet, but might be filled with content in the future. Furthermore, the simple mechanism of URL allows easy reference and thus, traceability of Wiki content into other software documents like code. For a further discussion on Wiki features, refer to Cunningham (2005).

Besides those technical aspects, Wikis foster a mindset of a fit-for-use, evolutional approach to requirements documentation and management. The approach of Wikis—in particular, Wikipedia as the most prominent representative (Wikipedia,

2006)—demands that an initially created document is adequate for its intended usage (fit-for-use). This initial version is then extended, based on the demand of the people using this document.

Software Engineering-Oriented Wikis

Wikis were initially used in a software engineering setting, namely the Portland Pattern Repository (Leuf & Cunningham, 2001). Furthermore, they are often used to support software development, in particular in the area of open source software. The Wikis of the Apache Foundation are a prominent example of this application scenario. Some examples of Wikis offer specific functionality for software engineering:

- **Trac** (Alrubaie, 2006) is a Wiki, written in python, that integrates an issue tracker, allowing it to relate Wiki pages to issues, and vice versa. Furthermore, the python code of a project can be integrated as read-only documents.
- **MASE** (Maurer, 2002) is an extension to the JSP Wiki that offers plugins for agile software development, in particular for iteration planning and integration of automated measurement results.
- **SnipSnap** (John, Jugel, & Schmidt, 2005) is implemented in Java and allows read-only integration of code documentation. Furthermore, it offers support for the integration of Wiki entries into the integrated development environment eclipse.
- **Subwiki** (SubWiki, 2005) is a Wiki implementation that uses the versioning system subversion as a data repository. Since subversion allows attaching metadata to files, the resulting Wiki is supposed to have the same features. However, this project has not released a stable version yet.
- **EclipseWiki** (EclipseWiki, 2005) is a plugin for the eclipse software development platform. It uses the workspace of a project as (local) data storage. By using a versioning system, the Wiki files can be shared and edited by a project team.
- **WikiDoc** (Oezbek, 2005) is a conceptual work that supports adding java code documentation via a Wiki interface. This allows nonprogrammers to participate in the creation of code documentation.

All those examples show that Wikis are increasingly being used as a platform for software development. However, "regular" Wikis (see (WikiEngines, 2005) for an overview of most of the Wikis currently available and WikiMatrix, (2006) for a configurable overview), as well as software engineering-oriented Wikis, build upon the fact that the relations between documents and further metadata are maintained by the users of those Wikis. This lack of explicit semantic information is addressed by an extension to the regular Wiki functionality that is developed in the RISE project. These so-called *semantic Wikis* are elaborated in the next section.

Semantic Wikis

In this section, we present further examples of semantic Wikis. Most of these examples are taken from the overviews presented in Dahl and Eisenbach (2005) and Semantic Wikis (2005). Those examples show that a) even "regular" Wikis offer some support for structuring their content and b) that semantic, RDF-based Wikis can be implemented. Most of those examples are general purpose Wikis that do not focus on software engineering in particular. A general overview of semantic Wikis can be found in Völkel, Schaffert, Kiesel, Oren, and Decker (2005):

- The most common way to categorize within Wikis is the usage of the backlink function of a Wiki (Aumüller, 2005). Basically, a page is created that represents a certain category. Pages belonging to this category have a reference to this page. The backlink function lists all of these references. However, this approach has one major drawback: pages that are used to navigate to the category entry (and thus do not semantically belong to this category) are also included in the backlink list.
- Some Wikis offer additional support for structuring content. For example, *TikiWiki*, (TikiWiki, 2005) allows assigning pages to structures (table of contents) and categories (taxonomy style classification). XWiki (2005) offers forms (templates) that contain metadata that are instantiated in documents derived from this form.
- From the area of SE-specific Wikis, TRAC offers a labeling feature for pages (smart tags) that could be used for a facetted presentation of the pages annotated with those tags. SnipSnap allows determining the template of a document and offers RDF export.
- *Platypus* (Platypus, 2005) and *SHAWN* (Aumüller, 2005) allow adding RDF annotations for each page. Pages within Platypus represent a concept. While viewing a page, the RDF triples are displayed that have the current page as object (in particular, pages that reference this page) and as subject (in particular, metadata about a page). SHAWN also offers navigation support based on the ontology information added to a page. Wiki.Ont is still in a preliminary version.

- *Rhizome* (Rhizome, 2005; Souzis, 2001) and *RDF-Wiki* (Palmer, 2005) are Wikis that provide their content in RDF, thus allowing to reason about their context.

Only the Wikis mentioned in the last two bullets can be seen as "real" semantic Wikis, since they allow relating their content to an RDF-based ontology. However, all of them—at least in their current state—do not integrate their ontology into the Wiki, for example, they neither provide metadata templates to be filled in based on an ontology nor do they check whether metadata entered is consistent with an ontology. Therefore, when related to the Semantic Web layer cake (Berners-Lee, 2005), all of these semantic Wikis implement the RDF and RDFS layer. The vocabulary layer of these applications is not domain specific and thus, does not allow inferring about domain specific relations.

Ontology Development

The development of ontologies to classify and structure knowledge—often called knowledge engineering—is a rather mature field that has its origins in artificial intelligence. Several methodologies, approaches, and standards have been developed that focus on ontology development in general, or resulted in an ontology for software engineering knowledge. This work is implicitly included in the RODent method presented later, and developers of Riki-specific ontologies might find these works helpful as a source of inspiration for their own ontology development. Furthermore, by adhering to the following standards, the tools and framework based on (some of) these standards can be employed for reasoning-specific tasks in RISE:

- **Ontology development:** CommonKADS (Schreiber, Wielinga, Hoog, Akkermans, & Velde, 1994) is a methodology for developing knowledge-based systems and contains guidelines for developing ontologies.
- **Ontology description standards:** The language set of RDF (Manola & Miller, 2004), RDF-Schema (Brickley & Guha, 2004) and OWL (Smith, Welty, & McGuinness, 2004) defines language constructs that can be used to define ontology in a way suitable for machine reasoning.
- **General ontology standards:** Ontology standards make use of those ontology description standards. In RISE, we referred to the Super Upper Merged Ontology (Legrand, Tyrväinen, & Saarikoski, 2003; SUMO Ontology), describing general relations (such as part-of) and the Dublin Core metadata to have a general set of document metadata (such as author, creation date) (2005).
- **Software-engineering-specific ontologies:** These ontologies define a general set of concepts and their relations in the field of software engineering. This allows the entries within Riki to be annotated with domain-specific meaning.

Examples of such ontologies are the software engineering body of knowledge (Software Engineering Body of Knowledge, Iron Man Version, 2004) and the classification of the Association for Computing Machinery (2005).

This background section illuminated the background of our work and gave a short overview of the application field of software engineering and software reuse, as well as the Wiki technology that was used in the RISE project. These fields represent the context in which several problems were encountered that are described in the following section.

Problems and Challenges

After the description of the background of software engineering and the application of techniques from knowledge management and learning management, we look at the specific problems addressed within the RISE project. As depicted in Figure 3, we identified several problems of knowledge and learning management in software engineering.

Figure 3. Problem overview

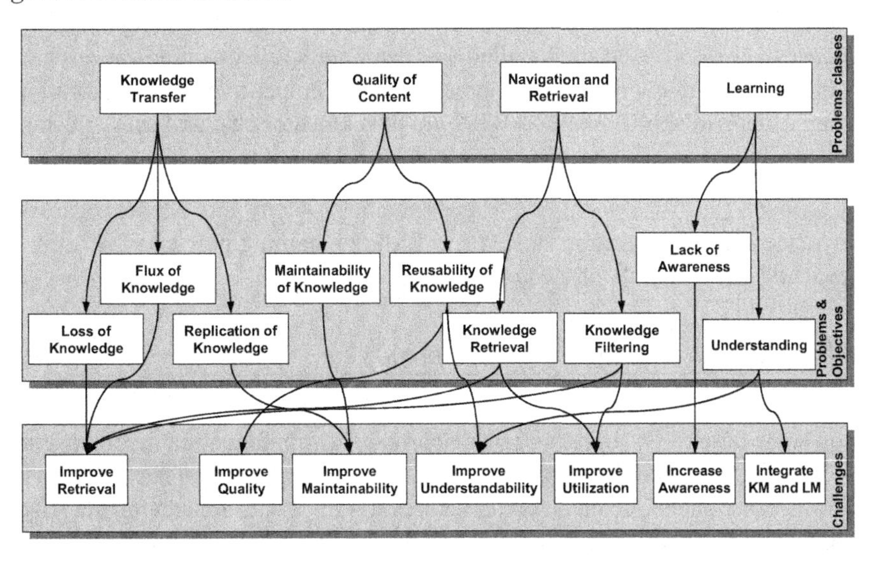

Problems of Knowledge Transfer and Reuse in Software Engineering

As motivated in *Software Engineering and Reusable Knowledge*, the development of software is a highly knowledge-intensive activity that produces many reusable documents, ideas, and experiences. The productivity as well as the quality of the products developed heavily depends on the efficient and effective storage and retrieval of knowledge in a socio-technical system. A knowledge management system should at least reduce or prevent the occurrence of the following basic problems in KM:

- **Loss of knowledge:** Key personnel with valuable or even critical knowledge about products, processes, or customers leave the organization and leave a knowledge gap. In a software organization, this might be a senior software developer who is the only person with critical information about the inner structure or function of a software system.
- **Replication of knowledge:** Products, intellectual property, or experiences are developed over and over again in slightly different versions. In a software organization, an algorithm might be developed twice because one project does not always know what other projects are doing. This might also apply to defects that are introduced to different parts of the software system and removed by different testers doing the same work (i.e., solving the same problem) twice.
- **Flux of knowledge:** The knowledge about new technologies, projects, processes, products, people, or standards is continuously subject to change. In order not to fall behind the innovations, competitors who are using these gaps have to be discovered and handled. For example, software organizations have to cope with many new open source projects, competitive systems, development standards, or frameworks that are developed or changed every year.

In the following sections, we have grouped specific problems into classes regarding quality aspects, the integration of KM and LM, the learning processes, as well as retrieval and reasoning about the content.

Problems Related to the Quality of Content

A knowledge base (KB) serves as an asynchronous communication medium or intermediary between people such as managers, developers, or even customers. The whole process is one of mediated communication (i.e., people are leaving messages to other people). Furthermore, there is the danger that relevant content from the outside is not considered, especially from outside the knowledge base (i.e., on the

Intranet), from the Internet, and from the social system at large (i.e., the people). Until today, there are several problems related to the quality of the content in a knowledge base that still represent a barrier in knowledge management:

- **Problem of reusability of knowledge:** The quality of the reported and recorded knowledge and experience highly depends on the individual skills of the contributor, for example, the ability to structure the content, to formulate the artifacts with accuracy, and to describe it properly according to the needs of the target audience. Without assistance, this leads to quality discrepancies and gaps in the knowledge base. To be included in the knowledge base, the new content must meet minimal quality requirements, such as described in a correct, complete, consistent, concise, and nonambiguous way, including information on the context of the specific content.
- **Problem of maintainability of the knowledge base:** A regular evaluation of all content and removal of outdated entries is required. Storing several contradictory solutions for a sole problem, originating from different persons at different points in time, is a source of confusion and mistrust. The capacity to retrieve previous related experiences exists in most KB approaches, but it requires time and effort to review them. The risk of applying outdated content is high if content does not have an attached expiry date, and on many occasions, these repositories become a sort of graveyards: some content is added, but nothing is ever thrown away. With the continually growing size of KBs, it is difficult to keep an overview in order to connect related packages and avoid inconsistencies.

While the use of Wiki systems, as applied in our project, facilitate and improve several of the previously mentioned problems due to the increased flexibility, agility, and simplicity, they also bring along their own new problems, such as the *motivation to contribute* or the *sustainability* of the Wiki system. Furthermore, the flexible and easy creation of links between Wiki pages (i.e., knowledge elements) leads to high cross-linking and hence, to the *deterioration and loss of structure*.

Problems Related to the Navigation and Retrieval

A long running KM system that is accepted by the users and continuously increases the amount of knowledge stored within it typically amasses a plethora of knowledge that is unstructured, not connected, or outdated. The retrieval of a specific knowledge component, either by navigation or search mechanisms, typically leads to an information flood. In order to enable and improve the elicitation, organization, retrieval, and usage of knowledge in software organizations, several problems have to be addressed:

- **Problem of knowledge retrieval:** Software development in general has to cope with the overwhelming amount of new processes, technologies, and tools that periodically appears. As a consequence, the fast retrieval of up-to-date information about new technologies, corporate software systems, or available experts becomes more and more important. Furthermore, there are many knowledge components that become outdated within a few years (e.g., information about Java frameworks).
- **Problem of knowledge filtering:** Searching for crucial information in a large knowledge base, especially if it is focused on a single topic such as software engineering, leads to a flood of results. The more similar the components are in a knowledge base, the more precise a search or navigational structure has to be in order to find the relevant information.

Problems Related to Learning

KM systems focus mainly on organizational learning, that is, where learning leads to collecting knowledge for the organization in order to be used by its employees or for the modifications of the software organization's processes, internal standards, objectives, or strategies. However, Rus and Lindvall stated that individual learning is considered to be a fundamental part of KM because employees must internalize (learn) shared knowledge before they can use it to perform specific tasks (2002). KM systems make the assumption that the problem of continuous competence development can be partially solved by using intelligent retrieval mechanisms and benefitting from innovative presentations of retrieval results. As a result, knowledge-based systems (KBSs) focus mainly on knowledge acquisition, storage, and retrieval, and less on the learning processes themselves, the integration with the work process, and the personal learning needs of the software developers. More specific problems related to experiential learning (i.e., learning from experience) are listed below:

- **Problem of understanding and applying of documented experience:** Experience is often documented by domain experts. A problem that occurs when expert knowledge is used for teaching novices is that there is a quantitative difference between expert and novice knowledge bases, and also a qualitative difference, for example, the way in which knowledge is organized (Ericsson, Krampe, & Tesch-Romer, 1993). Novices lack SE background knowledge and are not able to connect the experience to their knowledge base. Hence, they often misinterpret other people's documented experience. The organization of knowledge at the experienced provider's level and at the consumer's level makes the transfer of knowledge between different levels of expertise extremely difficult. Expert knowledge is somehow "routine." This makes it challenging for experts to document experiences appropriately and to make them reusable for others. A more detailed summary of problems related to learning from documented experience can be found in Ras and Weibelzahl (2004).

- **Problem of overview and lack of awareness:** Systemic thinking is the conceptual cornerstone of the "Fifth Discipline" (Senge, 1990). It addresses the problem that we tend to focus on the parts rather than seeing the whole, and fail to see organizations as a dynamic process. Unfortunately, learning by documented experience is limited to a very focused view of SE, and does not relate the experience to the whole SE context and related domains. Another problem is that systems do not point explicitly to other available SE methods, techniques, and tools that could be useful for the work at hand, which leads to a lack of awareness.

Objectives, Challenges and Research Issues

Most of the previously mentioned problems were tackled by several researchers in projects around the world, but a solution to them is still far in the future. We tried to improve the situation by using the open Wiki technology and integrated aspects of LM and KM to support reuse in software engineering. This system, which we call reuse-oriented Wiki (Riki), has to support the comprehensive reuse of the artifacts as described in Background, and has to help the users to collect, record, retrieve, reuse, and learn from them. Furthermore, the administrative staff needs to be supported in the packaging, formalization, aggregation, and generalization of artifacts in this knowledge base.

The overall goal of the RISE project was to integrate lightweight experience management with agile software development. RISE pursued the following specific objectives:

- **Improvement of the retrieval of knowledge and orientation** in a body of knowledge to optimize the amount of knowledge and accelerate the time to access relevant knowledge.
- **Improvement of the quality of transferred knowledge** by assisting software engineers in creating optimized artifacts (i.e., with optimized content and structure) based on didactical principles and by delivering didactically augmented experiences. These artifacts should easily be adopted and internalized

by users of different expertise levels to support them in their daily work and performance.

- **Improvement of utilization and usability of the KM systems** to allow the user the goal-oriented search for suitable solutions to his problem in minimal time, and to support him in the adaptation of the solution to his specific problems.
- **Integration of knowledge management and experience management** with e-learning and work itself in order to improve the reuse of documented experience and to bring learning to the work place.
- **Improving the understandability** of documented expert experience by explicitly offering additional SE learning components, and by explicitly stimulating learning activities through didactical principles.
- **Increasing the awareness of available but unknown SE topics** in order to increase the software quality based on the application of new software development approaches that have not been applied before.
- **Improve the maintenance of knowledge in KM systems**, and especially Wikis, in order to optimize the amount of potentially relevant knowledge.

Semantic-Based Reuse in SE: The RISE Approach

As we have argued, neither the technology nor the methodology currently available is sufficient to challenge the problems listed in *Problems and Challenges*. After introducing the basic concepts of Riki, we describe the methodology and technology that was developed and used in the RISE project.

Basic Concepts in RISE

In general, we use the model defined by Tautz: "*knowledge* is the range of learned information or understanding of a human or intelligent information system, experience is considered to be knowledge or practical wisdom gained through human senses, from directly observing, encountering, or undergoing things during the participation in events or in a particular activity" (Tautz, 2001).

Representation of Knowledge in Wiki Systems

After describing Wiki systems and the types of knowledge that might be stored in those systems (see *Wikis and Semantics in Software Engineering*), we shed some light on the storage of knowledge artifacts in a Wiki system. We use the following concepts:

- **Knowledge elements:** are the most basic containers for knowledge and cannot be further divided without destroying the ability to understand them using other knowledge elements.
- **Knowledge components:** are complete and self-sufficient (i.e., independent of other knowledge elements) descriptions of knowledge (e.g., a SE artifact). A knowledge component consists of one or more knowledge elements.
- **Learning elements:** are the most basic learning resources. They are the electronic representation of media, such as images, text, sound, or any other piece of data that could serve as a learning resource when aggregated with other learning elements to form a learning component (Note: Learning elements can be compared with assets of the SCORM content aggregation model).
- **Learning components:** are units of instruction that contain at least one learning element. A learning component represents the lowest granularity of a learning resource that can be reused by the system for learning purposes. The difference between a learning component and a learning element is that

Figure 4. Knowledge in Wiki systems

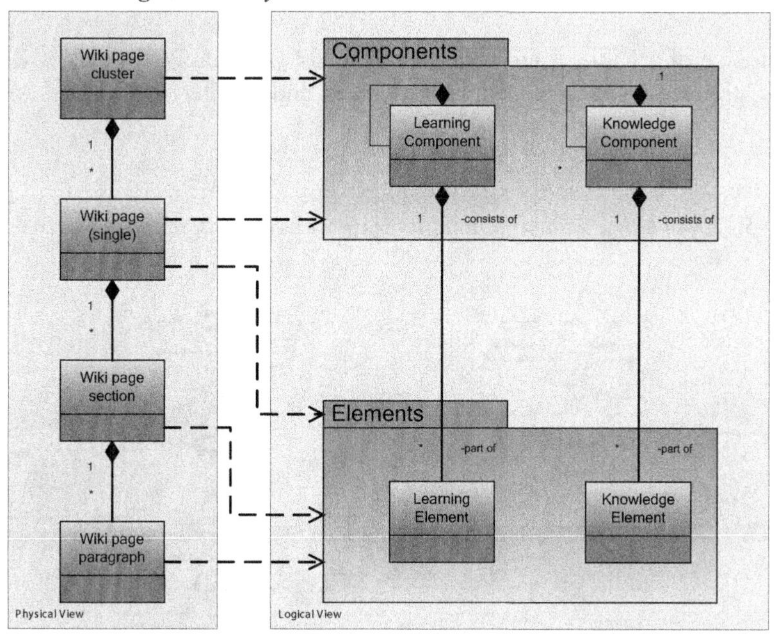

a learning component is related to a learning activity and a learning objective. In addition, it can be referenced as a learning resource by the system (e.g., by using hyperlinks). Another difference is that a learning component could possess contractually specified interfaces and explicit context dependencies when these are used within a so-called learning space (Note: Learning components are similar to sharable content objects of the SCORM content aggregation model).

- **Learning space:** consists of a hyperspace that contains at least one or more learning components that are presented, for example, by linked Wiki pages. A learning space follows a specific global learning goal, and is created based on context information of the current situation (e.g., learner needs, working tasks the learner is currently performing, or attributes of software artifacts). The goal of a learning space is to provide a learning environment for self-directed situated learning (see *Learning Space Analysis* for more details).

As depicted in Figure 4, knowledge elements are the typical content of a Wiki page, while a short knowledge component might equally fit. Furthermore, a knowledge element might have to be split into multiple Wiki pages if the content is too large or structured, as a training course.

Classes of Knowledge in a Riki System

The entrance of a Riki system consists of the six general classes of knowledge: projects, products, processes, people, customers, and (further) knowledge. Around

Figure 5. Knowledge component classes in an SE organization based upon O4PKC

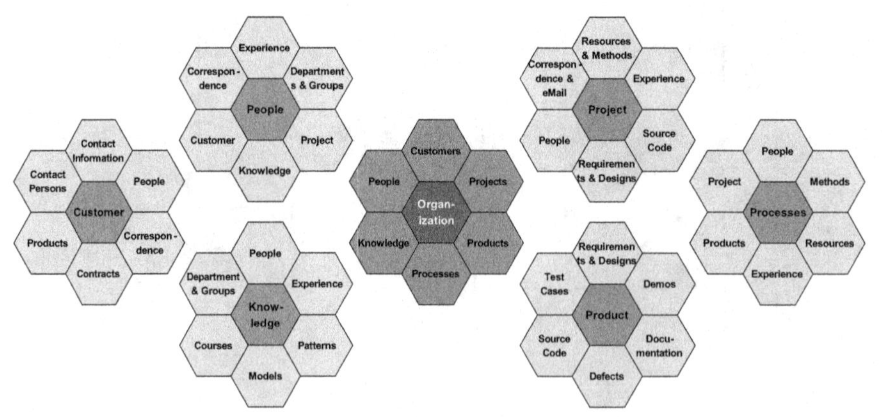

these classes, several knowledge leaves are developed, based on the knowledge types from *Software Engineering Experience and Knowledge* (i.e., know-how, know-where, etc.). Therefore, a specific project page (e.g., about the RISE project) includes information about the requirements and designs of the changes planned for the products involved in the RISE project, but the product page (e.g., about the Riki) will include all requirements relevant for this specific product. However, a single knowledge leaf is not always purely classifiable as a single knowledge type (e.g., know-how), but might include other types of knowledge (e.g., source code developed in a project might include know-where, (i.e., location) as well as know-when, (i.e., version) knowledge.

As depicted in Figure 5, the artifacts from *Types of Knowledge* might be grouped around several core artifacts, such as projects or products, and represent connection points usable for further inference. For example, in the configuration shown, one could easily infer employees who have worked in a project that was initiated by a specific customer and therefore might have valuable knowledge for further acquisition activities.

The more often these or similar artifacts are generated, the more probable it is that they might be reused in a new project.

Figure 6. The RIME components (ontology, learning space, and Riki system development)

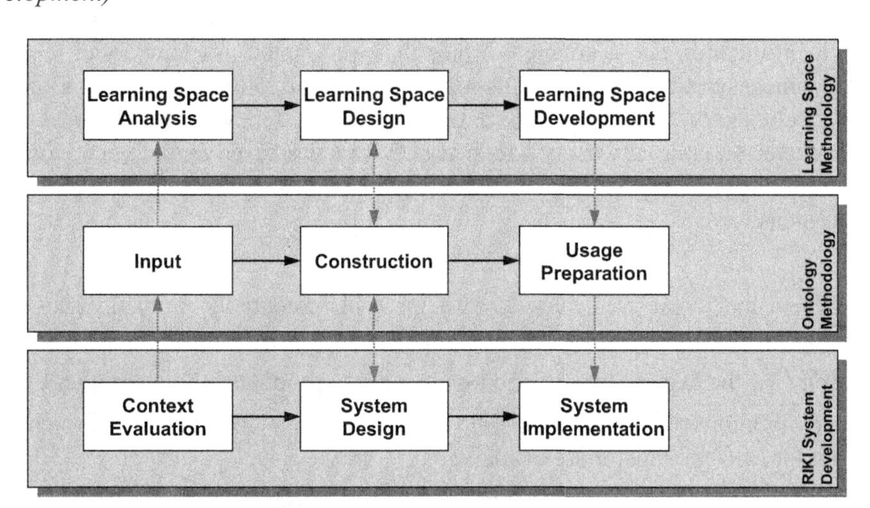

RIME: The RISE Methodology for Knowledge Transfer and Reuse

In this section, we describe three parts of RIME, including the design and development methodology for Riki systems, ontologies in a Riki, and learning spaces in a Riki. As depicted in Figure 6, all three are based on a detailed context evaluation in software organizations whose results were used for deriving the requirements for a Riki in the context to be addressed.

The RISE methodology represents a concept for the structuring, implementation, and operation of the Riki system.

Riki System Development

To develop a KM system such as Riki, we first analyzed and evaluated the context in two SMEs, which both develop search technologies systems. From the information we gathered in these context evaluations, we designed and developed the Riki system, considering the people, processes, and available technologies. Finally we developed, tailored, and implemented these systems in the organizations.

Context Evaluation: Analyzing the Existing Socio-Technical Infrastructure

The goal of our context evaluation step was to elicit the existing socio-technical infrastructure of the companies. Therefore, we developed a catalog of questions to elicit information about concrete topics that we wanted to know about (e.g., what technical systems are in use). In order to answer the following questions, and therefore elicit knowledge about the context the RISE system will be embedded in, we conducted an interview using a refined questionnaire based on the know questions from *Software Engineering Expereince and Knowledge*. The basic topics of the questions were:

- Where and what are technical systems with potentially valuable knowledge?
- Who are the experts for specific topics, such as products or technologies?
- How is knowledge transferred from tools to persons? What technical systems for knowledge transfer are available?
- How is knowledge transferred from person to person (interpersonal)? What social knowledge transfer techniques are used?
- How is knowledge collected from persons to tools?
- How is knowledge collected or transformed from tools to tools?

- Who needs and who produces new knowledge?
- What processes and tools are used to develop the software? Where can knowledge be collected and injected?
- When is knowledge collected, transferred, reused, needed, or produced?
- Why is knowledge currently being collected, transferred, or reused?
- What knowledge is (seemed to be) valuable for collection, transfer, or reuse? Which artifacts (as in *Types of Knowledge*) are used and should be reused?

Beside the use of questionnaires to query the employees of the companies, and elicit knowledge about the context a social-technical system has to be embedded in, we also conducted open group discussions and analyzed the existing artifacts and storage system ourselves. Overall, we used the following techniques to gather the knowledge:

- Goal-oriented, questionnaire-based *interviews* were used to put the previously listed questions to three to ten persons in two to four sessions. The collected answers were summarized and validated by the participants via e-mail.
- *Group discussions* were done at every company to collect any additional information, opinions, ideas, and so forth, that were not covered by the interviews. The discussion was started with a specific topic (e.g., why had the old Wiki not worked for you as a KM system?) ,and every person could state what they expected from an improved knowledge management infrastructure.
- *Artifact analyses* were conducted to identify knowledge sources, the type of knowledge within, as well as how people structure their documents and knowledge in existing storage systems (e.g., the hierarchy of directories in personal file systems or in pre-existing Wiki systems).

Using the information extracted with these techniques, we derived and created tailored versions for each company of:

- **Ontology** with metadata for all pages in the KM system (i.e., the Riki) and relations between them. This metadata is used for inference, search and presentation purposes. The ontology is based upon information from the existing artifacts of the company, the knowledge lifecycle, and standards of knowledge description such as LOM.
- **Templates** for every artifact type with a special focus on requirement documents. These help to record new knowledge of that type and are used in inference, for example, to find similar documents of the same type. The templates

represent the inner structure of artifacts and esp. Knowledge Elements on a Wiki page. Information to define the templates came from the identified knowledge artifacts, the knowledge lifecycle (i.e., how would a user read the document in a specific activity of the process?), and industrial best practices such as the Volere requirement template (Robertson & Robertson, 2005a) or the ReadySET requirements-engineering template.

- **Navigational structures** within the KM system (Riki) were created to support the goal-oriented and artifact-centric access to the knowledge. The structures are based upon information from the existing structures used by the employees of the company and the processes, products, and groups of the company.
- **Riki software system** with plugins to support the users with additional information from inference via the currently viewed knowledge as well as connectors to the technical infrastructure. The system design is based upon information from available software systems in the organization, established knowledge transfer techniques, and usability aspects.

System Design: Tailoring a Riki for a Learning Software Organization

After we elicited the information about the context our socio-technical system should be embedded in, we started the design of the system. Beside the information about the context, we needed further information about the technical features and the extensibility of the available systems. The following information was found to be useful for the design of the system:

- **Survey** of systems (e.g., open source), extensible without too much work, and flexible enough to realize the planned systems.
- **Selection** of an appropriate system that fulfills the optimal set of requirements by the specific customer based on the use cases and scenarios as defined by the customer's business or development processes.
- **Design of plugins and portlets** that give specific views on related articles, similar pages (of the same document type) as well as the plugin interface. In general, every know question from *Software Engineering Experience and Knowledge* represents one plugin that shows information related to the currently viewed knowledge element, for example, the persons who have further knowledge (i.e., know-who) or methods for post-processing (know-how).
- **Design of templates and interface masks** for every specific knowledge type [e.g., templates and masks for use cases (requirements)].

Furthermore, based on the features already existent in Wikis and extensions planned for the Riki, as well as on the features of the search and inference technology, we shaped the ontology and vice versa.

System Implementation: Introducing a Riki into a Software Organization

Based upon the information from the design, the system and required plugins are built using the chosen Wiki systems. During operation, the experiences acquired from the daily work (e.g., projects) are seized and didactically augmented to support users in current or future projects.

The operation and maintenance of the Riki system, its underlying ontology, and the knowledge stored within it is currently being done by the software organizations themselves.

RODent: Riki Ontology Development

This section explains the RODent method for the design and development of Riki ontologies. In parallel with systems building, we need to develop an ontology to be used by the Riki. In general, an ontology is defined as "an explicit and formal specification of a conceptualization" (Gruber, 1995).

In RISE, we instantiate this definition: An ontology is a set of templates, their metadata,and the relations among those templates. The role of the resulting ontology is to structure and relate the information captured inside the Riki. Therefore, the ontology can be seen as a link between the implementation of a Riki and the content of a Riki. The guiding idea is *Wikitology*, that is, that the Wiki is the physical representation of the ontology with pages as concepts and links as relations (Decker, Ras, Rech, Klein, Reuschling, Höcht, et al., 2005; Decker, Rech, Althoff, Klotz, Leopold, & Voss, 2005).

Besides the ontology itself, the result of this method is an initial set of document templates and content to seed a Riki. In the following sections, an overview of RODent is presented, using requirements engineering as an example application.

Outline of RODent

As depicted in Figure 7, RODent is divided into two groups of subtasks: *ontology construction*, where the concepts and their relations are identified, and *usage preparation*, where the usage of the ontology is defined. A more detailed description of the following tasks is presented in the subsequent sections:

- **Input** to RODent comes from two sources: The first source is the result of the context analysis, with the prioritized challenges of the organization and

Figure 7. Overview of RODent

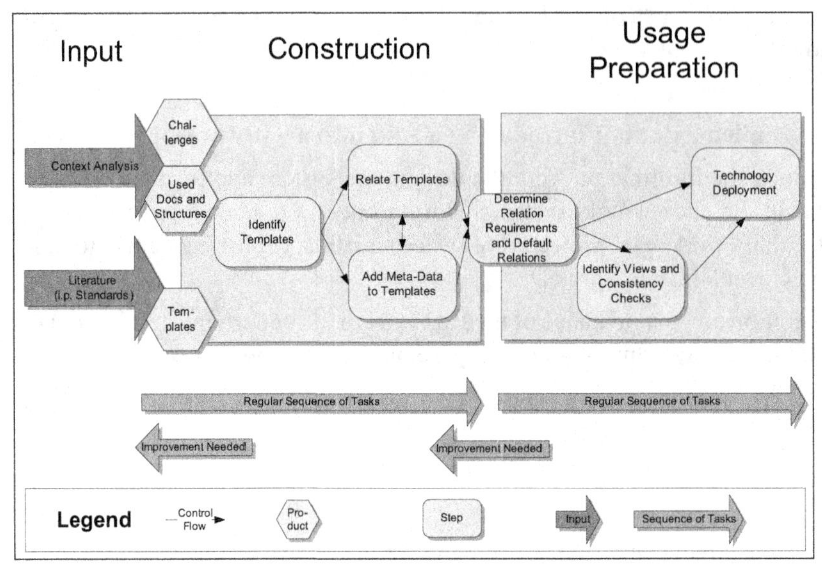

the currently used structures and documents defining the "asIs" status of the organization. The second source is an analysis of domain-specific literature relevant for the domain where the ontology should be built (in the example, from the area of requirements engineering). This literature will provide an initial set of templates.

- **Construction** as the first group of tasks uses this input as follows: First, the actual templates used in Riki are identified. Second, those templates are related with each other and "equipped" with metadata.
- **Usage Preparation** as the second group is about setting up a Riki to use the ontology defined in the subsequent phase. The task "Determine Relation Requirements and Default Relation" is a link between those phases since it refines ontology relations, but also covers aspects of ontology usage in the Riki. "Identify views and consistency checks" takes care of using the ontology for navigational and editing support as well as to define inconsistencies within the knowledge captured in Riki. In "Technology Deployment," it is defined where the ontology, the views, and consistency checks are put in the Riki.

The application of RODent—provided that no increments or iterations occur—is depicted from left to right in Figure 7.

The challenges, as well as the feedback when developing and using the systems, guide the execution of the method:

- In the first execution of the method, one has to concentrate on solving the most relevant challenges most of the people using the Riki are interested in. In particular, one should try to identify multipliers, that is, people in the organization who have a special stake in the Riki usage and support their daily work. For example, if inconsistent and outdated documentation is a challenge, then the resulting ontology should support the documentation author.
- During development and usage of the systems, increments and iterations are likely to occur. Since those terms are sometimes used with interchangeable meaning, we define their meaning within RODent and their impact on ontology development: Increments are additions to the current ontology without the need to change further parts. Iterations also include a change within the existing ontology.

Within the RISE project, we encountered several increments (e.g., adding an architectural description) and some iterations (e.g., rearranging use cases), but no severe change of the ontology occurred. This experience supports the demand-oriented approach that is the basis of RODent. However, this stability of the resulting ontology might be a result of the comprehensive context analysis and literature survey.

The following sections describe the task of RODent in detail and provide an example of the usage of this method for requirements engineering.

Identify Templates

The main objective of this task is to identify the templates capturing knowledge inside a Riki, and to create prototypes of the templates needed. As outlined in the method's overview, this task has the following two inputs:

- The result of the context analysis, with its overview of the currently used documents and the challenges of the organization.
- The literature survey identifying standards and other useful information to be used in template development.

During identification and development of those templates, we found the following guidelines to be helpful:

- **Split and link self-contained documents:** Resources found in the literature (e,g., standards) are normally part of a self-contained document written in a linear way. Since Riki is a hypertext-system, one needs split and link coherent information chunks found in those documents. Potential candidates are the different sections within these documents. For example, in the Volere Requirement Specification Template (Robertson & Robertson, 2005b), we identified the different user descriptions based on this approach.

- **Refactor documents covering multiple aspects:** The resulting templates should cover one aspect of information. Given a readable font, this guideline boils down to the following operational rules: (1) When a template is completed, it should not be shorter than one and not longer than five screens. (2) Each (main) section of the template should fit on one screen. Adherence to this guideline is the basis for the reuse of knowledge, since it allows referring to specific information.

When all templates concerning the current challenges are addressed in the first execution of RODent, further templates demanding too much additional effort should be left out. To find out about those templates, one should ask the user whether the information is relevant and whether the template would be completed.

As a preparation to the following steps, "Relate Templates" and "Add Metadata to Templates," the templates should be arranged into main categories according to their purpose. In RISE, we found the following categories helpful:

- **Context templates** like project and homepage of employees (people) based on O4PKC.
- **Navigation templates** like overviews about certain types of documents for specific reader groups.
- **Core templates** that define the structure of SE artifacts (cf. 0) directly related to software engineering activities (in the example, requirements engineering documents).

Finally, in order to test the templates, one should try to map some of the available information in the organization to the developed templates. This test might indicate hints that some of the information required by the templates is not available within the organization.

Add Metadata to Templates

After the templates and their contents are identified, they are annotated with metadata to support filtering and finding of relevant documents. To test which set of metadata is suitable, one should test it with a template. To identify relevant metadata, the following sources should be considered:

- **General standards:** Domain-independent, standardized metadata-sets like Dublin Core and Learning Object Standards (e.g., LOM) provide general-purpose metadata. This allows other applications that rely on these standards to reuse the content of a Riki.
- **Template-specific metadata:** Some templates derived from existing standards and documents might already contain a set of specific metadata to classify their content. Furthermore, similar templates that are on different sections of the outline of the document are candidates for identifing metadata. One example is the description of stakeholders and users in the Volere Requirement Template (Robertson & Robertson, 2005b), which has a similar structure.
- **Method-specific metadata:** Some metadata might not be directly related to a template, but to the underlying method. Using this metadata allows providing method-specific support in the form of know-how documents. An example from RISE is the TORE method (Paech & Kohler, 2003), which classifies requirements engineering documents (e.g., as description of the current state "As Is" and the system to be developed "to Be").

For adding metadata in general, remember the following guidelines: *Automatically derivable metadata* (like the author's name) can be added without further consideration. *Manually entered metadata* should only be considered if it is of direct benefit to the person who will enter it. In our experience, it is no sufficient benefit that the author is able to find this document based on the metadata entered: This search will be performed in later stages of the project. Therefore, improving the searchability of the document does not provide any direct benefit. An example of metadata with direct use is the use case classification, which can be used to generate overviews. Whether this direct use is actually taking place should be checked in the task "Identify view and consistency checks."

Relate Templates

The tasks before focused on identifying and creating single documents that have a high internal coherence. In this task, these templates are linked in order to define their semantical relations, which are later used by a Riki to identify relevant documents.

In the work, several general types of relations are identified that form the foundation for defining the relations within RISE:

- **Inheritance/Subclass:** This relation denotes that one subconcept (template) inherits the properties (in RODent, the metadata) of a super-concept (a generalized template).

- **Instantiation:** This relation denotes that an object (in Riki: a document) belongs to a certain class (in Riki: a template) and thus, inherits the properties of this class.
- **Part-of/composition:** This relation denotes that an object derived from a concept is supposed to be part of another object.
- **Temporal:** This relation denotes that there is a relation within time between one concept to another concept. For example, it is a temporal relation that one object is created before another one.

Within RODent, those general relations are refined further according to their interrelations between templates and their documents. The actual use of these relations for reasoning is described in the task "identify views and relations":

- **Hierarchy** among documents of the same templates (part-of type): Instances of templates might have a hierarchical relation. For example, one use case might have several subuse cases. It might be necessary to distinguish between different types of hierarchies for documents derived from one template: However, in RISE, we found one hierarchy to be sufficient.
- **Used in** (part-of type): This relation describes a "strong" relation between documents of different templates: If the content of a document is needed to understand another document. For example, the description of an Actor is part of the description of a use case. Without knowing the description of the Actor, the use case is not sufficiently understandable.
- **Refined in** (temporal): Refined in defines a temporal relation between documents. For example, a user story (a prose text of a certain requirement) is refined in a use case (a more structured representation).
- **Of Interest** (part-of type): This relation is used for weak relations between documents of different templates, that is, where information relevant to one document can be found in another one.
- **Context definition** (inheritance type, relation between context documents and other documents): This relation is used when additional context of a document is defined in another document. For example, the project context (like size, programming language) of a use case is defined in the project homepage. Simplified, when such a relation is established, the referencing document "inherits" the metadata of the document (in this case, the metadata about the project).
- **IsA** (inheritance type, between templates and documents): The IsA relation is reserved for denoting the relation between a template and an instance of this template.

Determine Relation Requirements and Default Relations

In the previous task, (relevant) potential relations between documents have been identified. In this task, those relations are annotated to define requirements concerning the relation itself. These relation requirements are used in the subsequent task to derive views and consistency checks. In addition to these additional relation requirements, a default relation between documents derived from a certain template is defined.

The additional requirements define the nature of a relation between templates and thus, the nature of the link between documents derived from those templates that have this relation. In other words, they define the nature of a link between the source document (i.e., where the link is defined) and the target document (where the links points to). In RISE, the following additional requirements concerning relations were identified:

- "*Required*," "*recommended*," "*optional*," and "*not allowed*" denotes the degree to which a link is supposed to be established between documents.
- "*Unique*" and "*multiple*" denotes the cardinality of the relation, that is, the source document can have only one relation to a target document, or it may have multiple relations.

Table 1. Ontology elements

Ontology element / structure	Views	Consistency Check
Metadata	Present metadata annotations	n/a
Inheritance	n/a	Is there a cyclic relation among subclasses?
Instantiation (IsA)	Show all documents belonging to a template	Does a template have documents? Does each document belong to a template?
Part-of	Show documents that are the target of a part-of relation	Are there cyclic relations among documents derived from templates that have a part-of relation (i.e., is the "higher" document part-of of a "lower" document")?
Temporal relationship	Show timeline of creation of documents	Does the document derived from the source template have an earlier editing date than the target document?
Quality of relation (i.e., required and not allowed)	Show documents derived from templates that are the target of the required relation.	Are all required or not allowed relations satisfied?
Cardinality of relations	n/a	Are cardinality constraints violated?

Based on this overview of relations between these templates, the default relation —that is, the one used most often—is determined. For example, the default relation between use cases and actors is Used In. As long as no other relation is stated, a Riki assumes that the link between those documents is the default relation. Therefore, a Riki must state less explicit information about the type of the link. In addition, a user not aware of the additional Riki features can use a Riki like any other Wiki system.

Identify Views and Consistency Checks

In the previous steps, the templates, their metadata, and relations were defined. In the task "Identify views and consistency checks," the actual use of these results is determined. In particular, the definition of views and consistency checks is based on the general types of relations and the additional requirements presented in the previous two tasks. For metadata, relation type and additional potential requirement views and consistency checks are presented in Table 1.

Technology Deployment

The task "technology deployment" covers how the templates, metadata, and their relations are implemented within Riki. The task itself is subdivided into two sequentially performed subtasks: 1) Deployment of templates, metadata, and ontology upon distinct Wikis (if any) and 2) the deployment of ontology concepts on native Wiki syntax, that is, how parts of the metadata and relations are expressed by using naming conventions.

The *deployment on different Wikis* is trivial if only one Wiki is used. However, based on the experience from RISE, it is sensible to use, at least in larger organizations, one Wiki for each group (in particular, projects) and one main Wiki for the whole organization. This separation between different Wikis has several advantages independent of whether or not Riki is used: First, it reduces the complexity of access right administration by dividing it into several sub-Wikis. Second, the possibility of name collision is lowered. An example of such a naming collision would be if two projects using the same Wiki have a meeting on the same day. If both want to use "meeting<date>" as the name for the document containing the meeting minutes, a name collision occurs. Furthermore, if there is no syntactical collision (i.e., the same name), a semantic collision might happen: Members of one project might link to the entry of the other project because they cannot differentiate between the two documents (e.g., "meeting<date>" and "<date>meeting"). Second, it is more likely that the group responsible for a Wiki accepts it as "their" Wiki. The separation into several Wikis also has an advantage for Riki: Since each group owns "their" Wiki, contextual information about this group can be derived. An example is project Wikis, where context information about the project could be derived from the metadata defined on the project homepage.

Figure 8. Development Dimension of Learning Space Engineering

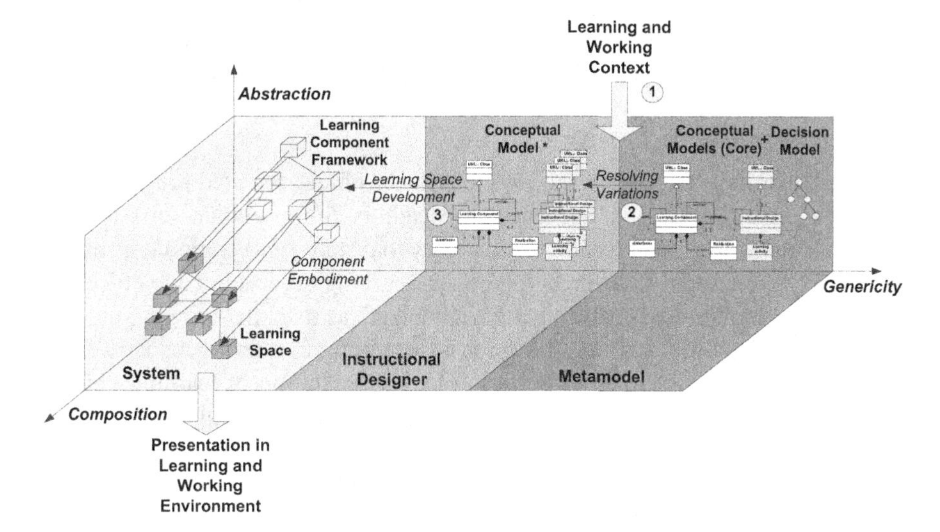

The *deployment on native Wiki syntax* is partially based on the deployment on several Wikis. By using the interwiki feature, the context of a document can be derived even if referred from a different Wiki. Another example for deployment of parts of the ontology into native Wiki concepts is the instantiation (IsA) relation. Within Riki, we had the following naming convention to denote this relation without the need to explicitly create a link: The instances of a template have the name of the template as prefix. For instance, documents of the type "Actor" are named "Actor_<NameOfActor>."

When an ontology developed using RODent is finished, it should contain the relevant information to execute the software engineering activities it is intended for. How it is actually used and gradually enriched with experience and further information on how to perform software engineering tasks is covered by the learning spaces described in the following section. These are an unintrusive approach for providing the procedural knowledge needed to perform a certain task.

Riki Learning Space Development

In many publications about learning objects, terminological issues are discussed, because there is a lack of solid theoretical foundation in the field of e-learning (Self, 1992), especially concerning learning objects. It seems that the main reason why learning objects have been invented is reuse and the desire for more flexible, adaptive learning systems. Current development efforts with learning objects are mainly concerned with metadata and content packaging aspects. Current object metadata says little about how to combine learning objects with others, and this will limit the success of the numerous repositories of learning objects that are being developed. Nevertheless, a model such as the SCORM *Sequencing and Navigation* is a first step towards a more systematic way for defining the sequencing of learning content and navigating through it.

Sometimes, learning objects are put into relation to object-oriented programming objects. The term "object" is somehow misleading. Some authors toss around theoretical connections to object-oriented theory that stem from computer science. One reason why many of us attempt to connect learning objects to code objects is that there is a grammatical affinity between "object" as used in "learning object" and object-oriented programming theory. It is not wrong to refer to concepts from object-oriented theory in order to increase our understanding of learning objects and our belief in successful reuse. Friesen states that there is not only a conceptual confusion in the literature between software objects and learning objects, it also seems that object-orientated programming objects and learning objects do not fit together at all (Friesen, 2001).

Therefore, we will use the term *learning component* instead of learning object. They should be considered as components instead of objects because their characteristics are similar to software components. A software component is a "unit of composition with contractually specified interfaces and explicit context dependencies only. A software component can be deployed independently and is subject to composition of third parties" (Szyperski & Pfister, 1997). Component-based software development is based on the principles of "separation of concerns" in order to decrease the complexity of system design and its latter embodiment with components. Therefore, a set of formal description models for components, their interfaces, and context dependencies are defined in a metamodel in order to develop components from an abstract, generic, and coarse-grained view of a conceptual component model into concrete, specific, and fine-grained learning material. This material is composed of learning components that can be integrated into a learning space (see Figure 9).

In order to develop learning spaces (see *Representation of Knowledge in Wiki Systems* for the definition of concepts used in these sections), the following three phases can be identified (see numbering in Figure 8):

- During the *learning space analysis* phase, the results of the context evaluation are analyzed. The main goals are to find out what types of content are available and useful for developing appropriate learning spaces, how learning needs can be identified based on analyzing the produced software artifacts, and in which way learning spaces can be connected to the working environment.
- During the *learning space design* phase, the analysis results are used to describe the learning space from a conceptual point of view. This means that appropri-

ate learning methods, learning goals, and a content classification have to be chosen. Based on this information, the metamodels of the learning components and the instructional design are adapted to the current learning context.

- During the *learning space development* phase, the physical learning space is created to be explored by the learner by transforming, in a first step, the metamodels into a framework with "empty" placeholders for learning components and learning elements (see *Representation of Knowledge in Wiki Systems* for the definition of these concepts). The automatic embodiment replaces the placeholders within the framework with concrete learning components and elements, that is, Wiki pages with appropriate links and navigation structures are created during run-time.

The subsequent sections explain the three phases, which have to be performed for setting up a learning space, in more detail. Each phase is described with a few main questions that cover the goal of that phase and end with a concrete example.

Learning Space Analysis

This phase can be motivated around the following four questions:

- What is the most relevant domain for improving task performance and competence development, and which target group do we address?
- What type of knowledge that is suitable for learning is available or created by the software engineers during work?
- Where are the triggers for learning space creation and how can a learning space be related to the working context?
- Which software artifacts could be used to identify (e.g., automatically) competence and skill gaps to be solved by a learning space/learning arrangement?

In general, learning spaces can have two different purposes. First, a learning space can improve short-term task performance, that is, by providing solutions in order to solve problems more efficiently, or by offering different methods or tools that enhance a specific well-known task. The domain under consideration is very narrow. Second, long-term competence development involves an analysis of a much broader domain software engineers are working in. Here, we would like to find our competence gaps that cover perhaps more than one software development phase, such as general software engineering principles or completely new technologies or development approaches.

Usually, a software project covers the whole development cycle from requirements elicitation to programming, testing, and delivery of the software to the customer.

The aim of the Riki methodology is not only to address the whole development process, but to focus on very specific tasks first and to extend the scope of the Riki later. This has the advantage that early successes on important and difficult tasks, in terms of better task performance and competence development, can be used to extend the system's scope. This step is called *domain scoping*, and will also influence the development of the domain ontology. We found out that, especially during the requirements and programming phase, suitable tasks can be found to get the system started. The information that is necessary to choose such tasks was gathered through personal interviews, by analyzing content available in knowledge repositories, and by looking at artifacts produced, such as code or software documentation. In addition, a rough process model and a role model are derived in order to relate the learning space to the well-known processes and roles. It is essential to ask software engineers what kind of problems bother them the most, and which tools, methods, and techniques they apply to create software artifacts.

During the context evaluation, available content was already analyzed and software engineering challenges were identified. In this phase, we check especially if this knowledge could be used for learning components and learning elements. The content is classified according to the knowledge dimensions and types (see Table 2 for details). Furthermore, metadata and granularity (i.e., size) are investigated in order to make first decisions about metadata extensions, respectively adaptations, to the metamodel of learning content. The idea is not to change existing policies and rules for content authoring. Learning spaces, and hence the learning components, should be adapted to the existing situation and content within the organization.

Another important issue is to find out which situations trigger a learning need. The generation of a leaning space is demand-driven, that is, learning spaces are created based on a trigger. We distinguish between two types of triggers. The human-based trigger is created by the software engineer himself, for example, by searching for specific information, documented experience, or solutions. These search results could be embedded in a learning space. The system-based trigger is related to an internal system event, for example, the technical software development environment analyzes a code artifact and finds a defect, which leads to a learning space where the engineer could learn how to remove this defect. Human triggers can be found by interviewing the engineers. System triggers have to be defined by Riki experts. Those triggers strongly depend on the capability of analyzing produced software artifacts such as code or other formally described documents. Based on those findings, appropriate learning spaces could be created in order to improve the quality of those artifacts or their development process.

The last aspect in this phase is to relate learning spaces directly to the working context. Since the learning space should be delivered as close to the work place as possible, connection points have to be found. In the domain where Riki can be implemented, those points are usually located within the technical development environment (e.g.,

Eclipse IDE) or within the knowledge management environment.

Learning Space Design

After finding out what domains are the most promising for learning (i.e., both long-term as well as short-term learning), and what kind of artifacts could be used to identify skill and competence gaps, this phase defines learning goals and appropriate methods to be applied for the learning space development in the last phase. This phase can be motivated around the following four questions:

- What kind of learning goals could be defined and how are they related to the knowledge dimensions/types and learning content?
- What are appropriate learning methods for the identified learning needs, triggers, and competence levels?
- How is the domain ontology used or adapted to meet the domain context and requirements for creating learning spaces?
- How is the instructional designer supported in adapting the core metamodels to the requirements for creating learning spaces?

Our learning spaces follow the constructivist learning theory and are related to the current working situation as closely as possible. Before we provide answers to these questions, we would like to say some words about learning theories and learning approaches that are suitable for the software engineering context.

First, following the constructivist learning theory, learning can be seen as a self-directed process where the focus lies on opening up information and on constructing individual knowledge, for example, (Bruner, 1973). Constructive learning theories criticize former learning methods for ignoring almost completely the transfer of lessons learned to new situations in practice, that is, knowledge remained in a latent condition and was not applicable.

Second, situated learning approaches developed mainly at the end of the 1980s emphasize that a human's tasks always depend on the situation they are performed in, that is, they are influenced by the characteristics and relationships of the context (Brown, Collins, & Duguid, 1989). Because of the relation between cognition and context, knowledge and the cognitive activities meant to create, adapt, and restructure the knowledge cannot be seen as isolated psychological products: they all depend on the situation in which they take place. Learning involves interpreting individual situations in the world based on one's own subjective experience structures. Learners have an active role and derive most of the knowledge from real situations by themselves, and this knowledge is afterwards integrated into their own knowledge structures. Learning and applying the lessons taught should happen in a situated context, that is, during the development of software artifacts.

Third, research in cognitive psychology has shown that students learn better when involved in solving problems. Collins' Cognitive Apprenticeship (Collins, Brown, & Newman, 1989), Schank's Goal Based Scenarios (Schank, Bermann, & Macperson, 1999), and the 4 Component Instructional Design (4C/ID) Model of Merriënboer (Merriënboer, 1997) are just three of the instructional models that address problem-based learning. Merrill proposed the *First Principles of Instruction*: Learning is facilitated when previous experience is *activated*, when the lessons learned are *demonstrated* to the learners instead of just being presented to them, when the learners are required to *apply* their knowledge or skill to solve a problem, and when the learners are motivated to *integrate* the new knowledge or skill into their daily work (Merrill, 2000).

In fact, instructional design could be handled in two obvious places: embedded within a learning component or as a separate object (e.g., by using specifications such as SCORM Sequencing and Navigation or IMS Learning Design). Riki handles the pedagogical rules of instructional design *outside* of the learning components in a metamodel for instructional design. By applying those didactical rules to this metadata, adequate learning spaces can be created that fit the current situation of the user.

Based on the identified triggers, appropriate learning methods are chosen. In the domain of software engineering, problem-based learning methods, as listed previously, and experiential learning (i.e., compared to experience-based learning, experiential learning integrates elements of reflection, support, and transfer) methods are a good starting set for creating learning spaces. The utilization of a knowledge management system is usually problem-driven, that is, a problem arising during the completion of a software engineering task motivates the software developer to search for suitable information or even complete solutions in the repository. When reusing an experience, a developer is usually engaged in active problem solving while reading, understanding, abstracting, or instantiating the experience, and trying to apply the gathered knowledge to the real problem situation. Ideally, software engineers could learn effectively from experiences when all four phases of Kolb's Experiential Learning Circle (Kolb, 1984) are passed: making a concrete experience, observing and reflecting about the occurrence, forming abstract concepts, and testing these concepts in new situations. When a software engineer documents an experience for later reuse (i.e., this is usually done by creating abstractions), he or she profits from being involved in the situation that leads to the experience, and his or her own observation and reflection about the happening. When a software engineer other than the experience's provider wants to reuse this documented experience, he or she will lack specific knowledge about the event that led to the experience, and the knowledge that results from observation and reflection. Hence, the learning space should focus on the delivery of appropriate content, in addition to the experience, in order to support knowledge construction as described in Kolb's learning cycle.

In addition to the triggers, the role and the competence level of the software developer plays a crucial role in how learning methods are implemented in a learning space. We follow a self-directed learning approach with a specific amount of guidance based on the capabilities of the learners, that is, learners proceed through the learning space at their own pace, and decide by themselves which learning components they want to access in which order. Nevertheless, when learning spaces are created, a certain amount of guidance and suitable content is provided to learners, depending on their competence level. Riki distinguishes between three competence levels: novice (knowledge dimension: declarative knowledge), practitioner (declarative and procedural knowledge), and expert (all kinds of knowledge).

Content for learning has been identified in the first phase, and domain-related basic software-engineering content that is not available has to be added to the repository. This content is now classified according to learning element types. A basic set, as listed in Table 2, is used to categorize the learning content. The set is a mixture of different instructional designs as well as software engineering specific types. This set could be extended if necessary. Learning elements could not be related directly to the cognitive processes categories, respectively learning objectives, because many learning elements could be used in different cognitive processes such as "Example."

We refer to Bloom's taxonomy of educational goals (Bloom, Engelhart, Furst, Hill, & Krathwohl, 1956), which is widely accepted and applied in various topic areas including software engineering (Dupuis, Bourque, & Abran, 2003). In addition, we refer especially to the revision of the original taxonomy by Anderson and Krathwohl (2001), which is briefly explained next. The new taxonomy can be explained by two dimensions: the knowledge and the cognitive processes dimension. Our work is based on a similar knowledge dimension as the one in this taxonomy. Regarding the cognitive process dimension, Anderson and Krathwohl distinguish between six different categories:

- **Remembering** is to promote the retention of the presented material, that is, the learner is able to retrieve relevant knowledge from long-term memory. The associated cognitive processes are *recognizing* and *recalling*.
- **Understanding** is the first level to promote transfer, that is, the learner is able to construct meaning from instructional messages. He/she builds a connection between the "new" knowledge to be gained and prior knowledge. Conceptual knowledge provides the basis for understanding. The associated cognitive processes are *interpreting*, *exemplifying*, *classifying*, *summarizing*, *inferring*, *comparing*, and *explaining*.

Table 2. Overview of educational goals and associated learning element types

Knowledge Type	**Knowledge Dimension**	The Cognitive Process Dimension (Learning Objectives)						Learning Element Types
		1. Remember	2. Understand	3. Apply	4. Analyze	5. Evaluate	6. Create	•Definition •Description •Example •Counterexp. •Analogy •History •Overview •Summary •Scenario •Procedure •Explanation •Theorem •Rule •Law •Principle •Model •Practice item •Checklist •Strategy •Reference •Learning Space Map • ...
Know-What Know-who	A. Factual Knowledge	LA 1						
Know-That	B. Conceptual Knowledge		LA2	LA4				
Know-how	C. Procedural Knowledge		LA3	Overall Learning Goal	LA5			
Know-if **Know-when** **Know-where** **Know-why**	D. Meta-Cognitive Knowledge			LA6				

- **Applying** also promotes transfer and means carrying out or using a procedure in a given situation to perform exercises or solve problems. An exercise can be done by using a well-known procedure that the learner has developed a fairly routinized approach to. A problem is a task for which the learner must locate a procedure to solve the problem. Applying is closely related to procedural knowledge. The associated cognitive processes are *executing* and *implementing*.
- **Analyzing** also promotes transfer, and means breaking material into its constituent parts and determining how the parts are related to one another, as well as to an overall structure or purpose. Analyzing could be considered as an extension of Understanding and a prelude to Evaluating and Creating. The associated cognitive processes are *differentiating*, *organizing*, and *attributing*.
- **Evaluating** also promotes transfer and means making judgments based on criteria and/or standards. The criteria used are mostly quality, effectiveness, efficiency, and consistency. The associated cognitive processes are *checking* and *critiquing*.
- **Creating** also promotes transfer and is putting elements together to form a coherent whole or to make a product. Learners are involved in making a new product by mentally reorganizing some elements or parts into a pattern or structure not clearly presented before. The associated cognitive processes are *generating*, *planning*, and *producing*.

Riki addresses all the categories of these dimensions, with the focus being on the first three categories, because these are important for reaching the upper levels and can be taught directly, while the fourth to sixth levels require a longer term and deeper understanding of a subject matter.

Common instructional design theories often speak of the following elements in the design of instruction: generalities, examples, explanations, practice items, test items, overviews, advance organizers, and analogies, among others (Yacci, 1999). Table 2 shows the educational goals and the related learning component types that were selected as a first set for a Riki in the domain of software engineering.

Although a lot of effort has been put into the definition of standards, and although the LOM standard seems to be widely accepted by now, "key issues related to global content classification such as a common schema, ontology, granularity, taxonomy and semantics of learning objects which are critical to the design and implementation of learning objects remain unsolved" (Mohan & Daniel, 2004). Hence, one of the key issues of this phase is to adapt the domain ontology in order to describe the semantics of learning components/elements and their relations, and to find a common vocabulary for describing learning components/elements.

The resulting ontology created by RODent covers the domain that was identified in the analysis phase. Learning spaces tie into this ontology. After defining the types of learning components, each learning component/element has to be related to the concepts of this ontology. This means that the ontology concepts are used for describing the learning components/elements with metadata. Riki will use LOM as metadata description. The suggested LOM vocabularies are adapted to the types of Table 2 (right column) in order to specify the value range of the LOM attributes.

The most complex task in this phase is the adaptation of both metamodels to the working and learning context where the Riki should be implemented. There exists one learning component core metamodel for defining the learning component and its composition of learning elements on a conceptual level, and one core metamodel for instructional design applied to this domain. The adapted metamodels are used to produce a learning space framework (i.e., a concrete implementation framework to create learning spaces). The types and relations between learning components (i.e., according to the relations defined by RODent) are explicitly modeled in the metamodels. The conceptual model covers aspects, such as the specification of metadata (i.e., by using LOM), containment rules that specify the parent-child relationships between learning components/elements within a containment tree (e.g., for modeling the location of learning components), specialization rules that define the types of learning components and their specialization (e.g., definitions-, examples-, table of content-, overview-, and summary-components). Furthermore, this model could contain elements that specify the kind of interaction between the system and the user, and adaptation rules for adapting the learning components to learner types or context aspects. These rules are very similar to the contracts used as specifications for interfaces. Beside the conceptual core model for instructional design that is based on learning objectives with related learning activities (see Table 2 right section), a decision model exists that enables the instructional designer to adapt the model. The decision model contains so-called variation points, their resolution space, and their effects on the conceptual model. The variation points mark variable parts of the model that are resolved by questions. The instructional designer uses these questions in order to change the conceptual model in a systematic way. The questions refer to the categorization of learning components (i.e., the instructional designer adapts the categories or the specialization structure), instructional design strategies (i.e., the instructional designer adapts the containment rules, for example, to an *experiential learning* strategy), or the questions consider adaptation aspects (i.e., the instructional designer changes the variable parts of the logical learning component such as their composition of learning elements, see Table 2, middle section). The answers to the questions include solution packages, so that the instructional designer gets support on how to adapt the model. One possibility for defining such solution packages is to use design patterns. They are very useful for describing instructional design strategies in a comprehensive manner. A design pattern can be understood as a transformation process from one conceptual model state to a new state. Each transformation step relates to specific parts of the model and tells the instructional designer how to change those parts.

Based on these models, frameworks can be derived that can be used for creating learning spaces. The next section describes how a pedagogical agent creates learning spaces.

Learning Space Development

After the selecting of learning goals and appropriate methods as well as the generation of the metamodels, this section explains how a learning space could be created based on a framework from the metamodels.

This last phase can be motivated around the following four questions:

- How can a framework be built from the adapted metamodels in order to develop learning spaces?
- How can this framework be embodied with learning components and elements?
- How can the learning space be presented by means of Wiki pages?
- How can sequencing of learning activities and navigation through a learning space be realized?

Figure 9. Details of an embodied learning space

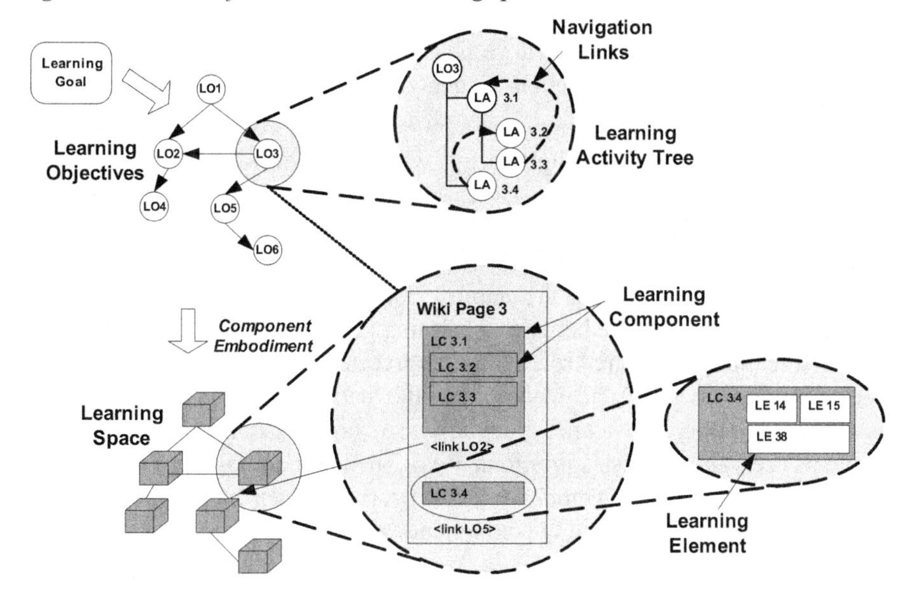

Before we answer those questions, a small excursus about pedagogical agents is given. A learning space is created automatically by a so-called pedagogical information agent. Information agents are a special kind of intelligent software agents (Wooldridge & Jennings, 1995). Software agent technology itself originates from distributed artificial intelligence. Software agents have access to multiple, heterogeneous, and geographically distributed information sources. Klusch provides an overview of information agents and describes their main tasks as performing proactive searches, as well as maintaining and communicating relevant information on behalf of their users or other agents. This includes skills such as retrieving, analyzing, manipulating, and fusing heterogeneous information, as well as visualizing and guiding the user through the available individual space (Klusch, 2001).

The pedagogical agent is a special type of information agent: it puts its emphasis especially on the mediation of information by taking into account learner profiles' learning preferences, such as preferred learning styles, presentation modes, and so forth, and creates their learning space based on the metamodel. The difference, as compared to instructional tutoring systems (ITS), lies in the fact that agents react proactively and take into account the current environment the learner is working in, instead of simply analyzing the current status of the learner's knowledge as ITS do. In our approach, a task agent observes specific software engineering tasks that are suitable for monitoring. For example, the activity of programming in an integrated development environment, such as the *Eclipse IDE*, can be monitored. Once a trigger condition, as specified in the design phase, has been observed, the task agent sends a notification message to the pedagogical information agent that has registered interest in the occurrence of particular triggers during the monitored task.

For each instructional design metamodel, a framework is derived that is consistent with the metamodel for learning components, which was developed in the previous phase. An instructional design refines a learning goal into several objectives (see values in the cells of Table 2). Each learning objective refers to a cognitive process (e.g., remember the task of refactoring). As illustrated in Figure 9, arrows between the learning objectives show how the learning objectives should be sequenced in a learning space. The difference between a learning goal and a learning objective is that usually, learning goals are broad, often imprecise statements of what learners will be able to do when they have completed the learning space. Learning objectives are more specific, have a finer granularity, and are measurable by performing assessments (i.e., through tests, questionnaires). The learning objective network is transformed into the learning component framework. The next step is the embodiment of this framework by learning components and elements.

Before the embodiment can take place, each learning object is refined in a learning activity tree (i.e., similar to the SCORM activity tree that could be derived from the SCORM content packages). The tree serves as a help structure for navigation. Each activity tree consists of learning activities that enable the learner to reach the related learning objective (e.g., reading, thinking about a question posed, removing a real code defect). In contrast to the learning objective network, this structure can only be created during run-time, that is, after a notification message has been sent to the pedagogical agent. This structure depends on the following factors: the learning objective, the addressed domain and topic, the available content, and the context. A default structure for each learning objective/topic category pair is defined in the instructional design metamodel. The two latter factors influence the adaptation of these structures during run-time, for example, learning activities have to be abandoned if suitable content is not available, or if the context allows transferring learning activities directly into the working environment instead of keeping it within the learning space environment. The embodiment creates learning components from learning elements by using the domain ontology. Afterwards, each learning activity of the activity tree is extended with a reference to learning components created.

The learning components are presented to the learner by means of Wiki pages. Wiki pages are used within Riki because of their advantages of relating pages; other technologies could also be used instead of Wiki pages. Each learning objective represents one Wiki page, respectively one learning activity tree. They are shown by sections and paragraphs using the Wiki syntax. The difference to a standard Wiki page is that only parts of the Wiki page can be changed by the learner. These parts usually consist of specific knowledge, such as project, customer, people, or product knowledge (see Figure 2 for the knowledge types), or assessment parts (e.g., answering questions etc.). General learning content cannot be changed (e.g., the definition of "Software Quality" or explanation of "Polymorphism"). Only one Wiki page is generated by the agent at a time. The activity tree sometimes offers alternative navigation options to proceed to the next learning objective, respectively to another Wiki page (see link of *LO3* Figure 9). When such a link is chosen, the agent creates the corresponding Wiki page by first resolving the references to learning components and second, by generating navigation options by means of links within the Wiki page or external navigation portlets on the Web site.

By default, sequencing of learning activities on a Wiki page is done hierarchically (see top of Figure 9). Beside the navigation options between learning objectives, additional navigation options could also be offered within the same Wiki page, that is, between learning components. Within the SCORM Sequencing and Navigation model, navigation requests are processed based on a kind of learner model, that is, data about, for example, answered multiple-choice questions that are stored. This data influences which navigation options are available, or whether they are not. In the Riki context, assessments play a minor role. Only data from the software development task and changing learner preferences will be used to adapt the navigation options.

In summary, a learning space consists of several Wiki pages with links forming a hypermedia network. Agent technology allows us to adapt the learning space dynamically during run-time, for example, while the user is browsing through the space and working on his task. Important triggers are forwarded by the task agent to the pedagogical information agent, who adapts the content selecting, sequencing, and navigation of the learning space. Observing certain tasks performed by a software engineer and the demand-driven creation of learning spaces ensures close integration of the learning process and the working task, and enables the provision of a situated learning environment for the user where he/she can construct his/her individual knowledge.

Figure 10. Infrastructure around a Riki system

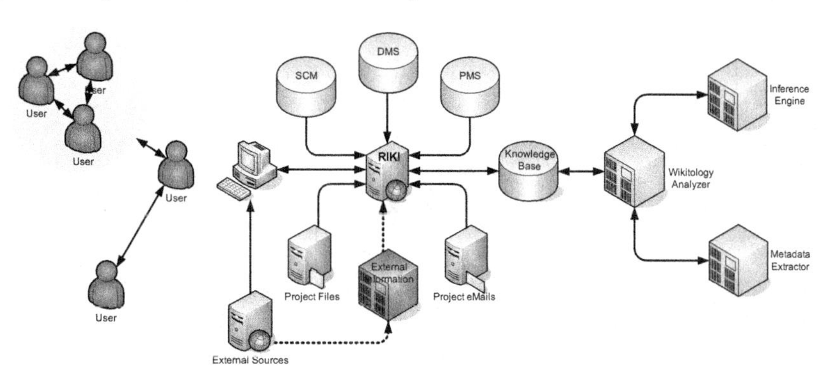

Riki: The Reuse-Oriented Wiki

In RISE, we developed a platform and a methodology for the management of experiences in SE organizations, which is integrated smoothly into the infrastructure. In this section, we will elaborate the architecture and technology of a plugin-based, reuse-oriented Wiki (Riki). This technical system sets the stage for the knowledge-based development of software systems strengthened via the support of social relationships, as well as competence development, and knowledge sharing in and between projects. As depicted in Figure 10, three domains or spaces are connected to the core system.

The social-technical system of RISE into which the Riki is embedded consists of the *social space* on the left side, the *technical space* symbolized in the middle, and the *logical space* on the right. The social space encompasses all users of the Riki from the target group(s). They are all accessible via the personal pages and references such as (co-) author or inspector (i.e., know-who entries). In the technical space, all hard- and software systems are collected. The Riki is statically or dynamically (i.e., online) integrated into the existing infrastructure and previously collected information. The integration of information includes internal sources such as software configuration management (SCM) systems, defect management systems (DMS), project management systems (PMS), as well as project files and e-mail messages.

Figure 11. Basic architecture of the Riki system (KC: Knowledge Component, LC: Learning Component, KE: Knowledge Element, LE: Learning Element, Onto: Ontology, Temp: Template)

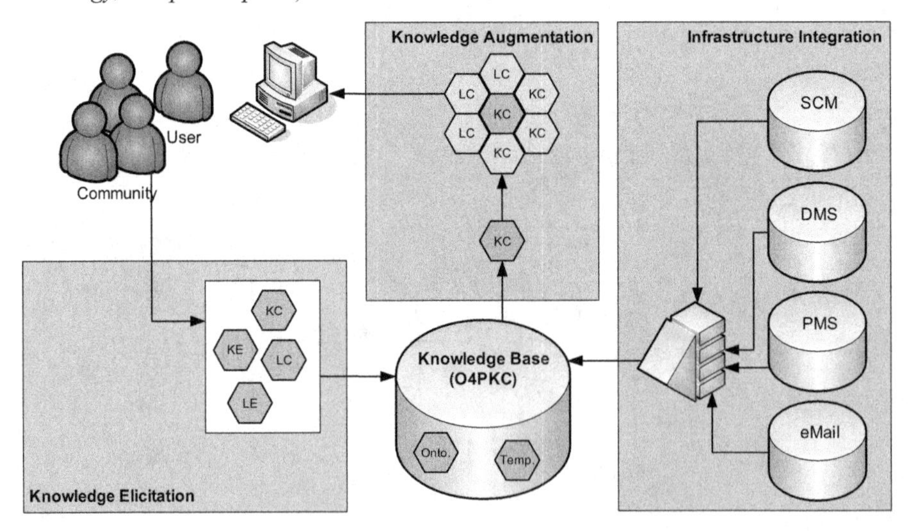

For example, SCM systems can be used to extract information about persons who have changed the source code over the different configurations. If a newbie (at least for this part of the system) needs more information about this subsystem, the newbie can directly access these persons and knowledge about it. Furthermore, information from external sources, such as technology specific mailing groups or search engines such as Google, are dynamically integrated.

The Riki Architecture

The general plugin concept of the RISE system is a service that is invoked via the Web service interface. The Web service approach was chosen to provide the added functionality independent of the actual implementation. The result of the Web service request is delivered text or simple html. The result is then integrated into the GUI via a content plugin, the templating mechanism of the Wiki, or as a pop-up window.

The RISE system has three different types of plugins that are differentiated based on their integration: Plugins that change the workflow of the underlying Wiki, plugins whose results are integrated into a single point on the GUI, and plugins whose results are integrated into the content.

This integration is supported by plugin interfaces that are already provided by some Wikis: First, Wikis might offer a plugin interface to add dynamic content to pages. The RISE system uses this interface by implementing a general plugin to request Web services and to present the result. Second, Wikis might provide an XML-RPC interface to read and write content of a page. The RISE system uses this interface to standardize the access to Wiki content independent of the actual Wiki used.

The basic knowledge flow of the Riki is shown in Figure 11. It depicts the *elicitation subsystem*, where information from the community of users (or experts) is injected into the system as a first pool of knowledge in the knowledge base. This knowledge as well as the created ontology and approach for creating learning space are used in the *augmentation subsystem* to construct the learning spaces and augmented knowledge (e.g., a knowledge component about a project with context-specific information such as similar projects) that are presented to the user. The *integration subsystem* provides additional knowledge and information from the existing infrastructure.

RISE in Retrospective

In this section, we will raise requirements and lessons learned from the development and application of a Riki in the context of two SMEs that one should keep in mind when building such a system.

Lessons Learned and Implications for Developing a Riki

During the RISE project, while building two KM systems for SMEs in the software industry, we developed the Riki technology and RIME methodology. From the development and evaluation, we extracted several lessons learned that are stated in the following:

- The KM system should be *tailored* to the characteristics and needs of the organization, its projects, and the target group(s). The process where knowledge is generated, how it is recorded, and who reuses it should be considered. In a medium to large organization (i.e., more than 100 persons), the knowledge should be far more general and self-sufficient than in a small organization (e.g., with five persons). The larger the organization, the more probable it is that the knowledge is used by persons with a totally different context, from another culture, or without the opportunity to ask the author.
- The KM system should be *integrated* into the existing tool landscape and socio-technical infrastructure of the organization. It should represent either integrated relevant information from other systems as a single point of consistent knowledge (SPOCK) or offer links to these other systems. Yet, another system that is used to store information will only be used at the start and then vanish over time as nobody cares to store information in multiple systems.
- The knowledge within the knowledge base should be *goal-oriented.* The author should have a clear organizational, project-specific, or personal goal in mind and identify the problem, potential solutions, and side effects. A simple observational experience that does not inform the reader about a specific problem or solution is of low interest and use in a KM system.
- The knowledge within the knowledge base should allow *individual structuring* by the users. Everybody structures his knowledge individually based on his personal worldview (in German, *weltbild*), which needs to be mapped to the general ontology as implemented in the KM system. This can be realized either by giving all the rights to insert personal links or by mapping between personal, project-specific, departmental, organizational, or community-specific ontologies.
- The knowledge in a knowledge base should be versioned and managed using *authorized groups*. For example, knowledge about marketing processes should only be modifiable by marketing personnel, while knowledge about the interface of two departments (e.g., travel application) should be modifiable by all those involved.
- The plugin-based design and development of a KM system allows defining development tasks for separate subgroups of the project. This enables the in-

dependent implementation of functionality and improves the further extension of the system. In contrast to a monolithic system architecture, this furthermore allows the independent testing of plugins, thereby reducing development risks.

- By abstracting from the actual implementation and by implementing plugins independently from other plugins, this architecture allows using different configurations of plugins for tailored KM systems. This is particularly important when functionality is provided by different partners that should work independently even after the project.

Patterns and Anti-Patterns in Knowledge Management

In the 1990s, a new concept was transferred from architecture to computer science, which helped to represent typical and reoccurring patterns of good and bad software architectures. These design patterns (Gamma, Richard, Johnson, & Vlissides, 1994) and anti-patterns (Brown, Malveau, McCormick, & Mowbray, 1998) were the beginning of the description of many patterns in diverse software phases and products. Today, we have thousands of patterns (Rising, 2000) for topics such as agile software projects (Andrea, Meszaros, & Smith, 2002) or pedagogies (http://www.pedagogicalpatterns.org/) (Abreu, 1997; Fincher & Utting, 2002). Many other patterns are stored in pattern repositories such as the Portland pattern repository (PPR, 2005) or the Hillside pattern library (HPL, 2005), and are being continuously expanded via conferences such as PLOP (Pattern Languages of Programming; see http://hillside.net/conferences/).

While there are similar concepts such as barriers (Riege, 2005; Sun & Scott, 2005) and incentives (Ravindran & Sarkar, 2000) in KM and software reuse (Judicibus, 1996), the identification of patterns seems to be underdeveloped and informal.

We will use the concept of patterns and antipatterns to describe the experience and knowledge we acquired during RISE and several other projects, such as indiGo (Rech, Decker, althoff, Voss, Klotz, & Leopold, 2005), V(I)SEK (Feldmann & Pizka, 2003), or ESERNET (Jedlitschka & Ciolkowski, 2004). In software engineering, design patterns are defined as follows:

- **Design pattern:** A design pattern is a general, proven, and beneficial solution to a common, reoccurring problem in software design. Built upon similar experiences, they represent "best-practices" about how to structure or build a software architecture. An example is the façade pattern that recommends encapsulating a complex subsystem and only allows the connection via a single interface (or "façade") class. This enables the easy exchange and modification of the subsystem.

By transferring the concept of patterns to knowledge management, we therefore define knowledge and knowledge management patterns as follows:

- **Knowledge pattern:** A knowledge pattern is a general, proven, and beneficial solution to a common, reoccurring problem in knowledge design, that is, the structuring and composition of the knowledge (e.g., on or via Wiki pages) or the ontology defining metadata and potential relationships between knowledge components.
- **Knowledge management pattern:** A knowledge management pattern is a general, proven, and beneficial solution to a common, reoccurring problem in knowledge management, that is, the implementation, interconnection, or interface of technical knowledge management systems (e.g., a Wiki system), as well as social methods or systems to foster knowledge elicitation, exchange, or comprehension.

Furthermore, we cluster the patterns into six groups ranging from KM system (Wiki) patterns via content patterns to KM maintenance patterns. We describe several patterns and anti-patterns from three of these groups. In the following, the format to describe these patterns consists of the pattern name, the description of the problem, the solutions or countermeasures, and causes or consequences. While patterns typically state and emphasize a single solution to multiple problems, antipatterns typically state and emphasize a single problem to multiple solutions.

Knowledge Content Patterns and Anti-Patterns

These patterns and anti-patterns apply to the content of knowledge components or elements and are typically used from the viewpoint of the reader or writer.

Name	***Knowledge Blob Anti-Pattern***
Problem	The description of an experience or knowledge component get's larger and larger over time and subsumes more and more information. The search for an arbitrary knowledge component will often include the knowledge blob. The knowledge blob can be used for different problems, has multiple solutions or contact data.

Solution/Countermeasures	• **Compact knowledge:** Summarize and rewrite the knowledge in a shorter form on one page. • **Extract elements:** Apply divide & conquer to create several mutually exclusive pages with parts of the original page. • **Extract commonalities:** Find elements on other pages with overlapping knowledge and extract this overlapping element from both (or all) pages to a new page.
Causes/Consequences	The KM system makes it easy to find and change (extend) a knowledge component; the users are not sensitized to create individual experiences; or there is no maintenance of the knowledge in the KM system.

Name	***Redundant Information Anti-Pattern***
Problem	The description of an experience or knowledge component is too long and has information that is either not relevant to the topic, already stored elsewhere, or outdated. The reader has to read more to get little relevant information, which might lead to an abandoned system. Furthermore, the description is longer than one page in the KM system and requires that the user scrolls (and has to interrupt his learning mode).
Solution/Countermeasures	• **Compact knowledge:** Summarize and rewrite the knowledge in a shorter form on one page • **Offer templates:** Find all knowledge components of a specific type and offer a distinct template for every type.
Causes/Consequences	The writer does not really know what to describe in order to produce a simple, short and comprehensive knowledge component.

Name	***Unnecessary Breakdown Anti-Pattern***
Problem	Multiple pages are used to describe one topic that is not reusable for other knowledge descriptions, and all have to be read to understand the knowledge. The reader has to read several pages in order to understand the knowledge; he/she interrupts his/her learning mode and might interrupt the learning activity altogether. Furthermore, a search on the knowledge base might return only a page within this knowledge chain.
Solution/Countermeasures	• **Compact knowledge:** Summarize and rewrite the knowledge in a shorter form on one page. • See Explicit Start Pattern
Causes/Consequences	The writer does not really know what to describe in order to produce a simple, short and comprehensive knowledge component.

Knowledge Maintenance Patterns and Anti-Patterns

These patterns and anti-patterns apply to the maintenance of knowledge components or elements and are typically used by the knowledge maintainer or gardener.

Name	*Duplicated Knowledge Anti-Pattern*
Problem	Multiple versions of the same information reside in different locations in the knowledge base. The change of one piece of information causes changes to be made on several pages of different knowledge components. If not all replications are changed as well, multiple, slightly different versions might exist in the knowledge base.
Solution/Countermeasures	• **Compact knowledge:** Summarize and rewrite the knowledge in a shorter form on one page • **Extract commonalities:** Find elements on other pages with overlapping knowledge and extract this overlapping element from both (or all) pages to a new page.
Causes/Consequences	Writers are not aware of or do not care about similar knowledge. Furthermore, either the knowledge base is not cleaned up from time to time, or similar knowledge components are not aggregated.

Name	*Dead Knowledge Antipattern*
Problem	Knowledge is considered useless, is not reused anymore by the users, and wastes space in the knowledge base or computational power (e.g., in search algorithms).
Solution/Countermeasures	• **Fuse knowledge:** Find a similar and "nondead" knowledge component and integrate the remaining useful information (i.e., combine, compact, or rewrite their descriptions). • **Forget knowledge:** Remove the knowledge from the knowledge base (maybe after an inspection by possibly interested parties).
Causes/Consequences	The knowledge is outdated, too specific, or too general.

Name	*Undead Knowledge Antipattern*
Problem	Knowledge is not used anymore by the system and undiscoverable by the users. While it might be useful to the users it, cannot be reused anymore and wastes space or computational power (e.g., in search algorithms).

Solution/Countermeasures	• **Reintegrate knowledge:** Reintegrate the component in the search index or an applicable navigational structure. • **Fuse knowledge:** Find a similar and "non-dead" knowledge component and fuse them together (i.e., combine, compact, or rewrite their descriptions). • **Forget knowledge:** Remove the knowledge from the knowledge base (maybe after an inspection by possibly interested parties).
Causes/Consequences	The knowledge is not linked anymore and does not show up in any navigational structures or search results.

Conclusion

We have shown that reuse in software engineering needs support in order to work in agile software organizations. Poor documentation and management of knowledge, experiences, decisions, or architectural information accompanies the development of software with agile methods in distributed software organizations. The Wiki technology promises a lightweight solution to capture, organize, and distribute knowledge that emerges and is needed fast in agile software organizations.

The RISE framework sketches our approach for agile reuse and tackles several problems in traditional KM and agile software organizations. Semi-automatic indexing of pages improves the retrieval and enables the semi-automatic creation and evolution of ontologies from Wikis (i.e., Wikitologies). The cooperative adaptation of knowledge to community needs, and the didactic augmentation of the content and interface are targeted to improve the usability of lightweight KM applications in agile environments.

As a basis, we are using Wikis as repositories with fast and liberal access to deposit, mature, and reuse experiences made in agile projects. Our next step is the design and implementation of additional functionality to Wikis with a first version targeted for 2006. In the context of our project, we pursue the following research questions:

- **Are free structures of knowledge and hierarchies more accepted by the users than fixed structures?** A long-term goal would be the development of dynamic or individual structures based on personal arrangement of documents.
- **Does the extraction of information from existing sources (e.g., versioning, defect tracking, etc.) improve the integration and interrelation of knowledge?** This will improve the access to experts and knowledge carriers and will facilitate the build-up of goal-oriented face-to-face communication.

- **Does the didactical augmentation of knowledge improve the understandability and applicability of the knowledge, compared to conventional, non-enriched knowledge descriptions?** A long-term goal is to improve the mechanism for creating learning spaces by considering different instructional designs tailored to software engineers.
- **Is Wiki-based management of knowledge better accepted by the users than classical knowledge management applications in agile processes?** Classical knowledge management applications need a well-defined process to be integrated. Wikis—in particular, if enhanced by ontologies—might provide a solution for agile and hence, less-structured processes.

By using a plugin-based architecture, the Riki system represents a flexible and expandable infrastructure to support reuse in software organizations of different shapes and sizes. The main variability mechanism in this infrastructure is realized by using the plugins as independent services. Currently, this includes only functional aspects of the developed system, but we plan to adapt this idea to knowledge inside the Riki system to improve the reusability of knowledge across software development organizations. By bundling content and functionality, additional complexity is introduced concerning the variability mechanisms needed to establish this product line. This interrelation between content and functionality is subject of the research area of knowledge product lines. The RISE project will provide a first step into this research area.

Future Trends

This section discusses future and emerging trends and provides insights about the future of knowledge transfer and reuse in software engineering. A system for knowledge reuse and transfer, such as the Riki, might not only be used in software engineering but also in other domains.

- **OSS reuse—from code to content:** Currently, most of the reuse within OSS is focused on software code. However, with Wikipedia and WikiCommons, there is a growing amount of content (such as music, videos, or research results) available under an open-source-style license. This content will help to overcome the initial seeding problem observed in current reuse systems.
- **Bi-directional openness:** Through open standards and APIs (Web 2.0, Semantic Web), future reuse systems can rely on content and functionality already

available to the public. For example, code search engines like Koders.com or Krugle.com can be integrated in reuse systems to provide reusable (code) artifacts from outside the organization.

- **Proactive suggesting instead of searching:** Future reuse systems will make even more use of the context of a user than depicted in Riki. Based on the metadata and their underlying ontologies, inference is done to support the user in generating more high-quality knowledge. In particular, showing similar and relevant content reduces redundancy because people are aware of available content and do not create the content from scratch. Hence, the content is subject to continuous evolution.
- **Amount of guidance during learning:** Riki provides a first significant step towards the integration of e-learning and knowledge management. Nevertheless, several problems remain to be solved and addressed. Riki intends for users to learn at their own pace, and decide which content is suitable. Self-directed learning requires that the system provides a certain amount of guidance and support during learning. For example, experts need a different kind and amount of guidance than novice people.
- **Support for situated learning:** These approaches, developed mainly at the end of the 1980s, emphasize that a human's tasks always depend on the situation they are performed in, that is, they are influenced by the characteristics and relationships of the context (Brown et al., 1989). Because of the relation between cognition and context, knowledge and the cognitive activities meant to create, adapt, and restructure the knowledge cannot be seen as isolated psychological products; they all depend on the situation in which they take place. This means that the Riki has to gather more context information in order to tailor the learning space for situated learning.

Further barriers to integrating learning management and knowledge management were identified during the LOKMOL2005 workshop (Ras, Memmel, & Weibelzahl, 2005). Examples are the lack of interactivity, lack of dynamic adaptation of content, or adequate presentation of content.

To cope with these problems, we see the need for further research and development in the following directions:

- **Ontology usage and development:** The content of reuse systems needs to be indexed according to currently available ontologies such as SWEBOK, Dublin Core, and FOAF, in order to make it available to inference support. This indexing should be done automatically wherever possible. Based on the experience gained during this indexing, the need for further software ontologies can be derived (e.g., an ontology of software engineering artifacts).

- **Integrated context models:** Besides indexing content according to ontologies, models for describing content information are another issue to be addressed further in the future. Based on context information, knowledge, and learning space can be tailored to the current situation. Different approaches in software engineering exist for describing domains and context. However, they mostly focus on one context dimension (e.g., organizational context, group context, activity context, project context, product context, individual or process context). Context models have to be developed that integrate the different dimensions in order to tailor the content delivery (e.g., by learning space) to the current situation and needs of the software engineer. Standards such as AttentionXML will play a bigger role in context description in the future (see http://developers.technorati.com/wiki/attentionxml).
- **Integrated user models:** In order to provide user tailored content, we need to know about the users' activities, their competence profiles, their learning and working preferences, their roles, and their relationships to other people and teams. The first challenge is to integrate this information in a standardized user model, and the second one is to investigate how this information can be gathered automatically during daily work.

Acknowledgments

Our work is part of the project RISE (Reuse in Software Engineering), funded by the German Ministry of Education and Science (BMBF) grant number 01ISC13D. We thank our colleagues Bertin Klein, Christian Höcht, Lars Kilian, Volker Haas, and Ralph Trapphöner as well as Prof. Klaus-Dieter Althoff, Dr. Markus Nick, Ludger van Elst, Heiko Maus, and Dr. Ingeborg Schüssler for their ideas during the first phases of the project.

References

Abreu, F. B. E. (1997). Pedagogical patterns: Picking up the design patterns approach. *Object Expert*, *2*(3), 37, 41.

Alrubaie, M. (2006). *A tagging system for Trac*. Retrieved 24/11/2006 from http://trac-hacks.org/wiki/TagsPlugin

Anderson, J. R. (1993). *Rules of the mind.* Hillsdale, NJ: L. Erlbaum Associates.

Anderson, L. W., & Krathwohl, D. R. (2001). *A taxonomy for learning, teaching, and assessing: A revision of Bloom's taxonomy of educational objectives* (Complete ed.). New York: Longman.

Andrea, J., Meszaros, G., & Smith, S. (2002). *Catalog of XP project 'smells'*. Paper presented at the 3rd International Conference on XP and Agile Processes in Software Engineering (XP 2002), Alghero, Sardinia, Italy.

Aumüller, D. (2005). *SHAWN: Structure helps a Wiki navigate*. Retrieved 29.9.05, 2005, from http://the.navigable.info/2005/aumueller05shawn.pdf

Basili, V. R., Caldiera, G., & Cantone, G. (1992). A reference architecture for the component factory. *ACM Transactions on Software Engineering and Methodology, 1*(1), 53-80.

Basili, V. R., Caldiera, G., & Rombach, H. D. (1994). Experience factory. In J. J. Marciniak (Ed.), *Encyclopedia of software engineering* (vol. 1, pp. 469-476). New York: John Wiley & Sons.

Basili, V. R., Costa, P., Lindvall, M., Mendonca, M., Seaman, C., Tesoriero, R., et al. (2002). *An experience management system for a software engineering research organization*. Paper presented at the Proceedings of the 26th Annual NASA Goddard Software Engineering Workshop, 2001.

Basili, V. R., & Rombach, H. D. (1991). Support for comprehensive reuse. *Software Engineering Journal, 6*(5), 303-316.

Bergmann, R. (2002). *Experience management: Foundations, development methodology, and Internet-based applications*. Spring New York ISBN 3540441913

Berners-Lee, T. (2000)*Semantic Web layer cake*. Retrieved 29.09.05, 2005, from http://www.w3.org/2000/Talks/1206-xml2k-tbl/slide10-0.html

Bloom, B. S. e., Engelhart, M. D., Furst, E. J., Hill, W. H., & Krathwohl, D. R. (1956). *Taxonomy of educational objectives; The classification of educational goals* (1st ed.). New York: Longmans Green.

Brickley, D., & Guha, R. V. (2004). *RDF vocabulary description language 1.0: RDF Schema*. Retrieved 24/11/2006 from http://www.w3.org/TR/2004/REC-rdf-schema-20040210/

Brown, J. S., Collins, A., & Duguid, P. (1989). *Situated cognition and the culture of learning* (No. 481). Champaign, IL: University of Illinois at Urbana-Champaign.

Brown, W. J., Malveau, R. C., McCormick, H. W., & Mowbray, T. J. (1998). *AntiPatterns: refactoring software, architectures, and projects in crisis*. New York: John Wiley & Sons Inc.

Bruner, J. S. (1973). *Beyond the information given: Studies in the psychology of knowing* (1st ed.). New York: Norton.

Collins, A., Brown, J. S., & Newman, S. E. (1989). Cognitive apprenticeship: Teaching the crafts of reading, writing and mathematics. In L. B. Resnick (Ed.), *Knowing, learning and instruction: Essays in honor of Robert Glaser* (pp. 453-494): Hillsdale, NJ: Lawrence Erlbaum Associates.

Consortium, R. P. (2005). *RISE homepage*. Retrieved from http://www.rise-it.info

Cunningham, W. (2005). *Wiki design principles*. Retrieved from http://c2.com/cgi/wiki?WikiDesignPrinciples

Dahl, I., & Eisenbach, M. (2005). *Anwendung: Semantic Wikis*. Unpublished Seminal Thesis, Karlsruhe.

Decker, B., Ras, E., Rech, J., Klein, B., Reuschling, C., Höcht, C., et al. (2005). *A framework for agile reuse in software engineering using Wiki Technology*. Paper presented at the KMDAP Workshop 2005: Knowledge Management for Distributed Agile Processes, Kaiserslautern, Germany.

Decker, B., Rech, J., Althoff, K.-D., Klotz, A., Leopold, E., & Voss, A. (2005). eParticipative process learning - Process-oriented experience management and conflict solving. *Data & Knowledge Engineering*, *52*(1), 5-31.

Dupuis, R., Bourque, P., & Abran, A. (2003). Swebok guide: An overview of trial usages in the field of education. In *Proceedings—Frontiers in Education Conference* (vol. 3).

EclipseWiki. (2005). *EclipseWiki Web site*. Retrieved 6 Oct., 2005, from http://eclipsewiki.sourceforge.net/

Enns, C. Z. (1993). Integrating separate and connected knowing: The experiential learning model. *Teaching of Psychology*, *20*(1), 7-13.

Ericsson, K. A., Krampe, R. T., & Tesch-Romer, C. (1993). The role of deliberate practice in the acquisition of expert performance. *Psychological Review*, *100*(3), 363-406.

Feldmann, R. L., & Pizka, M. (2003, 6 Aug. 2002). *An on-line software engineering repository for Germany's SME—An experience report*. Paper presented at the 4th International Workshop, Advances in Learning Software Organizations (LSO 2002), Chicago.

Fincher, S., & Utting, I. (2002). Pedagogical patterns: Their place in the genre. *SIGCSE Bulletin*, *34* (3), 199-202.

Friesen, N. (2001). What are learning objects? *Interactive Learning Environments*, *9*(3), 323-230.

Gagné, R. M., Briggs, L. J., & Wager, W. W. (1988). *Principles of instructional design* (3rd ed.). Fort Worth: Holt Rinehart and Winston.

Gamma, E., Richard, H., Johnson, R., & Vlissides, J. (1994). *Design patterns: Elements of reusable object-oriented software* (3rd ed. vol. 5): Addison-Wesley.

Gruber, T. R. (1995). Toward principles for the design of ontologies used for knowledge sharing. *International Journal of Human Computer Studies*, *43*(5-6), 907-928.

HPL. (2005). *Hillside Pattern Library*. Retrieved 10, Oct., 2005, from http://hillside.net/patterns/

Jedlitschka, A., Althoff, K.-D., Decker, B., Hartkopf, S., Nick, M., & Rech, J. (2002). The Fraunhofer IESE experience management system. *KI*, *16*(1), 70-73.

Jedlitschka, A., & Ciolkowski, M. (2004, 19-20 Aug. 2004). *Towards evidence in software engineering*. Paper presented at the International Symposium on Empirical Software Engineering, Redondo Beach, CA.

Jedlitschka, A., & Nick, M. (2003). Software engineering knowledge repositories. *Lecture Notes in Computer Science*, *2765*.

John, M., Jugel, M., & Schmidt, S. (2005). *Software development documentation —A solution for an unsolved problem?* Paper presented at the International Conference on Agility, Otaniemi, Finland.

Judicibus, D. D. (1996, 8-9 Jan. 1996). *Reuse: A cultural change*. Paper presented at the Proceedings of the International Workshop on Systematic Reuse: Issues in Initiating and Improving a Reuse Program, Liverpool, UK.

Klusch, M. (2001). Information agent technology for the Internet: A survey. *Data & Knowledge Engineering Archive*, *36*(3), 337-372.

Kolb, D. A. (1984). *Experiential learning: Experience as the source of learning and development*. Englewood Cliffs, NJ: Prentice-Hall.

Legrand, S., Tyrväinen, P., & Saarikoski, H. (2003). *Bridging the word disambiguation gap with the help of OWL and Semantic Web ontologies*. Paper presented at the EROLAN 2003, the Semantic Web and Language Technology, Budapest.

Leuf, B., & Cunningham, W. (2001). *The Wiki way. Quick collaboration on the Web*. Boston: Addison-Wesley.

Manola, F., & Miller, E. (2004). *RDF primer*. Retrieved 24/11/2006 from http://www.w3.org/TR/2004/REC-rdf-primer-20040210/

Mason, J. (2005). *From e-learning to e-knowledge. In M. Rao (Ed.), Knowledge management tools and techniques* (paperback ed., pp. 320-328). London: Elsevier.

Maurer, F. (2002). *Supporting distributed extreme programming*. Paper presented at the XP Agile Universe.

McIllroy, M. D. (1968, 7th to 11th October 1968). *Mass-produced software components*. Paper presented at the NATO Conference on Software Engineering, Garmisch, Germany.

Merriënboer, J. J. G. v. (1997). *Training complex cognitive skills: A four-component instructional design model for technical training*. Englewood Cliffs, NJ: Educational Technology Publications.

Merrill, M. D. (2000). *First principles of instruction*. Paper presented at the International conference of the Association for Educational Communications and Technology (AECT), Denver.

Mohan, P., & Daniel, B. (2004). *The learning objects' approach: Challenges and opportunities*. Paper presented at the E-Learn 2004, World Conference on E-Learning in Corporate, Government, Healthcare & Higher Education, Washington DC.

Naur, P., & Randell, B. (1968). *Software engineering: Report of a conference*. Garmisch, Germany: sponsored by the NATO Science Committee.

Nick, M. (2005). *Experience maintenance through closed-loop feedback*. Unpublished PhD thesis, Technical University of Kaiserslautern, Kaiserslautern.

Nonaka, I., & Takeuchi, H. (1995). *The knowledge-creating company*. New York: Oxford University Press.

North, K. (2002). *Wissensorientierte Unternehmensführung: Wertschöpfung Durch Wissen* (3., Aktualisierte Und Erw. Aufl. ed.). Wiesbaden: Gabler.

Oezbek, C. (2005). *WikiDoc homepage*. Retrieved September 28, 2005, from http://www.inf.fu-berlin.de/~oezbek/

Paech, B., & Kohler, K. (2003). Task-driven requirements in object-oriented development. In J. H. J. C. D. Sampaio do Prado Leite (Ed.), *Perspectives on Software Requirements* (pp. 45-67)

Palmer, S. B. (2005). *RDFWiki homepage*. Retrieved September 29, 2005, from http://infomesh.net/2001/05/sw/#rdfwik

Platypus. (2005). *Platypus Wiki Web site*. Retrieved October 6, 2005, from http://platypuswiki.sourceforge.net/

PPR. (2005). *Portland pattern repository*. Retrieved October 10, 2005, from http://c2.com/ppr/, http://en.wikipedia.org/wiki/Portland_Pattern_Repository

Ras, E., Memmel, M., & Weibelzahl, S. (2005). *Integration of e-learning and knowledge management - Barriers, solutions and future issues*. Paper presented at the Professional Knowledge Management (WM2005).

Ras, E., & Weibelzahl, S. (2004). *Embedding experiences in micro-didactical arrangements*. Paper presented at the 6th International Workshop on Advances in Learning Software Organisations, Banff, Canada.

Ravindran, S., & Sarkar, S. (2000, May 21-24). Incentives and mechanisms for intra-organizational knowledge sharing. In *Proceedings of 2000 Information Resources Management Association International Conference*, Anchorage, AK (p. 858). Hershey, PA: Idea Group Publishing.

Rech, J., Decker, B., Althoff, K.-D., Voss, A., Klotz, A., & Leopold, E. (2005). Distributed participative knowledge management: The indiGo system. In R. A. Ajami & M. M. Bear (Eds.), *Global entrepreneurship and knowledge management: Local innovations and value creation*. Binghamton, NY: Haworth Press.

Rhizome. (2005). *Rhizome Web site*. Retrieved October 6, 2005, from http://rx4rdf.liminalzone.org/

Riege, A. (2005). Three-dozen knowledge-sharing barriers managers must consider. *Journal of Knowledge Management*, *9*(3), p 18-35efs.

Rising, L. (2000). *The pattern almanac 2000*. Boston: Addison-Wesley.

Robbins, J. (2005). *Readyset requirements specification template*. Retrieved 24/11/2006 from http://readyset.tigris.org/

Robertson, J., & Robertson, S. (2005a). *Volere requirements specification template*, Version 10.1. Retrieved October 10, 2005, from http://www.volere.co.uk/template.htm

Robertson, S., & Robertson, J. (2005b). *Volere requirements specification template*. Retrieved November 24, 2006 from http://www.volere.co.uk/

Ruhe, G., & Bomarius, F. (1999, June 16-19, 1999). *Proceedings of learning software organizations (LSO): Methodology and applications*. Paper presented at the 11th International Conference on Software Engineering and Knowledge Engineering, SEKE'99, Kaiserslautern, Germany.

Rus, I., & Lindvall, M. (2002). Knowledge management—Knowledge management in software engineering—Guest Editors' Introduction. *IEEE Software*, *19*(3), 26-38.

Schank, R. C., Bermann, T. R., & Macperson, K. A. (1999). Learning by doing. In R. R. C. (Ed.), *Instructional design theories and models: A new paradigm of instructional theory* (vol. II, pp. 161-181). Mahwah: NJ: Lawrence Erlbaum Associates.

Schreiber, G., Wielinga, B., Hoog, R. d., Akkermans, H., & Velde, W. V. d. (1994). *CommonKADS: A comprehensive methodology for KBS development IEEE Expert: Intelligent Systems and Their Applications*, *9*(6), 28-37

Secchi, P., Ciaschi, R., & Spence, D. (1999). *A concept for an ESA lessons learned system* (No. Tech. Rep. WPP-167). Noordwijk: The Netherlands: ESTEC.

Self, J. (1992). Computational mathematics: The missing link in intelligent tutoring systems re-search? *Directions in Intelligent Tutoring Systems*, (91), 36-56.

Semantic Wikis. (2005). *Semantic Wiki overview*. Retrieved October 6, 2005, from http://c2.com/cgi/wiki?SemanticWikiWikiWeb

Senge, P. M. (1990). *The fifth discipline: The art and practice of the learning organization* (1st ed.). New York: Doubleday/Currency.

Simons, C. L., Parmee, I. C., & Coward, P. D. (2003). 35 years on: To what extent has software engineering design achieved its goals? in *IEEE Proceedings Software*, *150*(6), 337-350.

Smith, M. K., Welty, C., & McGuinness, D. L. (2004). *OWL Web ontology language guide*. Retrieved November 24, 2006, from http://www.w3.org/TR/2004/REC-owl-guide-20040210/

Software Engineering Body of Knowledge, Iron Man Version. (2004). Retrieved November 24, 2006, from http://www.swebok.org/ironman/pdf/Swebok_Ironman_June_23_%202004.pdf

Souzis, A. (2001). *Rhizome position paper*. Retrieved September 29, 2005, from Adam Souzis.

Stenmark, D. (2001). *The relationship between information and knowledge*. Paper presented at the IRIS-24, Ulvik, Norway.

SubWiki. (2005). *SubWiki Web site*. Retrieved October 6, 2005, from http://subwiki.tigris.org/

SUMO Ontology. from http://ontology.teknowledge.com/

Sun, P. Y. T., & Scott, J. L. (2005). An investigation of barriers to knowledge transfer. *Journal of Knowledge Management*, *9*(2), 75-90.

Szyperski, C., & Pfister, C. (1997). *Workshop on component-oriented programming, summary*. Paper presented at the ECOOP96.

Tautz, C. (2001). *Customizing software engineering experience management systems to organizational needs*. Unpublished PhD thesis, University of Kaiserslautern, Kaiserslautern.

Tennyson, R. D., & Rasch, M. (1988). Linking cognitive learning theory to instructional prescriptions. *Instructional Science*, *17*, 369-385.

TikiWiki. (2005). *TikiWiki Web site*. Retrieved October 6, 2005, from http://www.tikiwiki.org

Volere. (2005). *Requirements tools*. Retrieved from http://www.volere.co.uk/tools.htm

Völkel, M., Schaffert, S., Kiesel, M., Oren, E., & Decker, B. (2005). *Semantic Wiki state of the art paper*. Retrieved from November 24, 2006, from http://wiki.ontoworld.org/index.php/Semantic_Wiki_State_of_The_Art_Paper

Weber, R., Aha, D. W., & Becerra-Fernandez, I. (2001). *Intelligent lessons learned systems. Expert Systems with Applications*, *20*(1) 94-100.

WikiEngines. (2005). *WikiEngines Compilation*. Retrieved October 6, 2005, from http://www.c2.com/cgi/wiki?WikiEngines

WikiMatrix. (2006). *WikiMatrix—Overview of Wikis*. November 24, 2006, from http://wikimatrix.org

Wikipedia. (2006). *Your first article*. Retrieved from http://en.wikipedia.org/w/index.php?title=Wikipedia:Your_first_article&oldid=41631731

Wooldridge, M., & Jennings, N. R. (1995). Intelligent agents: Theory and practice. *Knowledge Engineering Review, 10*(2), 115-152.

XWiki. (2005). *XWiki Web site*. Retrieved October 6, 2005, from http://www.xwiki.org/xwiki/bin/view/Main/WebHome

Yacci, M. (1999). The knowledge warehouse: Reusing knowledge components. *Performance Improvement Quarterly, 12*(3), 132-140.

Appendix I: Internet Session: Knowledge and Software Reuse

http://www.sei.cmu.edu/productlines/index.html

Software product lines are a way to describe commonalities and variabilities in a software system that are used in different contexts by different groups of people such as embedded software systems on mobile phones (each with different hardware characteristics and software features).

Interaction

Survey the information presented at the websites on product-line software engineering (PLSE) and software reuse methods and theory. Prepare a brief presentation on the core concepts and history of software reuse with a focus on PLSE. Alternatively, transfer the ideas behind PLSE to knowledge or learning management and assume that "software = knowledge" or "software = course". How would a "knowledge product line" or "course product line" look like? Are there commonalities or variabilites in KM/LM systems or the knowledge/courses itself?

Appendix II: Useful URLs

RISE: Web site of the RISE project:

http://www.rise-it.info

SWEBOK: The software engineering body of knowledge, with more information on SE and software reuse (see page 4-4):

http://www.swebok.org/

ICSR-09: The Ninth Biannual International Conference on Software Reuse on June 12-15, 2006 in Torino, Italy:

http://softeng.polito.it/ICSR9/

Lombard-Hill's bibliography: The largest bibliography on literature about software reuse:

http://www.lombardhill.com/biblio1.html

The TOA bibliography: A similar large bibliography:

http://www.toa.com/pub/reusebib.htm

Sverker Janson: Internet survey on Software Agents and Agent-based Systems:

http://www.sics.se/isl/abc/survey.html

A collection of arguments why Wikis work:

http://c2.com/cgi/wiki?WhyWikiWorks and **http://en.wikipedia.org/wiki/Wikipedia: Our_Replies_to_Our_Critics**

An overview of Wikis with a comparison feature:

http://www.wikimatrix.org

Different types of knowledge that might be taken into consideration when building a KM system (e.g., for knowledge flow descriptions or templates in a KM system):

http://www.knowledge-sharing.com/TypesOfKnowledge.htm

Pattern in general: Descriptions of patterns with links to patterns in architecture:

http://en.wikipedia.org/wiki/Patterns

Software patterns: Starting page with information about patterns in software engineering:

http://en.wikipedia.org/wiki/Design_pattern_%28computer_science%29

Pedagogical patterns for seminars and teaching:

http://www.pedagogicalpatterns.org/

The Hillside Pattern Library:

http://hillside.net/

The Portland pattern repository:

http://c2.com/ppr/ and, http://en.wikipedia.org/wiki/Portland_Pattern_Repository

Classification and references for patterns based on the book "The pattern Almanac:"

http://www.smallmemory.com/almanac/

Hillside Pattern bibliography:

http://hillside.net/patterns/papersbibliographys.htm

Quality overview: The paper "Construction of a systemic quality model for evaluating a software product" gives a nice overview about several software quality models:

http://www.lisi.usb.ve/publicaciones/SQJ%2011%203%202003%20Ortega%20Perez%20and%20Rojas.pdf

ISO 9126: Part 1 of the Software Quality standard with a focus on Quality models:

http://www.iso.org/iso/en/CatalogueDetailPage.CatalogueDetail?CSNUMBER=22749

Dromey's quality model in the paper "A Model for Software Product Quality:"

http://www.sqi.gu.edu.au/docs/sqi/technical/Model_For_S_W_Prod_Qual.pdf

Appendix III: Further Readings

Biggerstaff, T. J., & Perlis, A. J. (1989). *Software reusability: Volume I, Concepts and models*. ACM Press.

Biggerstaff, T. J., & Perlis, A. J. (1989). *Software reusability: Volume II, Applications and experience.* ACM Press.

Cunningham, W. & Leuf, B. (2001). *The Wiki way. Collaboration and sharing on the Internet.* Addison-Wesley.

Fensel, D. (2000). *Ontologies: Silver bullet for knowledge management and electronic commerce.* Berlin: Springer-Verlag.

Fowler, M. (1999). *Refactoring: Improving the design of existing code* (1st ed.). Addison-Wesley.

Gamma, E., Helm, R., Johnson, R., & Vlissides, J. (1997). *Design patterns: Elements of reusable object-oriented software.* Addison-Wesley.

Jacobson, I., Griss, M., & Jonsson, P. (1997). *Software reuse: Architecture, process and organization for business success.* ACM Press.

Karlsson, E. (1995). *Software reuse: A holistic approach.* John Wiley & Sons Ltd.

Mili, H., Mili, A., Yacoub, S., & Addy, E. (2002). *Reuse-based software engineering.* John Wiley & Sons Inc.

Kerievsky, J. (2005). *Refactoring to patterns.* Boston: Addison-Wesley.

Rising, L. (2000). *The pattern almanac.* Boston.

Roock, S., & Lippert, M. (2005). *Refactoring in large software projects.* John Wiley & Sons.

Sametinger, J. (1997). *Software engineering with reusable components.* Springer-Verlag.

Schaefer, W., Prieto-Diaz, R., & Matsumoto, M. (1994). *Software reusability.* Ellis Horwood.

Staab, S. & Studer, R. (Eds.). (2004). Handbook on ontologies. In *International Handbooks on Information Systems.* Springer.

Possible Titles for Papers/Essays

- Commonalities and Variabilities of Software Reuse and Knowledge Management
- Software Patterns for Knowledge and Knowledge Management
- Knowledge Management in Learning Software Organizations: Methods and Tools
- An Effective Knowledge Management System
- Knowledge Management in Software Engineering: Problems and Research Directions

Chapter IV

Human-Centered Design of a Semantically Enabled Knowledge Management System for Agile Software Engineering

Christian Höcht, Technical University of Kaiserslautern Germany
Jörg Rech, Fraunhofer Institute for Experimental Software Engineering (IESE), Germany

Abstract

Developing human-engineered systems is considered as a challenge that addresses a wide area of expertise; computer scientists as well as social scientists. These experts have to work together closely in teams in order to build intelligent systems to support agile software development. The methodology developed in the RISE project enables and supports the design of human-centered knowledge-sharing platforms, such as Wikis based on standards in the field of education science. The project "RISE" (Reuse In Software Engineering) is part of the research program "Software Engineering 2006" funded by the German Federal Ministry for Education and Research (BMBF).

The goal was to improve the reuse of artifacts in software engineering, and brought together researchers from education science (The Department of Educational Sciences and Professional Development at the Technical University of Kaiserslautern) and computer science (Fraunhofer Institute for Experimental Software Engineering (IESE) and the German Research Center for Artificial Intelligence (DFKI)) with industrial partners (Empolis GmbH and brainbot technologies AG). This chapter gives an overview about the human-centered design of Wiki-based knowledge and learning management systems in software engineering projects, and raises several requirements one should keep in mind when building human-centered systems to support knowledge and learning management.

Introduction

The development of complex software systems is based on company- and domain-specific knowledge that has to be constantly cultivated among the employees, because the resulting quality of manufactured software systems depends on what degree the needed knowledge is actually available (Decker, Ras, Rech, Klein, Reuschling, Höcht, & Kilian, 2005). It is not only that the technical platform should release software engineers as much as possible from time-consuming retrieval-processes. At the same time the platform acquires valuable pieces of information from users, who publish their problems and experiences during work. Out of this process, company-based knowledge may be built and refined.

However, it is just because of the various possibilities of searching and browsing through artifacts that users feel overwhelmed by the flood of information. Therefore, the increasing amount of information itself is not the problem, but an unfiltered and unrated access to it. In fact, the main goal is to ensure that software engineers can deal with their daily tasks without burdening them with additional work. A systematic selection and presentation of content helps to avoid the feeling of being swamped with artifacts and so keeps, and even improves, the employees' motivation. For example, on the one hand, it is a good idea to offer plugins that provide visual representations of concepts, but on the other hand, offering totally unrestricted overviews is often too complex to be processed by the users (Tonkin, 2005).

Ballstaedt (1997) mentions four main types of artifacts considering textual content. As Wikis mainly consist of text, this typology is helpful to distinguish between different textual instances, as seen in Figure 1.

From the pedagogical point of view, artifacts in a knowledge management (KM) system are considered as not more than a faint representation of knowledge. In order to communicate knowledge to others, its complexity has to be reduced. This can be done, on the one hand, by picking out only those aspects that are necessary to deal

Figure 1. Different types of content

	Description	Example	Challenges in Knowledge Management related to Software Engineering
expository text	Expository text describes facts, explains the context, and thus provides conceptual knowledge.	dictionary entry	Information related to software products, solutions, or methods might expire very quickly, and would thus require much effort to maintain it.
narrative text	Narrative text reports actions or plots and events. It informs about specific situations, motives, decisions, acts, and their consequences.	blog entry	Narrative text might be rather helpful for some employees, but probably just a waste of time for others, because the individual usefulness of a specific narrative text is hard to evaluate.
instructional text	Instructional text provides procedural knowledge and enables people to do or not to do something.	help on Installation or maintenance	Providing useful instructional text assumes that the author respects different levels of knowledge and writes adequate content, keeping a specific target group in mind.
additional didactic text	Additional text that supports specific learning activities.	advance organizer	Additional didactic content requires deeper knowledge about reading and learning strategies and depends on rather static content like printed material.

with the artifact. The main idea of that principle is that these selected aspects allow one to indicate the underlying complexity. This can be done by letting the users assign adequate metadata to the given concept. Several methods to support the users by means of an intelligent application are discussed later in the chapter. But it has to be critically remarked that the validity of this assumption depends on the type of knowledge that has to be communicated and the given types of content.

This approach itself, which concentrates on essential aspects concerning a concept, does not yet allow other users to adopt the given artifact. It is rather necessary to restructure the chosen aspects in a different way. This method considers the previous knowledge as well as the interests of the targeted users, provided by semantics based on metadata, concept structures, and user profiles. These requirements can be addressed by means of a semantically enabled Wiki that, for example, arranges artifacts in a flexible way depending on the users' needs (e.g., artifacts written/read by the user and given interests or tasks of the user). Besides that, searching the whole system for certain artifacts should present results in a nested or context-based way (e.g., the artifact describing "Pair Programming" should be arranged under the parent concept "Extreme Programming"). This solution is based on underlying ontologies, as discussed later in the chapter. After the whole process of selecting certain aspects and restructuring them, users may be provided with complete, self-contained and motivating knowledge.

Figure 2. Human-centered design processes for interactive systems (Source: ISO 13407, 1999)

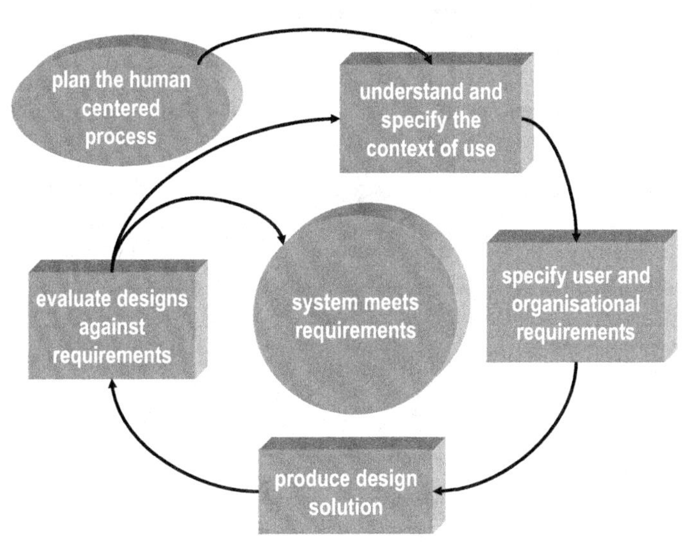

Based on the principles of a human-centered design process according to ISO 13407, expected users take an active part in the development process in order to get a clear idea of what might be specific requirements (ISO 13407, 1999). The early phase of the German research project, "RISE," therefore was dominated by context-analyses within the participating companies. Qualitative-centered studies delivered deep insight into organizational aspects and users' special needs. Two focus groups dealt with the drawbacks and opportunities of using conventional Wiki systems that were formerly introduced by the associated companies. Not only the focus groups, but also further analyses of existing artifacts allowed the allocation of functions among the technical system and respectively, the users themselves.

For example, the analysis of individually built file structures showed that an automatically enabled structuring of existing artifacts might be critical because people tend to use structures in different ways (hierarchical, time-based, priority-based, people-based, etc.) and with different granularity. This includes accessing existing artifacts as well as creating new ones. Teevan et al. discovered in a comparable study, for example, that people even use hierarchical organized structures if they do not maintain their individual structures hierarchically (Teevan, Alvarado, Ackerman, & Karger, 2004). This example shows, rather clearly, how important it is to allocate functions between users and intelligent systems. But it also gets clear that definite answers could not be found until final tests of the application.

Figure 3. Outline and structure of the following chapter

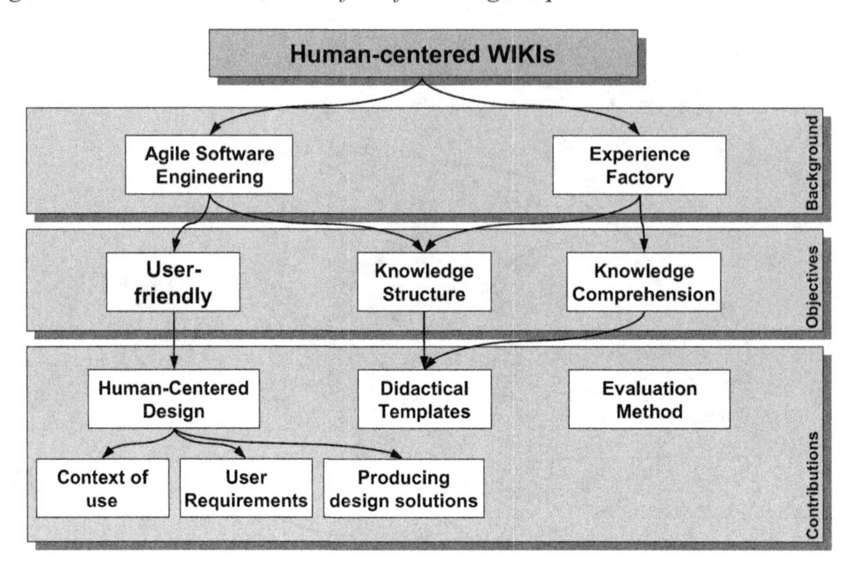

As depicted in Figure 3, we elaborate in the next section on the background regarding this chapter. This includes information on agile software engineering and software reuse based on the experience factory approach. Thereafter, in "Human-Centered Design in Software Developing SMEs," we describe the relevant objectives of the RISE project, as well as our contribution to human-centered design of Wikis in software engineering. Finally, we describe our evaluation method and results from the project evaluation.

Background

Centering the user during the software development process is especially important in engineering knowledge and learning management (KLM) as well as social software systems (e.g., Web 2.0) where users freely publish and consume information. Their efficient as well as effective interaction with the technical system gets more and more crucial for the overall success of the software product. The integration of users and users groups into the software systems is steadily increasing. This is also true in development methods such as extreme programming (i.e., an agile method), where the team members and the customer of a software system are deeply integrated to develop the envisioned software system. This section gives an overview about agile software engineering, as well as existing knowledge management approaches (i.e., the experience factory) that build the basis for collaborative human-centered software development.

Software Engineering and Reuse

Software engineering (SE) as a field in computer science is concerned with the systematic development of high-quality software systems. During the planning, definition, development, and maintenance of software systems, the people involved generate and require any information and knowledge to support them in their work or to back up their decisions.

This reuse of existing knowledge and experience is one of the fundamental parts in many sciences. Engineers often use existing components and apply established processes to construct complex systems. Without the reuse of well-proven components, methods, or tools we had to rebuild and relearn them again and again.

In the last thirty years, the fields software reuse and experience management (EM) are increasingly gaining importance. The roots of EM lie in experimental software engineering ("Experience Factory"), in artificial intelligence ("Case-Based Reasoning") and in knowledge management. EM is comprised of the dimensions methodology, technical realization, organization, and management. It includes technologies, methods, and tools for identifying, collecting, documenting, packaging, storing, generalizing, reusing, adapting, and evaluating experience knowledge, as well as for development, improvement, and execution of all knowledge-related processes.

The Experience Factory (EF) is an infrastructure designed to support experience management (i.e., the reuse of products, processes, and experiences from projects) in software organizations (Basili, Caldiera, & Rombach, 1994). It supports the collection, pre-processing, and dissemination of experiences of organizational learning,

Figure 4. The Experience Factory

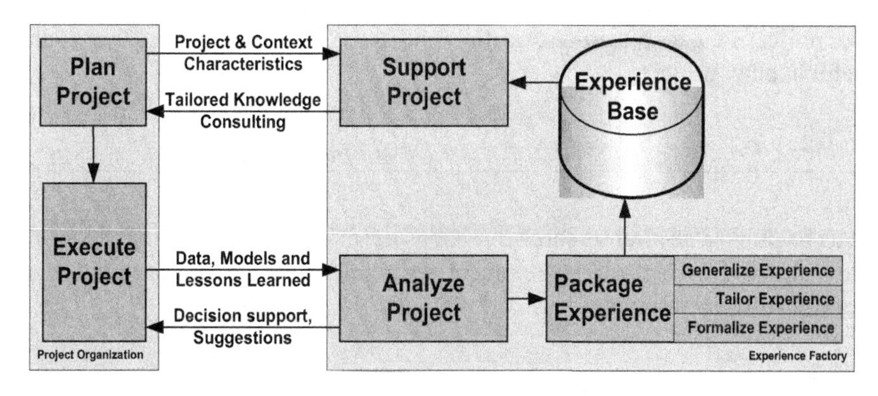

Figure 5. Software development reference model

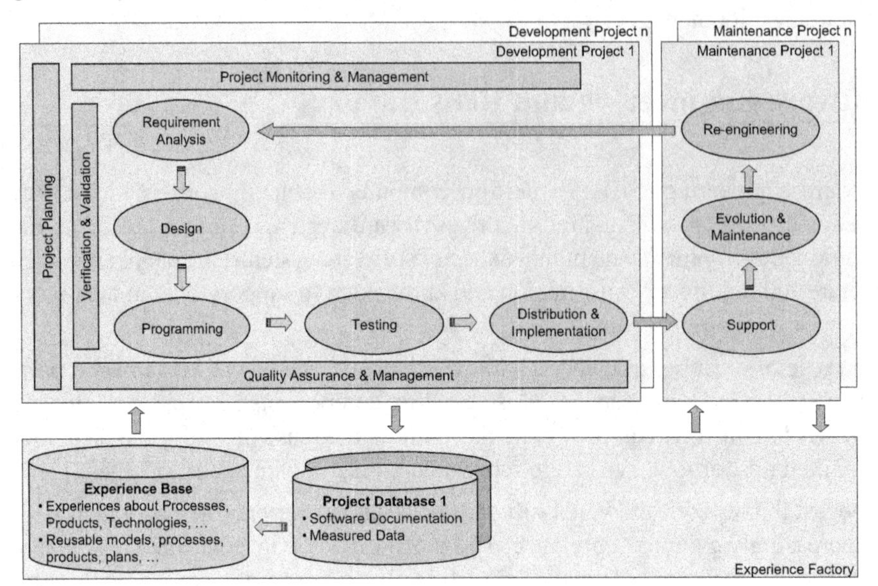

and represents the physical or at least logical separation of the project and experience organization, as shown in Figure 4. This separation is meant to relieve the project teams from the burden to find, adapt, and reuse knowledge from previous projects, as well as to support them to collect, analyze, and package valuable new experiences that might be reused in later projects.

For example, if we begin a project ("Plan project"), we might use the experience factory to search for reusable knowledge in the form of architectures, design patterns, or process models based upon our project context. In the execution phase ("Execute project"), the EF is used to retrieve knowledge "on demand" (e.g., to support decisions or reuse source code) and at the projects end, it is analyzed (i.e., a post-mortem analysis) in order to extract reusable knowledge, for example, in form of project data, architectures, quality models, or other experiences that might be useful in other projects.

Traditional, Process-Oriented Software Development and Reuse

Since its beginning, several research directions developed and matured in field SE. Figure 5 shows the software development reference model integrating important phases in a software lifecycle.

- *Project engineering* is concerned with the acquisition, definition, management, monitoring, and controlling of software development projects, as well as the management of risks emerging during project execution.
- Methods from *requirements engineering* are developed to support the formal and unambiguous elicitation of software requirements from the customers, to improve the usability of the systems, and to establish a binding and unambiguous definition of the resulting systems during and after software project definition.
- The research for *software design and architecture* advances techniques for the development, management, and analysis of (formal) descriptions of abstract representations of the software system, as well as required tools and notations (e.g., UML).
- Techniques to support the professional *programming* of software are advanced to develop highly maintainable, efficient, and effective source code.
- *Verification and validation* is concerned with the planning, development, and execution of (automated) tests and inspections (formal and informal) in order to discover defects or estimate the quality of parts of the software.

Research for implementation and distribution is responsible for the development of methods for the introduction at the customer's site, support during operation, and integration in existing IT infrastructure. After delivery to the customer, software systems typically switch into one of the following phases:

- In the *software evolution* phase, the focus of research lies on methods in order to add new and perfect existing functions of the system.
- Similarly, in the parallel phase, *software maintenance* techniques are developed for the adaptation to environmental changes, prevention of foreseeable problems, and correction of noticed defects.
- If the environment changes dramatically or further enhancements are impossible, the system either dies or enters a *reengineering* phase. Here, techniques for software understanding and reverse engineering of software design are used to port or migrate a system to a new technology (e.g., from Ada to Java or from a monolithic to a client/server architecture) and obtain a maintainable system.

Agile Software Development and Reuse

Beside the traditional or process-oriented software development another trend arose during the last years. *Agile software development* methods impose as little overhead

Figure 6. Agile software development (here the XP-Process)

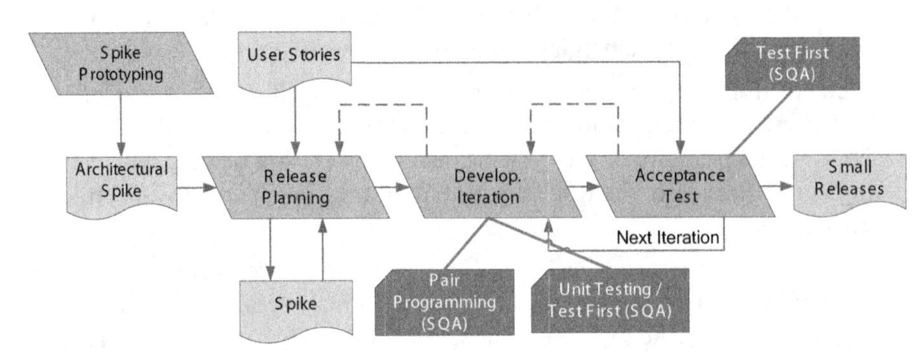

as possible in order to develop software as fast as possible and with continuous feedback from the customers. Agile methods have in common that small releases of the software system are developed in short iteration in order to give the customer a running system with a subset of the functionality needed. Therefore, the development phase is split into several activities that are followed by small maintenance phases. In contrast to traditional, process-oriented SE where all requirements and use cases are elicited, the agile methods focuses on few essential requirements and incrementally develops a functional system in several short development iterations.

Today, Extreme Programming (XP) (Beck, 2003) is the best-known agile software development approach. Figure 6 shows the general process model of XP that is closely connected to refactoring and basically its cradle (Beck & Fowler, 1999).

These agile methods (and especially extreme programming (XP)) are based upon twelve principles (Beck, 2003). We mention four of these principles, as they are relevant to our work. *The planning game* is the collective planning of releases and iterations in the agile development process and necessary to quickly determine the scope of the next release. Knowledge about the existence of existing code elements or subsystems relevant to the project can be used to plan the scope of the next release. *Small releases* are used to develop a large system by first putting a simple system into production and then releasing new versions in short cycles. The more an engineer can reuse, the faster his work is done and the quicker the customer gets feedback. *Simple design* means that systems are built as simply as possible, and complexity in the software system is removed, if at all possible. The more libraries are used and identified (via code retrieval), the less functionality has to be implemented in the real system. *Refactoring,* or the restructuring of the system without changing its behaviour, is necessary to remove qualitative defects that are introduced by quick and often unsystematic development. Decision support during refactoring helps the software engineer to improve the system.

Traditional software reuse initiatives and approaches that were developed for process-driven software development are inadequate for highly dynamic and agile processes where software cannot be developed for reuse and reuse cannot be planned in advance. Teams and organizations developing with agile methods need automated tools and techniques that support their work without consuming much time. Therefore, *agile software reuse* is a fairly new area where minimally invasive techniques are researched to support software engineers (Cinneide, Kushmerick, & Veale, 2004).

Typically, people in SME do not exactly know what additional knowledge and learning objects they need to support their work. The individual requirements of an employee in an SME will grow as they are working with a KLM system. Therefore, the agile approach to develop a software system; that is, incrementally developing the system with intense interaction with the user, is very important. The traditional approach of developing the system based on a final set of elicited requirements will probably result in an out-dated KLM system that does not fit the users needs.

Human-Centered Design in Software Developing SMEs

Software engineering, in general, aims at engineering-like development, maintenance, adjustment, and advancement of complex software systems. One characteristic of software engineering compared with classical engineering lies in the prevalent immateriality and the complexity and abstractness of software resulting from it. For this reason Broy and Rombach (2002), for example, point out the difficulty to gain vital working experiences, and point at deficits in the field of further training. Although many companies apply (agile) methods of software engineering, the transfer of the underlying complex knowledge is still a crucial problem.

Challenges in Software Development

The development of complex software systems requires specific knowledge about technologies, tools, processes, standards, and so forth. The quality of the outcome depends strongly on how successful existing knowledge and expertise of the employees can be provided and actually applied.

Considering that challenging situation, the German research project, "RISE" (http://www.rise-it.info), aims at a holistic support of software engineering tasks. Software engineers should be enabled to deal with their tasks and thus act more professionally. Furthermore, the transfer of existing knowledge within software-related companies has to be optimized. This should be accomplished by systematic reuse of experiences, methods, and models in different application contexts.

The project "RISE" is part of the research program "Software Engineering 2006," funded by the German Federal Ministry for Education and Research (BMBF). Project partners are Dept. of Educational Sciences and Professional Development at the Technical University of Kaiserslautern, Empolis Arvato GmbH, brainbot technologies AG, Fraunhofer Institute for Experimental Software Engineering (IESE), and the German Research Center for Artificial Intelligence (DFKI).

The vision of "RISE" is to develop a usable knowledge-management application for software developers that makes fun and requires minimum effort. Software developers are gently supported during teamwork and their reuse of working experiences and knowledge. Consequently, the organization itself should profit from improved productivity increases.

Based on the already stated special problems and situations, research also focuses on how high the impact of an intranet-based platform could be, in order to ensure the individual capacity to do successful work through reuse of experiences, methods, and models. Thus RISE tries to find answers to the question, *what are the main requirements for a knowledge-management platform from the view of employees?* In order to keep complex knowledge manageable so that it can be used individually and updated during work.

It has to be clarified in what respect a technical platform may allow an individually focused view of the information needed (knowledge management) and might facilitate (usability) use of it.

The participating companies already used Wiki systems as our project started. They provided initial data for the empirical study in the early project phase. In our case, we had to deal with technically and functionally rather different Wiki systems, which can all be summarized under the wide term "social software." Such Web-based content-management systems allow users not only to access content, but also to add their own pieces of information or to edit already available artifacts with as little effort as possible.

The underlying rationale is based on a strongly decentralized way of editing content. Early results of the evaluation, however, showed that a sophisticated methodology is required to successfully implement semantic based "social software" at the intranets of software-firms, in order to ensure a broad acceptance. In summary, we observed that our industrial partners had the following problems with KLM systems:

- The organizations used Wiki systems that few people used due to missing structure, participation, and documentation guidelines.
- The people stored their information in their own data repositories, network

drives, group directories, and so forth, with individual structures. This made the discovery and goal-oriented retrieval of important knowledge nearly impossible.

- The organizations used several other tools such as content management systems (CMS), e-mail, versioning systems, and chat tools (i.e., ICQ) that comprised valuable information, all unconnected and without a common structure or template support.

As observed, acceptance might decrease rapidly if the application system no longer represents a source of information that is usable, as described within the international standard ISO 9241-11: "*extend to which a product can be used by specified users to achieve specified goals with effectiveness, efficiency and satisfaction in a specified context of use*" (ISO 9241-11, 1998). So, if the systems fail to be usable, neither contents are published or edited nor even read in the worst case. The communication amongst software engineers will not be intensified, as intended, but stagnates to a total deadlock.

Understanding Context-of-Use and Defining User Requirements

It seems to be obvious that employees are responsible for an individual development of a vital knowledge basis. Not only that, this requires special abilities, resources, and strategies. Moreover, employees increasingly have to gather information and subsequently learn new things besides their working day, which is dominated by different peaks.

One kind of peak is, of course, caused by strict deadlines that temporarily raise the working load to a maximum. Besides those hard and rather ordinary kinds of peaks, there exists even a more elementary one: the problem-orientation that many software engineers cling to. One main hypothesis of the project "RISE" is that this kind of peak not only may provoke benefits, but also causes huge problems that eagerly demand a solution. The term "problem-orientation" refers to the assumption that software development predominantly is a rather trivial process: developers are provided with certain requirements and try to consider them while realizing software systems. But from time to time, that trivial process gets disturbed by rather tricky problems developers get stuck in.

Those more or less hard problems represent a kind of peak that has fatal consequences for knowledge management in software companies: developers that run into that peak are highly motivated to solve the problem and often try to solve it on their own. Probably, they spend hours and hours with their problem and do not bother about existing and proved solutions, concepts, or methods. In that case, reuse might not exceed accidental or sporadic access to available knowledge. Considering that the knowledge collected by means of a content management system, it seems to be almost impossible to build a shared repository. The result would be a collection of various problems (hopefully including a solution) that might resemble each other more or less. The so called "Experience Factory" approach has to be mentioned, which is considered as one answer to that challenge: "the Experience Factory approach was initially designed for software organizations and takes into account the software discipline's experimental, evolutionary and nonrepetitive characteristics" (Basili, Lindvall, & Costa, 2001, p. 1).

In addition to that, existing knowledge does not only grow rapidly, but can be accessed ever more easily. However, the technical feasibility itself does not actually pay off: employees might be overwhelmed by the huge amount of information they can access which suggests to them, despite (and just because of) various and omnipresent search possibilities, the feeling of just being swamped with artifacts.

Basili et al. (2001) see that problem too, and demand that the company has to *unload* its experts: "Experts in the organization have useful experience, but sharing experience consumes experts' time. The organization needs to systematically elicit and store experts' experience and make it available in order to unload the experts" (Basili et al., 2001, p. 2).

One-sided approaches to knowledge management often focus on gathering as much information as possible from experienced employees in order to preserve it. From an educational point of view, however, it neither seems to be reasonable nor possible to store that potentially relevant knowledge with its unreduced complexity if knowledge has to enable the individual capacity to act professionally as a software developer (Renzl, 2004, p. 36).

In fact, it is rather important to support the individual capacity to act professionally of each developer systematically. It is assumed that this individual ability will get more important in future. Employees will be faced with even more complex working conditions. Customized approaches to knowledge management for different kinds of enterprises should start just from the special abilities and needs of the employees, and thus help to prepare for that situation.

It is assumed that, by means of an adequate selection and presentation of content, the feeling of being swamped with artifacts can be reduced, and the software developers' motivation can be ensured or even be raised. This form of knowledge management centers the affected subjects. Thus, employees with huge expertise are no longer considered like a means to an end but, in fact, the technical knowledge management system.

- *First*, this application system acts as a flexible and customizable view (like a window) on the information needed during working-time. This system strongly relieves software engineers from time-consuming retrieval activities.

- *Second*, the system supports the collection and storage of vital working experience, which has to be subsequently formed and refined.

These are the two main factors of the RISE methodology, which were optimized during project time.

Producing Design Solutions and Evaluating Them Against Requirements

The survey that was dominated by qualitative social research methods revealed valuable insights about requirements of users and organizations. Two focus groups were dedicated to explore usage problems with the knowledge management platforms already introduced.

Especially, the collection of user requirements, related to Wikis as experience management systems for software engineering, important problem areas could be identified.

The gathered qualitative data is characterized by a very high validity, which means (given the background of user-centered design) that a common understanding of user requirements was developed and involved users agreed to high extent which user requirements should be realized in favor.

In order to classify the collected data, the Munich knowledge-management model has been used with its four categories: knowledge-representation, knowledge-usage, knowledge-communication, and knowledge-creation (Reinmann-Rothmeier, 2001):

- **Knowledge-representation:** Some employees tend to write down a minimum of information. It was observed that some of them document just as little as possible, so that they will be able to find out later what was meant by the given artifact. The main disadvantage of that behavior is that the saved data becomes hard or even almost impossible to understand for other employees accessing that content because they do not have the necessary knowledge to »decode« and to classify it. However, it seems to be a kind of game those developers are playing when doing some documentation: they rather puzzle together pieces of information than writing down supposedly redundant or superfluous information.
- **Knowledge-usage:** Crucial information about projects, products, or customers are distributed across various databases. This means that useful knowledge is hard to find and thus hard to be transferred in other contexts like new projects for example.

- **Knowledge-communication:** Employees who browse or search through Wiki content in order to find some special piece of information have to spend a lot of time. Moreover, editing content in most Wikis is rather uncomfortable: for example, adding a chart, a table or even a picture to Wiki pages requires special handling if it is even possible. As a consequence, information is being transferred by mail under pressure of time and not added to the Wiki site.
- **Knowledge-creation:** With increasing activity in a Wiki, it becomes harder for authors to integrate their piece of information into the existing structure. So, it becomes more and more likely that no new content is being added and already saved content gets orphaned.

Basically, using metadata is a good idea to keep heterogeneous and complex structures describable and thus technically manageable. But the problem is that users often fail to provide useful metadata, or simply do not bother about complex sets of metadata.

One very important hypothesis of the RISE project is that software-development teams that use a Wiki collaboratively to build knowledge repositories are actually about to **create a kind of semantic structure**, which users may not necessarily be aware of. This more or less refined structure, called "Wikitology," can be considered as a weakly formalized ontology. This has three main advantages:

- The *maintenance of metadata* is not considered as extra activity.
- *Ontologies* may always grow behind the content.
- Maintenance of ontologies is an expensive and time-consuming process. But, based on our assumptions, this work can be *automated more efficiently,* and thus releases employees from that job.

Another crucial approach of the RISE project is the **use of tags** as a very minimalistic but rather effective way of providing metadata. Any tags may be assigned individually to WIKI pages. So, each user is able to create his own view on any artifact by using his own depiction. Since in our approach all users are able to see the tags provided by the others, it is, of course, very probable that team members manage to create a shared set of tags as well.

Furthermore, **templates** for special types of content (bug report, use case, user story, etc.) help to provide a minimum of required information. Readers as "consumers" of the artifact can be satisfied, too. For example, the given structure helps them to browse faster through the content in order to find only some piece of information being of interest. Finally, this results in a higher acceptance of the system, which might also motivate employees to add their content to the repository.

Additionally, a **blog component** is added to the system. The blog contains not only news. In fact, the blog can be considered as a human-based *filter* on the Wiki content. For example, users might link to certain Wiki pages and provide some extra information along with the link. So, other users get useful assistance with the evaluation of artifacts.

Evaluation of Semantically Enabled KM Systems

The objective of the evaluation of a KM system, such as the Riki, is to show its effectiveness in a specific application context. The tailored instances of the system at different organizations are evaluated to identify the usefulness to the users, the examined applicability, the evolvability, as well as economic factors. The evaluation was split into two phases. The first phase, called *baseline evaluation,* at the start of the project was used to elicit the context and current state of knowledge transfer. From the information we gathered in this phase, we designed and developed the Riki system considering people, processes, and available technologies. The second phase, called *delta evaluation,* at the end of the project helped to evaluate the change on the socio-technical knowledge management system. In both phases, we used the following three techniques to elicit valuable information from the organizations and potential end users:

- Goal-oriented, questionnaire-based *interviews* were used to query the previously listed questions with three to ten persons in two to four sessions. The collected answers were summarized and validated by the participants via e-mail.
- *Group discussions* were done at every company to collect any additional information, opinions, ideas, and so forth, that were not covered by the interviews. The discussion was started with a specific topic (e.g., Why did the old Wiki not work for you as a KM system?), and every person could state what they expected from an improved knowledge-management infrastructure.
- *Artifact analyses* were conducted to identify knowledge sources, the type of knowledge within, as well as how employees structure their documents and knowledge in existing storage systems (e.g., the hierarchy of directories in personal file systems or in pre-existing WIKI systems).

These evaluation techniques helped to cover the following three topics:

- **Technology:** Elicitation of the existence and characteristics of the technical infrastructure, existing KM systems, and other software systems that might be integrated into or used as the KM system (i.e., the Riki system). Furthermore, these technological systems potentially have valuable information that can be utilized in a KM system.

- **Methodology:** Elicitation of the applied methodology for production (e.g., software development) and knowledge management (esp. knowledge transfer processes). This gives further information about how the KM system should be integrated into the social system of the organization and where, when, and by whom knowledge is produced or consumed.
- **Knowledge:** Elicitation of the existing knowledge components available in the organization, as well as their characteristics and interrelation (e.g., for the development of an ontology). Furthermore, the typical structure of documents that might be didactically enriched.

A more detailed description, as well as some results of the two evaluation phases, is described in the following sections. They address persons who want to evaluate a KM system, such as the RIKI in an organization.

Baseline Evaluation

The baseline evaluation is concerned with the determination of the organizational context a social-technical knowledge management should be embedded in. The core goal of the baseline evaluation is to measure and analyze the current status of the implicitly or explicitly performed KM processes, the used knowledge carrying or KM systems, as well as the knowledge culture itself. Baseline evaluations are typically applied only once to get a consistent view of the KM in the organization before larger changes. This section describes the basic process for the evaluation of a KM system as well as a summary of our baseline evaluation.

Baseline Evaluation Process

The baseline evaluation process (and similarly the delta evaluation) is structured into the three subphases: problem-determination, context-determination and knowledge-determination. As depicted in Figure 7, the steps in these subphases define a process that results in several documents (e.g., a problem description) usable for the specification of a socio-technical KM system integrated into the surrounding organizational context:

- **Problem-determination:** The problem determination serves to identify existing knowledge sources (e.g., in case of our partner, "empolis," a Wiki system named MASE) as well as emerged problems and challenges with it. Step 0a is used to determine existing information systems and technical knowledge sources using a systematic analysis method. By means of a group discussion in step 0b, the exchange of knowledge via existing technical (KM) systems in a typical project team is illuminated.

- **Context-determination:** This subphase is concerned with the determination of the context the socio-technical KM system is embedded in. The context determination produces information about the production processes, roles, documents, or sites that might be used in the KM system. The three steps in this subphase are concerned with the development processes that are to be supported by the KM initiative. Step 1a uses a group discussion technique to determine existing documents, templates, and other potentially reusable

Figure 7. Plan for baseline and delta evaluation

elements. To elicit or update the development process in use, we applied an interview with several product and project managers in step 1b.

- **Knowledge-determination:** The knowledge determination subphase targets the core information that should be made reusable via the KM system. The content, context, and structure of reusable elements is determined in step 2a using an interview. Based on this information, the knowledge transfer processes and the knowledge culture itself is analyzed in step 2b using a group discussion with several members of project teams.

Finally, step 3 is used to identify the technical infrastructure of tools and systems that are not used for knowledge management, but might be integrated and connected with the new or improved KM system (i.e., a new or improved Riki).

Results from the Baseline Evaluation

In the context of the RISE project, we applied step 0a to step 3 of the evaluation plan, as depicted in Figure 7. For the execution of the baseline evaluation one period, we required a time span of approximately 3 months, taking into account that not all employees are continuously available. Based on different vacation planning, holidays in summer, autumn, and Christmas, as well as other projects, one should take into account the time-consuming characteristics of such an evaluation.

During the group discussion concerning the usage of existing KM systems (cf. Figure 7, 0b) as well as the knowledge culture and transfer (cf. Figure 7, 2b), we determined the following status in the organization:

- The organization used a Wiki ("MoinMoin") that few people used, and contained partially documented concepts, ideas, comments, and larger documentations about planned as well as already developed software systems. Other information in the WIKI included customer information, dates, ToDo-lists, addresses, and absent lists.
- Important information about the software system itself is documented in the source code (in this case, Python and ePyDoc). To extract this information, one has to check out the whole software system from the versioning system and search for relevant information on file level.
- Important information about changes to the software system is documented in the used versioning system (in this case: Subversion). Changes at the software system are sent to all interested users by e-mail. To extract this information without the e-mails, one has to analyze every check-in into the system and appropriate comments.

- Internal information sources (i.e., repositories) with other project-relevant information are change tracking system, project folders, universal and private network drives, e-mails, and chat tools (e.g., ICQ), with information in files such as plain text or MS Word documents. Furthermore, task cards at a physical blackboard.
- External information sources are distributed over the whole Internet, but the employees had a focus on MSDN and Google if they required further information.

Positive characteristics: What goes well?

- The cooperation between two people closely working together, but who were distributed physically over two cities, worked very well using the old Wiki.
- The local teams worked on one floor and had only short distances to their colleagues. The face-to-face communication was very good (i.e., everybody was in "shouting" distance).

Negative characteristics: What runs badly?

- The Wiki was not used anymore at the beginning of the evaluation and the feedback indicated that most people were not pleased with the structure of the knowledge base.
- Neither the old Wiki nor the documentation language for Python (ePyDoc) permitted the integration of pictures or graphics.
- The search for information in the Wiki and file system is term based (i.e., no stemming or Boolean operators). This was perceived as insufficient and demotivating by the users. Furthermore, the search within the Wiki was impeded by the use of camel case (e.g., "MyProjectDescription") in the page names.
- The discovery of relevant information is perceived as complicated as they are distributed over multiple repositories that all use different (or nonexistent) search mechanisms.
- Access to the Wiki from a text editor (e.g., emacs under Linux/Unix) or a shell (i.e., command line interface) is impossible and/or uncomfortable. Nevertheless, some developers are biased or required to use these, and are not willing to install or use other operating systems (or Web browsers such as Internet Explorer™).
- Neither were the authors (resp. other observers) informed about changes done to the content in the Wiki, nor were they informed about changes to the navi-

gational or divisional structures (i.e., chapters and sections) of the content.
- It was not clear where to store information as they could be spread or duplicated in multiple repositories, for example, in the versioning system, change tracking system, or the code itself.

In summary, the knowledge transfer and management processes, as they were lived in the organization previously to the introduction of the Riki system, were determined by the baseline evaluation as follows:

- *Storage* of information is limited to few people in the organization and the documented information is only partially complete, consistent, or valid.
- *Reuse* of content is minimal, as the information is distributed over several sources with different search interfaces and techniques. Furthermore, the content of the documents have inconsistent structures, incomplete descriptions, or are simply outdated.
- *Workflow* for reuse of content and getting an *overview* is slow and typically demotivating, as multiple sources have to be searched manually and documents belonging together are not grouped or linked.
- *Sharing knowledge* is cumbersome, there are no templates, guidelines, or checklists to validate if the recorded information has some quality and might be easily reused by the colleagues.
- *Confidence* in the knowledge transfer system and *motivation* to share is low, as only few people are creating shareable documents and they are mostly not accurate or up-to-date. Nevertheless, the people would like to share their knowledge in a more persistent way.
- *Face-to-face communication* is strong, especially as most employees have short distances to their colleagues, are roughly of the same age, and see no need to hide their information (i.e., egghead's syndrome).

Delta Evaluation

The core goal of a delta evaluation is to measure and analyse the changes a KM system has inflicted on the affected organization. Delta evaluations can be applied multiple times during the lifecycle of a KM system (e.g., every year) to evaluate the effect on the organization.

Delta Evaluation Types

Since KM systems are usually used only irregularly in the beginning and not yet a firm part of the working process, the delta evaluation phase can be applied in three different types:

1. **Applicability:** The first type serves to examine how frequently the system is used, if it integrates into the socio-technical infrastructure, and if it helps the users during their daily work. In order to keep the effort of the evaluation down to a minimum, a lightweight evaluation is planned by reusing existing plans and other technology assessment or acceptance models.
2. **Usefulness:** In the second type, the results and experiences from the first type serve to sharpen requirements and improvement goals. The system has already demonstrated that it is applicable in the organization, and represents an integral component of the regular work routine. By means of structured evaluation processes, a formal evaluation plan is constructed to examine, in particular, the aspects usefulness, and ease-of-use for developers as well as management staff.
3. **Economy:** Finally, the third type serves to examine the economical aspects of the KM system. The system is already integrated into the regular work routine, and users share and reuse the knowledge within. An adaptive evaluation, reaction, and risk plan are developed to continuously monitor and improve the system. The focus of this type is the evaluation of the system and a forecast of the usefulness regarding the return on investment (ROI) and total cost of ownership (TCO).

To identify existing or potential problems, the entire system is continuously monitored during start-up phase. Logfiles help to drill-down into specific problems if the users observe a problem while using the system.

Results of the Delta Evaluation

In the context of the RISE project, we could only apply the first subphase and evaluate the applicability of the Riki system. Due to the short amount of time the system was used (two months) we could only get little insight into the usefulness of the system for the users in their daily routine. During the group discussion concerning the usage of the Riki (cf. Figure 7, 0b) as well as knowledge culture and transfer (cf. Figure 7, 2b), we noted the following characteristics the users liked very much about the Riki:

- Metadata elements that can be placed by every user (such as keywords in form of tags) can be very helpful in indexing the content of a Riki, and the users reacted very positively that they were able to *index every page* with their own metadata.
- The usage of metadata enabled the users to build up and use their own *individual ontology* (in form of individual tags) that is not bound to compromises or constraints from universal ontologies that might have been constructed in advance. Furthermore, metadata from the universal ontology (i.e., specified beforehand or as defined by other users) was partially used in their own ontology.
- *Searching* the information stored in the Riki is more accepted by the users when the metadata might be integrated into the search process. In the Riki, the results are *clustered* by this metadata and the metadata might be used to *refine* the search query. The search technology exploits co-occurring metadata from multiple users and applies "collaborative filtering" techniques (i.e., "metadata x you search for is also called y").
- Annotated pages that were listed in search results reminded the users that they already read them or were highly valuable and should be read again. Similar to the Memex concept by Vannevar Bush (Bush, 1945) (cf. http://en.wikipedia.org/wiki/Vannevar_Bush), the metadata might even be used to record a reading sequence for oneself.
- The integrated view of the Riki system, including various artefacts as well as repositories, enables the user to send links that are not subject to change as, for example, mounted devices in the Windows file system.

In comparison to the status, as determined by the baseline evaluation, the usage of the Riki system had the following subjective effect on the organization:

- *More storage* of information into the Riki than before as barriers (technological and social) are reduced.
- *More reuse* of content from the Riki as users are more likely to share and search for content.
- *Faster workflow* for reuse of content and an *improved overview* due to the integrative view over multiple systems (e.g., file system, e-mail, etc.) in a central integrated repository.
- *Less barriers for sharing knowledge,* as it is easier and faster to enter information, but this typically results in a *low quality* of the content. Most users embrace the Wiki idea and record even preliminary information that is revised by oneself or others over time.

- *Higher confidence* in the system and *increased motivation* as content is easier to find and more people are participating in the sharing process.
- *Consistent face-to-face communication* even as more information is reused from the technical system.

Further and more quantitative results about the usefulness and economical aspects, especially of the more SE specific features of a Riki such as ontology-based templates for requirements, will be elicited in later evaluations.

Conclusion

Although the importance of usability is broadly and increasingly accepted, user-centered design processes can hardly be found in software companies in general. Small- and medium-sized companies often fail to apply user-centered design methods due to poorly established role models. Even if user-requirements are (more or less) specified, the problem that remains is to guarantee that they are strictly followed during production.

The whole research process during the project "RISE" was strongly dominated by qualitative evaluation activities. They have been preferred because they helped to specify the context of use as well as user and organizational requirements. In general, empirical data, gathered by means of qualitative research methods, is characterized by its high validity. Unfortunately, it is rather difficult to extract requirements out of this data or to check to what extent those "implicit" requirements have been considered during the development process of the software system.

Strictly following the model of a user-centered design of an interactive software system, that problem could not be bypassed. It is rather necessary to provide prototypes, as soon as possible, that contain as much functionality as necessary in order to check current implementation states against more or less "implicit" requirements.

In terms of a rather comprehensive meaning of *usability,* it was not only about developing user interfaces and improving them. In fact, usability engineering is considered as a vital concept in software development. So, it is not only about describing, designing, or producing design solutions for user interfaces. It is rather about understanding and facilitating human-engineered socio-technical systems.

Acknowledgments

Our work is part of the project RISE (Reuse in Software Engineering), funded by the German Ministry of education and science (BMBF) grant number 01ISC13D.

References

Ballstaedt, S. (1997). *Wissensvermittlung.* Weinheim: Beltz, Psychologie-Verl.-Union.

Basili, V. R., Caldiera, G., & Rombach, H. D. (1994). Experience factory. In J. J. Marciniak (Ed.), *Encyclopedia of software engineering* (Vol. 1) (pp. 469-476). New York: John Wiley & Sons.

Basili, V., Lindvall; M., & Costa, P. (2001). *Implementing the experience factory concepts as a set of experience bases.* Retrieved May 12, 2006, from http://www.cebase.org:444/fc-md/ems_--_total_project/papers/SEKE01/seketalk18.pdf

Beck, K. (2003). *Extreme programming explained.* Boston: Addison-Wesley.

Beck, K., & Fowler, M. (1999). Bad smells in code. In G. Booch, I. Jacobson, & J. Rumbaugh (Eds.), *Refactoring: Improving the design of existing code* (1st ed.) (pp. 75-88). Addison-Wesley Object Technology Series.

Broy, M., & Rombach, D. (2002). Software engineering. Wurzeln, Stand und Perspektiven. *Informatik Spektrum, 25*(6), 438-451.

Bush, V. (1945). As we may think. *The Atlantic Online, 176*, 101-108, (Reprinted in 1996: *ACM Interactions, 3*(2), 35-46).

Cinneide, M. O., Kushmerick, N., & Veale, T. (2004). Automated support for agile software reuse. *ERCIM News, F* (pp. 22-23)

Decker, B., Ras, E., Rech, J., Klein, B., Reuschling, C., Höcht, C., & Kilian, L. (2005). A framework for agile reuse in software engineering using Wiki technology. *Wissensmanagement, 2005*, 411-414.

ISO 9241-11 (1998). *Ergonomic requirements for office work with visual display terminals (VDTs). Part 11: Guidance on usability.*

ISO 13407 (1999). *Human-centred design processes for interactive systems.*

Reinmann-Rothmeier, G. (2001). *Wissen managen* (Nr. 131). München: Inst. für Pädag. Psychologie und Empirische Pädag., Lehrstuhl Prof. Dr. Heinz Mandl.

Renzl, B (2004). Zentrale Aspekte des Wissensbegriffs – Kernelemente der Organisation von Wissen. In B. Wyssusek, M. Schwartz, & D. Ahrens (Eds.), *Wissensmanagement komplex*. Berlin: Schmidt.

Teevan, J., Alvarado, C., Ackerman, M. S., & Karger, D. R. (2004). *The perfect search engine is not enough: A study of orienteering behavior in directed search*. CHI 2004 Paper. Retrieved May 12, 2006, from http://haystack.lcs.mit.edu/papers/chi2004-perfectse.pdf

Tonkin, E. (2005). *Making the case for a Wiki*. Retrieved May 12, 2006, from http://www.ariadne.ac.uk/issue42/tonkin/intro.html

Appendix I: Internet Session: HCI and WIKI

http://c2.com/cgi/wiki?WikiEngines

http://en.wikipedia.org/wiki/Wiki

WIKI systems are a way to share knowledge and collaborate in a distributed environment with other people from different cultures and with different goals. They are used in different contexts by different groups of people, and are typically developed by software programmers with a very technology-centered view and without knowledge about usage scenarios or real-use cases.

Interaction

Survey the information presented at the Web sites on WIKIs and HCI methods and theory. Prepare a brief presentation on the core concepts and history of WIKIs with a focus on their HCI. Alternatively, analyze if the current WIKI systems are built human centered or technology centered. What would you change?

Appendix II: Useful URLs

Website of the RISE project:

http://www.rise-it.info

More information about WIKI systems on Wikipedia:

http://en.wikipedia.org/wiki/Wiki and http://en.wikipedia.org/wiki/List_of_wikis

A wikibook about WIKI systems:

http://en.wikibooks.org/wiki/Wiki_Science

More information about semantic WIKIs on Wikipedia:

http://en.wikipedia.org/wiki/Semantic_Wiki

More information about the topic "Social Software" on Wikipedia:

http://en.wikipedia.org/wiki/Social_software

A collection of arguments why WIKIs work:

http://c2.com/cgi/wiki?WhyWikiWorks and **http://en.wikipedia.org/wiki/Wikipedia: Our_Replies_to_Our_Critics**

The International Symposium on WIKIs (WikiSym):

http://www.wikisym.org/

Multilingual online journal for qualitative research:

http://www.qualitative-research.net/fqs/fqs-eng.htm

Appendix III: Further Readings

Beyer, H., & Holtzblatt, K. (1998). *Contextual design.* San Francisco.: Morgan Kaufmann Publ.

Cooper, A. (1995). *About face.* Foster City, CA: IDG Books Worldwide.

Fensel, D. (2004). *Ontologies: A silver bullet for knowledge management and electronic commerce.* Berlin: Springer.

Lauesen, S. (2005). *User interface design.* Harlow: Pearson/Addison-Wesley.

Leuf, B., & Cunningham, W. (2006). *The Wiki way.* Boston: Addison-Wesley.

Nielsen, J. (2004). *Usability engineering.* San Diego, CA: Kaufmann.

Shneiderman, B., & Plaisant, C. (2005). *Designing the user interface*. Boston: Pearson.

Shneiderman, B. (2002). *Leonardo's laptop*. Cambridge, MA: MIT Press.

Staab, S. (2004). *Handbook on ontologies*. Berlin: Springer.

Possible Titles for Papers/Essays

- Pedagogics in Knowledge Management: Socio-Technical Methods and Tools in a Phase of Convergence
- Knowledge Management Systems and Human Computer Interaction

Chapter V

Making Knowledge Management Systems Open: A Case Study of the Role of Open Source Software

Tom Butler, University College Cork, Ireland
Joseph Feller, University College Cork, Ireland
Andrew Pope, University College Cork, Ireland
Ciaran Murphy, University College Cork, Ireland

Abstract

This chapter presents an action research-based case study of the development of pKADS (portable knowledge asset development system), an open source, desktop-based knowledge management (KM) tool, implemented in Java and targeted at government and nongovernment organizations. pKADS was a collaborative project involving Business Information Systems, University College Cork, Ireland and the United Nations Population Fund (UNFPA), and was funded by the government of Ireland. Development of the application took just three months, using an agile development approach and some reuse of existing open source code. The chapter discusses the background to the pKADS project and prior UNFPA KM efforts, the technical and conceptual architectures of the pKADS application, the roles played by open source components and open data standards, the rationale for releasing pKADS as open source software, and the subsequent results. Future research, in the form of developing open source, Intranet/Internet-based KM tools for the Government of Ireland—eGovernment Knowledge Platform (eGovKP) is also briefly discussed.

Introduction

In the latter half of 2003, the United Nations Population Fund (UNFPA) and Business Information Systems (BIS) at University College Cork, Ireland, funded by the Government of Ireland (through the Department of Communication, Marine and Natural Resources (DCMNR)) undertook a collaborative research and development project to create pKADS (the portable knowledge asset development system), an open source desktop application that captured the core functionality of the UNFPA's internal knowledge management system (KMS). Development of the application took just 3 months, using an agile development approach and some reuse of existing open source code. The finished product was launched by UNFPA, BIS, and the Government of Ireland, at the *World Summit on the Information Society*, Geneva, Switzerland in December 2003. This chapter presents a case study of the pKADS project.

The remainder of the chapter is structured as follows. *Knowledge Management and Knowledge Management Systems in the Knowledge Society* presents a brief discussion of four key background concepts: the knowledge economy, knowledge management, knowledge management systems, and open source software. *The Portable Knowledge Asset Development System (pKADS) Case Study* describes case environment and findings of the study: the history behind the pKADS project, prior UNFPA KM efforts, the technical and conceptual architectures of the pKADS application, and so forth. In this section, particular emphasis is placed on the roles played by open source components and open data standards, on the rationale for releasing pKADS as open source software, and on the subsequent results of this decision. *The Future of pKADS and Related Work* describes the future of pKADS, and also related research building on pKADS in the form of developing open source, Intranet/Internet-based KM tools for the Government of Ireland eGovernment Knowledge Platform (eGovKP). The final section concludes the study. Additionally, the chapter includes recommendations for a variety of activities, exercises, and further reading.

KM and KM Systems in the Knowledge Society

In this section, we discuss four concepts that inform the research, namely the knowledge economy (KE), knowledge management (KM), knowledge management systems, and open source software (OSS). Figure 1 summarizes the relationships between these concepts.

The Knowledge Economy

The *information society* refers to the potential for information and communications technology (ICT) to play a pivotal role in a nation's economic growth and social well-being in a post-industrial society (Gualtieri, 1998). The information society offers the promise of an improved standard of living (e.g., through poverty reduction), economic growth for developing nations (ITU, 2003), and enhanced democracy by empowering individuals and offering enhanced governance (Mansell, 2002). In December 2003, the *World Summit on the Information Society* (WSIS) was held in Geneva, Switzerland in an effort to bridge the digital divide that exists between developed and developing nations. By pursuing an agenda of increased access to ICT, it is hoped that developing nations will experience some of the economic growth that characterises the information society.

Despite the promise of the information society, there is a danger that those countries without access to ICT infrastructure will become further marginalised (Mansell, 2002). There has been a gradual shift of emphasis, with researchers increasingly highlighting the important role of knowledge in today's world economy and a transformation from "information societies" to "knowledge societies' (Moser, 2003). Improvements in information and communications technology, globalisation, and increased economic competition have all combined to mark the arrival of a new "knowledge economy" (DTI, 1998). The OECD (1996, p.7) defines a knowledge economy as "economies which are directly based on the production, distribution and use of knowledge and information."

In the knowledge economy, knowledge has replaced land, labor, and capital as the key factor of production (Drucker, 1994), and represents the only source of sustainable competitive advantage (Nonaka, 1991). Knowledge, unlike the traditional factors of production, is not subject to diminishing returns. Rather, it is said to experience increasing returns, whereby every unit of knowledge used effectively can result in a marginal increase in performance (Romer, 1986). It has been argued that only those countries who exploit the opportunities presented by the knowledge economy will prosper, while those that fail to adapt will face economic decline (DTI, 1998). In order to succeed in the knowledge economy, it is vital that institutions and nations alike invest heavily in their knowledge and intellectual capital. In countries where natural resources are scarce, knowledge represents a valuable commodity that can be traded in the knowledge economy, and a means of narrowing the economic divide. An investment in social networks (e.g., communities of practice) as well as technical networks is required to promote knowledge sharing (Mansell, 2002; Mansell and Steinmueller, 2002).

KM

Knowledge management is a multidisciplinary domain of interest that has its origins in several fields, including philosophy, economics, organisation theory, information systems, marketing, management strategy, innovation research, and organisational learning (Earl 2001; Gray & Meister 2003).

Numerous claims have been made about the potential benefits that can be gained from using information technology (IT) to manage knowledge (for example, Duffy, 2000; Hildreth, Kimble, & Wright, 1998). Some of these benefits include increased innovation (von Krogh, Ichijo, & Nonaka, 2000); the bridging of geographical divides (Hackett, 2000); exploitation of intellectual capital (Petty & Guthrie, 2000); and improved cost effectiveness and problem solving ability (Zack, 1999). Although, it has been widely accepted that KM is supported by IT, it is looked upon by many as a panacea for all knowledge-related problems (Chua, 2004). This is illustrated by a McKinsey survey of 40 European, American, and Japanese companies, which revealed that most executives believed that KM was the outcome of implementing sophisticated IT (Hauschild, Licht, & Stein, 2001). This over-reliance on IT can be attributed to the fact that many of the early definitions of KM were based on the traditional view of computers as data processing devices (Butler, 2003). These definitions describe KM as a set of static processes and rules facilitated by the use of ICT (Malhotra, 2000). This IT-centric view of KM is not surprising given the number of technology vendors selling document and content management systems under the umbrella of knowledge management (Offsey, 1997).

The over-reliance on the technological support for the management of knowledge has weakened the effectiveness of many KM initiatives by ignoring the human processes that are intrinsic to knowledge sharing (McDermott, 1999). The IT-centric view of KM also ignores the tacit knowledge contained in people's heads, which is often difficult to codify and store using ICT (Butler, 2003). Drucker (1999) argues that while ICT supports operational aspects of organisational activities, it has not succeeded in supporting organisational knowledge work. Increasingly, KM authors are suggesting that technology infrastructures must be addressed in parallel with the cultural and social issues underpinning knowledge management (for example, Brown & Duguid, 1998; Davenport, De Long, & Beers, 1998; Davenport & Prusak, 1998; McDermott, 1999).

Malhotra (1998) states that KM allows organisations to adapt, survive, and compete in the face or environmental change. Thus, KM would seem to be ideally suited to dealing with the opportunities presented by the emerging knowledge economy. Following Malhotra (1998), this study views KM as a combination of organisational processes, the data and information processing power of IT, and the creativity of human beings. This definition proves useful as it incorporates the traditional information processing view of the firm without neglecting the vital social and cultural issues surrounding KM.

KM Systems

Knowledge management systems (KMS) are said to facilitate the capture, storage, and sharing of "knowledge" (Alavi & Leidner 1999). Alavi and Leidner (2001) outline the role IT plays in enabling various knowledge management processes such as knowledge creation, storage/retrieval, transfer, and application. They suggest that no one technology comprises KMS; rather KMS consists of a number of different technologies. These combined technologies fulfil three common KMS applications: (1) the coding and sharing of best practice in organisations; (2) the creation of knowledge networks; and (3) the creation of knowledge networks.

Many KMS implementations have proved unsuccessful as they merely supported data and information processing rather than the creation, storage, and dissemination of an organisation's experiential knowledge (Butler, 2003). As previously discussed, KMS failures have often been attributed to a neglect of the critical social, cultural, and motivational issues involved (Huber, 2001; McDermott, 1999; Schultze & Boland, 2000). According to Storey and Barnett (2000) IT/IS implementation can even serve to exacerbate communications problems by reducing the informal contact that takes place between social actors.

Brown and Duguid (1998) argue that for technology to be effective, it must be implemented in response to real social issues. McDermott (1999) suggests that although IT has inspired KM, it has failed to realise its promise. McDermott attributes this to a failure on the part of organisations to create a culture that promotes collaborative thinking and values knowledge sharing. Too much emphasis has been placed on creating systems to store knowledge without promoting knowledge sharing and knowledge use (Fahey & Prusak, 1998). As a result, high KMS implementation failures have been reported (Schultze & Boland, 2000). Storey and Barnett (2000) report failure rates as high as 80%, with many projects being cut back within two to three years of initiation.

Open Source Software

Open source software is software released under terms (see http://www.opensource.org) that allow users to freely use, modify, and redistribute the software without being required to pay royalties to the software author (although acknowledgement of the author is generally required). As a prerequisite to these freedoms, the underlying source code of the application must be made freely available to the user. Open source software release terms are carefully worded extensions of international copyright law, and open source is not synonymous with the concept of "public domain" (in which the intellectual property rights of the software author are completely abandoned) or "freeware" (in which the executable software is freely redistributable, but the underlying code is not available or modifiable).

The implications of open source licensing are many fold. These include:

- Potential reduction in the total cost of ownership (through zero-cost acquisition and avoidance of supplier lock-in).
- Potential increase in the total value of ownership (through modification, customisation, and participation in the developer and user communities).
- Potential increase in the speed of application development (through reuse and extension of existing open source code and leveraging of community-based development processes).
- Potential increase in the quality of software (through massively-parallel peer review and debugging, and user-driven software evolution).

The case for open source software for governments in developing countries is a compelling one. OSS lends itself to creating an ICT platform that provides increased ownership and local autonomy (Dravis, 2003). It also provides increased flexibility to address localisation issues and extensibility. There are also numerous cost benefits to be gained from the use of OSS. In addition, the open source community is characterised by geographically independent actors collaborating without traditional control mechanisms to create software faster and cheaper than using traditional methods (Awazu & Desouza, 2004). Such characteristics make OSS an ideal candidate for use by governments and non-government organisations (NGOs).

The culture and ethos of OSS represents a real-world example of knowledge sharing in action. It would also appear to address some of the concerns that have been voiced over the high cost of KMS development. Although it has long been advocated that ICT can serve to improve the standard of living in developing countries, prohibitive costs can serve to exacerbate the digital divide. OSS represents a very real strategy to overcome these hurdles. It can be concluded that very clear synergies between the

Figure 1. Open source, knowledge management and the knowledge economy

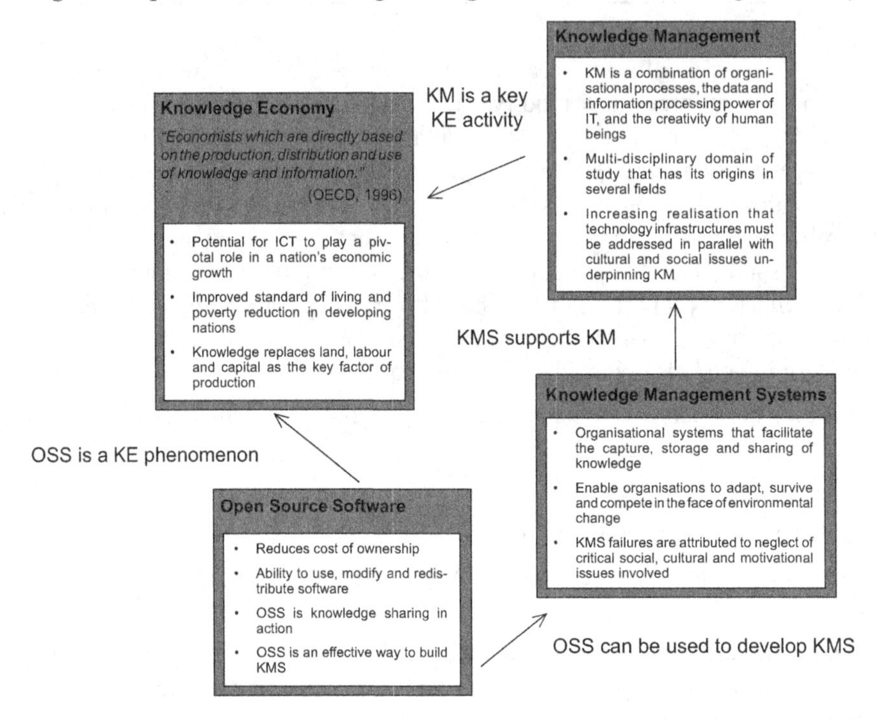

open source movement and knowledge sharing could be leveraged by developing nations to attain the benefits of the "knowledge economy."

The Portable Knowledge Asset Development System (pKADS) Case Study

The United Nations Population Fund (UNFPA)

The United Nations Population Fund (UNFPA) began operations in 1969 as the United Nations Fund for Population Activities. UNFPA works with governments and non-governmental organisations (NGOs) in 142 countries and territories in four regions. The organisation supports developing countries through the promotion of reproductive health and the equality of women. UNFPA also works with governments to formulate policies and strategies to achieve sustainable development. The organisation has provided close to $6 billion in aid to countries in the developing world, making it the largest international source of funding for population and reproductive health programs.

An Overview of UNFPA's Knowledge Sharing Strategy

The UNPFA Knowledge Sharing Branch was established in 2000 to manage UNFPA's transition into a "a community that dynamically generates and uses knowledge to affectively accomplish its mission." In 2001, UNFPA's new Executive Director, Dr. Thoraya Obaid, launched a new change management process known as "The Transition." The objective of this change management effort was to improve the work process of the organisation and allow it to respond dynamically to its ever-changing operating environment whilst also leveraging the opportunities presented by the Millennium Development Goals. "The Transition" was composed of six working groups, including the Knowledge Sharing Branch, and was supported by a variety of outside consultants. Brendan O'Brien, Chief of the Knowledge Sharing Branch, was responsible for guiding the change management process and ensuring that knowledge sharing was integrated into the change process. In 2002, a formal Knowledge Sharing Strategy (KSS) was formulated and adopted. This marked the beginning of a number of knowledge sharing pilot projects including the development and deployment of UNFPA's Knowledge Asset Development System (KADS) in 2002/2003.

Knowledge sharing in UNFPA is viewed as a synergistic relationship between people and organisational processes, enabled by technology (see Table 1). Central to UNFPA's approach to knowledge sharing is the collection, synthesis, and dissemination of UNFPA worker's know-how and experience. UNFPA acknowledges that guidelines and operational procedures drafted in their New York headquarters must be adapted and leveraged to suit a myriad of different operating environments. UNFPA does not entertain the idea of disparate information silos; rather there is an emphasis on creating a living repository of knowledge that is constantly refined and updated based on the experience of their workers and other NGOs. UNFPA's knowledge sharing pilot projects saw the continuous collection and refinement of the organisation's internal and external knowledge so that inexperienced workers would complete their work with the benefit of a more-experienced worker's insight and know-how.

UNFPA strives to achieve their operating objectives in a number of different geographic locations. Although many of the projects undertaken are similar, the environments in which they are undertaken vary greatly with regard to operating conditions, timescales, and cultural differences. UNFPA's ability to learn from the its past mistakes and to capitalize on its successes will allow it to eliminate costly and unnecessary repetitive mistakes while also encouraging best practices and nurturing

Table 1. UNFPA's knowledge sharing strategy

People	Process	Technology
• Employee education programs • "Knowledge Sharing" added to employee job descriptions • Communities of Practice • Knowledge Networks • Incentive Schemes	• "The Transition" change management process • Field reports • Lessons learned reports • Knowledge Asset (KA) concept	• Knowledge sharing portal • Corporate calendars • Development gateway • Collaboration software • KADS • pKADS • Internet Supermarket • Staff Directories

core competencies. Thus, members of UNFPA's Knowledge Sharing Branch argue that its IT-enabled strategy allows relatively unskilled workers to perform tasks immediately "with the competence of an old hand—even hundreds of old hands —without always having to ask the old hand for help and advice."

People

Critical importance is placed on the role of people in UNFPA's knowledge sharing initiative. UNFPA has invested considerable effort in educating employees about the benefits and goals of the organisation's knowledge sharing strategy. To this end, employees are motivated to think beyond job titles and description and consider their role in the larger international development learning community. A UNFPA employee that contributes to knowledge sharing can expect the same cooperation in return. Similarly, the act of sharing knowledge has now been added to the job description of each new employee. As such, each employee is aware that knowledge sharing is fundamental to the organisation's growth and survival. Integrating knowledge sharing into the work processes of the organisation provides knowledge sharing incentives to workers by way of career advancement and performance related rewards.

UNFPA is keenly aware that knowledge sharing is a fundamentally social process and has strived to create an environment that facilitates such interaction. Two social groups are considered vital to the success of the organisation's knowledge sharing initiative: *communities of practice* (COP) and knowledge networks (KN). Communities of practice (COP) are an example of the intricate and social nature of knowledge of creation. Wenger et al., (Wenger, McDermott, & Snyder, 2002, p.

4) describes a COP as "groups of people who share a concern, a set of problems, or a passion about a topic, and who deepen their knowledge and expertise in this area by interacting on an ongoing basis." As communities of practice are informal by nature (Wenger & Snyder, 2000) UNFPA has also put in place a formal social structure to encourage knowledge sharing. Knowledge networks are structured teams of individuals that focus on knowledge domains that have been identified as being of critical strategic importance to UNFPA. The roles and responsibilities of KN members are strictly delineated. KN members must actively collaborate as part of their job descriptions and their knowledge sharing efforts are fully accountable. The formal nature of the grouping means that the social process of knowledge sharing can be managed in a way that is not possible with COPs.

Process

Efficient and consistent processes are required to enable knowledge sharing. Rather than allow workers to share knowledge in an *ad-hoc* way, UNFPA provides a number of mechanisms to help workers share their experiential knowledge in a structured manner. UNFPA workers use a number of instruments including field reports, lessons learned, and annual reports to capture their experiential know-how so that it can be leveraged by other workers in future activities. Increasingly, such reports are seen as an unnecessary burden that can actually serve to hamper knowledge sharing. For example, an employee's trip report is adequate in summarising an agenda but often lacks information that would make it useful to others in the organisation. In order for information to become knowledge it needs to be timely, relevant, and provide an adequate descriptive context so that it can be applied. This requires a process that provides relevant data, insights, ideas, rules of thumb, and contextual information so that it is useful to others in the organisation. UNFPA's adoption of the widely used knowledge asset (KA) concept is considered to be a major component of UNFPA's knowledge management process. KAs will be discussed in detail later in this paper.

Technology

Staff at UNFPA's Knowledge Sharing Branch believes that an over-reliance on the technology component of knowledge management dilutes the concept by ignoring the vital role of tapping into the knowledge contained in people's heads. UNFPA's use of technology includes the provision of tools to capture, store, and disseminate data, information, and experiential knowledge. As of 2004, UNFPA's knowledge sharing toolset consists of a knowledge sharing portal, a corporate calendar, a development gateway, an Internet supermarket, a collaboration workspace, staff directories, and the Knowledge Asset Wizard, which is used to create new knowledge assets.

The availability of technology support for knowledge sharing does not guarantee knowledge sharing (Butler, 2003). Brendan O'Brien cites the example of the World Bank that, despite an expenditure of over $220 million on corporate networks and regional knowledge sharing activities and over $60 million on three global knowledge sharing initiatives over a period of six years, failed to integrate knowledge sharing into its work processes (World Bank, 2003). O'Brien is eager to avoid the mistakes made by the World Bank, and believes that the lessons learned in the World Bank report have been incorporated into UNFPA's Knowledge Sharing Strategy, thereby ensuring its success.

The Knowledge Asset Concept

Knowledge assets are "stocks of knowledge from which services are expected to flow for a period of time that may be hard to specify in advance" (Boisot, 1998, p. 3). Although the knowledge asset concept is widely used in business and academia, the UNFPA approach has specific idiosyncrasies. Knowledge at UNFPA is seen in terms of "how to do things," "where to find examples," and "who to ask for help." UNFPA knowledge assets (KAs) are described as containing the distilled experiential knowledge of organisational actors on a well-bounded subject area or topic of interest.

KAs are typically based on the work processes of the organisation. They provide an intuitive, empirically grounded, logical structure to capture, store, and share knowledge. The key conceptual vehicle is the knowledge map, which enables users to navigate and explore a knowledge asset. At the centre of the map is the name of

Figure 2. Structure of a knowledge map (Based on UNFPA 2002)

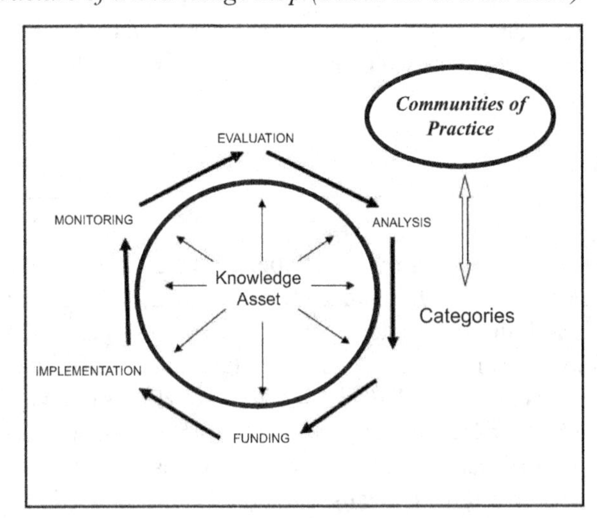

the knowledge asset, while the circumference is ringed by the named categories for that asset (see Figure 2).

Knowledge assets are structured into categories in order to make them accessible. A category is a subtopic or component of a knowledge asset. Categories are further divided into, and described by, a set of questions and answers. UNFPA posits that to be effective; a KA should have about eight categories. A category should have one or more question and answer pairs, the number of such pairings depending on the complexity of the category. Hence, at a fundamental level, a KA presents information in a question and answer (Q&A) format. Questions should be straightforward and should be designed to elicit essential information. Answers should be concise (typically 200 words) and to the point. Finally, questions and answers should be supplemented with informational resources external to the KA, including examples and further reading (these can be uploaded documents and/or Web references).

In addition to "examples" and "further reading" resources, a KA also has links to experts or individuals who can provide additional information or offer guidance. A knowledge asset may have several contributing authors, called KA network members. In single author scenarios during KA creation, the author/expert adopts all the roles in a knowledge network, while other members of a community of practice constitute the target audience for the asset. As knowledge is distributed in organisations and across societies, a dynamic KA will have a network of contributing authors and a ready audience. In such scenarios, a network member will be responsible for each category. The same and/or other network members will be responsible for the various questions and answers that constitute a category; these are called the primary and other contributors.

Knowledge assets are grouped into knowledge domains called super assets; a knowledge domain simply describes the context for a collection of related knowledge assets. KAs that are grouped by domain or super asset describe the various areas of interest, activities, and so forth, which together constitute a recognizable body of knowledge.

UNFPA Knowledge Asset Development System (KADS)

In order to provide technical support for their knowledge sharing strategy, UNFPA commissioned the development of an Intranet-based knowledge asset wizard and viewer, using Lotus Notes and Domino technology, in 2002. Christened the Knowledge Asset Development System (KADS), this was deployed on a pilot basis initially in 2003 (see Figure 3).

January 2004 saw preparation for the incremental deployment of KADS throughout UNFPA as the organisation's performance appraisal and development system (PAD) incorporated knowledge sharing as a vital staff competency; it also set

Figure 3. UNFPA's knowledge asset development system (KADS)

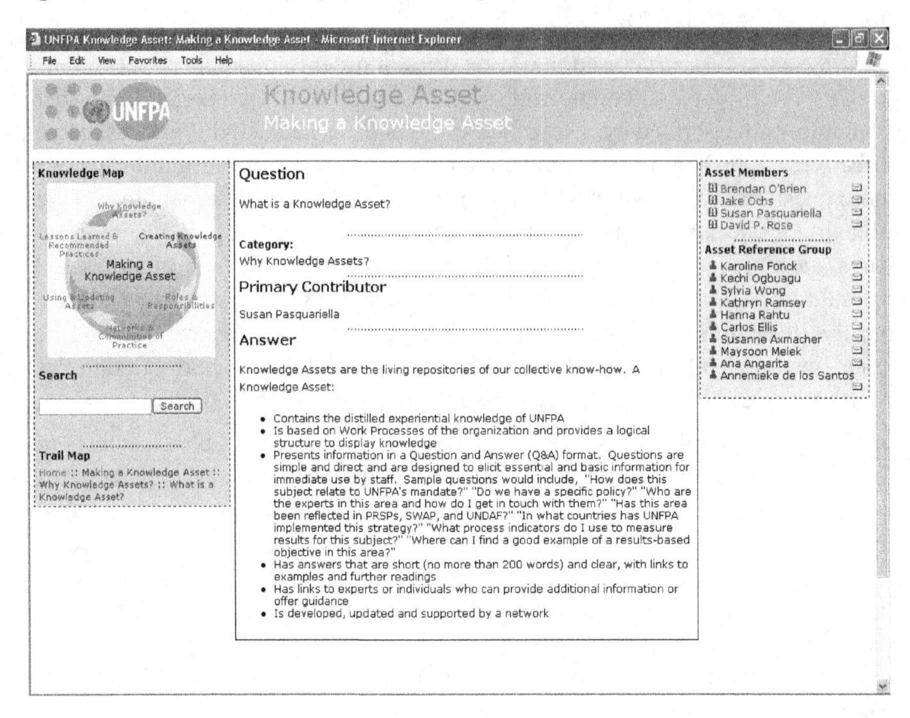

out guidelines and responsibilities for the creation of knowledge assets. UNFPA launched an extensive education program as part of the change management process surrounding the implementation of KADS: this sought to explain fully all elements of the transition process, especially the knowledge sharing strategy. This education program consisted of running over 90 workshops over a period of three months in late 2003. These workshops helped educate staff about their new roles and responsibilities, and also the strategic goals and objectives of the organisation. Prior to this, several attempts to educate staff via circulars, videos, Intranet sites, and formal presentations proved unsuccessful. Consequently, Brendan O'Brien believed that the effectiveness of the training sessions was due to a combination of factors *viz.* the presence of a facilitator, good informational materials, and effective staff participation in each office.

A Portable Knowledge Asset Development System

UNFPA's KADS comprises an online collection of HTML documents and forms, and client- and server-side scripts, and requires a dedicated database server. However, this software architecture was limited in its scope and its application outside of UNFPA, primarily because it lacked portability, as it was tied to proprietary enterprise technologies (Lotus Notes and Domino). UNFPA wanted a portable solution that they could share with other organisations in order to promote knowledge sharing and enhance UNFPA's standing among government and non-government organisations alike.

In the beginning of September 2003, staff from Business Information Systems, University College Cork, met with representatives from UNFPA in their New York headquarters to discuss the possibility of producing a portable version of KADS in time for the *World Summit on the Information Society* in December 2003. In late September 2003, Business Information Systems, with funding provided by the Government of Ireland, undertook a research and development project to create a *portable knowledge asset development system* called pKADS. This task had to be accomplished in over six weeks, a tight timescale for a project of this nature and complexity.

Technical Requirement for pKADS

In mid-September, the project feasibility team investigated the initial scope and technical architecture. The project feasibility team identified the following criteria as critical to the success of the project:

- **Stand-alone:** The pKADS architecture should not be based on a complex relational database management system (RDBMS) or other server software for its knowledge base.
- **Portable:** Due to the wide variety of operating systems and hardware platforms used by UNFPA's partner organisations and clients, pKADS would need to be platform independent to ensure compatibility.
- **Extensible:** Many of UNFPA's partners and clients operate in geographically disperse locations with differing work processes and working environment. In order for the system to be extensible, users of the system would require the ability to modify the system at the data and source levels.
- **Flexible output:** Knowledge asset would have to be output in a number of different formats. For example: XML for sharing between pKADS applications, HTML for the Web, and other formats for print, and so forth.
- **Create a community of practice:** pKADS would have to be freely available, modifiable, and redistributable in order to foster a community of practice. This would ensure an increased uptake in the number of users and developers involving themselves in the project.

pKADS Implementation Details

pKADS is a desktop application written in Java 2 standard edition, with an extensible markup language (XML) data storage and exchange layer. Java was chosen for several reasons, including its (relative) platform independence and sophisticated support for localisation, graphical interface elements, event driven execution, and so forth. The software architecture follows the Model-View-Controller (MVC) design pattern, which improves performance and robustness by decoupling code related to data access, business logic, and data presentation/user interaction (see Figure 4).

pKADS presents the user with a Java Swing interface for data entry, and also accepts input in the form of XML data (individual KA files), XML schemas (used for validation) and XSLT stylesheets (used to control output). The pKADS system has three main forms of output (see Figure 5):

1. The individual KA files (XML).
2. A Web-ready view of the KA (HTML, JavaScript and CSS) (created using XSLT).
3. A zip archive containing both the XML file and the Web-ready view.

Figure 4. The Model-View-Controller (MVC) design pattern (Source: Sun Microsystems, http://java.sun.com/blueprints/patterns/MVC-detailed.html)

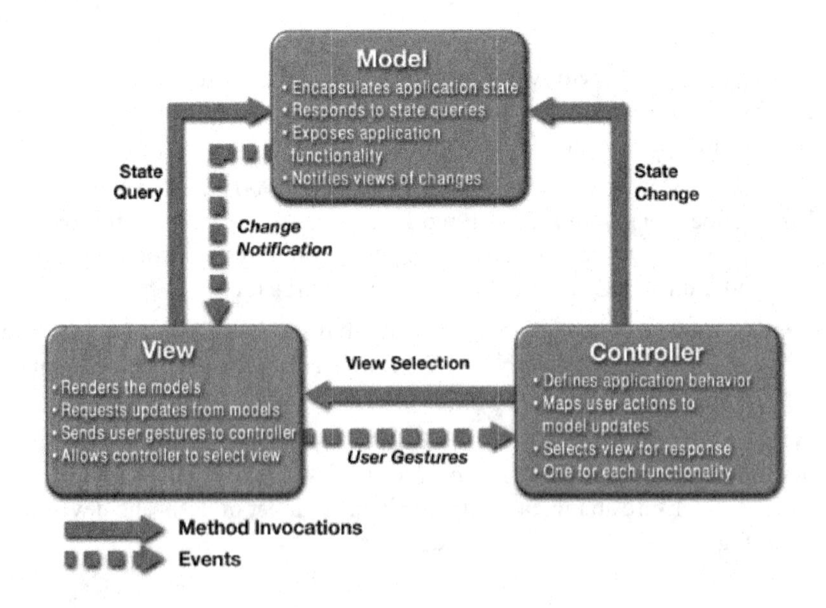

Figure 5. pKADS inputs and outputs

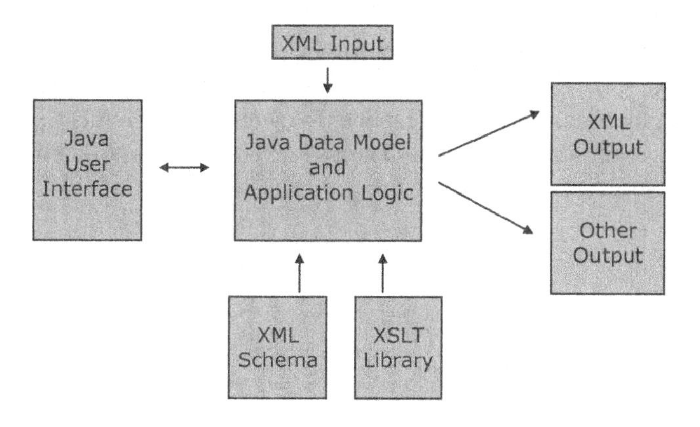

The Role of Open Source Software and Open Standards

As described previously, the Java programming language was used to support the design goal of portability, and open data (XML), and data processing standards (XML schema and XSLT) were used to address the technical requirements of the pKADS project *vis-à-vis* independence from external data sources, flexible output, and extensibility of the data model. XML was also used in implementing localisation by removing all Swing GUI text to a separate XML configuration file. As will be discussed in the next section, the use of XML in this capacity, combined with the MVC application architecture, was advantageous in stimulating software translation.

In addition to utilising open standards, open source software played an important role in the pKADS development process. Firstly, open source development tools (such as Ant, JUnit, and CVS) were employed as components within the pKADS development environment. CVS served a traditional version control role, while Ant and JUnit supported the agile methods employed in the development process. Secondly, the open source Xalan XSLT parser from the Apache Software Foundation was used as a testing and development environment for the XSLT transformations. Because pKADS needed to support transformations with multiple output documents, the XSLT stylesheets utilised Xalan extensions to the XSLT standard. The ability to directly include modified code from org.apache.xalan.xslt.Process package was instrumental in rapidly including this functionality into pKADS. Finally, pKADS also made use of org.jibx.runtime (developed by Dennis M. Sosnoski, see http://jibx.sourceforge.net/jibx-license.html) and of Dean S. Jones' Icon Collection (see http://sourceforge.

net/projects/icon-collection/). In all instances, the availability of open source code and other software artefacts improved development speed and quality.

Perhaps the most important requirement for the pKADS project, given the organisational goals of UNFPA, was that pKADS be readily available to, usable to, and adaptable by a global community of practice. To meet this requirement, pKADS was released itself as open source software. The pKADS license is a simple modification of the Apache Software Foundation license (see Figure 6).

Figure 6. The pKADS license

Copyright (c) 2003 UNFPA, United Nations Population Fund. All rights reserved.

Redistribution and use in source and binary forms, with or without modification, are permitted provided that the following conditions are met:

Redistributions of source code must retain the above copyright notice, this list of conditions and the following disclaimer.

Redistributions in binary form must reproduce the above copyright notice, this list of conditions and the following disclaimer in the documentation and/or other materials provided with the distribution.

The end-user documentation included with the redistribution, if any, must include the following acknowledgement: "This product includes software developed by UNFPA, United Nations Population Fund (http://www.unfpa.org/) in collaboration with Business Information Systems (BIS) at University College Cork, Ireland (UCC) through the pKADS Project (http://pkads.bis.ucc.ie/)." Alternately, this acknowledgement may appear in the software itself, if and wherever such third-party acknowledgements normally appear.

The names "UNFPA," "United Nations Population Fund," "BIS," "Business Information Systems," "University College Cork," and "UCC" must not be used to endorse or promote products derived from this software without prior written permission. For written permission, please contact (http://www.unfpa.org/) or (http://pkads.bis.ucc.ie/) as appropriate.

Products derived from this software may not be called "pKADS," nor may "pKADS" appear in their name, without prior written permission. For written permission, please contact (http://pkads.bis.ucc.ie/).

THIS SOFTWARE IS PROVIDED "AS IS," AND ANY EXPRESSED OR IMPLIED WARRANTIES, INCLUDING, BUT NOT LIMITED TO, THE IMPLIED WARRANTIES OF MERCHANTABILITY AND FITNESS FOR A PARTICULAR PURPOSE ARE DISCLAIMED. IN NO EVENT SHALL UNFPA OR ITS CONTRIBUTORS BE LIABLE FOR ANY DIRECT, INDIRECT, INCIDENTAL, SPECIAL, EXEMPLARY, OR CONSEQUENTIAL DAMAGES (INCLUDING, BUT NOT LIMITED TO, PROCUREMENT OF SUBSTITUTE GOODS OR SERVICES; LOSS OF USE, DATA, OR PROFITS; OR BUSINESS INTERRUPTION) HOWEVER CAUSED AND ON ANY THEORY OF LIABILITY, WHETHER IN CONTRACT, STRICT LIABILITY, OR TORT (INCLUDING NEGLIGENCE OR OTHERWISE) ARISING IN ANY WAY OUT OF THE USE OF THIS SOFTWARE, EVEN IF ADVISED OF THE POSSIBILITY OF SUCH DAMAGE.

The Future of pKADS and Related Work

Since its launch at *WSIS 2003*, pKADS continues to attract attention from a variety of organisations (government, nongovernment, and private sector) across the globe. Over 1,400 downloads of the application have been recorded from the pKADS Web site; server log analysis indicates that these downloads were made by individuals from various private and public institutions from all parts of the globe, including developing nations. Interest in pKADS from those attending the summit was likewise considerable. This level of attention is indicative of the need for such an application and its potential for use in organisations, particularly government and nongovernment institutions.

Significantly, the Knowledge Sharing Branch of UNFPA leveraged the pKADS experience and the launch at *WSIS* to get top management commitment to the full deployment of KADS. Subsequently, UNFPA Knowledge Sharing executives employed pKADS as a training platform and promotional tool in the full implementation of KADS. They also used it as a tool to promote knowledge sharing for development by getting other NGOs and UN agencies interested in adopting the tool.

Although pKADS has attracted a user community, this community has not, to date, been active in modifying and extending the application. The one exception to this is in translation of the software. Spanish and French translations are available from the pKADS Web site, the government of Jordan has translated pKADS into Arabic, and a computer science postgraduate student in Greece has undertaken a Greek translation. The translation of pKADS is facilitated jointly by both the architecture of the system (MVC, XML-based UI text) and the open source license (allowing for the translation of XSLT code and the modification of Swing UI code to accommodate other character sets and language directionality.

In April 2004, the engineering division of the Department of Communications, Marine and Natural Resources (Government of Ireland) began using pKADS as part of their knowledge-sharing pilot project. The group's activities involve consulting with local fishermen, local interest groups, and local authorities on issues such as preparing design and contract documents, conducting surveys, and marine construction. The work conducted by the marine engineers is knowledge intensive. In an effort to quickly train new recruits and disseminate their acquired knowledge, the marine engineers used pKADS to identify critical domains of knowledge. This resulted in two sample knowledge assets: "Aquaculture" and "Foreshore Development." The system was found to be useful both in cataloguing existing knowledge and also identifying knowledge gaps.

The major limitation of pKADS is that it is a single-user application, notwithstanding that it can import and export knowledge assets. On the other hand, UNFPAs' original KADS system, while multi-user, is proprietary and limited in other ways, as described in this paper. The UNFPA and researchers at Business Information Systems expect that, in time, pKADS will be improved upon by the global user-developer community, both in terms of additional features and the evolution of its architecture to accommodate multi-user collaboration (as either a peer-to-peer or client/server application—or, perhaps, both). The future evolution and improvement of the software is important, as BIS researchers found that users reported problems with pKADS when it was deployed on a pilot basis in one division of the Department of the Communications, Marine, and Natural Resources. The application's limitations did not, however, detract from its utility as a knowledge-sharing tool. Users were unanimous in their praise for the underlying concept and its implementation. Such was the enthusiasm within this government department for an IT-based solution for knowledge capture, storage, and sharing, that researchers at BIS are currently undertaking the research and development of a Web-based KMS called the eGovernment Knowledge Platform (eGovKP). This R&D project is being funded by the Irish Government, which is deploying the system within the DCMNR. The UNFPA also plans to undertake the research and development of an enterprise-wide KADS (eKADS) for use in their organisation. Neither of these developments would have been possible without pKADS.

Conclusion

In conclusion, an analysis of the pKADS case study makes several important contributions to research in the information systems field and related disciplines. First, it describes one organisation's (UNFPA) success in implementing its knowledge sharing strategy and in developing its knowledge asset concept. Second, it illustrates the relevance and importance of knowledge management in the context of multinational, citizen-facing NGOs, as indicated to the research team by delegates to the *World Summit on the Information Society 2003*. Third, the architecture of *p*KADS has been described in detail, with emphasis on the importance of open source software and open standards, and on robust software architectures. Fourth, the study presents an analysis of interest in, and the uptake of, the *p*KADS application. Finally, contrary to points made by Alavi and Leidner (2001), it highlights how a single knowledge-management tool can provide IT support for knowledge creation, storage/retrieval, transfer, and application. Indeed, the subsequent development of a Web-based KMS through a government-funded R&D is tangible evidence of the ability of IT to deliver on the promise of knowledge management.

References

Alavi, M., & Leidner, D. E. (1999). Knowledge management systems: Issues, challenges, and benefits. *Communications of the Association for Information Systems, 1*(7), 1-37.

Alavi, M., & Leidner, D. E. (2001). Knowledge management and knowledge management systems: Conceptual foundations and research issues. *MIS Quarterly, 25*(1), 107-136.

Awazu, Y., & Desouza, K. C. (2004). Open knowledge management: Lessons from the open source revolution. *Journal of the American Society for Information and Technology, 55*(1), 1016-1019.

Boisot, M. (1998). *Knowledge assets: Securing competitive advantage in the information economy.* Oxford: Oxford University Press.

Brown, J. S., & Duguid, P. (1998). Organizing knowledge. *California Management Review, 40*(3), 90-111.

Butler, T. (2003). From data to knowledge and back again: Understanding the limitations of KMS. *Knowledge and Process Management: The Journal of Corporate Transformation, 10*(4), 144-155.

Chua, A. (2004). Knowledge management system architecture: A bridge between KM consultants and technologist. *International Journal of Information Management, 24,* 87-98.

Davenport, T. H., De Long, D. W., & Beers, M. C. (1998). Successful knowledge management projects. *Sloan Management Review, 39*(2), 43-57.

Davenport, T., & Prusak, L. (1998). *Working knowledge: How organisations manage what they know.* Boston: Harvard Business School Press.

Dravis, P. (2003). *Open source software: Perspectives for development.* Retrieved January 13, 2006, from http://www.infodev.org/symp2003/publications/OpenSourceSoftware.pdf

Drucker, P. (1994). The age of social transformation. *The Atlantic Monthly, 274*(5), 53-80.

Drucker P. (1999). *Management challenges for the 21st century.* New York: Harper Business.

DTI. (1998). *Our competitive future—Building the knowledge driven economy.* Retrieved January 13, 2006, from http://www.dti.gov.uk/comp/competitive/main.htm

Duffy, J. (2000). The KM technology infrastructure. *The Information Management Journal, 34*(2), 62-66.

Earl, M. (2001). Knowledge management strategies: Toward a taxonomy. *Journal of Management Information Systems,* 18(1), 215-233.

Fahey, L., & Prusak, L. (1998). The Eleven Deadliest Sins of Knowledge Management, *California Management Review*, *40*(3), 265-276.

Gray, P. H., & Meister, D. B (2003). Introduction: Fragmentation and integration in knowledge management research. *Information Technology & People*, *16*(3), 259-265.

Gualtieri, R. (1998). *Impact of the emerging information society on the policy development process and democratic quality.* OECD Publications. Retrieved January 20, 2006, from http://appli1.oecd.org/olis/1998doc.nsf/linkto/puma(98)15

Hackett, B. (2000). *Beyond knowledge management: New ways to work and learn.* Report 1262-00-RR. New York: The Conference Board Publications.

Hauschild, S., Licht, T., & Stein, W. (2001). Creating a knowledge culture. *The McKinsey Quarterly*, *1*, 74-81.

Hildreth, P., Kimble, C., & Wright, P. (1998). Computer mediated communications and communities of practice. *Proceedings of Ethicomp 1998* (pp. 275-286).

Huber, G. P. (2001). Transfer of knowledge in knowledge management systems: Unexplored issues and suggested studies. *European Journal of Information Systems*, *10*(2), 72-79.

ITU. (2003). *Declaration of principles - Building the information society: a global challenge in the new millennium*. Retrieved February 1, 2006, from http://www.itu.int/dms_pub/itu-s/md/03/wsis/doc/S03-WSIS-DOC-0004!!PDF-E.pdf

Malhotra, Y (1998). Tools@work: Deciphering the knowledge management hype. *The Journal for Quality and Participation*, *21*(4), 58-60.

Malhotra, Y. (2000). From information management to knowledge management: Beyond the 'hi-tech hidebound' systems. In K. Srikantaiah & M. E. D. Koenig (Eds.), *Knowledge management for the information professional* (pp. 37-61). Medford: Information Today.

Mansell, R. (2002). Constructing the knowledge base for knowledge-driven development. *Journal of Knowledge Management*, *6*(4), 317-329.

Mansell, R., & Steinmueller, W. E. (2002). *Mobilising the information society: Strategies for growth and opportunity.* Oxford: Oxford University Press.

McDermott, R. (1999). Why information technology inspired but cannot deliver knowledge management. *California Management Review*, *41*(4), 103-117.

Moser, C. (2003). *Transforming the information society into knowledge societies.* Retrieved February 7, 2006, from http://www.developmentgateway.com/node/130685/special/wsis/interview.pdf

Nonaka, I. (1991). The knowledge-creating company. *Harvard Business Review, 69*(6), 96-104.

OECD. (1996). *The knowledge based economy*. Retrieved February 7, 2006, from OECD, http://www.oecd.org/dataoecd/51/8/1913021.pdf

Offsey, S. (1997). Knowledge management: Linking people to knowledge for bottom line results. *Journal of Knowledge Management, 1*(2), 113-122.

Petty, R., & Guthrie, J. (2000). Intellectual capital literature review: Measurement, reporting and management. *Journal of Intellectual Capital, 1*(2), 155-176.

Romer, P. M. (1986). Increasing returns and long-run growth. *Journal of Political Economy, 94*(5), 1002-1037.

Schultze, U., & Boland, R. (2000). Knowledge management technology and the reproduction of work practices. *Journal of Strategic Information Systems, 9*(2), 193-212.

Storey, J., & Barnett, E. (2000). Knowledge management initiatives: Learning from failure. *Journal of Knowledge Management, 4*(2), 145-156.

Von Krogh, G., Ichijo, K., & Nonaka, I. (2000). *Enabling knowledge creation: How to unlock the mystery of tacit knowledge and release the power of innovation.* Oxford: Oxford University Press.

Wenger, E., McDermott, R., & Snyder, W. H. (2002). *Cultivating communities of practice: A guide to managing knowledge.* Cambridge: Harvard Business School Press.

Wenger, E., & Snyder, W. (2000). Communities of practice: The organizational frontier. *Harvard Business Review, 78*(1), 139-145.

World Bank. (2003). *Sharing knowledge: Innovations and remaining challenges.* Retrieved January 2, 2006, from http://www.worldbank.org/oed/knowledge_evaluation/

Zack, M. H. (1999). Managing codified knowledge. *Sloan Management Review, 40*(4), 45-58.

Appendix I: Internet Session: pKADS and Knowledge Sharing at UNFPA

http://pkads.bis.ucc.ie

http://www.unfpa.org/knowledgesharing/

Choose one site that you find related to your chapter main issue and provide a brief synopsis of its offering. Choose a case of Web site that can provide interactions. It is something like a guided tour that in the next section will be specified.

Interaction:

From the UNFPA Web site, visit the sample knowledge asset on Quality of Sexual and Reproductive Health Care.

Appendix II: Case Study: Building a Knowledge Asset

Download the pKADS application and user manual from http://pkads.bis.ucc.ie. Consider the following knowledge-sharing scenario:

You are a member of a university student government body, charged with creating a knowledge asset for the student KMS on the topic of student health and safety.

Questions

1. What asset categories would you create?
2. What kind of community would be needed to support the asset (i.e., what different "experts" are needed)?
3. What kind of resources (links to documents, examples and experts) would become a part of the asset?

Appendix III: Useful URLs

pKADS Web site:
http://pkads.bis.ucc.ie

UNFPA Knowledge Sharing:
http://www.unfpa.org/knowledgesharing/

Open Source Initiative:
http://www.opensource.org

Free Software Foundation:
http://www.fsf.org

Appendix IV: Further Readings

Butler, T. (2003). From data to knowledge and back again: Understanding the limitations of KMS. *Knowledge and Process Management: The Journal of Corporate Transformation*, *10*(4), 144-155.

Feller, J., & Fitzgerald, B. (2002). *Understanding open source software development*. London: Addison-Wesley.

Feller, J., Fitzgerald, B., Hissam, S, & Lakhani, K. (Eds.). (2005). *Perspectives on free and open source software*. Cambridge: MIT Press.

Gottschalk, P. (2005). *Strategic knowledge management technology*. London: Idea Group.

Schwartz, D. (2005). *Encyclopedia of knowledge management*. London: Idea Group.

Possible Titles for Papers/Essays

- People, Process, Technology: Components for a Knowledge Management System
- From Data Processing to Knowledge Management
- Capturing Experiential and Tacit Knowledge: Techniques and Tools
- Why Knowledge Management Systems Fail
- Tools are not Enough: Getting People to Use Knowledge Management Systems
- Knowledge Hording and other Fears: Creating Incentives for Knowledge Sharing
- The Politics of Knowledge: Impediments to Organisational Knowledge Sharing

Chapter VI

Evaluating Open Source in Government: Methodological Considerations in Strategizing the Use of Open Source in the Public Sector

Christian Wernberg-Tougaard, Unisys A/S, Denmark
Patrice-Emmanuel Schmitz, Unisys, Belgium
Kristoffer Herning, Unisys A/S, Denmark
John Gøtze, Copenhagen Business School, Denmark

Abstract

The use of free and open source software (F/OSS) in the public sector has been accelerating over the last ten years. The benefits seem to be obvious: No licensing costs, unlimited flexibility, vendor independence, a support community, and so forth. But as with everything else in life, a successful implementation of F/OSS in government is not as simple as it might look initially. The implementation of F/OSS should build on a solid evaluation of core business criteria in all their complexity. In this chapter we analyze the evaluation considerations that government bodies should undertake before deciding between F/OSS and traditional software (SW), including the way knowledge networks and communities of practice work, total cost of ownership, and core functional requirements. The chapter presents a methodology conceptualizing this process in a comprehensive framework, focusing on the interaction between the strategic and business process level and the SW/infrastructure level. The chapter aims at presenting a framework enabling IT strategist and management from the "business side" of public sector institutions to evaluate F/OSS vs. traditional SW in tight cooperation with the IT side of the organization.

Introduction

Free and open source software (F/OSS) has become a major issue during the last decades, as Dedrick and West (2005) describe. We will not make a difference between "free software" as specified by the Free Software Foundations (FSF) and "open source" as this would be out of scope. For a discussion between the legal differences, see Stallman (2002) and Bessen (2002, p. 13).

With the rise of the Internet, the accessibility, communication, and distribution side of F/OSS projects has become much easier, giving a boost to the use of F/OSS in general. Outside the academic world, F/OSS has increasingly made its way into the public sector over the past decade, also as a consequence of budgetary and efficiency demands. Another reason for this phenomenon seems to be the political reluctance to channel substantial amounts of taxpayers' money into the pockets of a few private companies.

In this chapter, we will try to identify and analyze some of the mechanism of why public sector entities select and use F/OSS. We believe that, too often, the choice between F/OSS and traditional SW solutions is made on the basis of either "religion" or beliefs: Dedrick and West (2005) describe it as either a normative preference in one direction or simply a non-empirically based conception of the various solutions' pros and cons. Schmitz (2001) contends that experience shows that making a decision about, for example, fundamental platform and business application environments without a thorough analysis will most likely lead to loss and decreased efficiency in the business operations.

The non-holistic approach to evaluating different solutions is sometimes also mirrored in a too-narrow IT strategy. We all agree that strategy is good when strategy relates to agreeing on some general goals and thoroughly considered priorities that guide the organization in a designated direction. But strategy can also be a vendor-specific or technology-specific strategy, and this type of strategy is much more dangerous.

Of course, it makes good sense to seek general complementarities and inter-linkage in the IT environment. However, this ambition should not limit a public sector institution (PSI) to one technology or vendor. Instead, strategy should be the overall guiding principle for how the IT department seeks to support the core business processes of the PSI. Dedrick and West (2005) emphasize that vendors and technology (e.g., F/OSS vs. traditional SW) should be selected in each individual case according to which product is the best and has the lowest cost in supporting this strategy. As simple as this may sound, vendor and technology strategies are too often the primary evaluation criteria for PSIs (and private organizations, for that matter). In this chapter, we urge PSIs to pursue the principle of "best and cheapest," rather than specific vendors and technologies.

A substantial number of evaluation parameters should be established as the basis of decision-making. With reference to Brooks (1987), it is important to initially stress that there are no silver bullets, meaning there is no generic lump of criteria that will always satisfactorily cover every evaluation situation. Every PSI is different, is based on different business processes, and faces different challenges and opportunities. Consequently, every evaluation should be structured according to the context in which the PSI and its IT systems operate.

Nevertheless, there are software evaluation criteria that should always be included in an IT strategy assessment or an IT purchase evaluation. Schmitz (2001) explains how F/OSS will grow into covering more and more domains, as also complex and sensitive software areas will experience the emergence of F/OSS knowledge communities and, as a consequence, a gradual "OSS-ization" of former proprietary domains. This creates a dynamic demand for conceptual models analyzing how F/OSS affects the linkage between business strategies, business processes, application portfolios, and infrastructure in organizations within these domains. We will argue that this becomes evermore relevant in a public sector increasingly faced with efficiency, budgetary, and productivity demands. Later in the chapter, we develop a model that, on an experience and research-based basis, summarizes how public sector entities should evaluate the choice between F/OSS and traditional SW. We will dedicate separate sections to the core criteria, the vital knowledge communities, and the legal matters surrounding F/OSS.

Finally, we sum up our findings in a matrix listing some of the generic, basic economic, functional, and additional evaluation criteria in the four different layers of the business: strategy, business processes, applications, and infrastructure. These should, in most cases, all be taken into account when choosing between F/OSS and traditional SW solutions. This segregation is inspired by the enterprise architecture methodology, especially the Zachman framework put forward by Zachman (1987) and Zachman and Sowa (1992), and the Unisys 3DVE methodology developed by Malhotra and Maksimchuk (2005). We will then try to join these in a simple evaluation diagram linked to the weighted compliance to the strategies and priorities of a non-existing, illustrative PSI.

We stress that we have no ambitions of creating a generic master model applicable to all PSIs in all situations. The exercise is rather to draft some conceptual models illustrating the holistic methodology and approach necessary for an evaluation where more than just the short-term cost of ownership and upfront technical compliance is included.

Background

Denmark offers an example of a wave of new public management that has forced PSIs to utilize IT in order to increase efficiency, and cut costs. A variety of innovative solutions have been developed and deployed in Denmark, making the Danish public sector one of the most heavily digitalized in the world. While IT and management interact with each other on a daily basis, there is still a great need to make IT and the business layers of the organization connect better.

F/OSS illustrates this challenge. Even the most basic evaluation criteria for deciding whether to pursue an F/OSS solution rather than a traditional SW solution, or vice versa, has effects in every corner of the organization. The IT layers—applications and infrastructure—should support the business processes and the overall strategy and vision of the PSI. At the same time, the decision makers at the IT layers will, to an increasing extent, realize that business decisions will create new demands for flexibility, scalability, openness, and so forth. This interrelation is depicted in Figure 1.

Fortunately, the IT department has left the role of "an independent state in the state"; a department that, because of its novelty and alleged complexity, was exempt from the demands facing other departments. Considering this, a decision regarding F/OSS should be made with the primary purpose of supporting the overall strategy and business processes of the PSI, and the decision should be made in a dynamic evaluation and feedback process of between the two layers. This process is also depicted in Figure 1. The strategy and business processes should decide which criteria are

Figure 1. Strategic dynamics in OSS

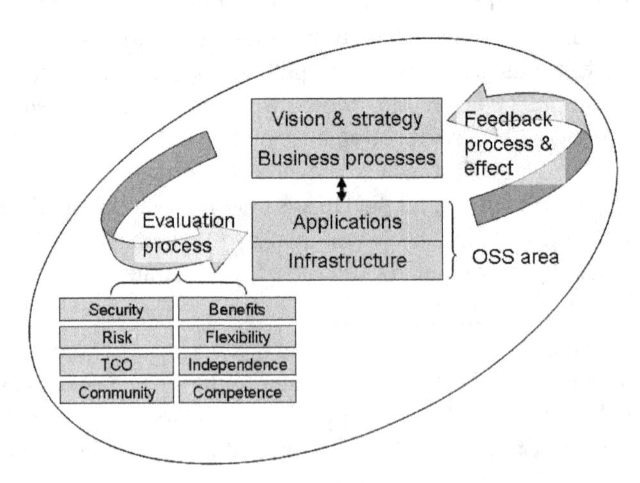

relevant to evaluate. Those listed in Figure 1 are merely illustrative and should, of course, mirror the context of the PSI and its environment.

Case Study: A Brief Description of a Successful Software Evaluation

When the Danish government, in 2001, established the cross-governmental Project eGovernment and the Digital Taskforce as the national knowledge centre and program management office, a Web site—http://www.e.gov.dk—was established. At the time, a proprietary and commercial content management system (CMS) was procured.

The Web site was evaluated after 2 years, and a number of critical issues were identified. Among these were:

- Usability and accessibility problems
- Lack of standards compliance
- Inflexible data management
- Costly development of new services
- Vendor dependence

Over the following year, the task force staff, who had expertise in conducting business case studies of large digitalization projects, took their own medicine and conducted a thorough business case study for their Web site and its underlying CMS.

They identified a number of key criteria for a new CMS. First, the TCO should be good; the economic case was essential, the task force residing in the Ministry of Finance and their preaching about cost-effectiveness taken into consideration. Second, it was decided that the Web site should be standards compliant, highly usable, and accessible. Third, the CMS should be flexible and extensible, and have good local support.

Although initially not defined as a selection criterion, licensing and reusability became a further criteria, especially since several candidate systems were open source systems. Not only could the task force get a cheaper CMS by selecting an open source solution, but they could also offer their solution to others if they went for an open source system.

The task force, in the end, opted for TYPO3, a mature, open source CMS system with a stronghold in Denmark (lead developers are Danish). The task force financed some custom development that was given back to the TYPO3 community, and later became integrated into the main product.

In late 2005, half a year after the new site opened, it was awarded the prestigious national Top of the Web award. The site scored 85.7% of the maximum score, which was the highest score of all 58 sites in the category "cross-governmental portals." The average score in the category was 61%. In particular, http://e.gov.dk scored 90% on usability and 91% on accessibility. The Web site was awared five Net Crowns, the highest score.

The Dynamics of F/OSS Environments

While F/OSS is highly visible, it is, in fact, only one example of a much broader social-economic phenomenon, and Benkler (2002) suggests that we are seeing the broad and deep emergence of a new, third mode of production in the digitally networked environment. Benkler calls this mode "commons-based peer-production," to distinguish it from the property- and contract-based models of firms and markets. The argument is that groups of individuals successfully collaborate on large-scale projects following a diverse cluster of motivational drivers and social signals, rather than either market prices or managerial commands.

Commons-based peer production is particularly effective when the object of production is information or culture, and where the capital investment (applications, infrastructure) necessary for production is widely distributed instead of concentrated. Benkler argues that peer production better identifies and assigns human capital to information and cultural production processes, in that it effectively approaches the "information opportunity costs." As Benkler also points out, the "production mode" allows very larger clusters of potential contributors to interact with very large clusters of information resources in search of new projects and collaboration enterprises. Participants and contributors can review and select which resources to work on, which projects to be involved in, and with whom they will work. Metcalfe's Law[1] applies: The networks become more and more valuable as they grow, and the peer-production mode thrives.[2]

How F/OSS Development Moves Over Time, and can F/OSS Capture all Areas?

One of the core issues in the F/OSS debate is the ability of F/OSS to become usable within all SW areas. Schmitz (2001b) describes how, within technical backend areas like Web servers, F/OSS has had great success. But what about the front end, the desktop, mission-critical SW, and a variety of other SW with extensive non-technical user interaction? We believe that, over time, F/OSS will engulf a wide variety of functional areas; however, some areas may experience an increasing "commercialization" of the OSS applications, which will transform the process from community driven into a more business-oriented F/OSS development. We will describe the F/OSS in more detail later in this chapter. This could potentially limit the progress of development within some areas, since the Comino, Manenti, and Parisi (2005) studies show that the more restrictive the licensing within an area, the smaller the chance for OSS projects to reach a profound level of maturity.

One exception to this trend might be global domains. A global domain refers to sectors with comparable global challenges; sectors such as the healthcare sector. This field or sector might contain "enough" F/OSS-programmers to form a community, and hence to secure a proper and best practice-based development of source code, reducing the risk of increasing proprietary commercialization.

The process of F/OSS for reaching maturity is described in Figure 2. The figure illustrates the process in which inadequacies of traditional SW create a knowledge community that develops OSS products. Over time, these products, while still being open and free, become commercially competitive as functionality and user friendliness evolves. The dynamics of OSS communities spill over into formerly proprietary domain-specific SW types and ultimately, companies and public institutions can rely on an almost entirely OSS-based IT environment. This model actually describes the development process both within specific SW areas (e.g., Web servers or OS) and with IT in general (end-to-end environment).

Furthermore, we believe that there is a relationship between a specific type of software and the possible emergence of knowledge communities. A strong community is a necessity for the development and maturing of "real" F/OSS. Hence, more and more sectors will experience development of competitive F/OSS, which will put traditional SW under continuous pressure. This means that in just a matter of years, the range of business-ready F/OSS will be far greater than what exists today, as illustrated in Figure 3.

Figure 2. OSS life cycle development

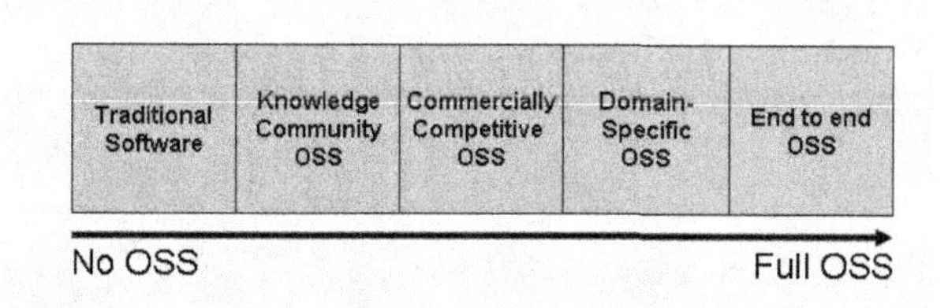

Figure 3. Community growth and software types

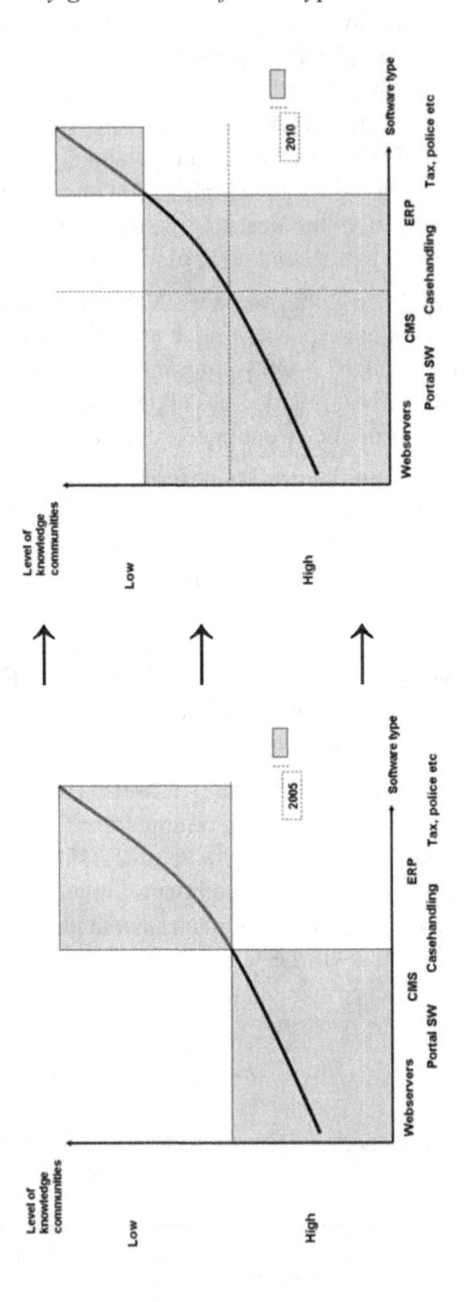

While more and more F/OSS applications will be developed for remaining functional, uncharted areas, other areas still exist that seem to be unsuitable for community growth and, subsequently, competitive F/OSS. The upper-left corner of Figure 3 illustrates these remaining areas. In the figure, we list examples of software types that will witness a low concentration of knowledge communities also in the future.

This can be explained by the need for a necessary, critical mass within the specific sector and secondly, the complexity of the sector's operational demands. The last element should not be understood as technical complexity but rather functional complexity, since business processes, business needs, legal and conceptual frameworks, standards, and user specific priorities vary greatly from one solution to another. Examples include police, tax authorities, defense solutions, and so forth.

This is not to say that these types of organizations cannot and will not use F/OSS software. In fact, most of them already do. Rather, it is a result of the complexity in applying "out of the box" code to the mission-critical business processes in these organizations. Additionally, some of the sectors might be reluctant to use systems that are too transparent to the public, because of the very nature of their field of work.

These organizations will still develop proprietary mission-critical SW, whether doing so internally or in cooperation with trusted external partners. These institutions are, however, looking for the same flexibility, independence, and cost-effective infrastructure as their more open counterparts. Herning, Wernberg-Tougaard et al. (2005) describe how these organizations subsequently often turn to a standards-based, service-oriented architecture, where COTS products leverage and handle

Figure 4. Critical mass and complexity in diverse applications

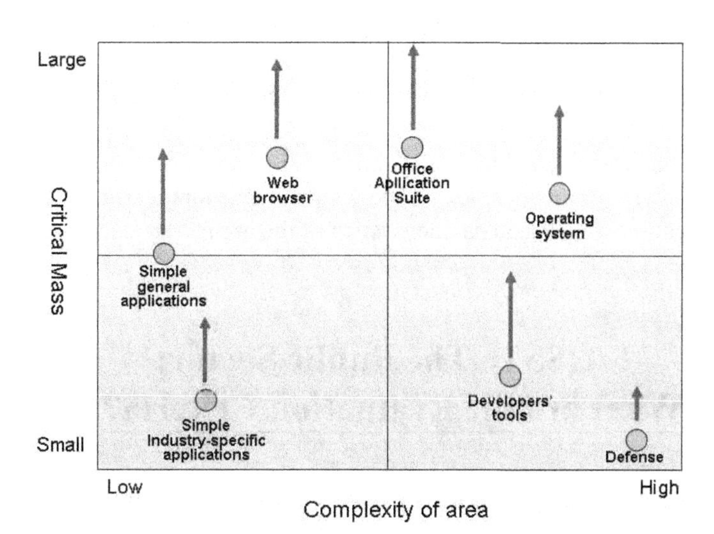

individual and generic business processes, while the overall operational infrastructure is developed for, and alternately by, the specific organization.

In Figure 4, we have tried to show that critical user and community mass and complexity of the functional processes does not only relate to the sector, but also the type of software. For a not solely illustrative example of maturity development within different domains see Schmitz (2001). As mentioned, F/OSS operational systems for defense might experience the combination of high complexity and a small critical mass, since defense systems developers normally do not share their findings.

A small critical mass of users and developers is not necessarily a sign of strategically chosen secrecy, and neither is it a sign of an inactive community within the sector. Software developers might experience a small critical mass of users and a high degree of complexity for SW tools with a very narrow but highly specialized audience. However, these areas are likely to survive and develop as well-functioning and very active F/OSS areas. In fact, studies by Comino et al. (2005) show that, in general, development projects targeted at a sophisticated audience have the greatest chance of survival. Also developers' communities can be small, but the user communities large. An operating system is a very complex piece of software, but can reach a large critical user mass. Web browser and simple applications, in comparison, have low complexity, but can still obtain a large critical mass. Other small applications developed for a specific industry or purpose might be both simple and have a small critical mass.

These examples simply go to show that some SW types and functional sectors are more likely to experience stronger user and developer communities than others, and that the size of the user community is not always a sufficient indicator for the sustainability of the knowledge community. When evaluating F/OSS, the PSI should consider the maturity of the area that it seeks to support by using F/OSS software. Is the domain F/OSS well developed and widely applied? Is it an F/OSS frontier with a small but strong community developing within it? Or is it still an area where F/OSS has not matured into basic business appliance? Such an analysis will also help to shape the future IT strategy, such as choosing one platform over another, or assessing whether the domain or the functional application, which the PSI is evaluating, is likely to undergo heavy open source development, or will remain proprietary because of the basic characteristics of the area?

F/OSS in The Public Sector: What are the Evaluation Criteria?

Historically, the public sector seems to have been somewhat more reluctant to embrace the usage of F/OSS than the private sector. This can partly be explained by the time lag that is often observed between the private and the public sectors' embracing new technology. The constant application of new technology has been seen as a way of realizing the private sector's ambition of driving down costs and raising profits, while the public sector historically has operated with alternative strategic goals ,imposing a more incremental adoption to new technological challenges and possibilities.

Nevertheless, over the past decade, we have seen a steady increase in F/OSS implementation in government. According to Ghosh et al. (2002) and Free/Libre and Open Source Software (2005), this growth is expected to continue and intensify over the coming years. It is outside the scope of this chapter to further investigate why some F/OSS technologies have had an extensive penetration in the public sector while others are still very rarely used.

It is worth noticing that there, according to Schmitz (2001b), is a significant difference between, for example, the server market and the workstation market. F/OSS for Web servers is widely used and F/OSS for general-purpose servers (on LANs, Intranets, etc.) is experiencing a substantial growth. The usage of workstation F/OSS is, on the other hand, very limited in the public sector. This partly mirrors the general picture of F/OSS usage for professional purposes, but there are some special features related to public sector F/OSS. For a thorough description of some of the differences see Schmitz (2001b). The public sector's gradual embrace of F/OSS will substantially impact the future of F/OSS; some analysts even suggest that the public sector could become the key driver of F/OSS usage. Additionally, several governments have introduced open source policies. Unites States (http://www.whitehouse.gov/omb/memoranda/fy04/m04-16.html) and the UK: (http://www.govtalk.gov.uk/policydocs/policydocs_document.asp?docnum=905) are great examples. Now we must ask, what has driven this radical change in the public sector's approach to new technologies and its role in the technological ecosystem?

In order to understand this change, we should look at what generally drives public sector decision makers today. While the public sector still aims to fulfill goals (legitimacy, accountability, transparency, objectivity, equality, etc.) substantially different from those of the private sector (profit maximization, cost reduction, increased efficiency), the two worlds seem to have grown closer in the last decade or two. With the emergence of the new public management theories and practices in the 1990s, the public sector was forced to apply a private sector mindset to all of the processes deemed operational in contrast to political. That is, once political decisions are made, administrative and operational implementation of the policies should focus on economical, managerial, technological, and organizational efficiency, as well as the traditional, distinct public considerations. This development is described in Table 1.

As a consequence, top decision makers in the public sector have been forced to pay close attention to the operations and efficiency of their institutions. Terms

Table 1. Changing demands facing public sector institutions

New demands to Public Sector institutions	
Traditional demands	**New demands**
Continuity	Flexibility
Bureaucratic correctness	Efficiency
Standard procedures	Adaptability
Adjust budget	Reduce costs
Push information	Make information available
"Protectionist" institutions	Transparent and open institutions
Accordance with regulation	User and customer satisfaction
We know what's good for you	Learn from the best
Contractually managed dependence on suppliers	Independence from single suppliers

like return on investment, total cost of ownership, activity based costing, business process reengineering, customer self-service, and digitalization are now common vocabulary amongst senior public sector managers, and success in these areas plays a significant role in the evaluation of their managerial achievements.

Ghosh et al. (2002) contends that the increased focus on F/OSS in the public sector can partly be explained as one of the consequences of this development. In the following section, we will investigate which parameters influence the decision of integration F/OSS in the IT strategy of PSIs.

Wheeler (2005) lists and analyzes a number of generic parameters for evaluation of F/OSS. These are functionality, cost, market share, support, maintenance, reliability, performance, scalability, usability, security, flexibility/customizability, interoperability, and legal/license issues. While all of these are indeed important to PSIs, we have chosen to focus on a more coarse-grained range of parameters. Schmitz (2001) describes how many criteria might be in play, but to strengthen the operational capacity of our analysis, we have decided to focus on the following criteria:

- Flexibility and interoperability
- Security
- Independence and anti-monopoly
- Legal issues
- Costs and benefits

- Support and development in the F/OSS ecosystem
- Internal or external resource building

Flexibility and Interoperability

The ability to adapt to new challenges in the market has long been a key success parameter in the private sector. However, in the last decade, flexibility and adaptability have played an increasing role in the ambitions of PSIs as well. Not only does the environment in which the PSIs have to operate change rapidly, but the legal foundation for their work can also change from one day to another. The same goes for political agendas and resulting priorities.

An example of flexibility and adaptability demands is user's demand for self-service, or a whole new pattern in the public's usage of certain public services, functions, and/or agencies. An example of the changing environment is the frequently changing tax regulations forcing the tax authorities to operate with high levels of flexibility. Another example is the political agenda changing in favor of new public services and processes.

According to Hahn (2002), flexibility is essential in both cases, not only from an organizational point of view, but also from a software point of view. The Free/Libre and Open Source Software (2005) report describes how, at the same time, interoperability is essential not only from a technical point of view, but also from an organizational point of view. One of the major consequences of the ongoing digitalization of public services and functions is that PSIs are not only enabled by technology to run new procedures or offer new services, they are also intensely relying on, and limited by, technology. At a conference on IT architecture recently held in Denmark, the CIO of the Danish tax authority told the audience how his greatest nightmare involves telling his management that an important political decision or priority cannot be carried out because of insufficient IT flexibility and interoperability between IT systems. Hardware, in most cases, can be easily purchased or scaled to match new performance needs. Dissimilarly, the applications and OS carrying out the institutions' core business processes are often complex and are highly specialized, reflecting the specific PSI's business needs. A consistent, open, standardized, and adjustable architecture is obviously a perquisite for obtaining necessary flexibility. But also, an F/OSS-based application portfolio is seen by some as another important step in pursuing the independence and dynamics supporting swift and efficient compliance with new demands from the political and administrative management. For a study on IT managers valuation of access to free source code, see Dedrick and West (2005). The application of F/OSS is seen as a way for the public CIOs and IT managers to reclaim full control of their software portfolio; its structuring, development, and operation.

In this context, according to Hahn (2002), the open source code allows IT departments to make necessary adjustments on an *ad-hoc* basis. Further, Tuomi (2005) explains how some find that sparring with a strong development community ensures that the changes are coded and implemented much faster than the case where proprietary software developers are involved. Many IT managers also contend that COTS products will not meet many non-generic work processes, which are unique to a specific PSI. Reengineering the application in order to support very specific work processes can either prove difficult because the proprietary SW provider does not see a business case in engaging in developing the application, or it can prove very costly because it requires consultants with no or limited prior understanding of the specific business area. Hence, the force of F/OSS is the possibility for the IT department to code corrections, add-on's, new functions, and so forth, themselves. This is possible because the department already holds in-depth knowledge of the specific business domain, or can engage in appropriate knowledge communities to find a solution.

This possibility heavily decreases the need to pass tacit knowledge of the business domain to an external party. Many IT managers claim that the resources needed for making external developers fully understand the details of the complex business processes supported by a given application far exceed the actual development. This also explains why many software houses hire developers with hands-on, domain-specific knowledge, to try to in-source the resource-demanding process of realizing the tacit knowledge crucial to the area.

Security

According to Ghosh et al. (2002), another key issue in the ongoing debate on F/OSS vs. traditional software is whether OS platforms and applications offer better performance in relation to security.

Security is a key concern in the public sector in general and in the public sector's use of IT in particular. Ghosh et al. (2002) uses the debate arising from the German Parliament's decision to equip workstations with Windows XP, which eventually forced MS to reveal the source code to a panel of security experts, as an example. When security is compromised in a private company, it can lead to severe loss and jeopardize the commercial sustainability of the company. While the IT security threat to private companies is a serious issue, it is nevertheless dwarfed by the security concerns in the public sector. Tuomi (2005) emphasizes how absolute trust in the confidentiality of information given to and stored by the public sector is a perquisite for the citizens' willingness to deal with the public sector in general, and even more when it comes to engaging in digitalized processes with the public sector. The known cases of security breaches in the public sector's handling of citizens' information have been widely criticized in the press and have raised demands by citizens to take immediate action. This proves that when public sector managers regard security as a main concern, they are in sync with the public opinion.

Wong (2004) describes how the increasing risk of identity theft, cyber terrorism, and other forms of IT-enabled crime have helped to put IT security high on the public sector agenda. Public IT systems play a key role in avoiding the wrong people gaining access to confidential or/and sensitive information.

As a consequence, most new digital administration initiatives in the public sector will consider the level of security as a main evaluation criteria.

For the past two to three decades, digitalization has been a high agenda item among government agencies all over the world. Digitalizing citizens' interaction with PSIs offers a way to pursue goals of increasing service towards citizens while reducing costs and optimizing work processes. With security being one of the most important criteria in new projects, the security of applications and platforms become a key issue in the digitalization process itself. Hence, public IT management considers (or should consider) IT security as a strategic concern, since operating on safe platforms and using secure applications impacts the PSIs overall possibility of pursuing the benefits of digitalization.

So how does F/OSS affect public sector IT security? Unfortunately, there is no easy answer to this question. Furthermore, answers vary greatly depending on who you ask. On one hand, there is no doubt that traditional, proprietary software suppliers have been forced to increase their focus on security, as customers have demanded secure solutions. At the same time, most studies prove that F/OSS has less security breaches than proprietary software. Since one explanation for this could be that more attacks are launched towards proprietary software than F/OSS, it is far more relevant to investigate which overall product development strategy is best to avoid security breaches from emerging in the first place. This question also divides the two proponents' groups. According to Ghosh et al. (2002), some claim that only by having a closed source code can suppliers hide potential weaknesses in a product and close the gaps that emerge during its usage. This group will point to the fact that open source code gives IT criminals the exact same knowledge of weaknesses and security holes as those trying to close them. The first-mover advantage will always allow IT criminals to be one step ahead when it comes to abusing security breaches for criminal purposes.

According to Ghosh et al. (2002), the OSS front will claim that only open source code gives the entire user community the possibility of dynamically contributing to closing and concealing security gaps. This, according to Wong (2004), gives users the possibility of proactively enhancing the software's security level, hence eradicating the IT criminals' first-mover advantage. The argument, explains Wong (2004), is that very few software houses, if any, can keep track of the rapid development in IT crime. The numerous security breaches and successful attacks against software from the world's largest suppliers are presented as proof for this claim. The only way to ensure safe software is by inviting users to participate in identifying and closing the holes that will inevitably be identified and become subject to abuse by IT criminals, no matter how well developed the software is.

The two camps mentioned are mirrored in the public sector's IT managers' approach to IT security and the use of F/OSS. In general, experienced users of F/OSS normally consider F/OSS safer, both regarding application portfolio and platforms. On the other hand, typical users of traditional software will consider this the safest choice. Consequently, there is no clear answer as to how the question of security should be integrated into the evaluation process.

That there is no general answer to the security question does not mean that security should not be a criterion in the evaluation process. The PSI should still conduct an analysis of the security consequences of selecting one or another application or platform. In this process, a series of criteria can be deployed:

1. Number of security breaches in the proprietary solution as number of breaches per year over the past years.
2. Number of security breaches in the F/OSS solution as number of breaches per year over the past years.
3. Has the supplier of the proprietary software historically shown dedication to resolving security issues and has this work been timely and efficient?
4. Has the F/OSS community, including commercial F/OSS actors (consultants, etc.), proved capable of closing security holes and has this been done in a timely and efficient manner? Here special focus should be given to the communities' ability to-through the availability of the source code-proactively identify and close security gaps.
5. What is the criticality of security breaches? Criticality is defined as the impact of a potential security breach. One should ask questions such as will a breach result in momentary breakdown of non-critical citizens' services from a closed environment Web site or will a breach potentially give intruders access to highly sensitive citizens' data. The lower the level of criticality, the lower the security criteria should impact the overall assessment.
6. Finally, does the competencies of the organization best support maintaining high and proactive security standards with traditional software or F/OSS?

An assessment should be made of all these elements to identify a) the advantage of selecting closed- or open source-based products, respectively, and b) the overall impact of the security level on project.

The result of the criticality assessment can turn out to be one of the main determinants in the evaluation process. This is particularly the case if the projects take place in an environment where security is essential (e.g., in military, intelligence or police sectors). As we will describe later, these very specialized sectors often lack the open-user communities. This is due to no tradition of openly sharing experiences and exposing potential vulnerabilities in sectors where protecting information is not one of the evaluation criteria, but *the* evaluation criteria. Hence, in some cases, the security element might be the key determinant in deciding which software strategy to pursue.

Independence and Anti-Monopoly

Another criterion in choosing one software strategy over another is the level of independence that the chosen software is estimated to bring the PSI. According to Ghosh et al. (2002), most PSIs consider it very important to be able to make independent decisions that, at the given point in time, are expected to best support the opportunities and challenges in the PSIs environment. As mentioned earlier, this independence and the resulting flexibility is essential in order to support the overall strategy and vision of the PSI in a world where most of the core business processes have been digitalized.

Relying on too few software providers and products is seen by many IT managers in the public sector (as well as in the private sector) as limiting flexibility. Hence, the essential question for IT managers is how to avoid dependence on a single supplier.

For some, the answer has been utilizing OSS. Open source offers applications and platforms that, in general (or in theory), are independent of profit-oriented suppliers. As a consequence, explains Ghosh et al. (2002), the PSI does not rely on the suppliers' development of the product and subsequent limitations. According to Hahn (2002), proprietary software suppliers have historically shown some reluctance toward establishing open and standard-based interfaces and genuinely open APIs. There are, says Hahn (2002), even examples of proprietary suppliers frequently changing their APIs to discriminate third-party developers. Instead, the interfaces and APIs have mirrored the strategic goals of the supplier, that is, seamless integration with the rest of the supplier's product suite or with partnering companies' applications, rather than genuinely open and transparent interfaces with "equal access" for all.

Demand from users has not always been capable of putting the question of openness on the agenda. Hence, IT managers in PSIs have felt locked in with a sole supplier or a tight oligarchy of suppliers pursuing profit goals rather than putting user needs at the center of development. If the options of substituting the supplier have not been adequate, this has obviously limited the independence of the PSIs IT strategies, and overall strategy of the institution. Obviously, the situation has been worst in those domains of the markets characterized by a very limited number of suppliers and where users, as a consequence, have had no or very limited possibility of substitution.

The days of pure monopoly in the software world are over in almost every corner of the market. There is obviously still strong dominance in some markets (e.g., operating systems), but the fact that possibilities of substitution exist result in a far greater focus on flexibility and, as a minimum, genuinely open APIs from most suppliers. It is reasonable to assume that part of the desire for independence from suppliers derives from bad memories from earlier times. At the same time though, some software suppliers still seem to hang on to the idea that only by locking their clients into an isolated, one-supplier, IT environment can they maintain their share of the market. That lack of independence is not a concern that is only promoted by hardcore F/OSS-disciples; it is illustrated by the frequent outcries from public IT managers complaining about the lack of the most basic cooperation from the long-term suppliers who, in some cases, basically own the PSIs IT infrastructure, business logic, data, application portfolio, and so forth. A recent (and still relevant) example from Denmark is the complaints from a substantial number of municipalities that cannot access their own data (e.g., various citizens' data) without having to pay a supplier to provide/release it. Further, there is evidence that a variety of highly domain-specific applications still succeed in maintaining their market share with predominantly closed and inflexible APIs. According to Tuomi (2005), the customers relying on these applications complain that the suppliers limit their flexibility by abusing the dependence to ignore customer demands (e.g., concerning open interfaces, standards, and the ability to provide Web services as part of an overall IT architecture).

Though examples like the ones mentioned still exist, it would be reasonable to conclude that most software suppliers no longer rely on a single-minded, protectionist strategy. In a parallel development, the isolationistic strategies of some software suppliers, especially regarding proprietary file formats, have been undermined by the emergence of a variety of brokers and converters with the capability of transforming, for example, one format or protocol into another.

From an operational standpoint, many public IT managers prefer not to put all their software eggs into one basket. Alone, the possibility of being able to pick and choose from different functionality in different applications empowers the IT managers to pursue the PSIs operational goals. According to Ghosh et al. (2002), many public IT managers also have a more normative approach to choosing F/OSS over traditional software. Every single IT manager has his or her own reasons for this, but in general, it seems that the idea of supporting the development of non-commercial software pleases many public IT managers.

Legal Issues

Although the technology and the processes by which software is developed collaboratively are important, the real nature of F/OSS is not technical, nor organizational; it is legal. This legal essence is expressed by the license-a text summarizing all rights and obligations provided by the author of the software (the licensor) to the users (the licensees) under the copyright law.

As soon as a license claims to be "open source," the rights are basically the same, responding to the 10 conditions of the Open Source Initiative (OSI). In summary, the license has to grant freedoms regarding:

- Access to source code
- Permission to modify the work, provided attribution marks are respected
- Redistribution
- Absence of discriminations regarding purposes or persons
- Absence of additional licenses or conditions mandating, for example, to the inclusion of the work in particular products or distribution
- Absence of restrictions applying on other software and of conditions to use exclusively specific individual technology or style of interface

Despite common points, there is not one, but multiple (hundreds) models of license that are usually not compatible with each other. The real differences are related to provisions organizing the redistribution of work. If these provisions state that the redistributed work has to be licensed under the same original license, the text is said to be "Copyleft," while if redistribution is not restricted to original terms, it is said to be "Permissive."

License incompatibility creates huge conflicts as soon as you want to combine various existing software components into a single new application. Fortunately, the number of relevant licenses—we mean licenses used for the most vital and basic components, and by a significant number of developers—is much more reduced; it numbers less than 10.

The GNU GPL (General Public License) is among the less permissive; all software redistribution (of the same software, of improvements, of inclusion into a broader piece of software) must be done under the same conditions. It may be less generally attractive for the software industry, but will guarantee that no version of the software will be "appropriated" in the future.

On the contrary, the BSD (Berkeley Software Distribution)/Apache or MIT licenses permit the widest panel of uses, especially when collaborating with the software industry; the software developed may become proprietary.

Other licenses, such as the MPL, provide compromises where the code and the executable binary may sometimes be dissociated. With these licenses, the code will stay open (Copyleft effect); in some cases the original author asks to be notified with all improvements, and the binary object may be distributed with a proprietary license (to avoid redistribution by simple end-user media duplication).

For historical reasons (because the movement was born there 20 years ago), nearly all relevant licenses are written under U.S. law. Applied to European context, this raises a number of issues.

In general, the copyright framework is similar enough to answer positively to questions related to enforceability of U.S. licenses. The Munich district Court enforced the GPL on 19 May 2004; however, a number of differences are making European legal services insecure about the responses provided by U.S. licenses in all possible circumstances. Some examples include:

- Copyright law and author rights are not applied in the same way; particularly concerning specific provisions related to "communication to the public" and moral rights (right to withdraw, to modify, to stay anonymous...).
- The impact of the applicable contract law (often designated as the law of the U.S.) is difficult to appreciate by European judges, and is not fully compatible with mandatory European provisions concerning, for example, consumers information protection and the warranty and liability clauses.
- The determination of the competent jurisdiction is generally ignoring European context.
- U.S. texts are only printed in English and their authors often refuse, for integrity reasons, to provide any official value to translations.

Released by IDABC on 23 June 2005, the European Public License (EUPL) approach addresses these issues, in order to facilitate open source licensing by local, national, and community authorities. Its merits are to reduce legal flaws in the European context and to highlight contributions from European parties in an area that was occupied exclusively by U.S. lawyers. Its weakness is that it is a new license, but it does not have the projects' and developers' base that made existing free software licenses (and in particular the GNU GPL) a success. License is the most visible part of the iceberg, but other legal issues exist:

- The validity, justification, and non-discriminatory character of dispositions mandating open source in public call for tenders.
- The relationship between public administrations and open source developers and the possible incentives to maintain a "community."

- The real impact of warranty and liability (for example in the case of patent infringement) and the possibility of insurance.

By imposing patent conditions on the software distributors, the GPL (and the EUPL) intend to significantly reduce risk to their users.

Recently, the Lloyds Company announced the first insurance policy around the use of open source software. Such policy is aimed at corporate customers that might be redistributing software in violation of open-source licenses. Other companies, including Open Source Risk Management, Palamida, and Black Duck Software, have emerged to assure corporate customers they comply with open-source license provisions. This indicates that the potential risks associated with open-source software have become quantifiable, and allows additional opportunities for pooling software in Europe.

Costs and Benefits

One of the major debates over the last few years has been on the cost of software. According to Tuomi, (2005), there is no doubt that one of the main drivers for PSIs when selecting an F/OSS solution is the possibility of cost saving. Studies by Dedrick and West (2005) actually show that to many IT managers, the cost issue is often more important than, for example, the possibility of customizing software. The debate has been particularly focused on the licensing issue; "why pay when you can have it for free" seems to be the most used argument. The problem with this argument is that the "total cost of ownership" (TCO), defined broadly, is completely missing. To paraphrase Keynes: "There is no such thing as a free lunch"—which also includes open source software.

When dealing with total cost of ownership (TCO) of F/OSS, one should note that even though TCO normally would consist of many individual components, according to Ghosh et al. (2002), the pure license costs have a tendency to dominate the discussion. This argument is what we would call the "black hole TCO-argument," as it has the magic ability to draw focus away from all other selection or TCO criteria.

In a study financed by the Danish Board of Technology (Danish Board of Technology, 2002) the researchers concluded that the savings arising from utilizing F/OSS on the desktop within the Danish public sector could yield a yearly saving of €275 per desktop, resulting in total public sector savings of more than €123 million per year. This figure stirred a political demand for more use of F/OSS in the public sector. It also explains why the Danish Ministry of Science, Technology, and Innovation, in its Software Strategy, MSTI (2003), promised "...development of a TCO-model (total cost of ownership)" that could assist in selecting between F/OSS and traditional SW. As part of the validation of the model, six pilots were arranged.

Figure 5. PNP analysis

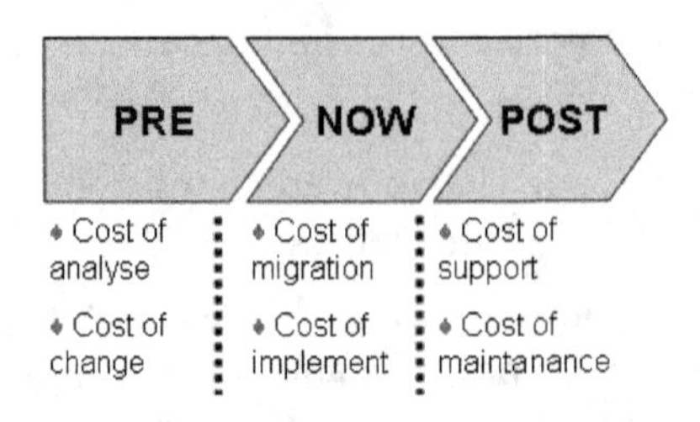

In the evaluation report, MSTI (2003), it was concluded that the pure licenses cost element yielded a mere 4% of the TCO. The final TCO model was released in 2005, MSTI (2005).

The focus of politicians, media, vendors, and so forth, traditionally has been on the fact that license fees on F/OSS are zero, while on traditional software it is higher than zero. When studying empirical data, however, the "black hole" argument is faulty, or a non-stringent criteria for evaluation of SW. The evaluation of F/OSS vs. traditional SW should be stringently calculated based on pricing of all the criteria mentioned in this chapter. When evaluating the cost consequences of choosing F/OSS compared to traditional SW, the holistic business case should be analyzed. The business case should be the analytical tool with which public sector organizations should steer and find decision support when determining whether F/OSS or traditional SW is the right choice for an organization.

We suggest that in evaluating SW, one should adopt a life cycle view that holistically spans all significant areas.

The PNP model in Figure 5 captures the life cycle approach from pre to post. The "pre" is capturing all the effort made before selecting and implementing SW (e.g., analysis of different possibilities). "Now" is the actual cost incurred by the SW-choice (e.g., migration). "Post" covers the costs that arise from further support and maintenance of SW (e.g., code maintenance). In this study, we do not dive into the details of these cost elements. We will now describe some basic concepts of the PNP analysis:

- **Pre:** As always, it is good to ask open-ended "W" questions to gain knowledge: why, what, who, when, and so forth. But knowledge gathering also has a price, costly consultants or internal working groups that shift resources from "doing business" to "analyzing." In order to adopt a proficient approach to "cost of analysis," management should clearly state directives on measures and targets. Another driver is the "cost of change," measured as the implication of change of

SW on the way business processes are conducted and the way the organization is structured. This is normally a large task, as most public sector institutions (as well as private) do not have easy access to digitized workflows, allowing them to make assessments on implications of SW costs of changes.

- **Now:** When installing and implementing the chosen SW, one should be aware of the cost of implementation. This cost normally covers program management, project leaders, architects, and programmers; but also training of new users. The costs would often be straightforward, based on normal good practice. The other issue, migration cost, can actually prove to be much more challenging. Often the use of one specific software product derives a large number of modifications and additional add-on contingents to the core SW product. One example is Microsoft Office, in which many organizations have programmed business processes into the package in the shape of various macros, and these are not easily migrated. Consequently, migration to a new product can imply significant costs. These should be taken into consideration and calculated as part of the evaluation.
- **Post:** After implementation, when everything is in operation, there will be a need for support and maintenance. The support costs might cover everything from super users to a full-blown ITIL organization, yet the cost should still be estimated beforehand. Maintenance costs are also difficult to estimate and have several traps. When dealing with F/OSS, a key feature is the access to the source code, which will give the organization a high level of flexibility. But the associated risk is that the IT department might conduct more and more ad hoc development. Mismanaged code alterations can make the F/OSS product more and more complex, specialized and un-transparent. Continuous development of the source can lead to complications, for example, when upgrading the source code. We comment further on this in the later section on code management.

The PNP-model indicates the areas that should be covered by a business case and the overall issues on which public sector managers should focus their analysis. PSIs can only perform a qualified, knowledge-based analysis of F/OSS and traditional SW, respectively, by assessing all TCO-areas and evaluating all relevant criteria.

The aforementioned study, MSTI (2005), conducted by the Danish Ministry of Science, Technology, and Innovation provides a good detailed model and an Excel sheet to calculate the TCO of a desktop. However, a holistic model covering all business aspects of PSIs use of F/OSS is yet to be developed. We suggest that the methodology described in this chapter should be followed as guidance. Still, a series of puzzling questions remain to be resolved: Is the scrap time of HW delayed by using F/OSS? How is the learning curve with regards to F/OSS user interfaces in terms of intuitive and user-friendly designs? And does "contract management," as a parameter for the CIO, need to be higher with traditional SW than with F/OSS?

All these questions will generate cost elements to be considered and evaluated in a holistic model.

When dealing with cost elements it is important, from a government perspective, to include the potential development of a supporting industry, or the risk of not having such a supporting infrastructure. We believe that as F/OSS becomes more and more viable, a highly value-adding service industry will evolve around it. This, according to Kim (2005), has been the case in countries like Korea, Venezuela, and Brazil. Firms that support and develop F/OSS to meet specific business needs are growing rapidly. One of the driving factors of this growth is the way in which PSIs demand solutions that are open, both with regards to open standards and open code, but also have domain specific requirements that can only be met by coding executed by commercial OSS professionals. This will continue to drive open source development forward and, at the same time, create a service industry supporting this process. This development is consistent with the research conducted by Garelli (2005) and Knowledge@Wharton (2005), which concludes that products are not viable by themselves, but need to be wrapped in services to become competitive.

In *Roadmap for Open ICT Ecosystems*, The Open ePolicy Group (2005) presents a holistic view on open ICT ecosystems. The *Roadmap* argues that open ICT ecosystems drive efficiency, growth, and innovation for enterprises, government, and society. For further insight into the macroeconomics of F/OSS please see Lerner and Tirole (2004), Wong (2004) and Frost (2005)

Support and Development in the F/OSS Ecosystem

We have mentioned what is often promoted as the single greatest advantage of F/OSS: the existence of devoted non-commercial user forums where applications are dynamically developed and redeveloped as a consequence of the users' hands-on experience and needs.

A large quantity of academic, scientific, and business studies have analyzed the dynamics and structures of F/OSS communities. Social scientists have analyzed the special social and cognitive attributes of different F/OSS communities, as well as how they emerge, develop, and how knowledge is generated and shared in the communities. Computer scientists have studied the advantages of the code generated in developers' communities and how the application development is much more aligned with user needs when developed in communities rather than by private companies. Economists have looked at the commercial and socioeconomic consequences of F/OSS and have, together with business researchers, been somewhat puzzled by the mere existence of these apparently altruistic communities that often develop products that could easily be developed commercially.

This bulk of academic literature does not satisfactorily deal with how these findings should be included when evaluating F/OSS vs. traditional software solutions, nor if PSIs should include specific criteria in this process. We believe that in the process of evaluating an F/OSS solution against a solution with traditional software, the existence of a strong user and developer community and a supporting environment should not only be considered an extra bonus, but should be considered a key parameter in the evaluation process.

The actual benefit of choosing F/OSS over traditional software is closely interlinked with the existence of a strong community, as mentioned earlier. There are numerous examples of F/OSS application projects that have been launched and then rarely or never touched again (this problem seems somewhat smaller for non-application F/OSS. [The Roadmap for Open ICT Ecosystems, http://cyber.law.harvard.edu/epolicy/]). This obviously limits the long-term usability of the application since, for example, user needs and development in the "market" will not be reflected in the F/OSS development. Therefore, an evaluation of the long-term sustainability of an F/OSS application should (a) analyze the historic characteristics of the user and developers community and (b) estimate the long-term solidity of the community.

Scoping—setting priorities and understanding your baseline—requires evaluating what you can control or influence and prioritizing needs with early input from users and partners. Scoping means assessing what competencies exist within your organization, and which can be tapped externally.

The Roadmap for Open ICT Ecosystems from The Open ePolicy Group (http://cyber.law.harvard.edu/epolicy/) suggests using three tools for scoping: baseline audits, an Openness Maturity Model, and the business case.

Baseline audits (e.g., benchmarking) must be used selectively as they require time, money, and personnel. It is necessary to focus on the services and functionality most critical to the business. Mapping standards, business processes, and existing services can help identify "siloed" processes or systems. Failure to identify and document business processes and requirements before deployments can be costly.

To complement baseline audits, the Roadmap offers a diagnostic tool, the Openness Maturity Model, to assess where an ICT ecosystem is and where it should be headed. Many capability maturity models exist to guide change management in an ICT environment (CMMi, etc.). None, however, gauge openness across an entire ICT ecosystem, and the Openness Maturity Model is a first attempt to provide such a tool. The model does not precisely measure openness, but describes the road to open ICT ecosystems based on an examination of certain fundamental features, including interoperability, open technology usage, business process linkages, acquisition strategies, and collaborative development. By organizing baseline data into a broader framework, the Openness Maturity Model identifies areas where the balance between open and closed technologies is not producing optimal performance,

Table 2. Business needs and IT effectiveness

Adequacy of Meeting Business Needs	IT Effectiveness
• Functional Fit • Collaboration • Usability • Performance • Security • Flexibility • Support and Accountability • Education	• Interoperability • Reusability (Development/Maintenance) • Standards Compliance • Scalability • Flexibility • Administration • Security (Vulnerability) • Market evolution expectations • Independence • Total Cost of Ownership (TCO)

interoperability, or competition. Also, it can inform the assembly of a business case for any ICT initiative or deployment.

The Roadmap's third tool for scoping, the business case, is critical for generating high-level support and wider organizational "buy in." The Roadmap emphasizes two points when building a business case: Consider more than just acquisition costs by applying a full cost accounting, and do not pay for anything you do not need.

To reduce costs, it is necessary to decide what functionality is really needed, and this is not always easy to do. According to Tuomi (2005), open ICT ecosystems offer the flexibility to add components and functionality as needs change or services expand.

To determine F/OSS efficiency and ability to meet business needs, many issues must be considered. At the application level, F/OSS should be considered "just another" software solution. Adequacy of meeting business needs relates to the application's ability to support the business functionality of the enterprise. Pepple (2003) suggests that adequacy of meeting business needs can be defined as follows:

- The time required to introduce new features
- The ease of use of the application
- The ability to support the functional requirements of the enterprise
- The ability to support the future growth of the enterprise

Hence, the adequacy of meeting business needs relates to the application's ability to meet the current and projected functional needs of the enterprise. These considerations are strategically important; however, other considerations and assessments must be made. To compare these perspectives, it is necessary to evaluate a number of concerns on each side. Such concerns could be similar to the ones described in Table 2.

Evaluating the F/OSS Knowledge Communities

The knowledge communities should be learning communities, and evaluations must take a learning perspective in order to grasp the full value of the community building via collaborative learning. Basically, communities of practice (CoPs) differ in how effective they are as learning communities. Some provide few opportunities for what Wenger (1998) calls "legitimate peripheral learning," and make it difficult for novices to gain entry and contribute to the community efforts, while others are very inclusive and have various ways to involve people at different levels of competence. Some blindly follow long-established traditions and are fundamentally not learning oriented; others are more reflective about their own status and practices as a learning community. The learning architectures (ibid) vary.

Wenger, McDermont, and Snyder (2002) define communities of practice (CoP) as having the following characteristics:

- Groups of people who share a concern, a set of problems, or a passion about a topic, and who deepen their knowledge and expertise in this area by interaction on an ongoing basis.
- They typically share information, insight, and advice with each other; help each other solve problems, discuss situations and their aspirations and their needs, ponder common issues, explore ideas and act as sounding boards, and may create documents.
- They are informally bound by the value they find in learning together.
- The value they derive is not merely instrumental, but also adds to the personal satisfaction of knowing others who share/understand your perspective.
- Their sense of identity is created through interactions and exchanges over time, which continually combines the personal/social and instrumental/business concerns of members.
- They may create a body of knowledge, practices, and approaches.

The tangible outcomes of communities of practice, which include reports, documents, and F/OSS CoPs software as well as improved skills, are central to their legitimacy. Wenger et al., however, notes that it is the intangibles such as sense of trust, increased ability to innovate, relationships and intimacy built amongst people,

Figure 6. OSS community resource profiles

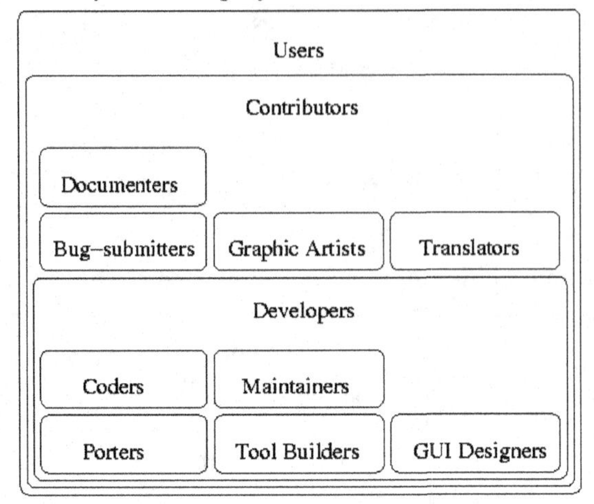

sense of belonging, spirit of enquiry, professional confidence, the identity conferred to members, pockets of support created, and the ability to transcend multiple boundaries both within and outside one's organization that become especially important toward building a sense of community among participants.

As Tuomi (2001) points out, an open source development community does not only produce software. It also produces the interacting system of knowing, learning, and doing that organizes the community and its relations with other communities. Tuomi's empirical analysis shows that the open source development model is a heterogeneous network of communities and technologies.

Yeates (2004) describes the community roles in F/OSS communities as depicted in Figure 6.

The three generic roles—users, contributors, and developers—are all essential to the community. User roles (end-users, super-users) are naturally fundamental, although their community participation might be peripheral. Contributor roles cover all those who make an explicit contribution to the project (potential users). The developer roles are more specialized, and often considered to be the elite roles in open source projects. PSIs are often users, are sometimes contributors, but rarely developers.

Holck et al. (Holck, Larsen, & Pedersen, 2004) proposes several ways in which PSIs and other organizations can participate in and contribute to an F/OSS project:

- **Source code:** improvements and corrections in-house (competence building), which are offered to the developer community
- **Documentation:** both in-house and for the developer or user community

- **Error reports:** assisting in bug finding and removal for the developer community
- **Suggestions:** for improvements to the developer community
- **Technical infrastructure:** supply and maintain for the community (or donate money to do this)
- **Participation:** in management of the community F/OSS organization
- **Response:** to requests for help in user communities
- **Participation and support:** in local chapters of developer/user communities

Keil and Carmel (1995) remind us that in a commercial setting, it is important for a software vendor to establish good links to customers, and that there are many ways to establish these links (e.g., bulletin boards, customer groups, prerelease demonstrations, etc.). In the F/OSS world, both "old economy" and "new economy" are at stake. As the *Cluetrain Manifesto* in Locke et al. (Locke, Levine, Searls, & Weinberger, 2000) claims, "markets are conversations," and this is especially relevant to F/OSS, since the traditional market relation (vendor-customer) is disruptively changed.

Despite the notably democratic features of the open source community, Kipp (2005) describes how individuals take on leadership positions in various projects. Raymond (1999) suggests that software project management has five functions: defining goals, monitoring progress, motivating participants, organizing people's work, and marshalling resources for the project.

Hence, when analyzing the characteristics of the community, the following elements should be observed:

- Does the community have a traceable history? This simply identifies whether the community has just emerged around a temporary application concept/experiment or if it is a robust community with shared business and technical interests. When analyzing the history of the community, the following parameters should be included:
  - How long has it existed?
  - Is it reasonably formalized?
  - Is its work reasonably well organized and documented?
- Does the community have a satisfactory size and competence? This parameter is of course dependent on the application type and, therefore, the potential community size. In general, it is important to estimate if the community has a size that indicates certain sustainability and whether it represents the necessary competence, that is, do the users and developers in the forum represent organizations of a satisfactory size and skill?

- How does the community function? When choosing an F/OSS solution, it is of utmost importance that the solution is supported and developed by both a proactive and a reactive community. The reactive ability of the developers' community is simply its ability to effectively solve the problems that emerge over time, and to develop new functionality that complies with the users' stated needs. It is useful to try to analyze how the community has historically reacted to the feedback that flows back into the community. That is, whether the input- output (technical and "business" feed back results in new code development) mechanism seems to work. An example could be a security breach members of the community observe that is dealt with effectively by the developers in the community.

It is also relevant to try to estimate the proactive capabilities of the community. It is the community's ability to proactively solve problems and meet challenges that evolves in the user environment. An example could be development of the application to meet changes in the legal regulation of the area in which the F/OSS application is in use, even before the changes occur. This indicates a (pro) active community that is up to speed with both the users' technical and business needs.

Evaluating Other Actors in the F/OSS Ecosystem

Finally, another essential part of the F/OSS environment involves the commercial players in the field: consultant companies, implementers, commercial developers, integrators, and so forth. It is essential, when trying to understand the dynamics of F/OSS, that we acknowledge that much of the development is driven by volunteer and non-paid developers, but is capitalized on by the same actors in the roles of consultants, and so forth. Hahn (2002) describes how:

In a sense, open source provision is an extension of the market, not an alternative. Private agents meet private needs. As I explain below, instead of providing software in exchange for money, open source developers provide software in exchange for a (sometimes informal) promise to improve the product and return the fruits of their invention to the community.

The F/OSS communities deal with problems, challenges, and issues relating to the application itself, as well as issues of general interest to the community. If a PSI faces a problem relating to an F/OSS application, but the problem is not related to the core purpose of the application or is very unique to the PSI, the community will often be reluctant to "code an answer." The obvious advantage of F/OSS is that the IT department of the PSI is allowed to code the appropriate modification itself.

Since it is too costly for most PSIs to hold application development competencies in house, this coding is outsourced to the commercial part of the F/OSS ecosystem, the private, commercial companies we mentioned before that offer services relating to F/OSS. This, of course, means that the PSI is not only depending on the community as a supporting institution, but also the commercial actors in its periphery. The PSIs evaluation should include the existence and presence of supporting institutions outside the community. In this context, the "supporting periphery" should be evaluated with the normal software evaluation criteria, such as:

- Presence in the local area
- Language issues
- Cost and supply of support
- Competencies in support environment (proven success record)
- Sustainability of support environment

The key parameter, which sounds simple but is often ignored due to either lack of attention or "dogmatic reasons," involves investigating how the support community and the commercial F/OSS ecosystem support the business needs of the PSI both in the short and in the long term. There may be a mature technical community developing solutions that function well, but lack basic user friendliness and the ability to dynamically adopt to new business needs. At the present time, according to Schmitz (2001b), this holds true for some types of desktop and business application F/OSS, whereas Web server and data center F/OSS seem to perform better.

Figure 7. Public sector institutions in the OSS environment

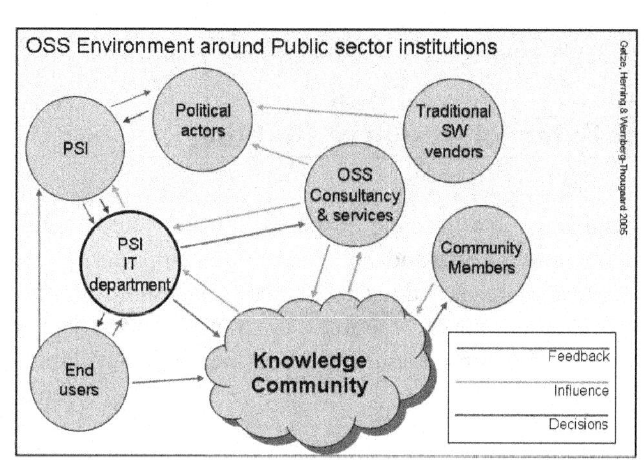

One reason for this could be that these "back office" and infrastructure related areas can develop quickly without the need for costly and time-consuming desktop user testing. Additionally, in these areas, the need for functional adoption is less apparent than the need for technical adoption, and a community of primarily developers can react to these changes more effectively.

According to Murdock (2005), these factors influence the commoditization of software and services, where the open source movement can be seen as "just another commoditization event and that, like other commoditization events, it represents a disruptive shift in the software industry." It has, adds Asay (2005), been in the "back office" that open source first found viable business models. The "front office" has more recently seen a rapid growth in various areas such as Web browsers (Firefox) and office packages (OpenOffice). Walli (2005) describes the new business models evolving around these applications.

According to Schmitz (2001), it is important to realize that the ecosystem surrounding the PSI is often a complex one, with many actors deciding over, influencing, and giving feedback to one another. The dynamics and dependencies within each type of F/OSS can vary substantially. In Figure 7, we have tried to outline a generic picture of dependency in the F/OSS environment surrounding the PSI.

The challenge is to identify the strongest and the weakest links in this relational diagram of influents, and evaluate the F/OSS accordingly. Who does the PSI rely on and to what extent, and how is the community and other influents capable of supporting technical, operational, or business changes? The scenarios should be evaluated against the overall goal of the PSI and the political or/and strategic goals defined by the ruling political actors.

Everybody agrees that a modern IT environment should be characterized by flexibility and adaptability, and should be based on future proof architecture, standards, and technologies. In the area of F/OSS software, these priorities should be reflected in a thorough analysis of these elements and a clear picture of the present future priorities and dependencies in the environment surrounding the potential F/OSS solution.

Internal or External Resource Building

A substantial challenge is estimating how to best utilize the internal and external resources, and measure the pros and cons of various set-ups against these particular dependencies. The next step is to decide whether the PSI should focus on recruiting, training, and developing internal resources, or should rely partly or completely on assistance from external, commercial F/OSS partner (e.g., developers, integrators, implementers, consultants, etc.)

This choice depends on a variety of parameters. An initial concern relates to the organization's overall IT strategy. Does the PSI focus on a lean and mean IT organization with primary role of controlling suppliers, or is the focus on maintaining and developing in-house competencies? Depending on the present PSI, the IT operations can either be seen as a non-core business function or as a key determinant for success in a digitalized reality.

This discussion influences the priorities within the F/OSS domain. Even if the PSI is free to choose its F/OSS strategy, there are criteria that should be evaluated before deciding to either in-source or outsource the F/OSS maintenance and operations. These criteria are listed in Figure 8. Before the PSI decides to in-source, it should evaluate its internal competencies in maintaining and developing a dynamic F/OSS environment.

This evaluation is rather basic and simply analyzes the level of F/OSS experience amongst the staff, its existing interaction with F/OSS communities (an optimal use of an F/OSS community requires some experience), whether in-sourcing the resources affects the flexibility of the IT department's IT usage; and finally, the department's track record in maintaining and developing a dynamic IT environment in support of the PSIs overall business goals. At the same time the knowledge community around the F/OSS solution(s) should be evaluated (as mentioned earlier). Finally, the supporting commercial actors should be evaluated. Most PSIs will not be capable of fulfilling all development and maintenance tasks despite choosing to in-source the function. Hence, concludes Hahn (2002), the commercial F/OSS environment's ability to support the IT department when necessary should be evaluated.

Figure 8. Sourcing strategy for OSS maintenance and development

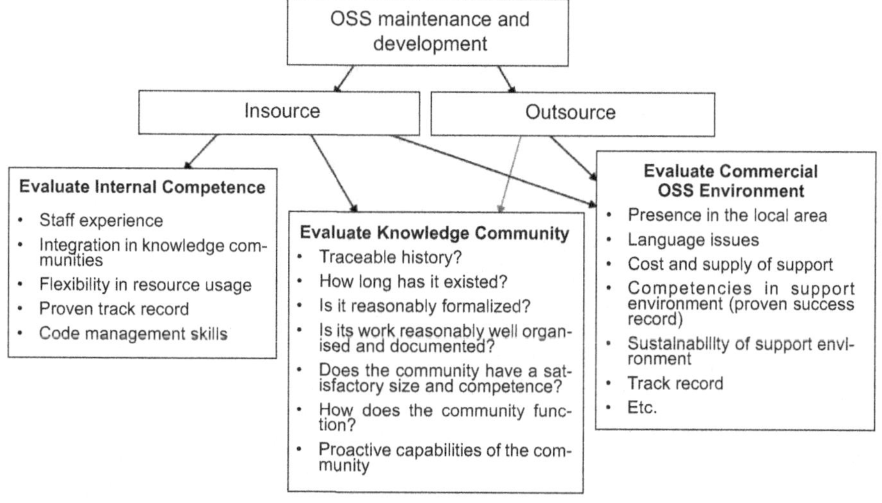

When choosing to outsource the implementation, development, and maintenance of the F/OSS solution to a commercial company, the market players should be thoroughly analyzed. The criteria for an evaluation like this should resemble an ordinary vendor selection process, and include criteria like those mentioned in Figure 8. Even in an outsourced F/OSS process, the PSI should investigate the function of the knowledge community to identify the dynamic knowledge base, which the outsourcing partner can utilize.

Code Management

Another important consideration when deciding to in- or outsource involves the capability to perform what we call *code management.* In F/OSS, code management is distributed in a complex ecosystem as illustrated previously. New functionality is often coded in subcommunities, or by users or user groups. At the same time, primary application code will be developed by the main community, and bug fixes, patches, upgrades, and so forth, will be rolled out from time to time.

A competent PSI might generate its own moderations to the code supporting specific business needs. Consequentially, code management becomes an important issue in the depicted distributed system. It requires a certain level of not only technical insight, but also organizational competence to manage the stress field between own development, decentralized development in the community, new primary code roll outs, and other distributed inputs. The capability of code management, especially within complex F/OSS areas, should be an evaluation criterion against both internal and external resources. Studies, among these Dedrick and West (2005), show that this concern is gradually becoming a concern for IT managers.

There will also be the challenges of shifting from "add-on" programming to "full-scale" programming, as new skills and education will certainly be needed. And the art of software engineering (SE) is timely, costly, and demands maturity of processes and tools, some of which F/OSS projects might lack.

After realizing that most F/OSS projects will not exceed one or two developers and never gain critical mass, Scacchi (2004) states that: "*... F/OSSD in general is a risky undertaking, at least in terms of the probability of achieving critical mass, as well as realizing a faster, better and cheaper way to develop complex software products or services. Accordingly, F/OSSD is not well suited for adoption in hierarchical organizations that develop software products or services through rational management schemes traditional to SE principles and practices.*"

As PSIs often are very formalistic and hierarchical, the adoption of "good programming practice" and SE-skills could be a determining factor when evaluating uses of internal and external resources.

Overall Evaluation Criteria

We have listed some criteria that we find particularly relevant when evaluating F/OSS against traditional SW. We have identified key parameters within costs (TCO), functional demands, and what we have called *additional requirements*. As described earlier, these elements should be evaluated holistically, that is, in a manner that mirrors the complexity of modern PSI, from the board of directors to the server room. In the matrix, this consideration assumes four layers: vision and strategy, business processes, applications, and information and infrastructure.

In Table 3, we have tried to gather all the elements illustrating what an evaluation scheme for a PSI might look like. Again, each individual scheme should mirror the actual PSI, its goals and strategies, and its environment.

All of the evaluation criteria listed do not need to be applied to every evaluation. However, the exercise of discussing the listed criteria is beneficial, and can prevent future discord between priorities and consequences at different business layers and within each evaluation criterion area. Evaluations that focus solely on any one of the listed cells in the matrix (and many do) will eventually lead to trouble, since interdependence and reliance between business layers is evident in all complex PSIs.

The next proposed exercise is to attempt to quantify the evaluation. Quantification is not a goal in itself; instead, the next exercise attempts to visually link evaluation criteria to various compliance solutions.

Table 3. Evaluation criteria divided on business layers

Vision and strategy	Business processes	Applications and information	Infrastructure
TCO evaluation			
• Support costs • Implementation costs • Long term time consumption • Scalability	• Effect on business processes • Possibility of optimizing business processes • Learning costs • Process change costs	• Licenses • Updates and maintenance • Cost of security breaches • Migration costs • Scalability	• Costs from hardware requirements • Costs from future hardware requirements
Functional evaluation			
• Compliance with overall PSI strategy • Compliance with political priorities • Compliance with IT dep.'s goals and targets • Openness	• Functional fit with existing business processes • Flexibility in supporting specific business processes • Support of workflows • Information infrastructure • Customizability	• General flexibility in application • Possibility of individualization • Security • Standards based • User friendliness • Information infrastructure • Reliability	• Standards based • Compliance with present hardware set-up • Impact on future hardware decisions • HW Performance
Additional evaluation			
• Independence from vendor • Knowledge sharing • Supporting org. evaluation • Legal evaluation	• Internal/external resources • Community evaluation • Legal evaluation • Code management capacity	• Future proof? • Market trends • Reputation • Code management capacity • Interoperability	• Compliance with hardware strategy • Interoperability

Table 4. Weighted evaluation score card

	TCO	Flexibility/interoperationability	Security	Independence	Community and Support	Total weighted score
Strategic weight	2	4	4	2	3	
OSS Solution 1 Compliance	4	3	1	3	2	
OSS Solution 1 Weighted score	8	12	4	6	6	36
OSS Solution 2 Compliance	3	3	3	4	5	
OSS Solution 2 Weighted score	6	12	12	8	15	53
Traditional SW 1 Compliance	1	2	5	1	2	
Traditional SW 1 Weigthed score	2	8	20	2	6	38
Traditional SW 2 Compliance	2	3	2	2	3	
Traditional SW 2 Weigthed score	4	12	8	4	9	37

First management and IT management need to agree on which evaluation criteria are the most important and how important they are compared to each other. An example could be a health sector application with a very static functionality. In this situation, flexibility is of limited importance, but security might be the key evaluation parameter, because the application holds sensitive data and is Web accessible. Another example could be an application serving an extremely dynamic business area with great need for flexibility and strong knowledge communities, but with less focus on TCO because of a limited license need.

In Table 4, we have chosen five criteria that are identified as the core evaluation criteria for a non-existing PSI. The criteria are listed on top of each column. The first row lists the strategic weight that the PSI places on the different criteria. Again, the identification of core evaluation criteria is a business decision that should be based on a discussion between all the layers of the business, and documented in a matrix similar to the one depicted in Table 4. Each criterion is then given a certain weight between one and five. In Table 4, the key criteria are flexibility/interoperation ability and security, which each receive a score of four.

The next task asks the IT department (and perhaps internal or external business analysts) to rank each solution's compliance with the listed criteria. In the example, F/OSS solution one is low cost and therefore scores four on the TCO criterion. However, the security standard in this solution is rather poor and scores only one. The compliance score is then multiplied with the strategic weight assigned by the

Figure 9. Evaluation compliance graph

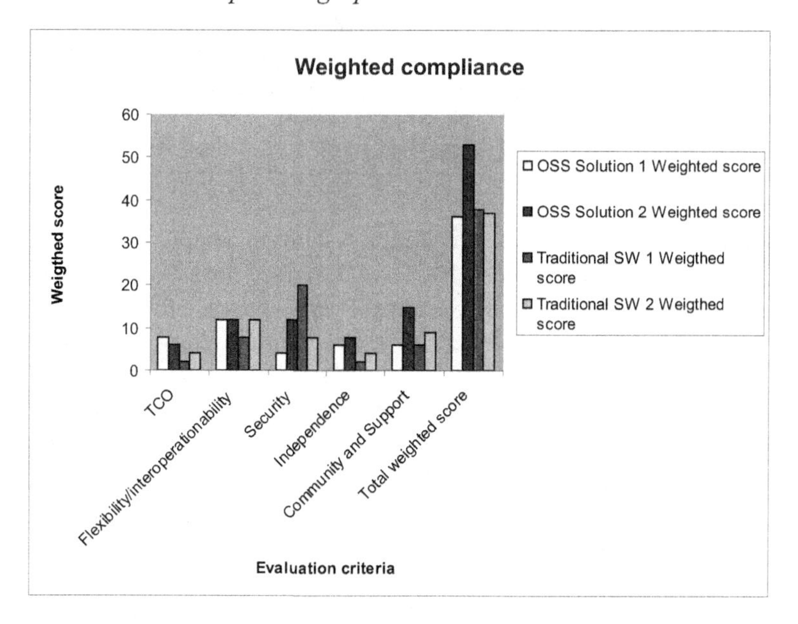

PSI to the given criterion. For example, since the PSI only weights the TCO of the solution two, the weighted score is eight, and so forth. The solutions that are being evaluated are all analyzed and ranked against the weighted criteria of the PSI.

The exercise is simple, but allows for the strategic- and business-process layers of the organization to express the key business-related criteria for the solution, as well as for the IT department to use their technical expertise to analyze various solutions against these requirements. In this way, we achieve the dynamic relation between the business layers in the evaluation, a key question in Figure 1 in the very introduction to this chapter. It is important to notice that each evaluation conducted by the IT department (or external consultant) can utilize the large variety of technical evaluation tools available[3]. For example, the criterion "security" can be analyzed using hundreds of technical compliance criteria also including an analysis of the solution's affect on the existing IT environment.

Finally, the matrix can be transformed into a diagram visualizing the findings, as illustrated in Figure 9.

This diagram visualizes each solution's weighted compliance with the core evaluation criteria and the total weighted score of each solution. The columns to the right illustrate each solution's aggregated weighted compliance.

As simple as it seems, a process resulting in a diagram, like the one in Figure 9, allows for business and IT to "speak the same language" and select an F/OSS or traditional SW solution that is best and most cost-effective in supporting the business needs, as requested by Dedrick and West (2005).

Conclusion

We started out by emphasizing the need for IT systems to comply with the business needs of PSIs in a dynamic process. Next, we described how we expect F/OSS to spread to more complex areas, and how critical mass of users and knowledge communities will evolve in areas that are, today, strictly proprietary. We claimed that PSIs will increasingly turn to F/OSS to pursue cost savings and increase efficiency. We contend that this will create a need for conceptual models for evaluating F/OSS against traditional SW.

We than listed various criteria that will almost always play a key role in such conceptual evaluation models, describing the importance of each. In conclusion, these (and other suggestions) were gathered in a matrix combining the different groupings of criteria with business layers. Finally, we proposed a conceptual process for merging business needs and IT evaluation competencies into a consistent framework.

We conclude that successful IT implementation and operation is always subject to the important provision that comprehensive and empirically-based evaluations are carried out prior to pursuing one solution over another. The choice between F/OSS and traditional SW poses a number of parameters to consider. As Schmitz (2001) concludes, making this decision based solely on religion or beliefs seldom leads to success.

It is our hope that the identification of key PSI evaluation criteria, and our simple evaluation model, will inspire PSIs to focus more on the holistic aspects of evaluation software, and prevent decisions based on solutions that do not match business needs or where the evaluation criteria have been too narrowly defined.

References

Asay, M. N. (2005). Open source and the commodity urge: Disruptive models for a disruptive development process. In C. DiBona, M. Stone, & D. Cooper (Eds.), *Open sources 2.0: The continuing evolution*. O'Reilly Media.

Benkler, Y. (2002). Coase's penguin, or Linux and the nature of the firm. *Yale Law Journal, 369*.

Bessen, J. (2002). What good is free software? In Hahn, R.W. (Ed.). (2002). *Government policy toward open source software.* AEI-Brookings Joint Center for Regulatory Studies. Retrieved from http://www.aei.brookings.org/admin/authorpdfs/page/php?id=210

Brooks, F. P. (1987).No silver bullet: Essence and accidents of software engineering. *Computer, 20*(4), 10-19.

Comino, S. Manenti, F. M., & Parisi, M. L.. (2005). *From planning to mature: On the determinants of open source take off* (Discussion Paper No. 2005/17). Università degli Studi de Trento.

Danish Board of Technology. (2002). *Open-source software in e-government. Analysis and recommendations drawn up by a working group.* Retrieved from http://ww.tekno.dk/pdf/projekter/p03_opensource_paper_english.pdf

Dedrick, J., & West, J. (2005, March 11). *The effect of computerization movements upon organizational adoption of open source.* Presented at the Social Informatic Workshop: Extending the Contributions of Professor Rob Kling to the Analysis of Computerization Movements. Retrieved from http://www.crito.uci.edu/si/resources/westDedrick.pdf

Fitzgerald, B., & Kenny, T. (2003). *Open source software can improve the health of the bank balance—The Beaumont Hospital experience.* MIT Sloan Free/Open-Source Research Community Online Papers. Retrieved from http://opensource.mit.edu/papers/frost.pdf

Free/Libre and Open Source Software. (2005, August 25). *Policy support. FLOSSPOLS. Results and policy paper from survey of government authorities.* Maastricht.

Frost, J. J. (2005). *Some economic & legal aspects of open source software.* University of Washington.

Garelli, S. (2005). *The world competitiveness landscape in 2005*, Executive Summary, IMD, Lausanne, Swiss. Retrieved from http://www.imd.ch/documents/wcc/content/eSummary.pdf

Ghosh, R. A., Krieger, B., Glott, R., & Robles, G. (2002). *Open source software in the public sector: Policy within the European Union.* International Institute of Infonomics, University of Maastricht, The Netherlands.

Gosain, S., & Stewart, K. J. (2005). The impact of ideology on effectiveness in open source software development teams. *MIS Quarterly, 30*(2).

Hahn, R. W. (Ed.). (2002). *Government policy toward open source software.* AEI-Brookings Joint Center for Regulatory Studies. Retrieved from http://www.aei.brookings.org/admin/authorpdfs/page/php?id=210

Herning, , K., Hornemann, K., Hornemann J.,Wamberg, J., & Wernberg-Tougaard, C. (2005). *Sikkerhed og sikring i Danmark.* Post-konference strategirapport om national sikkerhed i Danmark.

Holck, J., Larsen, M. H., & Pedersen, M. K. (2004). *Identifying business barriers and enablers for the adoption of open source software*. Copenhagen Business School, Dept of Informatics. Retrieved from http://ep.lib.cbs.dk/download/ISBN/x656409451.pdf

IDA, (2004, June). OSS Competence in the Public Sector. In *Proceedings of the IDA Open Source Software Workshop*.

Keil, M., & Carmel, E. (1995). Customer-developer links in software development. *Communications of the ACM, 38*(5), 33-44.

Kim, E. (2005). *F/OSS adoption in Brazil: The growth of a national strategy*. Retrieved from http://www.ssrc.org/wiki/POSA/index.php?title=F/OSS_Adoption_in_Brazil:_the_Growth_of_a_National_Strategy

Kipp, M. E. I. (2005). Software and seeds: Open source methods. *First Monday, 10*(9). Retrieved from http://firstmonday.org/issues/issue10_9/kipp/index.html

Klincewicz, K. (2005). *Innovativeness of open source software projects*.Tokyo Institute of Technology. MIT Sloan Free/OpenSource Research Community Online Papers. Retrieved from http://opensource/mit.edu/papers/klincewicz.pdf

Knowledge@Wharton. (2005). *Globalization forum: Looking at the market's successes and failures, interviews with Prof. Garelli about management, services and products*. The Wharton School, University of Pennsylvania.

Lerner, J., & Tirole, J. (2004). *The economics of technology sharing: Open source and beyond* (Working Paper 10956). Retrieved from SSRN: http://ssrn.com/abstract=620904

Locke, C., Levine, R. Searls, D., & Weinberger, D. (2000). *The cluetrain manifesto: The end of business as usual*. Perseus Books Group. Retrieved from http://www.cluetrain.com

Malhotra, S. S., & Maksimchuk, R. A. (2005). *Unisys 3D-VE Strategy*. Unisys white paper. Unisys Corporation. Retrieved from http://unisys.com/eprise/main/admin/corporate/doc/clarity/Services/3D_Visible_Enterprise_Strategy.pdf

MSTI. (2003). *The Danish software strategy.* Retrieved from http://www.oio.dk/files/Softwarestrategi_-_Engelsk.pdf

MSTI. (2004). *Selection of desktop applications for the office*. Retrieved from http://oio.dk/files/Desktop-evalueringsrapport__V1-2_.pdf

MSTI. (2005). *Desktop applications for the office: Decision support evaluation*. Retrieved from http://oio.dk/files/VTU_Kontorpakke_-_beslutningsstotte.pdf

Murdock, I. (2005). Open source and the commoditization of software in open sources 2.0. In C. DiBona, M. Stone, & D. Cooper (Eds.), *Open sources 2.0: The continuing evolution*. O'Reilly.

Open ePolicy Group (2005). *Roadmap for Open ICT Ecosystems.* Harvard Law School. Retrieved from http://cyber.law.harvard.edu/epolicy/

Pepple, K., Levy, D., & Down, B. (2003). *Migrating to the Solaris Operating System: The discipline of UNIX-to-UNIX migrations.* Prentice Hall PTR.

Raymond, E. S. (1999). *The cathedral & the bazaar: Musings on Linux and Open Source by an accidental revolutionary.* Retrieved from http://www.catb.org/~esr/writings/cathedral-bazaar/cathedral-bazaar/

Scacchi, W. (2004). *When is free/open source software development faster, better, and cheaper than software engineering*? Working paper. Institute for Software Research, UC Irvine. Retrieved from http://www.ics.uci.edu/%7Ewscacchi/Papers/New/Scacchi-BookChapter.pdf

Schmitz, P.-E. (2001a). *Study into the use of open source software in the public sector.* Part 1. OSS fact sheet.. An IDA Study. Interchange of Data between Administrations. European Commission, DG Enterprise.

Schmitz, P.-E. (2001b). *Study into the use of open source software in the public sector. Part 2. Use of open in Europe.* An IDA study. Interchange of Data between Administrations. European Commission, DG Enterprise. Retrieved from http://ec.euopa.eu/idabc/servlets/Doc?id=1973

Schmitz, P.-E. (2001c). *Study into the use of open source software in the public sector. Part 3. The open source market structure.* An IDA study. Interchange of Data between Administrations. European Commission, DG Enterprise. Retrieved from http://www.ec.europa.eu/idabc/servlets/Doc?id-1974

Stallman, R. M. (2002). *Free software, free society: Selected essays of Richard M. Stallman.* Philosophy of Software Freedom Series. GNU Press. Retrieved from http://www.gnu.org/doc/book13.html

Tuomi, I. (2001). Internet, innovation, and open source: Actors in the network. *First Monday, 6*1. Retrieved from http://firstmonday.org/issues/issue6_1/tuomi/index.html

Tuomi, I. (2005). The future of open source: Trends and prospects. In M. Wynants & J. Cornelis (Eds.), *How open is the future? Economic, social and cultural scenarios inspired by free and open source software* (pp. 429–459). Brussels: Vrjie Universiteit Press.

Walli, S. R. (2005). Under the hood: Open source and open standards business models in context in open sources 2.0. In C. DiBona, M. Stone, & D. Cooper (Eds.), *Open sources 2.0: The continuing evolution.* O'Reilly.

Wenger, E. (1998). *Communities of practice. Learning, meaning, and identify.* Cambridge: Cambridge University Press.

Wenger, E. McDermot R., & Snyder W.M. (2002). *Cultivating communities of practice: A guide to managing knowledge.* Havard Business School Publishing.

Wheeler, D. A. (2005). *How to evaluate open source software/free software (OSS/FS) programs*. Retrieved fromhttp://www.dwheeler.com/oss_fs_eval.html

Wong, K. (2004). *Free/open source software: Government policy*. Asia-Pacific Development Information Programme. Retrieved from http://www.apdip.net/publications/fosseprimers/foss-gov.pdf

Yeates, S. (2004). *Roles in open source software development*.Retrieved from http://www.oss-watch.ac.uk/resources/roles.xml

Zachman, J. A. (1987). A framework for information systems architecture. *IBM Systems Journal, 26*(3).

Zachman, J. A., & Sowa, J. F. (1992). Extending and formalizing the framework for information systems architecture*IBM Systems Journal, 31*(3).

Endnotes

1. Metcalfe's law states that the value of a network equals approximately the square of the number of users of the system (n^2). Since a user cannot connect to itself, the actual calculation is the number of diagonals in an n-gon: n(n – 1)/2. The limit inferior of this number is n^2 (even though that it is disputed whether n in networks are large enough to ensure approximation to n^2). [http://en.wikipedia.org/wiki/Metcalfe's_law].
2. Reed [http://en.wikipedia.org/wiki/Reed's_law] claims that Metcalfe's law understates the potential value by not including subgroups and suggests 2^n – n – 1, which grows exponential compared to Metcalfe's law.
3. Within the security area e.g. the BEATO (Benchmark Assessment Tool) security evaluation tool, the NIST "Security Self-Assessment Guide for Information Technology Systems." and the growing bulk of specific F/OSS evaluation models.

Appendix I: Useful URLs

The Roadmap for Open ICT Ecosystems from The Open ePolicy Group:

http://cyber.law.harvard.edu/epolicy/

Cluetrain Manifesto:

http://www.cluetrain.com

Study into the use of Open source Software in Public Sector (2000 – 2001):
http://europa.eu.int/idabc/en/document/2623#study

Pooling Open source Software (roadmap for Public Sector software sharing) done in 2002:

http://europa.eu.int/idabc/en/document/2623#feasibility

Open Source Observatory. A (first) two year mission (2004-2005) to collect News, Events, Case Studies and Advices on Open Source:

http://europa.eu.int/idabc/oso

Open Source Licensing of software developed by The European Commission (2004):
http://europa.eu.int/idabc/en/document/3879/471

eLearning at the workplace. This 2005 report is not dedicated to open source, but the recommendations stress on the need for an open source "Wikipedian approach":

http://europa.eu.int/comm/education/programmes/elearning/doc/studies/vocational_educ_en.pdf

Guidelines for Public Sector when collaborating with Open source communities (2005):

http://europa.eu.int/idabc/en/document/3879/471

The new European Union Public License (EUPL) – an open source license adapted to the EU legal framework (2005):

http://europa.eu.int/idabc/en/document/2623/5585#eupl

Patents and Open Source software (2005):

http://europa.eu.int/idabc/en/document/3879/471

European Biometrics Portal. (This is not a study but a development based on 100% open source technology – 2005):

http://www.europeanbiometrics.info

Appendix II: How to Get Started with this Type of Evaluation Process

When applying the methodology described in this chapter, a constructive way to initiate an analysis is by asking and investigating a series of questions. The questions should be investigated for the various software alternatives that are being analyzed:

1. What are the known costs: licenses, implementation, hardware, and so forth.
2. What are the support costs?
3. What are the implementation costs?
4. What is the estimated time consumption—implementing, training, analyzing?
5. Is the solution scalable?
6. To which extent does the solution support our business needs?
7. To which extent does the solution optimize our business processes?
8. Is the solution adjustable, customizable, and flexible?
9. Is it user friendly and in accordance with our end-users' needs?
10. Is the solution in sync with our strategy of best and cheapest?
11. Is the solution open and standards based?
12. Can it communicate with the rest of our environment?
13. Does our organization hold the competencies needed for managing and further developing/adjusting the solution in the future?
14. Do we hold the necessary code management resources?
15. How does the solution affect the security level of our environment?
16. Does the solution perform satisfactorily?
17. Does the solution seem to be future proof in terms of core technology? (Code language, protocols, APIs, and so forth.)

Trying to answer these questions in, for example, a workshop, with participants from both IT and the business side, will be an excellent way of launching a more formalized evaluation process. The reason is that the questions will force IT to explain the basic technical implications arising from choosing one application over another, while the business side is forced to be very concrete in formulating their business needs.

This will help create a framework that can, later in the process, be intensively refined and detailed and, in the end, serve as listing graded-evaluation parameters.

Chapter VII

Open Culture for Education and Research Environment

Ernesto Damiani, University of Milan, Italy
Paul G. Mezey, Memorial University of Newfoundland, Canada
Paolo M. Pumilia, 'Open Culture' International Association, Europe
Anna Maria Tammaro, Parma University, Italy

Abstract

Some contemporary theoretical and technological issues that are becoming of paramount importance for building a cross-disciplinary research and knowledge-sharing environment are outlined, pointing out those cultural changes implied by the increasing adoption of the ICT. In the unprecedented abundance of information sources that can be reached through the Internet, the growing need for reliability will not be met without a major change of scholar's, teacher's, and learner's attitudes to foster enhanced trusted relationship. In this chapter, emphasis is placed on the open source organizational model, highlighting some of the key elements of the open culture: knowledge-sharing technologies, interoperability, reusability and quality assurance.

Introduction

The spreading of the ICT in a variety of contexts is raising the urgent need for a transformation in how we experience and exchange knowledge and will have substantial impact in scientific and commercial production, as well as in the learning process. Lifelong learning and cross-disciplinary collaboration competencies will be more and more required by scientific institutions and enterprises, while knowledge sharing will become the *sine qua non* of collaborative research.

Boundaries between research areas are increasingly blurred, and growing numbers of investigations are being carried out by larger and geographically distributed teams composed of different kinds of professionals working in close contact.

The ability of sharing knowledge is getting more and more important in universities. The patterns and cadences of interaction among faculty members, learners, instructional development staff, knowledge management staff, and expert practitioners will assume new forms. The ability of generating just-in-time knowledge will spread in parallel with a decline of the relative importance of static knowledge. Pervasive, perpetual learning, richly supported by knowledge management, will become the new "gold standard" for many learners' experience (Collier, 2003).

It is clear that we cannot naively rest and merely rely on the power of the ever more-advancing new technologies to successfully face such challenges.

More efficient organizational frameworks for the production of knowledge components and for their sharing and reuse are to be devised and fine-tuned, together with aptly suited international laws to regulate authorship management, and a stronger commitment to manage and assess the quality of information.

But the establishment of such infrastructure will not be enough. Ability to create and maintain new relationships with coworkers, often outside the institutional context, and the attitude to emphasize truthfulness of such relationships should be tied with these changes, thus positively affecting the whole spectrum of interpersonal relations and driving the same kind of thorough cultural change that can be already witnessed by some successful open source software projects.

In fact, a response to such challenges is provided by the people involved in the open source phenomenon, where peculiar collaborative methodologies and organizations, rooted into a freely accessible digital infrastructure, are brought out, aimed at designing, assembling, maintaining, and delivering knowledge objects; thus, increasingly shifting the locus of innovation toward users, so that an economical system consisting of complete user-to-user innovation systems can be foreseen (Barron, 2000).

We all have to reeducate ourselves: the culture of open source brings very-high new demands on data quality, information quality, and source code quality, as well as on accountability of all those contributing code and data, and of those who merely use the benefits of open source. These traits countersign the new phenomena of open access repositories and open content for e-learning as well as traditional open source software development, although rules governing the conduct of participants are still evolving and somewhat unclear.

In our opinion, this process will trigger cultural changes leading to new demands for higher degrees of responsibility to everyone and, in the fullness of time, to a new, cross-cultural code of Internet Integrity. In other words, the most profound effect of open culture is the actual development of a new culture, incorporating the needs for openness, as well as the requirements of a new level of "integrity." Openness provides the benefits, whereas the new levels of integrity provide some of the safeguards against misuse of the powerful tools involved.

We argue that such open culture will have greater impact in the interdisciplinary fields, where a certain lack of familiarity of experts in one field with the subject matters of the other fields is the grounds for a natural caution, slowing down both communication and progress. Thanks to the increased levels of trust generated by the open culture approach, these difficulties will be reduced.

This demands a proper attitude by researchers, as well as proper tools to help researchers to grasp concepts when reading papers or following seminars in different fields. Much of the actual developments are still ahead of us and, by extrapolation, from the developments of the recent past, the effects of attitude changes originating from open cross-disciplinary interactions may provide for many surprises.

Although such exciting turmoil promises great opportunities and brings out new business models, scholars are often unaware of such possibilities or unable to exploit them properly, and the standing commercial interests are often opposing the trends, denying, restricting, or delaying easy access to publications, especially to students and to researchers from the less rich countries.

This chapter outlines some contemporary theoretical models, and discusses emerging technological platforms in which the issues of reuse and integrity are becoming of paramount importance. Emphasis is placed on the three key elements of the open culture: interoperability and open assets; reuse and intellectual property rights management; quality assurance and integrity.

Towards Open Culture

There is a growing number of ever larger communities supporting the principles of open source (software with available source), open access (based on interoperability of digital resources), open content (easy-to-deploy and reuse of learning material), sharing the belief that knowledge cannot be considered as exclusive property of those who made the discovery and that inventors will benefit, in terms of feedback from peers and also financially, by spreading out the obtained results, under the least restrictions as possible, while benefiting from the international laws to preserve authorship[1].

There is room for plenty of synergies among those communities, once the common ground for acting openly is firmly established. What does it mean to be open? Originally, open has meant free sources available for the open source community, the oldest and most organized of the participating communities. Open means interoperable for the open access community, starting with open archives experiences and representing an alternative or subversive proposal to the current scientific publication structure. Finally, open means encouraging reusability and free spreading of digital resources for improving learning and teaching for the e-learning community.

"Open culture" appears as the unifying perspective around which the different communities can meet, as Lawrence Lessig claimed before (Lessig, 2004). Echoing the "global brainstorming" and cultural change ideas put forward by one of the authors (Mezey, 2004), an intriguing description of that concept has been recently given by Mark Hemphill[2]:

Open culture is like a cross disciplinary brainstorming. Sharing information and knowledge stimulates cross disciplinary interactions and gives additional significance to individual knowledge. Before Internet, there was the practice of brainstorming, now Internet and communication methodologies offer a new level of integration. Sharing and exchanging knowledge is good not only for me, as an individual but for the entire society, however there is a cultural resistance. Sharing knowledge throughout Internet should have the same integrity as in interpersonal communication.

It is also worth noting that there are differences between science and humanities communities, as the latter is more individualistic than the former. In any case, change agents are needed to move people to the culture of knowledge sharing. As Fred Friend puts it[2], referring to the "open archives":

If they do not know how, can we address this problem? Key questions are: who owns the fruit of academic research? And what is the value of dissemination of research results (often publications)? What libraries pay?

The required cultural changes will lead to new demands for higher responsibility by everyone, and to a new, cross-cultural code of Internet integrity. The more profound effect of open culture is the actual development of a new culture, incorporating the needs for openness, as well as the requirements of a new level of "integrity." Openness provides the benefits, whereas the new levels of integrity provide some of the safeguards against misuse of the powerful tools involved.

Community-Based Knowledge Sharing Platforms

As noted, in the scenario of the knowledge-based, open-culture society, communities are emerging as a new organizational form supporting knowledge sharing, spreading, and application processes. Communities do not operate in a vacuum; rather they have to confront a huge amount of digital information, such as text or semi-structured documents in the form of Web pages, reports, papers, and e-mails. Experience has shown that basic communication and data processing technology is not enough to support community-based knowledge sharing. The capability of extracting and handling classifications of heterogeneous documents produced by multiple sources is an essential requirement for information sharing; it can dramatically improve the effectiveness of community-wide cooperation.

From an architectural point of view, a community-based knowledge-sharing platform is composed of two main parts: a *knowledge interchange infrastructure* and a *metadatabase*. Recent research and development has proposed a number of architecturally diverse platforms, going from service-oriented distributed architectures like `DSpace`, `CDSWare`, and `Ariadne` to "pure" peer-to-peer ones like `Edutella` (Nejdl, Siberski, & Sintek, 2003).

These platforms are called digital asset management (DAM) systems. DAM allows organizations to maximize the use of these resources, ensuring that their value is maintained while generating institutional savings. DAM involves:

- Creating an efficient archive that can hold digital resources (such as images, audio, and text) and the metadata that describe them.
- Implementing an infrastructure to ensure that these electronic data are managed and preserved in such a fashion that they will not become obsolete.
- Implementing search facilities that enable users to identify, locate, and retrieve a digital object.

The benefits of implementing DAM include:

- Centralizing discovery and access.
- Coordinating disparate projects as part of a coherent whole.
- Centralizing authorization, validation, security, and tracking systems.
- Unifying organizational solutions to managing copyright and IPR.
- Reducing duplication of effort and resources.
- Saving time for the creators and users through organizational structure and centralization of data.

Regardless of the architecture chosen by DAM, metadata plays a crucial role when it comes to the integration of existing infrastructures.

Multiple attempts at standardizing general metadata have been independently made both by the e-learning and the digital libraries communities. The latter have a much longer history, and resulted in the development of a number of heavyweight standards like Z39.50, aimed at large scale cataloging of non-digital resources. More recently, attention focused on lightweight metadata standards aimed at the description of digital objects, with the aim of supporting, besides learning, creative innovation and research. For the purposes of this section, after a brief review of available standards for knowledge-description metadata, we shall take as a reference the metadata and the technical infrastructure chosen for the DSpace repository to be used as a pilot implementation within the project *European meta-database of E-Academic resources* (EUREA).

Dublin Core is a library-oriented standard aimed at defining a bare minimum (*core*) set of metadata elements (such as author, title, etc.), for digital libraries' cataloging and interchanging purposes. Special profiles (e.g., the Education Profile) have been defined for adding domain-specific elements to the DC standard.

MARC (Machine Readable Cataloging) is the metadata format originally defined for the U.S. Library of Congress. It provides a mechanism for computers to exchange and process bibliographic data. There are several variations of MARC, the latest being MARC 21. This standard divides each bibliographic record into logical fields (like author, title, etc.), in turn subdividing into subfields. The repertoire of MARC fields and subfields is encoded as a set of numerical tags whose meaning is spelled out in MARC documentation. The MARC format is semantically rich and widely used by the digital libraries community. However, it is aimed at the specific institutional purposes of a librarian (classification and conservation) rather than at the free interaction style of research communities.

IEEE-LOM (learning object metadata) is a standard published by the Institute of Electrical and Electronic Engineers (IEEE). It is composed of multiple parts, including a data model describing a set of elements with a defined semantics. These elements are grouped into nine categories: General, Life-Cycle, Meta-Metadata, Technical, Educational, Rights, Relation, Annotation and Classification. These nine categories, forming LOM *base schema*, were designed as a refinement of the three main ones of descriptive, technical, and administrative metadata introduced previously. The LOM model is a hierarchy of elements whose leaves are either *simple* (i.e., containing a single value) or *aggregated* (containing multiple values). Each leaf element has a name, an explanation, a size, an order, and a usage example. This complex structure was designed to be machine rather than human-readable, and is aimed at fostering interoperability and free interchange of heterogeneous objects between platforms. LOM intricacies discouraged developers from attempting full-fledged implementations of it, although many partial ones exist.

SCORM (Sharable Content Reference Model) is a standard developed by the U.S. Department of Defense for technology-based learning across the federal and private sectors. SCORM deals with sharable content objects (SCOs), that is, a collection of multimedia assets (image, text, sound) that becomes an instructional unit. SCORM metadata schema is based on LOM's nine categories.

Of course, current technological platforms for knowledge exchange do not support all these standards; for instance, at the moment, `DSpace` only supports the Dublin Core Metadata Element Set, plus some extensions conforming to the DC Library profile. In other words, items available for exchange in a `DSpace` all have a single Dublin Core Metadata record. The development team behind `DSpace` at MIT has announced its intention to support a subset of the SCORM element set within `DSpace` in the year 2006.

An important and often neglected step in metadata lifecycle is *harvesting*, that is, metadata collection and processing by software agents (*harvesters*), for example, to create custom views and, more importantly, registries and cross-references. As will be recalled in the next section, *Open Archives Initiative Protocol for Metadata Harvesting* (OAI-PMH) provides an application-independent interoperability framework for metadata harvesting that collects metadata from different repositories and creates an *open registry* where each metadata entry links back to the original metadata item. From an architectural point of view, main assumption behind OAI-PMH is a clean separation between data and service providers. Data providers establish an OAI-PMH-based interface to their own local digital resources, while service providers collect and integrate metadata from multiple repositories. Harvesters like ARC (Liu, Maly, Zubair, & Nelson, 2001) provide facilities for searching across multiple archives plus other value-added features like resource ranking. OAI-PMH supports dissemination of multiple metadata formats, but for interoperability purposes, it mandates dissemination of Dublin Core without additional profiles. Mapping complex metadata formats to unqualified Dublin Core may be difficult or even unfeasible without severe loss of semantics.

In service-oriented architectures like `DSpace`, metadata are treated differently from ordinary data, especially as far as modification permissions are concerned. In `DSpace`'s metadata registry, entries can be edited only via a custom administrative interface to be used at certain preset steps of the `Dspace` population workflow. The workflow process in `Dspace` is supporting self-submission of digital objects (e.g., learning objects or scientific "grey literature" items) on the part of their authors, but monitor the submission process in order to guarantee that the objects' self-descriptions will be standard enough to support effective query and retrieval.

The rationale behind this choice is that metadata cannot be treated lightly: they map data items to the shared conceptual space, and changing them freely would inevitably bring in errors, potentially even loss of resources ending up associated with the "wrong" metadata elements. Also, even on occasions when `Dspace` users are allowed to modify the values of the Dublin Core description fields, in principle, they should use only terms from a shared, controlled, resource classification.

Technological platforms and their architecture are not neutral with respect to the modalities of knowledge sharing. In a recent paper (Stuckenschmidt, Siberski, & Nejdl, 2005), W. Nejdl argues that the combination of advanced metadata and peer-to-peer (P2P) technologies is suited to deal with most problems of inter-organizational knowledge management; his research group has also presented search techniques specifically aimed at distributed research communities (Chirita, Damian, Nejdl, & Siberski, 2005). Concrete applications and scenarios, including cooperative research, have specific requirements and constraints that may require *ad-hoc* design decisions. A crucial point is the role shared vocabularies and ontology play in these different areas. Service-oriented architectures support a shared metadata structure aimed at integrating different points of view in a common domain model, for example, providing the community with common description vocabulary or domain ontology. The peer-to-peer approach tolerates (and indeed encourages) a certain degree of inconsistency among individual domain models, in order to effectively support a high rate of change. Inconsistency between local models and vocabularies will eventually be resolved via continuous interaction among community members.

A second major aspect, where the choice of a service-oriented vs. a "pure" P2P platform architecture is not neutral, is metadata harvesting. As we have seen, OAI-PMH defines service relationships between the data provider, the service provider, and the final clients. However, digital libraries, in most cases, act both as a client and as a server, trying to obtain outside material for their internal users and offering resources to other libraries. A standard OAI service-oriented architecture has a many-to-many structure: multiple service providers harvest multiple data providers. This is a potential cause of inefficiency: when a user queries multiple service providers the results might overlap, and duplicates handling will become necessary. Also, the conventional service-oriented architecture is prone to the well-known "cold-start problem": new sources of knowledge may find it difficult to attract the attention of a service provider, be harvested, and have their voice heard.

In a "pure" P2P harvesting system (Ahlborn, Nejdl, & Sierski, 2002), there is no separation at all between service and data providers: each peer maintains two separate subsystems for metadata storage and query handling. Of course, hybrid approaches are also possible: even P2P networks may require additional service providers that replicate metadata, greatly enhancing the system's overall performance and reliability.

Finally, the underlying technical platform is not neutral with respect to *intellectual property rights* (IPR). The protection of intellectual property was introduced a long time ago before any computer or even electrical device was invented: IPR are rights granted to persons and aimed at protecting their intellectual creations, whether technical, scientific, or artistic. Copyright grants to the author of such material a right to control the exploitation of his/her work, including the right to allow/disallow reproduction and any other form of public communication; therefore, it is a central entity in any knowledge exchange infrastructure. A key requirement for any platform is supporting some form of digital right management (DRM), avoiding unauthorized use of protected multimedia contents while supporting integration and use of open objects.

While some "open" objects may well (and usually do) adopt their own access policy; for example, one imposing some limits to commercial secondary uses of their content, the DRM approach appears to be in conflict with the "open content" features, as summarized in the following section. However, creative exploitation of such technologies cannot be completely ruled out, in principle. As Weber noticed, the open source movement's distinguishing characteristic is its concept of intellectual property, which is centered on "the right to distribute, not the right to exclude." (Baker, 2005)

The European Union's 2001 Directive on Copyright in the Information Society has tried to provide a list of exceptions to IPR protection that member states are expected to uphold. Among the list of exceptions, some look relevant to creative cooperation and learning. Two major exceptions are *illustration for teaching* and *library privileges*. The former exception wording allows free use of copyrighted material for (noncommercial) teaching purposes: however, in some countries, it applies to the material's reproduction in the classroom and not to its communication to the public, which means that free teaching use of IPR-protected material on open e-learning platforms might be challenged by owners.

Integration and Decentralization of Repositories through Interoperability

In a technical sense, *open* means, first of all, *interoperable*. Interoperability is the common ground to develop open architectures, fostering integration and decentralization both of research papers and educational materials. In the future, this will include the whole complexity of integration not limited to protocol and standard.

As far as interoperability of the scientific literature archives and data are concerned, there will be considerations of the possibility of multiple choices and options, from simple adoption of OAI-PMH protocol and metadata indexing to ontology driven integration and to content publishers (digital asset management systems, portals, content management systems, and unstructured data-handling solutions).

In the educational context, the adoption of Internet technology as a support to education has also resulted in an abundance of Web-ready learning resources, often learning objects (LO), containing lessons as text form, audio-visual, or interactive applications (IMS Technical Board, 2003). Yet, despite their apparent ubiquity, locating and reusing LOs is hampered by a lack of coordinated effort in addressing issues related to their storage, cataloguing, and rights management, although large efforts have been made to create portal repositories by communities such as Merlot.

A variety of repositories is inevitable, being the reflection of different organizational needs, so probably attention should be addressed to interoperability of such networks.

The e-learning community has seen fruitful initiatives in the standardization of learning object metadata by IEEE and the emergence of specifications towards the standardization of other aspects of learning objects and learning processes by organizations such as IMS and ADL. More recently, the e-learning community has been focusing on the ability to connect and use resources located in distributed and heterogeneous repositories. This process closely resembles the initiatives in the domain of digital libraries, to the extent that there are initiatives such as the recent Alt-i Lab meeting at MIT to bring these two communities together (Hatala, Richards, Eap, Willms, 2004).

Interoperability allows for decentralized architectures to be established, especially peer-to-peer (P2P) networks to grow, thus allowing for network usage optimization by distributing loads throughout the community of network users and thereby avoiding bottlenecks. This will allow researchers and academics to be able to exchange extremely large files that would not otherwise have been transferable. Additionally, while most centralized, non-P2P systems are limited by their rigidity, the user-centered-approached P2P architecture is one that will maximize the users ability to control the sharing, downloading, and organizing of digital media while providing direct collaborative tools for individuals, departments, and organizations.

Many instructors, scholars, researchers, and librarians across higher education institutions have "hidden" repositories of digital content (images, audio, video, research papers, learning resources, learning activities, etc.) used for teaching, research, and outreach, stored on their networks or even individual hard drives. This content is "hidden" in the sense that other potential users at their own and other institutions have no way to discover these resources. In short, there is a distribution problem for the digital content. A peer-to-peer distribution network would solve this problem via a federated search and retrieve strategy that allows a single search query to reach all available repositories.

The convenience of small-scale open access archives has been explored, and the evolving structure of distributed repositories and independent services, as sources for automated data search and aggregation, has been vastly considered by the Open Access Initiative (OAI) since 1999. The OAI has been a first step for developing the architecture of information and knowledge sharing, distinguishing data providers and service providers on the net. The OAI-PMH (protocol metadata harvesting) represents the core requirement for interoperability and the unifying link between the two communities.

No simple solutions are available, and there are many factors to be taken into account for new scholarly communication using OAI-PMH. Ultimately, the opportunities and risks of the OAI Initiative, the good balance between commercial service providers and cultural institutions, content providers and their different points of view, should be better analyzed and determined to build an efficient way of academic publishing.

Currently, the OAI is representing a revolutionary threat for the conventional academic world. In this regard, an interesting example is evidenced by an English project (Jeffery, 2005). Linking CRISs (current research information systems) database and OA (open access) systems brings together systems for managing research and development (R&D) in universities with systems for providing open access to scholarly publishing. The major visible outputs of R&D and scientific publications are using the emerging European GRIDs infrastructure.

The debate over OAI is very active, with the components "green" (institutional and thematic repository for self-archiving) and "gold" (author/institution pays publishing at publishers' server) as competing, but also complementary processes. The project gives evidence that the scientific process can be treated as a workflow, with recording of outputs at various stages, from initial research ideas to project proposals to interim reports and final publications, along with the produced data, software, and cross-references to other works. The knowledge base considered by the project consists not only of the white literature (publications which have had a formal publication process), but also the "iceberg" of gray literature, encapsulating the know-how of the organization in technical reports, instruction manuals, training materials, and so forth. Furthermore, increasingly, the information process and the knowledge base rests in datasets (e.g., results of drug clinical tests), in databases (e.g., customer relationship information) and in software (which encapsulates much of the business processes of the organization).

The consequences and the impact of interoperable repositories and common access services could be very important for a change in scholarly communication. For example, research quality could be measured not only as publications produced and by other bibliometric indicators. The project CRISs provides both a context for evaluation of, and understanding the background to scholarly publication. CRISs also provides a management framework for R&D in academic institutions from funding agencies through national laboratories to universities, as well as a mechanism for interoperating research and development information.

Open Content for Creating and Reusing Knowledge

While the crisis of access to digital content and the difficulties associated with rights management are some of the most pressing issues in cyberspace today, the open content appears as a new, although still somewhat fuzzy, concept coming to the rescue by prompting the search for peculiar balances between the need for access vs. control. Generally speaking, the open content would allow copying of content without restrictions, provided that authorship is acknowledged; in some way, authors might provide for content modification as well. The public domain should be included as a special open content case.

For this vision of worldwide access to information to become a reality, knowledge must be created, organized, and stored in formats and architectures accessible to everyone (Mason, 2005). The author proposes a conceptual framework for thinking about knowledge management in the context of digital libraries that may serve multiple cultures. The framework is grounded in the context of boundary spanning, a concept that acknowledges the need for mechanisms for communication across the boundaries between domains of knowledge and experience.

Digital libraries are trying to identify barriers and obstacles to knowledge sharing, while paying attention to preservation issues, highlighting possible mixed business solutions involving open content creation, also recognizing success factors for using and reusing open contents besides the target community, and looking for agreements with common quality criteria and definitions of rules involved for creating collaboration frameworks.

In the framework of digital libraries, knowledge creation and reusing of content have three main types: community-centered, product-centered, and systems-centered.

- **Community centered:** Rather than focusing solely on the individual user who interacts with open content, digital libraries consider the group, organization, and community activities and concerns which give rise to information-related behavior. There is evidence of more convergence of information and communication technologies, blurring the lines between tasks and activities and between knowledge creation, e-learning and digital content. This trend extends not only to commercial content, but also into the open content of cultural heritage institutions wishing to benefit from digital content, in such scenarios as e-learning, e-government, cultural tourism.

  For Nancy van House, digital libraries should support the cognitive work, bringing to creation a new knowledge and facilitating learning. Cognitive work is characterized by three elements:

- It is situated in a cultural context
- It is distributed
- It is a social work

Among others, Wenger (Wenger, 1998) spoke about the theory of community of practice and community of interest aimed at knowledge work in a particular context.

- **Product centered:** Digital collections, open digital content, the Web, e-commerce developments, together with DRM systems or other suitable legal framework, combine to create myriad opportunities for repurposing content into diverse distribution channels, to maximize revenue for service providers, but also for reusing content for learning and teaching purposes. This theme focuses on digital document granularity and format, including metadata, bibliographic control, and semantic indexing.

  According to Lynch (Lynch, 2000), enabling the identification of digital works is not the only purpose of bibliographic control, but it is certainly one of the most important and most widely relied-upon aspects. But the practices of information finding are changing in a world of digital information and computer-based search systems. The real revolution in access is going to be driven by the availability of massive amounts of content directly in digital form rather than print, and by the emergence of network-based computer systems that provide an environment not just for identifying content (which historically existed in print form and was used offline, independent of systems like online catalogs), but for its subsequent actual use and analysis within the access system.

- **Systems centered:** open culture expands the interest of digital repositories in information storage and retrieval to include preceding and succeeding phases, incorporating the processes of creating, using, and disposing of information. The trend toward knowledge management as an overarching learning architecture philosophy and methodology is evidenced in the myriads of technological artifacts, such as digital repositories and learning content management systems (LCMSs), which have emerged to capture, categorize, and manage digital instructional content or learning objects.

  Diaz V. and McGee P (Diaz & McGee, 2005) identify the need to examine existing knowledge management models from a planning and decision-making perspective. They discuss four current models of knowledge management found in higher education:

  - The *traditional model* they call "pre-digital," which is teacher-centered and based on textbooks.
  - The *intellectual capital/appropriative model*, called "intellectual capital," characterized by education as a market product or process and by the

diversity of students, and where the intellectual property rights govern the systems (using learning management systems as WebCT, etc.).

- The *sharing/reciprocal model*, where the prevailing organizational form is that of a consortia of educational institutions, controlling intellectual property rights with licenses like Creative Commons[3], and based on networked directories of learning objects and institutional repositories distributed worldwide like DSpace (see next section).
- The *contribution/pedagogy model*, based on the requirement of a learning community sharing its knowledge, that is, moving on from the transmission to the cooperative creation of knowledge, for example, with tools as Wiki, OSCAR, and so forth.

They propose a new, relativist model of knowledge management that accommodates cross-institutional cultures and beliefs about learning technologies, construction of knowledge across systems and institutions, and the trend toward learner-centered environments, disaggregated and re-aggregated learning objects, and negotiated intellectual property rights. Further, they examine and showcase institutional instances of various knowledge management models, and propose the open knowledge model, developed to address learner-centered environments.

Quality of Knowledge Exchanges

Just because the quantity of educational and research materials increase does not mean its average quality rises.

Quality is a slippery concept, depending on the stage of the lifecycle of a given resource, that is, factors that affect on quality when producing the resource (pedagogical/technical/semantical), when it is put in a repository and meta-tagged (interoperability standards), when it is retrieved from the repository (rating by other users/peers/experts) and when it is actually used in a learning context.

We can say that quality is, to a certain degree, subjective, and has to be negotiated between stakeholders/user groups at each step. Therefore, validating educational content on the Web may be tricky, since a lot of the material is culturally biased, and also might need to be related to a national curriculum to be able to be validated for a national agenda, for instance. So validation should be done within each user community using either professionals/experts or peers to review the content, having recourse to structured user feedback from people who have used the content in their teaching. This is, for example, done in the Merlot repository (R. Vuorikari, personal communication).

Add to this the low diffusion of the open content ideas, it is easy to understand how difficult, at the present stage, to determine how quality of open content production can be maintained, and which conditions should be matched so as to let it rise.

One possible way to explore is the peer-to-peer technology endowed with authentication capability, like the LionShare project, providing access to both centralized databases of academic institutions and groups, and users' personal files, with only one search query. LionShare includes a permanent storage space for selected personal files to be shared even when the user is not logged on, increasing accessibility and convenience (LionShare, 2006).

In the following, the general issues pertaining to quality of resources are outlined.

Of particular relevance to the quality issue is to start with the distinction between an objectivist perspective, in which knowledge is considered as an "object" existing in a number of forms and locations, and a practice-based perspective in which knowledge is considered not to exist independent of human experience and social practice (Hislop, 2005).

Pedler (1991) considers the learning organization a vision of what might be possible, but he lists some unavoidable conditions: "...It's not brought about simply by training individuals; it can only happen as a result of learning at whole organization level. A Learning Organization is an organization that facilitates the learning of all its members and continuously transforms itself."

Conversely, this vision can be contrasted with more bottom-up or democratic approaches such as that adopted by Watkins and Marsick (1992) and Senge (1990); according to them, the pillar of a learning organization is team work: an organization can grow only if there is a sharing of ideas, opinions, and abilities among the staff: "Learning Organizations are characterized by total employee involvement in a process of a collaboratively conducted, collectively accountable, change directed towards shared values or principles."

Reviewing the literature, what is apparent is that there is general agreement that the primary objectives of knowledge management (KM) are to identify and leverage the collective knowledge in an organization to achieve the overriding goal of helping organizations compete and survive (Choo, 1996).

Kakabadse, Kakabadse and Kouzmin, (2003) say that there are as many KM models as there are practitioners and theorists alike, and they distinguish among different models, that is, the philosophy-based model of KM, the cognitive model of KM, the network model of KM, the community of practice model of KM. The philosophical model is concerned with the epistemology of knowledge or what constitutes knowledge. It is based on the Socratic definition of knowledge and a search for the highest knowledge—wisdom; this model holds that KM needs not to be technology intensive and should not be technology driven, rather, it is actor intensive and actor centered.

The cognitive model is deeply embedded in positivistic science, and for this model of KM, knowledge is an asset. The organizational focus is to ensure the efficient exploitation of the technology, which is achieved by making explicit the rules, procedures, and processes surrounding its use.

The networking perspectives of KM emerge parallel with the theories of the network organization and focus on acquisition, sharing, and knowledge transfers. This perspective acknowledges that individuals have social as well as economic motives, and that their actions are influenced by networks of relationships in which they are embedded. The term "community of practice" was coined by Lave (1991), and this model is widely distributed and can be found at work, at home, or amongst recreational activities (Kakabadse et al., 2003).

The starting point is the processes of codifying relevant knowledge, converting tacit to explicit knowledge. The next stage in the KM process involves collecting all the codified knowledge together into a central repository, and then structuring it in a systematic way. Finally, technology plays a key role in knowledge management processes utilizing the objectivist perspective.

On the other hand, one of the central components of the practice-based perspective on knowledge management is that it eschews the idea that it is possible for organizations to collect knowledge together into a central repository (Hislop, 2005). From this perspective, the sharing of knowledge does not involve the simple transferal of a fixed entity between two people. Instead, the sharing of knowledge involves two people actively inferring and constructing meaning. The perspective-making and the perspective-taking processes typically require an extensive amount of social interaction and face-to-face communication, which is a conclusion reached by a number of empirical studies (Hislop, 2005).

In a knowledge-based society, the organization of research and education systems must have the ability to contribute with quality-based contents and services in accordance with changes in the world of work and society. Specific emphasis is:

- On the development of an internal quality culture, strengthening institutional and community (as peer review) quality evaluation together with external evaluation processes
- How to agree with common quality criteria and definition of roles involved for creating open collaboration framework (for example for e-learning, scholarly communication, etc.)

This work is based on the evidence that knowledge is culturally derived, acquired, and applied, and that learning—the acquisition of new knowledge—is enabled by skills that are culturally dependent. These cultural bases (Mason, 2005) for knowledge creation and absorption mean that knowledge management systems, especially those supporting digital libraries, must take culture into consideration in their design and implementation if they are to realize their potential for providing access to the widest range of knowledge.

Mason proposes a conceptual framework for thinking about knowledge management in the context of digital libraries, which may serve multiple cultures. The framework is grounded in the context of boundary spanning, a concept that acknowledges the need for mechanisms for communication across the boundaries between domains of knowledge and experience. The relationship between culture and learning (the acquisition of new knowledge) suggests that knowledge management techniques that are appropriate in one culture may not be effective for digital libraries that seek to serve multiple cultures.

Boundary spanning has been recognized as a necessary component in processes that require coordination and translations among diverse groups (Star & Greisemer, 1989) and different functional groups or 'thought worlds' (Dougherty, 1992). Individuals within communities of practice (CoPs) share similar experiences, a similar language, similar ways of learning, and similar values. We might extend the CoP concept to virtual communities' individuals linked through information and communications technologies, and refer to these communities as "networks of practice" or NoPs (Brown, 2001).

Finally, an important role in quality assurance is provided by software environments suitable to be heavily customized and improved according to community needs, and to be adapted to the hardware devices of the future, thus giving users a sense of ownership and empowering them to take care of their tools.

Open technologies can fully meet such requirements, and there are currently a number of solid open source projects aiming to exploit this potential. Among others: Zope/Plone[4], Cocoon/Lenya[5], OpenACS[6]. In the appendix, interesting real life implementations of Plone in education will be described.

A Case Study

The much broader involvement of a very large number of individuals and organizations who can now participate in collective thinking and brainstorming, and the very construction, as well as continuous improvement of new intellectual products, allowed by the described technologies, are especially affecting cross-disciplinary research.

The open source and open access approaches suggest that higher and quicker results can be reached when an enhanced, trusted relationship can be established, thus allowing for institutional borders to be lowered a bit, and encouraging contributions by scholars outside the acknowledged group. While this potentiality has always been realized to some limited degree, especially within the scientific communication, for diffusing theoretical concepts and ideas, only with the development of the ICT has this approach a truly realistic and widespread opportunity.

As in the open source software case, exploiting such a possibility is not straightforward and cannot be taken for granted. Conditions have to be met, including 1) Proposers of an exciting scientific project have to be well involved in that field; 2) they have to be able to explain their newly acquired knowledge clearly, both to colleagues and to people involved in very distant fields; 3) they have to have the ability to leverage and coordinate contributions from different scientists and scholars for the progress of the actual study.

An example in which the open culture approach proved to be effective, and attitude changes helping the interconnections were evident, comes from interdisciplinary scientific modeling studies: Toxicological risk assessment of poly-aromatic hydrocarbons, using computational molecular shape analysis and plant grows monitoring (Mallakin, Mezey, Zimpe, Berenhaut, Greenberg, & Dixon, 2005).

This study, involving plant-biologists, chemists, toxicologists, physicists, and computer scientists, is truly interdisciplinary, where the open culture elements are evident.

As witnessed by one of the authors (Paul G. Mezey), by breaking down barriers between different fields and bridging the differences in the focal points of result analysis and interpretation, not only the overall goals of the actual project have been met, but a mutually beneficial attitude change also has occurred that has broadened the perspectives, and also the scientific efficiency, of all participants of the project. Not only the perspectives of the participants have broadened, but actual methodologies have been adopted in fields where they have not been used before, and methodologies tested and well established in one field have become accepted tools in a much broader area of science. Furthermore, this example also has indicated that broader society issues, such as fighting pollution in the environment, can also benefit when a cross-disciplinary, open culture approach is applied in science.

Conclusion

In this chapter, the issues of sharing and reuse of knowledge in digital format have been framed within some contemporary theoretical models centered on interoperability and emerging technological platforms. In so doing, we outlined how future interdisciplinary research and knowledge-sharing environments will have to take into account some key elements of the open culture.

Acknowledgments

The authors would like to thank Richard G. Baraniuk, Brent Hendricks, Michael Piotrowski, Mario Amelung, Dietmar Rösner, John Dehlin and David Ray for their invaluable contributions to this chapter.

References

Ahlborn, B., Nejdl, W., & Siberski, W. (2002). OAI-P2P: A peer-to-peer network for open archives. In *Proceedings of the IEEE International Conference on Parallel Processing Workshops*.

Baker, E. (2005) Open source, open market for ideas. *CIO Insight*. Retrieved November 3, 2006 from http://www.cioinsight.com/article2/0,1540,1837245,00.asp

Barron, J. (2000) Something for nothing. Interview with Eric von Hippel and Karim Lakhani. *CIO magazine*. Retrieved November 3, 2006, from http://www.cio.com/archive/101500/something.html

Brown, J. S., (2001). Knowledge and organization: A social-practice perspective. *Organization Science*, *12*, 198-213.

Chirita, P. A., Damian, A., Nejdl, W., & Siberski, W. (2005, November). *Search strategies for scientific collaboration networks*. Workshop on Information Retrieval in Peer-to-Peer-Networks, ACM Fourteenth Conference on Information and Knowledge Management (CIKM 2005).

Choo, C. (1996). The knowing organization: How organizations use information to construct meaning, create knowledge and make decisions. *International Journal of Information Management*, *16*(5).

Collier, G. Lefrere, P., Mason, J., Norris, D., & Robson, R. (2003). Share and share alike: The e-knowledge transformation comes to campus. In *Proceedings of the National Learning Infrastructure Initiative Conference*, 2003. Retrieved from http://www.scup.org/eknowledge/case_studies/ShareandShareAlike.pdf

Diaz, V., & McGee, P. (2005). Developing functional policies for learning object initiatives. Planning for higher education and distributed learning objects: An open knowledge management model. In A. Metcalfe (Ed.), *Knowledge management and higher education: A critical analysis*. Hershey, PA: Idea Group Inc.

Dougherty, D. (1992). Interpretive barriers to successful product innovation in large firms. *Organization Science*, *3*, 179-202.

Hatala, M., Richards, G., Eap, T., & Willms, J. (2004, May 17-22). The interoperability of learning object repositories and services: Standards, implementations and lessons learned. In *Proceedings of the Conference WWW2004*. Retrieved from http://www.www2004.org/proceedings/docs/2p19.pdf

Hislop, D. (2005). *Knowledge management in organizations: A critical introduction*. Oxford: Oxford University Press.

IMS Technical Board (2003) *Learning design specification*. IMS Global Learning Consortium, Inc. retrieved from http://www.imsglobal.org/learningdesign/ [registration required]

Jeffery, K. G. (2005, August 14-18). *CRIS + open access = The route to research knowledge on the GRID*. Paper presented at the 71th IFLA General Conference and Council "Libraries—A voyage of discovery," Oslo, Norway.

Kakabadse, N. K., Kakabadse, A., & Kouzmin, A. (2003). Reviewing the knowledge management literature: Towards a taxonomy. *Journal of Knowledge Management*, *7*(4), 75-91.

Lessig, L. (2004). *Free culture*. Penguin Press. Retrieved from http://www.free-culture.cc/freeculture.pdf

LionShare (2006). Pennsylvania State University. Retrieved on November 03, 2006 from http://lionshare.its.psu.edu

Liu, X. Maly, K., Zubair, M., & Nelson, M. L. (2001). *ARC: An OAI service provider for cross-archive searching*. ACM/IEEE Joint Conference on Digital Libraries.

Lynch, C. (2000). *The new context for bibliographic control in the new millennium*. Paper presented at the Bibliographic Control for the New Millennium conference, Library of Congress.

Mallakin, A., Mezey, P. G., Zimpel, Z. L, Berenhaut, K. S., Greenberg, B. M., & Dixon, D. G. (2005). Quantitative structure-activity relationship to model the photoinduced toxicity of anthracene and oxygenated anthracenes, *QSAR & combinatorial science*. In press (34 ms pages, accepted 2005 Feb.19). Published online June 1, 2005.

Mason, R. M. (2005, August 14-18). *The critical role of librarian/information officer as boundary spanner across cultures. Humans as essential components in global digital libraries*. Paper presented at the 71th IFLA General Conference and Council "Libraries—A voyage of discovery," Oslo, Norway.

Mezey, P. G. (2004). Open source: The goals, the tools, and the culture. In *Open Source Contents Workshop, Didamatica 2004 Conference*, Ferrara University, Ferrara, Italy, 2004 May 10-12.

Nejdl, W., Siberski, W., & Sintek, M. (2003). Design issues and challenges for RDF- and schema-based peer-to-peer systems. *SIGMOD Record*, September.

Nejdl, W., Wolf, B., Staab, S., & Tane, J. (2002), *EDUTELLA: Searching and annotating resources within an RDF-based P2P network*. International Workshop on the Semantic Web, WWW2002.

Pedler, M. (Ed). (1991). *Action learning in practice*. Gower Publishing.

Popper, K. R (1996). *The open society and its enemies* (5th ed.). London: Routledge and Kegan Paul.

Robinson, L., & Bawden, D. (2001). Libraries and open society: Popper, Soros and digital information. *Aslib Proceedings*, *53*(5), 167-178.

Senge, P. (1990). *The fifth discipline: The art and practice of the learning*. London: Random House.

Star, S. L., & Greisemer, J. R. (1989). Institutional ecology, translations and boundary objects: Amateurs and professionals in Berkeley's Museum of Vertebrate Zoology, 1907-39. *Social Studies in Science*, *19*, 387-420.

Stuckenschmidt, H., Siberski, W., & Nejdl, W. (2005) Combining ontologies and peer-to-peer technologies for interorganizational knowledge management. *The Learning Organization*, *12*(5)

Van House, N., (2003). In Bishop, Van House, & Buttenfield (Eds.), *Digital library use: Social practice in design and evaluation*. Cambridge, MA; London: MIT Press.

Watkins, & Marsick. (1992). Building the learning organization: A new role for human resource developers? *Studies in Continuing Education*, *14*(2), 115-29.

Wenger, E. (1998). *Communities of practice: Learning, meaning and identity*. Cambridge: Cambridge University Press.

Endnotes

1 The Conference held from June 27-29, 2005 in Milan University has been the first opportunity, to the authors' knowledge, for such diverse communities to meet. Proceedings of the Conference Open Culture—Accessing and sharing knowledge, June 2005, Antonella De Robbio and Valentina Comba, Anna Maria Tammaro, Paolo Pumilia, and Luigi Colazzo (Eds.), are also available on the Web as Open Archive: http://openculture.org/milan-2005. Further info about the Open Culture Committee initiatives can be found at the Website http://eexplor.org.

2 A thoughtful description of the impending risks over the open knowledge flowing in the digital era can be found in The Second Enclosure movement and the Construction of the Public Domain, by James Boyle, published in

the Law & Contemporary Problems Journal, vol. 66, 2003, Duke Univ. The author is hoping specialized organizations will rise, aimed at investigating and divulging the emergent concept of public domain in our time. The paper can be read at http://www.law.duke.edu/journals/66LCPBoyle or downloaded at http://www.law.duke.edu/pd/papers/boyle.pdf

[3] Creative Commons is a nonprofit organization that offers flexible copyright licenses for creative works, http://creativecommons.org/ .

[4] Zope/Plone—Zope is an application server for building content management systems, http://zope.org/. Plone is a Zope-based, technology-neutral content management system; it can interoperate with most relational database systems, open source and commercial, and runs on a vast array of platforms, http://plone.org/

[5] Apache/Cocoon is a Java/XML-based server-side application development framework, http://cocoon.apache.org/; Lenya is a content management system, incubating Cocoon subproject, http://lenya.apache.org

[6] OpenACS (Open Architecture Community System) is a toolkit for building scalable, community-oriented Web applications, http://www.openacs.org; it includes .LRN (http://dotlrn.org) Originally developed at MIT, it is used in higher education, government, nonprofit, and K-12.

Appendix: Zope/Plone in Education

Rhaptos: The Plone-Based Authoring and Publishing System Supporting Connexions

Richard G. Baraniuk and Brent Hendricks—Rice University

Rhaptos: (adj) - stitched or sewn together (Ancient Greek)

Rhaptos is a collaborative authoring and publishing system built by Connexions (cnx.org) for open educational resources. It is based on the Plone open-source content management system, and is available from rhaptos.org. Rhaptos supports three types of users:

- **Authors:** collaborate to write content in bite-sized chunks called *modules*.
- **Instructors:** arrange and re-contextualize modules into sequences called *courses*. (Think of them as online books.)
- **Learners:** read and discuss content.

To date, the following features have been implemented in Rhaptos:

- **Work areas:** Rhaptos features private workspaces, as well as shared, collaborative areas called *workgroups*. Content in a work area is not publicly visible until it is published in the repository.
- **Modules:** Modules are the basic building block on content in the Rhaptos system. Each module maps to a single Web page, but may also be viewed as a PDF. Modules have metadata like keywords and an abstract, may have multiple authors, and a set of supplementary links. Modules are written in CNXML (the Connexions XML language), but users can import content from a variety of sources, including Microsoft Word and Open Office files.
- **Courses:** A course is a collection of related modules; think of a course as an online textbook. Courses allow instructors to provide custom titles, annotations, supplementary links, and even mathematical notation for modules viewed in the context of the course. The same module may be customized in completely different ways in different courses.
- **Repository:** All content is stored under version control in the Rhaptos content repository. This allows earlier versions to be viewed and compared at any time. The repository can be browsed via the Web by title, author, keyword, or popularity. It can also be queried using the Open Archives Initiative protocol or the OpenSearch protocol.
- **Collaboration:** There are many ways authors can collaborate with Rhaptos, including co-authorship, adding additional maintainers, adding content to a collaborative workgroup, suggesting changes to an author, and deriving a new copy of existing content.

Rhaptos is designed to be scalable to large numbers of users. In February 2006, for example, the Rhaptos server at cnx.org handled over 16 million hits representing 1.1 million page views from 520,000 unique visitors.

Plone Education Case Study: Plone, eduCommons, and OpenCourseWare

John Dehlin and David Ray—Utah State University Center for Open and Sustainable Learning (COSL)

In 2001, the Massachusetts Institute of Technology (located in Cambridge, MA, USA) launched the OpenCourseWare (OCW) initiative. The goal of MIT OCW is to use the Internet to freely share the materials used in all MIT courses. MIT realized that a content management system would be needed to handle the workflow for all of its content, and for several reasons chose to customize and use Microsoft Content Management Server.

In early 2004, the William and Flora Hewlett Foundation awarded a grant to the Center for Open and Sustainable Learning (COSL) at Utah State University to create an open source alternative to the proprietary system developed at MIT, with the goal of making OCW projects affordable by any organization.

During the planning phase, Brent Lambert, Chief Technical Architect at COSL, made the decision to build upon an existing open source content management system. After evaluating several options, he settled on Plone:

Plone became our platform of choice for a number of reasons. First of which is the ease of use of the development tools. All of our projects based on Zope and Plone were alive and useful from the day we started, because we were able to quickly prototype functionality directly through use of a web environment. Expanding these prototypes into a source code base was made much more simple by the fact that we were able to take advantage of Python as the underlying programming language. Third, we have been continually able to take advantage of the fast moving development pace of the Plone community. Our releases have many additional features, which we have been able to incorporate without having to put in long hard hours of development time. Due to the community's hard work, we are able to develop software much more quickly, with the result of being able to better serve those wanting to both gain and provide access to freely available high quality educational materials. The fact that Plone is so closely aligned to what our project does and needs to do makes it an excellent development platform.

In January of 2005, eduCommons 1.0, a full service OpenCourseWare management system, was released, followed immediately with its first live deployment—Utah State University's OpenCourseWare (http://ocw.usu.edu).

Marion Jenson, the Director of USU OCW, has nothing but praise for both Plone and eduCommons:

We have found that Plone and eduCommons allow for the flexibility to do just what we need it to do. Almost without fail, when we've asked if Plone or eduCommons can do X, the answer has been yes. Stability has never been an issue, and the system is intuitive such so that our students can quickly learn how to build our OCW courses. Plone and eduCommons are exactly what we've needed to establish and grow USU OCW.

Several other universities worldwide have chosen eduCommons as their OpenCourseWare management system, including the University of Notre Dame, the University of Michigan, and the University of Kyoto. eduCommons is also in pilot at several other universities around the world.

To learn more about eduCommons, go to: **http://cosl.usu.edu/projects/educommons/**

EduComponents: Educational Components for Plone

Michael Piotrowski, Mario Amelung and Dietmar Rösner—Otto-von-Guericke-Universität, Magdeburg

Despite the advances in information technology and the spread of e-learning, many, if not most, face-to-face courses at universities are still organized in traditional ways. For example, in the exercise courses accompanying our lectures, the students had to bring their solutions on paper to the course and present them on the blackboard. This offered only relatively little motivation for students and permitted only restricted conclusions about the students' performance during the course, whereas the administration of the courses required a lot of work.

To make our courses more efficient, and also more effective, we decided to develop modules for the Plone (http://plone.org/) open-source content management system (CMS) to support the management of tests and assignments.

We selected Plone for several reasons. First, we were already successfully using it for our Web site, which includes online course material for the courses offered by our research group. Plone components would therefore fit seamlessly into this framework. Second, Plone is extensible through so-called products. Products can add new types of content objects to the CMS. They share the same look and feel, and they can leverage the facilities provided by the CMS framework, for example, user management, access control, and data storage. Custom content types also automatically benefit from Plone features like timed publication, metadata, or indexing and retrieval. Third, building on portable open-source software avoids license fees and vendor lock-in, and offers benefits like complete control over the software and the data, the possibility of adapting it to one's specific needs, and benefits from a large developer community.

Based on our experience gathered with previous partial implementations, we have, up till now, designed, implemented, and deployed EduComponents, a suite of educational extension modules for Plone. The main goal of these components is to reduce the workload of teachers and to improve the effectiveness of face-to-face courses. EduComponents currently consists of four products: ECLecture for managing lectures, seminars, and other courses, LlsMultipleChoice for the creation and delivery of multiple-choice tests, ECAssignmentBox for the creation, submission, and grading of online assignments, and ECAutoAssessmentBox, a variant of ECAssignmentBox, providing special support for automatic evaluation of student submissions, for example, for programming assignments.

We have been using online multiple-choice tests and automatic testing of programs since winter semester 2003/2004 in various courses offered by our research group. Since winter semester 2005/2006, students are required to submit their assignments through ECAssignmentBox. At the end of the semester, we asked our students to complete a questionnaire on their experience with the new system. The results were very positive and provide evidence that our approach makes sense. Students especially valued the reporting and statistics features, which help them to track their learning progress, resulting in better motivation. Furthermore, students find it helpful that their assignments are stored centrally, and can be quickly accessed for discussion during the course session. They also reported that they worked more diligently on their assignments because, unlike before, the teachers can now access and review all assignments. Teachers report that they have a much better overview of students and assignments, helping them to improve their teaching.

The implementation as Plone products has proven to be a good decision: The EduComponents can be mixed and matched with other Plone products (e.g., for bibliographies or audio data) to create flexible learning environments, while at the same time Plone ensures a uniform look and feel. The CMS also serves as item bank, a central repository of tests and assignment, enabling the reuse of teaching and learning materials. In the long run, when the repository of learning materials is large enough, it might even be conceivable to create personalized tests and assignments based on the metadata stored with the objects.

EduComponents is licensed under the GPL and freely available from our Web site: **http://wwwai.cs.uni-magdeburg.de/software**

Chapter VIII

European National Educational School Authorities' Actions Regarding Open Content and Open Source Software in Education

Riina Vuorikari, European Schoolnet (EUN), Belgium
Karl Sarnow, European Schoolnet (EUN), Belgium

Abstract

This chapter provides an overview into policies in the area of e-learning that ten European countries, all members of European Schoolnet, have taken regarding open content and free and open source software (FOSS) to be used to support and enhance learning. Additionally, it elaborates on European Schoolnet's initiatives to support open learning resources exchange in Europe. European Schoolnet (EUN) promotes the use of information and communication technologies (ICT) in European schools, acting as a gateway to national and regional educational authorities and school networks towards Europe. A variety of actions have been initiated by a number of European educational authorities from analysis and feasibility studies to the development of educational software based on open source as well as open educational content.

Introduction

European Schoolnet is a network of 27 national educational authorities in Europe in the area of compulsory education (K-12). European Schoolnet provides insight into the educational use of information and communications technologies (ICT) in European schools for policy-makers and education professionals. This goal is achieved through communication and information exchange at all levels of school education using innovative technologies, and by acting as a gateway to national and regional school networks.

In recent years, European Schoolnet and a number its members have, little by little, begun a trend towards awareness building, piloting, development, and the rolling-out of open source software programs for schools, as well as investigating open content as a possible addition to a more conventional content provision.

This chapter introduces some of these policy-level actions; however, it cannot be regarded as an exhaustive summary of policy initiatives in the field of ICT and education. There are two main focuses for the chapter, the policy initiatives and EUN initiatives.

First, the chapter introduces a number of emerging initiatives lead by ten EUN member countries in the area of open source and content for education. Initiatives are categorized in four main sections: awareness raising of Free Open Source Software (FOSS), development of LMS and learning platforms, promotion of the use of Linux on desktops and educational servers, and finally, the promotion of open content. The following countries are featured: Estonia, Spain, and Slovenia as an example of countries basing part of their policy initiatives and actions on open source development; Belgium's Flemish Community and the Netherlands, which run major campaigns to raise awareness of the FOSS issues; Ireland and Finland, as well as France, with smaller scale policy initiatives to familiarize schools with alternative solutions; and finally the UK and Lithuania carrying out feasibility studies with FOSS.

The second part presents two European Schoolnet's recent initiatives in this regard: Xplora, which promotes science education in Europe, and secondly, the EUN's Learning Resources Exchange, which promotes the use and reuse of educational content across Europe. The latter introduces the implementation of a digital rights management framework and briefs on the current development of a learning toolbox to support collaborative learning based on open source development.

Background

European Schoolnet (EUN) was funded in 1996 with the mandate of the Council of the European Union. The members of European Schoolnet represent national and regional educational authorities such as the Ministry of Education (MoE) or National Board of Education. Its mission is twofold: on the one hand, EUN works closely with national and regional policy-makers and shapers by setting up special interest committees, involving them in transfer of best practices, and in e-learning research and development. On the other hand, EUN works directly with a large network of European schools through special online events organized in collaboration with a variety of stakeholders.

European Schoolnet is committed in following open standards in e-learning research and development that it conducts in the field, partnering up with different stakeholders from public, private, and industry partners. This has resulted in services that allow multiple players' access to the field. Furthermore, the use and development of open source software in education is becoming more of a concern in different EUN member countries, whereas the promotion of interoperable content-based services, such as federations of learning resources repositories, has long been in the centre of EUN's attention. It is important to note that the members of EUN all lead their own policies based on their national policymaking, and that EUN only has an advisory role for its members.

Apart from reporting on European Schoolnet's partners on their national initiatives, this review will also extend to other national policymakers whenever the information was made available. Mostly, this review relies on contributions from European Schoolnet's partners.

EUN's Members Actions in the Quest for Educational Openness in Software and Content

A number of European Schoolnet's partners have explicit roles in promoting the use and development of open source software as an alternative choice for schools. A review on a selection of partners acting upon this challenge is provided in this section presenting the Ministry of the Flemish Community, Education department in Belgium, Kennisnet in the Netherlands, Becta in the UK, Tiger Leap foundation in Estonia, the Ministry of Education and Sport in Slovenia, the National Centre for Technology in Education in Ireland, National Board of Education in Finland, and the Ministry of Education and Science of the Republic of Lithuania. Additionally, some development is reported from Spain and France.

Table 1. Main action areas of a number of EUN member countries in FOSS and open content

Country	Awareness building/FOSS distribution	Feasibility studies	Common development of software	Development of GNU/ Linux	Open content
Flemish Community of Belgium	x				x
Estonia	x		x	x	x
Finland	x				
France	x		x	x	
Ireland	x				
Lithuania		x			
Netherlands	x	x	x		
Slovenia	x		x	x	x
Spain	x			x	x
UK	x	x			

The actions, initiatives, and policies that countries have undertaken in this regard vary throughout Europe. Table 1 presents the main action areas, which can be classified as following; awareness building and distribution of open source software for schools, feasibility studies regarding the deployment of open source software and/or open content, initiatives or pooling resources in the area of software development of learning management systems (LMS) and learning platforms, development or localization of GNU/Linux distributions for schools' use in native languages, and finally, in the area of open content. The list presented in this report does not cover equally all the European countries and is not exhaustive by any means; rather, it serves the purpose to highlight some of the good practices and initiatives.

Estonia: Tiger Leap Foundation (Tiigrihüppe Sihatusutus)

In 2004 in Estonia, the Tiger Leap Foundation (TLF) initiated a project for distribution and promotion of freeware in schools. The project aims at releasing a Linux distribution that is suitable for schools, preparing training materials, and training teachers. Furthermore, since the spring 2005, TLF only supports projects that will be released under general public license for the code; as for the content, a creative commons license will be required.

A number of Estonian educational open source software applications have been developed, with the financial support of TLF in collaboration with Tallinn University (TU). The development of virtual learning environment VIKO started in 2001. Schools do not have to set up their own server, VIKO is offered as a free service by Tallinn University. Furthermore, KooliPlone, a Plone-based content management system for school Web sites is developed in TU.

Another large-scale development of a learning management system, called IVA, was supported by Estonian Ministry of Education and Science, the Estonian Information Technology Foundation, and Hansapank, the largest bank in Estonia. IVA is also developed in TU, based on Zope and an existing educational platform called Fle3. It has Estonian, Russian, and English user interfaces, and is currently used by more than 2,000 users in TU.

Additionally, Estonia being a country representing a small market, the government has funded the translation of OpenOffice's spell-check program in Estonian.

Slovenia: Actions by the Ministry of Education and Sport

Slovenian Ministry of Education and Sport has a focus on three main areas providing basic tools, didactic tools, and promoting open source for teachers, headmasters, and pedagogical specialists.

To the category of providing basic tools, the Ministry includes Linux, OpenOffice.org, CMS, LMS, as well as some distance learning services. First of all, all new computers in schools, which are co-financed by the Ministry of Education and Sport, have a dual boot for Windows and Linux, and have OpenOffice.org installed for both operating systems. The Linux distribution is called Pingo and is provided in Slovene. Pingo has been developed by a local association, called Lugos, with the Fedora Linux 3 open source community in Slovenia. For the last two years, the Ministry of Education and Sport, the Ministry of Information Society and the (governmental) Centre for Informatics have financed the localization in Slovene language. Currently, a tender to co-finance the localization for the next two years is under preparation.

Another example of learning management and learning content management system that is available free of charge for academic institutions is E-CHO, developed by the Faculty of Electrical Engineering, University of Ljubljana. It enables simple course creation, extensive content management, and it supports entire learning process.

Secondly, in the area of basic teacher training, among other ICT skills, the programs include the use of Windows Office as well as OpenOffice.org. The Ministry financed an expert group that supports schools with open source software, such as some CMS and LMS, and support books have been distributed to schools about the use of Linux and OpenOffice.org. Moreover, the Ministry with National Education Institute and

Center for Vocational Training promotes the use of open source software among teachers, headmasters, and didactic specialists.

As for didactic tools and open content, the Ministry finances teacher training in the area of open source didactic materials (i.e., open content). It has also co-financed some new open content didactic material on the Web for the use in classrooms, with some support given for teachers in training to use this material. As well, the Ministry will co-finance, in the future, creation of didactic material that is not open source, but can be used freely by schools.

To promote the use of open source and open content, the Slovenian Ministry of Education and Sports has started the portal OKO. This project is with the intention to make the introduction of open source and free educational software into education environments faster and more efficient. The OKO project was started in 2003.

Spanish Initiatives

Spain has had some regional policy initiatives to promote the use of open source, and especially Linux use, in school servers and desktop. Probably, the region of Extremedura is the best-known large-scale example in Spain, where the local information strategy is based on the use of free and open source software. The local authorities decided to boost development in the region, which is prone to high unemployment, by delivering over 150 000 cd-roms containing a localized Linux distribution, Linex, along with dedicated office software. It has been distributed in different ways. In Extremadura, schools are immersed into using Linux; it has been deployed on around 70,000 desktop PCs and 400 servers in schools. Some other communities in Spain who have decided to do so are at least Andalucia, Madrid, and Valencia. In two of them, the school's workstations are delivered with a dual boot configuration, so that the users have the option to work either on Linux or Windows, and can familiarize themselves with two different operating systems. In the community of Galicia, new computers to schools are delivered with Linux installed.

Belgium: The Ministry of the Flemish Community, Education Department

The Ministry of the Flemish Community, Education Department in Belgium has an explicit role in promoting the use of open source software as an alternative choice for schools. In 2004, the former minister of Education, Ms. Marleen Vanderpoorten, commissioned an advisory on the issue, which led to a vision and a proposed action plan.

In 2005, a large campaign was organized to introduce free and open source software in Flemish schools, aiming to highlight its educational possibilities. In this campaign, a publication, a CD, and an educational tools database were drafted and a conference was organized.

By means of the publication "free software in the education," a practical guide for the use of FOSS and open educational tools is spread amongst all schools. Besides general information on the "what and how" of FOSS, one finds descriptions of a number of interesting open source applications. In association with the educational portal Klascement, an educational tools database was developed for these applications. This is also the general campaign Web site. Moreover, a conference was organized addressing FOSS and open educational tools, targeting audiences such as teachers, headmasters, and ICT co-coordinators.

The Education Department in Flanders has created didactic sheets on the use of educational freeware and open content, based on the primary education curriculum topics. The didactic sheets have been published as a book, "ICT on the menu," and are searchable in a database through the portal. The scenarios are a helpful means to make the ICT integration in primary education more concrete. In 2005, a similar project was developed for secondary education. This time, the work was carried out by teachers from the secondary ENIS schools. The result is a publication, both on paper and online, called "Digital resources for secondary education." In 2006, a CD was published, with open learning tools and open source educational software that is currently under a validation process by the European Network of Innovative Schools (ENIS).

The Netherlands: Open Source and Open Standards in Education (OSS in het onderwijs)

Since 2003 in the Netherlands, the government has brought open standards and open source into the central focus of its attention. A variety of initiatives have been set up to work on cross-sectoral issues that touch upon open standards, as well as open source development. As for the education, there are initiatives, programs, and actions taken to foster the efforts in the field and to muster the common efforts.

The program "OSS in het onderwijs," translated as open source and open standards in education, is a joint initiative between Kennisnet, ICT op School, and a government-wide program called OSSOS, the Program for Open Standards and Open Source Software. Additionally, to involve a diversity of partners in the field of education, an association called EduStandaard has been set up. The association aims to manage the standards that are used in the Dutch educational field, comprising stakeholders such as publishers, schools and so forth.

Kennisnet promotes a program to improve the use of open standards for content. A central point for "OSS in het onderwijs" is a Webspace where the Dutch education community can discuss open source and open standards aiming at both the novices and experts. The main focus is on primary and secondary education, but also on the field of vocational training. The program is informative, aiming at offering alternative solutions for schools that have an independent budget to spend on educational technologies. The program targets mainly the IT coordinators, administrators, and teachers who are responsible for IT set-ups in schools, but also at teachers who use computers and ICTs in their lessons.

One powerful means to transfer good practices and ideas of the use of FOSS in education are the case studies that can be found at the Web site of "OSS in het onderwijs". These case studies are simple descriptive interviews with practitioners on topics such as how to use GIMP for manipulating images, and so forth.

"OSS in het onderwijs" has also prepared an info package, on a CD, that focuses on the use of open standards in all processes in school that can involve the use of information technologies from administrative tasks to using applications for learning purposes, gathering content about the student for portfolios, as well as other actions for creation, exchange, and alteration of the content. The idea was to identify all actions and propose alternatives where closed systems or standards are used. This aims at better overall interoperability within schools' information systems. The CD was released in the end of 2005. In the same spirit, a booklet on open source software was created in 2004 for schools. These information packages can be requested from the Web site, but they are also handed out at local ICT conferences.

The program "OSS in het onderwijs" can help schools to implement open source, not only in advisory terms, but they can make small amounts of money available to pay for a third-party programmer or consultant to, for example, find compatibility solutions between an existing system and the new one based on open source and standards. On the Web site, there is also a FOSS helpline for schools to help them to solve small-scale problems. In this regard, the program tries to match the need that schools have for support with existing supply in the market. On the Web site, one can find an overview of companies with experience of FOSS and education.

"OSS in het onderwijs" has been running for 3 years, 2005 being the final year with a big push, the continuation for the next year is still unsecured. A conference, with 1-day education track on the topics, was held in December 8 2005.

France: Distribution of FOSS

In France, the National Centre of Pedagogical Documentation (SCÉRÉN-CNDP) has led a working group that evaluated some 30 educational open source software packages, with an emphasis on multiplatform usage. The software, and accompanying educational guidelines for its use in the classroom, was made available for schools, in the format of a CD, through a network of regional centers, at minimum charges, in 2004. The CD has had a good success, and its distribution continues.

On the school server level, advances have been made to introduce GNU/Linux for school servers. An initiative, SIIEE (service intranet-internet in educational establishments and schools), has deployed about 15, 000 Linux-based servers throughout the country.

Furthermore, some regional French authorities have also embraced FOSS. For example, the Pays du Soissonnais has declared as its ambition to become an axle of excellence in open source, making it part of its regional policy, grouping a variety of local actors together to find ways to benefit from open source. The Region of Picardie participates in the initiative; already since 2004, each school receives earmarked money to be spent on open source software to buy services or to hire someone to do the work locally. Partially, the idea behind this initiative is to boost local economy (Picardie ranks high for unemployment), but the objective is also to use public money for the public good. Picardie, as a region, also has a high profile on free and open source software, and participates actively in the annual trophy competition for the best educational software.

Finland: Informing about Educational FOSS

In 2006, the National Board of Education in Finland launched an initiative to gather an information package for schools about the use of open source software and content for educational purposes. The aim is to distribute information on how open source software can be used to support educational purposes for creating educational content, as well as for school administrational matters, but also to clarify the basic terminology to be used in the area. The target audience is teachers, the ICT coordinators, and school heads. The information is gathered in collaboration with local experts in the field, as well as practitioners who have been using and adapting FOSS solutions in their schools and educational establishments.

Another type of interesting initiative can be reported from Finland, although it does not directly receive any educational attention. To make open source development rooted into a variety of sectors within society, including education, a sustainable plan for services and support should be in place. The Finnish Centre for Open Source Software (COSS) aims to help its building. COSS started at the beginning of 2004 with basic funding, granted by Finland's Ministry of the Interior, to help to build an ecosystem within business, research, and education. Currently, the Häme Centre of Expertise, as a partner of COSS, is responsible for developing open source based business in the field of e-learning. It could be contemplated that this type of idea and innovation feeding across sectors has a positive value for the uptake of open source software in educational establishments, as they will have local businesses to rely upon for the support, sale, and delivery of these e-learning services.

Ireland: Star Office for all Irish Schools

In late 2004, the National Centre for Technology in Education (NCTE), the Irish Government agency established to provide advice, support, and information on the use of ICT in education, concluded a licensing and distribution agreement with SUN Microsystems to provide all Irish schools with Star Office, an office suite based on open source OpenOffice.org. The offer was made to schools in a joint move by the NCTE and SUN Microsystems.

To help schools appreciate the opportunity and to explore the implications of taking up Star Office, or substituting the commonly used MS, schools were notified and local information sessions were organized for school representatives. These sessions were well attended and, following participation, the take up has been significant to date. Schools receive a free CD that allows unlimited copying for staff and students.

Prior to the large-scale offer of Star Office in 2004, the NCTE carried out a number of evaluations of Star Office in a number of schools in order to assess the appropriateness of this software for schools. The outcome of these trials proved very positive. Star Office was identified as being a relevant and very useful software tool, particularly for schools at primary level.

The UK: Evaluation on Open Source Software in Schools

In May 2005, the British Educational Communications and Technology Agency (Becta), released an evaluation on the use of open source software within a number of schools. In the UK, some previous government studies have suggested that the use of FOSS within the UK public sector can provide a viable and credible alternative to propriety software, and lead to significant cost savings.

The study, funded by the Department for Education and Skills, had three main aims: to examine how well the open source software approach works, compared with proprietary offerings, in supporting delivery of the school curriculum and administration; to compare the total cost of ownership (TCO) of using FOSS within school environments against that of non-open-source solutions; and to highlight examples of successful school-based open source implementations.

The report, "Open Source Software in Schools: A study of the spectrum of use and related ICT infrastructure costs," demonstrates that although the implementation of FOSS in schools needs careful planning and support, it can offer a cost-effective alternative to proprietary software. For the ways forward with FOSS, the report examines cost-effective models of support in OSS schools; best practice in licensing solutions; successful implementation to run the school's servers to provide school-wide facilities, operating systems, and administrative PCs, and FOSS applications on classroom and administrative PCs.

According to Becta's chief executive, Owen Lynch, Becta believes that software used in schools should be of a high quality and adhere to open standards, enabling compatibility and interoperability between products. Becta will now be undertaking more extensive research across a wider range of institutions to allow further analysis of these issues.

Lithuania: Research Study and Recommendations for Actions in Open Source in Education

The Ministry of Education and Science of the Republic of Lithuania commissioned a study in 2004 to further investigate the possibilities of open source software in education in Lithuania. The global fight against the use of illegal software and piracy, and the openness of the source code to guarantee more transparency and ease of localization, were mentioned in the goals of the study as important to go forward with.

The conclusions of the study outlined the following; open source software has an indirect positive impact on the economy of education through the emergence of a competitor to commercial software, forcing a reduction in the price of commercial software and translations into the languages of small nations spoken by few people.

The study furthermore proposed some actions both at the state level and ministerial level. The state level proposal included, among others, the following: it is necessary to ensure the adaptation and localization of general purpose open source software at the state level; it is necessary to take care of the cultural and linguistic quality of open source software; the promotion and support for open source software could help solve the problem of the legality of software.

At the ministerial level of the Ministry of Education and Science, the proposed actions included analyses of localization of educational Linux distributions and open source virtual learning environments to determine which one would be appropriate to be localized and used in Lithuanian schools. As to introducing FOSS in education, the following was proposed: higher schools' training educators should introduce their students to both commercial software and equivalent open source software necessary for teaching and learning; at school, students should be introduced to general purpose software of both types: commercial software necessary for teaching and learning, as well as to equivalent open source software. Furthermore, to assure the quality of localization, an interesting proposal was made: a course on localization of software for some students specializing in information technologies and philology.

European Schoolnet's Projects Dealing with Open Content and Open Source

This section presents the Xplora project, which promotes science education in European schools, and briefly presents the work that EUN carries out in the area of learning resource exchange (LRE), where digital learning resources and/or their metadata are exchanged between educational repositories.

Xplora, Distributing Science for Education in its True Way: Openly

Xplora, the European Science Education Gateway, is operated by European Schoolnet. Xplora portal is supported by the PENCIL project, a project funded by the European Commission's Directorate General for Research as part of Science and Society.

Xplora offers science teachers tools, information, and resources to help them to conduct engaging science lessons that make students attracted to science. Commonly, with 30+ students in classes, science teaching is somewhat blocked by poorly equipped school laboratories. Among the resources that Xplora offers are the usual Web-based tools like online games, downloadable materials, and guides to software that is usable in science lessons.

Xplora portal also offers new tools that have not been used in the classroom before. Among these tools are the Web experiments or remote controlled experiments (RCL), in which real experiments are shared via the Internet. Such experiments do not only solve the problem of the true way of science teaching by experiments, but it also opens new pedagogical concepts for science classes. These Web experiments deliver results that students have to process in order to get a lab report.

Using Software: A Key Skill in Scientific Research

Participating in science education today means extensively using software. For instance, for the Web experiments where, in many cases, students get the result of an experiment as an image, the image analysis is a fundamental task. The main tasks for students in science education are (1) create a lab report with mathematical

Table 2. Open source software with open source-like licenses for use in science teaching

Name of software	URL	Description	Application
OpenOffice.org	http://www.openoffice.org	The Open Source office software for scientific text processing, database applications, graphics creation.	Lab reports. Calculation of results Creation of simple charts
LyX	http://www.lyx.org	Scientific text processor software, making use of LaTeX properties. Full support of mathematical expressions and all Postscript output from scientific programs.	Lab reports with even the equations, and output of all X11.
Xfig	http://xfig.org	Vector drawing program with a large and extendable parts library.	Preparation of schematic drawings (experimental setups) for lab reports.
Grace	http://plasma-gate.weizmann.ac.il/Grace/	Data analysis program	Plots diagrams of every complexity. Good software for creating regression and line fit.
GIMP	http://www.gimp.org	Graphics program to analyze images	Image analysis (length, angle)
ImageJ	http://rsb.info.nih.gov/ij/	Image analysis program	Analysis of intensity distribution in an image.
Xdrawchem	http://xdrawchem.sourceforge.net/	Program to draw chemical structures	Report on chemistry lab exercises.
OpenRasmol	http://www.openrasmol.org/	Program to visualize 3d molecules	Chemistry classroom use and creating images for reports.
Feynman	http://rpmfind.net/linux/RPM/suse/9.0/i386/suse/i586/feynman-1.00-581.i586.html	A program to create Feynman graphs	Particle physics teaching.
Ghemical	http://www.uku.fi/~thassine/ghemical/	A molecular modeling software package	Chemistry teaching in high schools
Gcompris	http://www.ofset.org/gcompris	A software package for the kids	For elementary schools. Many different applications around elementary schools teaching
KDE Edu	http://edu.kde.org/	The KDE Education project	Many educational software packages mainly focusing on lower-level education.

expressions, chemical formulas, Feynman diagrams, images, tables, and graphs; (2) analyze images, for example, measure length, angles, area, and intensity; (3) calculate results, for example, numerical processing, creating graphs, regression, and curve fitting; (4) create animations; (5) run simulations; (6) create and play with mathematical models, and (7) use CAS software to verify results of calculations.

While office suites text-processing software is useful and broadly applicable to be used in schools, it is, in many cases, not sufficient for specific science tools. One of the examples is simple text editing. For science lab reports, a text writer must be able to handle mathematical equations, chemical formulas, and Feynman diagrams, just to mention the most exotic pitfalls.

Many of the open source software packages have origins in scientific environments. Thus, there are many applications that can be used for science teaching in classroom, with some prior training. Xplora recommends the use of the following software packages, displayed in Table 2, for science teaching. On the portal, one can find articles and short descriptions for their usage.

Xplora-Knoppix, Making Science Accessible for Schools

To ease some of the organizational problems that schools face in terms of software availability, installation, and access in general, the Xplora team developed a live bootable DVD called Xplora-Knoppix. It is a based on the Linux Debian distribution, and completely contained on a self-booting DVD. As this Knoppix version is especially mastered for Xplora, the team has added software applications needed for science education (Table 2), as well as a number of educational materials from the Xplora repository. The Xplora-Knoppix has multilingual support. This concept ensures easy access to scientific tools for education. Being open source software, it can be given away freely and copied as many time as needed.

Xplora produced 600 DVDs to be given freely to schools. Moreover, the ISO image of the DVD is freely downloadable from the Internet and can be used to produce the copies needed for the students. This DVD is occasionally updated. Additionally, Xplora has partnered with a company that sells the Xplora-Knoppix DVD for the production plus shipping cost.

EUN Content Services in Pipeline

Since 2000, European Schoolnet has lead EU-funded projects to give better access to digital educational resources for teachers and learners across Europe. The CELEBRATE project (2002-2004) provided the first large-scale demonstration and evaluation of learning object (LO) interoperability and the use of LOs in schools at a European level.

In 2004, a survey of 13 Ministries of Education participating in European Schoolnet also indicated that they wished to take forward the vision of learning resource exchange (LRE) based on the architecture demonstrated in the project. Furthermore, many communicated that LOs are increasingly seen as an important, and in some cases, a key component in the content development strategies of Ministries of Education. Also, the majority expressed interest in open source content development strategies where "learning object economy" was created for open source and commercial content to coexist.

EUN continues its work towards an enhanced architecture for learning resources in Europe. EUN will continue to lead the development of the LRE based on a brokerage system architecture (of which the code for the brokerage system is licensed under the LGPL) involving a variety of stakeholders, from content providers, both public and commercial, to end users in European schools.

A set of more tailored services will be offered to the members of LRE, such as federated searches, learning resource exchanges, and digital rights management. It is envisaged to support multiple digital rights expression languages, and permit content providers to select the level of digital rights management that best fits their needs in terms of intellectual property protection. This requires a proper digital rights management (DRM). The objective is to design and implement a DRM framework that takes into account requirements from all stakeholders; thus, supporting available DRM standards like ODRL and Creative Commons.

European Schoolnet supports the use of Creative Commons licenses within its services, and has already implemented an integrated interface for its users to choose an option of Creative Commons license for the resources that they submit to various EUN projects.

Open Source Learning Toolbox to Support Collaborative Learning

European Schoolnet's research into the use of learning environments confirms that a number of its members flavor the development of open source VLEs. Moreover, many expect the next generation of new learning platforms to facilitate the adoption of more learner-centered and collaborative pedagogical approaches. However, the same survey and subsequent observations suggest that these high expectations are not yet being met. Most teachers are still using VLEs as little more than a "digital distribution" space, somewhere to upload, store, and distribute content, and to issue assignments to students.

EUN, among the CALIBRATE project partners, will lead the development of a VLE that brings together two quite distinct and somewhat opposing methodologies for pedagogical affordance; the first comes from a background of social constructivist pedagogies and collaborative knowledge building, whereas the second has a background in SCORM and LCMSs. By drawing on both these approaches, a new open source toolbox will be built using the existing code from Future Learning Environment 3 (FLE3) based on Plone/Zope. The VLE will offer a richer feature set that will be developed with the help of practicing teachers.

Conclusion

Currently in the European educational policy and practices landscape, the existing open content and free and open source software initiatives are rather dispersed on a local, national, and European level, as well as being spread throughout all educational levels and systems. It is challenging to get a comprehensive overview on the state of the art being available, as well as capitalizing on the transfer of knowledge gained in one context. However, as this report clearly summarizes, European Schoolnet and its members are more and more focusing on the issues around open source and content development. It must be stated, though, that these activities still remain somewhat marginalized in discussions, country reports, and conferences; they rarely receive the limelight that they merit.

When it comes to actions taken by European Ministries of Education and other national educational authorities, it seems like they are keen to explore the advantages that open source software and content can offer to education. According to the interviews conducted for this chapter, it can be stated that 10 out of 25 EU member states have taken policy-level actions in e-learning to better exploit the use of FOSS in education. In this report, we looked at five different categories where attention is given: awareness raising of FOSS as an alternative solution for e-learning tools; feasibility studies regarding the use of FOSS to support education, both in teaching and administration; development of learning platforms based on FOSS; localization of GNU/Linux desktops to be used in schools; and finally, open content as an alternative means for digital content provision. It appears that the featured countries have taken actions in all these areas, some in all, whereas others in one or two. Moreover, some of the countries seem to have ventured into the area of FOSS just to find out more about it, whereas the others have embedded FOSS into their policy-making strategies and initiatives in a more integrated way.

This chapter attempts to report on these developments, rather than going further to analyze them in details. Many interesting questions have been raised regarding these policy-level initiatives, more importantly, what are the synergies between grass-root actions in schools and the policy and decision-makers responsible for these initiatives, their continuation, their accountability, and so forth? Are these policy-initiatives a response to the demand in the field, or do they support the further uptake of FOSS in education?

It seems that it would be important to bring these somewhat disparate, but very pertinent national and regional initiatives into the European level to better help the transfer of good practices and to learn from one another. Furthermore, peer-learning possibilities on the policy level should be better exploited in this area, as have been done in other areas of ICT implementations.

Xplora carries out important work promoting science in education in European schools. The multiple ways to distribute software that is suitable for scientific studies allows schools a better access to the core of science: participate by practicing it.

Finally, the work EUN has carried out in publishing the Insight Special Reports has given a more prominent voice for FOSS in education, and been an important source of information for EUN's members and audiences on national levels.

The area of open content seems to be rather well accepted concept among EUN's partners. Thus, creating infrastructure and facilitating the content exchange of learning resources in schools is one of EUN's core areas where significant work is conducted to facilitate the coexistence of open and "closed" content. For example, the implementation of digital rights management framework is a step towards the coexistence of multiple stakeholders in the field of educational content. Also, some important work will be carried out in the context of EU-founded projects such as where the development and implementation of an open source collaborative "learning toolbox" for schools is being done.

Appendix I: Internet Session: INSIGHT, Observatory for New Technologies and Education

http://insight.eun.org

Insight is a service focusing on e-learning in schools in Europe. It is provided by European Schoolnet (EUN) in collaboration with its consortium members.

Interaction

We publish news, reports, and analysis on e-learning policies, school innovation, and information communication technology (ICT) in education. In the section of Insight Special Reports, three relevant reports are found dealing with FOSS for Education in Europe. http://insight.eun.org/ww/en/pub/insight/misc/specialreports.htm

Appendix II: Useful URLs

- **Links Related to *Introduction* and *Background***

LRE: **http://lre.eun.org**
EUN: **http://www.eun.org; http://www.europeanschoolnet.org/**
CELEBRATE: **http://celebrate.eun.org**
CALIBRATE: **http://calibrate.eun.org**

- **Links Related to Estonia**

Tiger Leap Foundation: **http://www.tiigrihype.ee/eng/arhiiv_1.php?uID=49**
VIKO: **http://www.htk.tlu.ee/viko/, IVA http://www.htk.tpu.ee/iva/**

- **Links Related to Slovenia**

OKO **http://oko.edus.si**
E-CHO, developed by the Faculty of Electrical Engineering, University of Ljubljana **http://dl.ltfe.org**

- **Links Related to Spain**

Article on the use of FOSS in education:
http://insight.zdnet.co.uk/software/linuxunix/0,39020472,39197928,00.htm
Brings hope to Spain's poorest region:
http://news.zdnet.co.uk/

- **Links Related to Belgium**

The Flemish advice on FOSS in education, is available in English at **http://www.ond.vlaanderen.be/ict/english/**

Portal Klascement: **http://vrijesoftware.klascement.net**

ICT on the menu: **http://www.klascement.net/ictophetmenu**

Digital resources for secondary education: **http://digitaalso.klascement.net, ENIS: http://enis.eun.org**

- **Links Related to The Netherlands**

Kennisnet **http://www.kennisnet.nl**

In the section "voorbeeldprojecten," one can find short descriptions of different case studies OSSOS, Open Standards and Open Source Software in Government in English **http://www.ososs.nl/index.jsp?alias=english**

ICT op School **http://www.ictopschool.net**,

Dutch association for a wide range of stakeholders in e-learning standards **http://www.edustandaard.nl/**

Kennisnet on content: **http://contentketen.kennisnet.nl/**

Conference announcement: **http://www.ossos.nl/article.jsp?article=1820**

- **Links Related to France**

Information on FOSS for education at **http://logiciels-libres-cndp.ac-versailles.fr/**

press release about the CD **http://logiciels-libres-cndp.ac-versailles.fr/IMG/CP_Logiciels_libres.pdf**

information about the school server program SIIEE: **http://www.solutionslinux.fr/fr/conferences_detail.php?id_conference=64**

Region of Picardie: **http://www.cr-picardie.fr/article.php3?id_article=374**

- **Links Related to Finland**

Finnish Centre for Open Source Software **http://www.coss.fi/en/**

EduCoss http://educoss.org/

- **Links Related to Ireland**

Irish news on Star Office **http://www.ncte.ie/NewsandEvents/Newsletter/d2413.** HTML.html, press release in pdf-format: **http://www.ncte.ie/documents/pressreleaseforStaroffice.pdf**

- **Links Related to The UK**

Open Source Software in Schools: A study of the spectrum of use and related ICT infrastructure costs – Project report **http://www.becta.org.uk/corporate/publications/documents/BEC5606_Full_report18.pdf**

Open Source Software in Schools: A case study report **http://www.becta.org.uk/corporate/publications/documents/BEC5606_Case_Study_16.pdf**

Using Open Source Software in Schools: Information sheet **http://www.becta.org.uk/publications/documents/BEC5606_Information_Sheetrev.pdf**

Previous UK Government studies include: Office of Government Commerce [2004] "Open Source Software Trials in Government: Final report" **http://www.ogc.gov.uk**

- **Links Related to Lithuania**

The Ministry of Education and Science of the Republic of Lithuania, Centre of information technologies of education, Institute of mathematics and informatics: Report of the research study open source in education **http://www.ipc.lt/english/apie/skelbiami_dok/2004/Open Source in Education. Abstract of Research Study.doc**

- **Links Related to Xplora**

http://www.xplora.org

Web experiments: **http://www.xplora.org/ww/en/pub/xplora/megalab/web_experiments.htm**

Xplora Knoppix DVD **http://www.europeanschoolnet.org/ww/en/pub/eun/news/news_headlines/1107.htm, Linux-cd.info: http://linux-cd.info/**

- **Links Related to Learning Resources Exchange**

http://lre.eun.org
CALIBRATE **http://calibrate.eun.org**
FLE3 **http://fle3.uiah.fi**

Appendix III: For Further Reading

Flosse Posse: Free and open source for education: http://flosse.dicole.org

Insight policy brief: VLEs, open standards and open source in European schools

Insight special report: Software patents - a potential hindrance of ICT in education http://insight.eun.org/ww/en/pub/insight/misc/specialreports.htm

Insight special report: Why Europe needs free and open source software and content in schools

Naeve, A., Nilsson, M., Palmér, M., & Paulsson, F. (2005). Contributions to a public e-learning platform: Infrastructure, architecture, frameworks, and tools. *International Journal of Learning Technology, 1*(3), 352-281.

Open source for education in Europe: Research and practice: http://www.openconference.net/index.php?cf=3

Possible Titles for Papers/Essays

- Examples on How the Support from Local Authorities Can Effect the Good Practices in the Field: Case Studies of Foss Implementations on the Regional and National Level
- Examples on Efficient Grass Root FOSS Actions in Education, and How It Has Had an Effect on Local Policy Making (look for examples where national and regional policy and decision makers have created support systems for FOSS in education, and try to find whether it has had an effect on the larger-scale uptake)
- Attitudes of Local and Regional Educational Authorities Towards FOSS in Education
- Future Scenarios for Adapting and Rooting FOSS in Regional, National, and European Level Policy Making in Education
- If I Were a Local Educational Policy Maker, What Would I Do for FOSS in Education?

Chapter IX

Using Open Source to Building and Accessing Learning Objects and Online Courses

Christos Bouras, Research Academic Computer Technology Institute and University of Patras, Greece
Maria Nani, Research Academic Computer Technology Institute and University of Patras, Greece

Abstract

As e-learning continuously gains the interest of the scientific community, industry, and government, a wide variety of learning technology products have been incorporated into the marketplace. Advances in information and communication technologies are in favor of the incorporation of innovative services and functionalities in such systems, though content creation and delivery remain the two key factors in any e-learning system. Therefore, in this chapter, we present the design and implementation of a tool targeted at building and accessing learning objects and online courses through the Web.

This tool aims to facilitate instructors and trainers to easily develop accessible, reusable, and traceable learning content that can meet their distant students' needs for anytime and anyplace learning. Learners are able to access learning content, in addition to consulting, at any time, reports on their interactions within a course and get support by subject experts. Furthermore, all users can request to upgrade their role in the system and, thus, actively participate in the learning process. Special attention has been paid on the utilization of reliable and qualitative open source technologies and Web standards so that the proposed solution can form an easily accessible system.

Introduction

Nowadays, the wide expansion of the Internet, in combination with the time and place limitations that traditional learning implies, as well as the current Web infrastructure, are in favor of the effective and efficient application of distance learning, otherwise e-learning. In many cases, actually, e-learning is used as a complement to face-to-face education in order to meet students' need for "anytime" (and/or "anyplace") learning.

Depending on whether learners interact in real time with their instructors and/or with each other, distance leaning is distinguished into asynchronous and synchronous learning. According to Midkiff and DaSilva (2000), synchronous and asynchronous distance learning classes each have their own strengths, which allow them to meet the needs of different markets. Asynchronous distance learning, though, gains the interest of a wider audience and thus, it is likely to grow at a faster rate than synchronous distance learning, due to its inherent flexibility and the ever-increasing bandwidth of Internet connections and capabilities of Internet applications. In this mode of learning, learners and instructor(s) can be separated in both time and space, and neither must be physically tied to anything except a computer and the Internet. More to the point, studies have shown that the achievements of individually tutored students may exceed that of classroom students. As a result, the majority of the up-to-date e-learning systems support, mainly, asynchronous distance learning in the sense of the asynchronous mode of learning content delivery. They include, though, some kind of real-time interaction among the users so that learners have the feeling that they are not isolated, but active members of a virtual community, and that they can get support whenever they need it.

Despite the different characteristics and services up-to-date e-learning platforms present, according to the pedagogical approach they follow for serving their end-users needs, as well as the technological solutions they adopt to support the learning process, they are all organized into three fundamental macro components (Colace, De Santo, & Vento, 2002):

1. A learning management system (LMS)
2. A learning content management system (LCMS)
3. A set of tools for distributing training content and for providing interactions among users

The elements shared by all LCMSs are (Wan, Zhao, Liu, & Sun, 2005) a learning-object repository; an authoring tool for creating learning objects; a dynamic publishing tool for delivering personalized-learning content; and an administration tool for providing management function. An advanced LCMS should, further, deploy and manage content that can be easily searched and retrieved during an auto-training phase and reused for different educational purposes (Bouras & Nani, 2004). To that end, learning resources would be described using metadata. Another functionality that LCMSs are expected to expose is the storage of the learners' interactions with the content. This enables the system to gather information about the content's usage, and report on learners' progress and performance.

As far as the LMS is concerned, this integrates all the aspects for managing online teaching activities. The LMS adds users, traces courses, stores data of the users, and generates reports for management, and it is designed to manage multiple courses (Álvarez-González, Sandoval, Ritter, & Berger, 2005). According to Colace et al. (2002), a state-of-the-art LMS should enable learners to consult, at any time, the results they have reached, and thus, monitor their preparation level. This information can be exploited by the system in an attempt to diagnose the learners' needs and advise them on the most suitable learning content.

The set of tools, lastly, is essential to differentiate the kind of provided services in accordance with the user. In particular, instructors should be provided with tools that will enable them to manage teaching processes for single individuals or groups, as well as all the interactions, including asynchronous discussions or live events. Instructors should also be provided with updated reports on the learners' performance in order to facilitate their activities. Above and beyond, it is necessary to allow learners to communicate, synchronously or asynchronously, with both the instructor and other members (Colace et al., 2002).

Overall, distance-learning platforms should present characteristics that make the training process functional and available, encouraging and accepting the learner autonomy and initiative. They should be Web-based, run on many computers and operating systems and follow one or more learning technology specifications. Yet, the two key factors in any e-learning system, according to Jesshope and Zhang (2002), are content creation and delivery.

To that end, this chapter presents the design and development of a system targeted at **B**uilding and **A**ccessing **L**earning **O**bjects and **C**ourses through the Web (BALOC). BALOC is an LCMS that incorporates all the innovative features an up-to-date LCMS is expected to expose, but also integrates a number of services for managing online training activities (LMS functionality), as well as tools that enable the users to asynchronously interact with each other. The learning process, inspired by the mindful learning theory (Langer, 1997) and other contemporary learning or instructional design theories, encourages learners to take risks and work things out for themselves. All BALOC users are able to upgrade their role within the system by becoming a learner, mentor, author, or a member of the Editorial Board (or to withdraw it) and, thus, actively participate in the learning process.

BALOC has been designed and developed based on Web standards, taking also into account leading learning technology specifications, such as SCORM. Special attention has been paid on the utilization of open source technologies, as such technologies are often of high reliability, and have the best performance and security, perhaps due to the possibility of worldwide review (Wheeler, 2005).

The following section provides an overview of the most known standardization efforts made so far in the learning technology field, focusing especially on ADL SCORM, as it references the most significant e-learning specifications and describes how these can be used together. We also identify, and shortly present, existing SCORM-conformant LCMSs in an attempt to understand their capabilities, and gain an appreciation of their possible weaknesses. Thereafter, the BALOC design characteristics and

Figure 1. Chapter overview

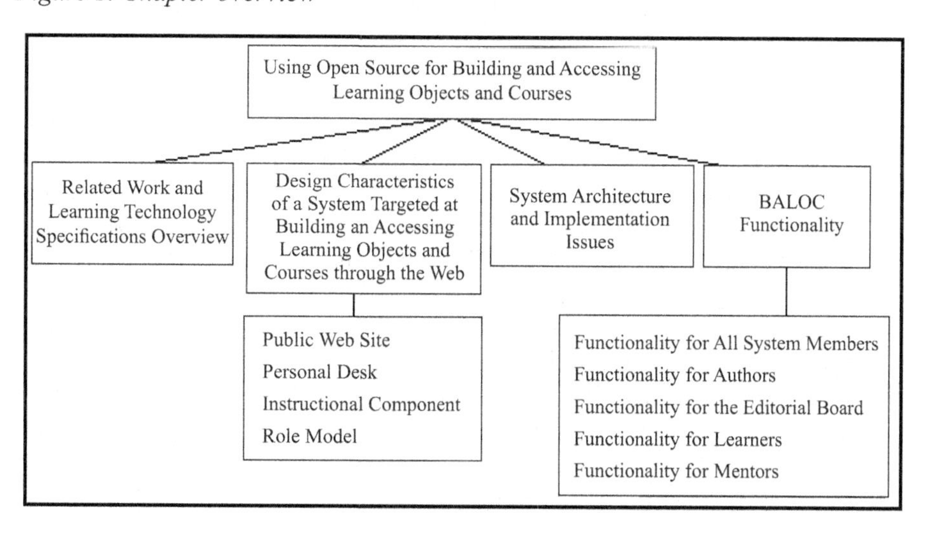

the role model adopted to differentiate the rights and access levels to the provided functionality are presented. Subsequently, we introduce the system architecture, and we discuss issues raised during its implementation. Key characteristics and services BALOC provides to its end users, depending on their role, are also presented. We end up by providing future directions and conclusions.

Related Work and Learning Technology Specifications Overview

In the last few years, a great number of LCMSs have emerged for deploying e-learning. The tools they provide for creating and maintaining learning content and infrastructure applications vary a lot in capabilities and complexity. In order to achieve the obvious benefits of learning content reusability and accessibility in a variety of learning, performance, and knowledge management requirements, organizations, committees, and initiatives from the academic, industrial, and governmental sector put special efforts into developing learning technology standards. The most well known are the efforts made by the IEEE Learning Technology Standardization Committee (LTSC), the ARIADNE Foundation, the CEN/ISSS, the Aviation Industry CBT (computer-based training) Committee (AICC), and the IMS Global Learning Consortium. The Department of Defense of the US government has undertaken the role of the coordinator, and the Advanced Distributed Learning (ADL) initiative it has established has presented a reference model that is known as "Shareable Content Object Reference Model," or SCORM.

The three main areas of interest of all the standardization efforts concern (Bouras, Nani, & Tsiatsos, 2003; Kaliakatsos, Malamos, & Damianakis, 2002):

- **Metadata:** how a learning resource can be described in a consistent way regardless of a specific learning context or a specific educational purpose. The IEEE LTSC Learning Object Metadata (LOM) is the first accepted standard regarding metadata. It is referenced by the IMS LOM specification as well as the ADL's SCORM. The ADL initiative actually applied the IMS LOM specification to the three components of the content model adopted in SCORM. This "mapping" has been considered as the missing link between general specifications and particular content models.
- **Packaging:** how learning resources, together with information about the intended behavior of the content, can be aggregated into useful packages. Even

if, the last few years, a number of content packaging implementations revealed, the IMS Content Packaging Specification seems to be the most flexible and feasible solution. According to the IMS specification, a content package includes information regarding the metadata of a whole course (using elements form LOM), the structure (for chapters etc.) and the resources (a full list of the files or URLs used) of the course. This specification is also referenced by SCORM.

- **Communication interface or API (application programming interface):** how the learning resources can communicate with external systems. The communication interface refers to the way learning resources can exchange information, in run time, with an LMS. The first API has been presented by AICC. However, the current trend is the substitution of the AICC communication protocol by the one presented in SCORM, which actually presents a very fast rate of adoption.

Compatibility with e-learning standards is essential to the future growth and success of an LCMS in education. To that end, many efforts have been made to develop LCMSs for producing multimedia educational material for the Web, compliant with e-learning standards. TotalLCMS, for example, a well-known platform for learning-content management and assembly as well as for personalized learning content delivery, conforms to SCORM and AICC specifications. The same applies for TopClass LCMS, which is part of the TopClass e-learning suite. Another recognized learning content management system is Learn eXact, which allows for automation and production of different versions of the same learning contents, based on different standards such as SCORM, IMS, and AICC, and commonly used peripheral devices. Xtention Enterprise is another SCORM-compliant LCMS that provides the infrastructure for enterprise training and management needs.

Despite the wide variety of the LCMS currently available, digital learning materials do not yet play the central role that they could in the learning process (Papadakis & Hadzilacos, 2005). Content creation and production of e-learning material has been proved to be a time-consuming and costly process, and questions have been raised about the time and effort required by instructors/authors to generate effective e-learning materials. There is indeed an increasing need for LCMS authoring and assembly components to expose a user interface tailored to the specific task of developing learning content. Furthermore, to make e-learning material really good, a number of users have to participate in its creation, such as authors and didactic workers. These are some of the issues that affect instructors today, and which BALOC will have to tackle.

Design Characteristics of a System Targeted at Building and Accessing Learning Objects and Courses through the Web

In this section, we present the design characteristics of the Web-based tool we propose for building and accessing learning objects and online courses. The following scenarios would sound familiar to distance learners and instructors to whom this writing is directed, and would raise some issues associated with the implied developments in BALOC tools and services.

- **Scenario 1: The instructor's view.** Maria is a radio-pharmacy lecturer in Athens University. Due to the lack of teaching courses and teaching material available to the community of radio-pharmacists, she is interested in developing a course on the generation, preparation, and quality control of radiopharmaceutical elements. She discussed this issue with a radio-pharmacy practitioner in London she had worked with a few years earlier, who encouraged her and decided to support her in this task. He also promised that he would try to get in contact with some other practitioners and researchers in Portugal and Belgium, inviting them to participate. These experts could bring in texts, simulations, videos, and other material they had at their disposal.
- **Scenario 2: The students' view.** Tom is a radio-pharmacy student in the U.S. He decided to use distance-learning courseware as a source of scientific information in order to increase his knowledge in the field. He prefers the traditional situation of material being presented as standard lectures from an instructor, favoring written material, graphics, illustrations, and interactive materials. He wants to determine, on his own, the pace and intensity of learning, and get support by an expert only in the cases he really needs it. Furthermore, as he is already working in the field, he does not require a full course.

Based on these usage scenarios, as well as the requirements an up-to-date e-learning system should meet (as they have been presented in the introductory section), and the theories and principles of the mindful learning theory (Langer, 1997) and other contemporary learning or instructional design theories, the functional specifications of the BALOC system have been extracted.

According to them, the system requirements concerning the learning content creation and delivery through the Web can be summarized as follows:

- The system should support the import of a wide variety of file types, with an emphasis on multimedia files.

- The learning resources should be easily merged and aggregated to produce a modular repository of training material.
- The courseware should be divided into small modules, so that it can be used by those not wanting to complete the entire course.
- Learning content should be used and reused within different learning objects and instructional units, thus avoiding content duplication within the system.
- The system should provide online examinations with feedback. Examinations may include multiple-choice, matching, fill-in-the-blanks, and open short-answer questions.
- The learners' interactions with the content should be tracked. On accessing a course, a learner could choose whether his/her interactions with the content will be tracked. These interactions include, among others, the time the learner spends on a learning resource, other related learning resources he/she selected to view, as well as answers on assessment objects.
- Learners should be provided with courses related to the field of interest, which should be accessed on a distance basis through the Web.
- The courseware should be designed to be delivery-platform independent.
- The system should provide mentors with whom the learners can communicate online.
- The design and the technology to be used should not demand any particular computer science or e-learning skills.

These requirements have next been transformed into system functional specifications. BALOC was intended to be an open and user-oriented environment that would facilitate users to take part in it. Therefore, the system was distinguished into three main-components, three functional areas: (a) the Public Web Site, (b) the Personal Desk component and (c) the Instructional component.

Public Web Site

The Public Web Site constitutes the introductory system component and it is accessible by all users. Its main aim is to present the system to the wide audience by supplying general information about it, and by encouraging potential system members to take part in or request more information. Users accessing the Public Web Site can be informed of the available courseware as well as the technology exploited to implement the whole system. The Public Web Site also acts as a gate for the already registered users.

Personal Desk

The Personal Desk area addresses users that have been subscribed to the system. In this area, a system member can be informed of all the registered users, and communicate with them via private messages or e-mails. A system member can fill in a card with personal information (personal card), such as his/her username, e-mail address, and interests, and part of this information may be viewed by other system members. In the Personal Desk area, users are also provided with tools that allow them to request, for undertaking or withdrawing, certain roles in the Instructional Component (i.e., the role of a learner, mentor, author, or member of the Editorial Board, as discussed in *Role Model*).

Instructional Component

The Instructional Component consists of the core functional area of BALOC. Its main aim is to support the creation of, and access to, the learning content, and facilitate learners, mentors, authors, and members of the Editorial Board in interacting with each other. The Instructional Component consists of an LCMS integrated with a learning-management element.

The LCMS provides tools and services, and exposes an intuitive user interface that allows authors to easily develop accessible, reusable, and traceable learning objects and courses. In particular, the LCMS, in line with the system functional requirements, provides an authoring tool that enables content authors to:

- Import content of various file types.
- Create learning objects that incorporate one or more of these files, and define how these will look.
- Create assessment objects consisting of a matching, fill-in-the-blanks, open short answer, or multiple-choice question (true/false and multiple answer questions are also included).
- Develop courses that are made up of one or more learning objects and/or courses, define the order in which these are intended to be delivered to the learners, and include them in specific catalogs.
- Describe learning resource using metadata.
- Edit the structure of a course.
- Edit metadata elements.

Learning content imported or created by means of the LCMS will be stored in the system. Though, only content that has been reviewed and approved by the Editorial Board would be made available while developing new learning objects or courses, or for being delivered to the end-users. In this way, it is assured that learners are delivered with content of high quality. The LCMS is also responsible for monitoring the learners' interactions in terms of their learning activities. This "interaction monitor" tool will extract the details of the interactions from messages sent for the Web pages. Users' actions within a Web page, such as the information about the time a user spends viewing a page and answers to assessment questions, will be tracked. Such information about the learner will be made available to his/her mentor.

The BALOC learning management element has as main goal to encourage and facilitate the learners' access to pedagogical resourses. Before accessing a course, learners would fill in a form with information about their educational and professional background. The pedagogical resources will contain a complete representation of the courseware, the relationships between learning assets both within a page and across pages, conceptual relationships, and recommended answers to self-assessment quizzes. This may be thought of as an expert's view of the courseware. It is this information that mentors will use to analyze the learner's interactions with the system and offer pedagogic advice.

Within the Instructional Component, the Editorial Board, apart from being responsible for reviewing any change in the learning content, will also decide on the assignment of the learner's, mentor's, or author's role to system members wishing to upgrade their role in the system, as well as their expulsion from the Instructional Component.

Role Model

A significant factor that has been taken into account during the BALOC design phase was the definition of the users' roles and the access levels each role involves. Therefore, this subsection is dedicated to the policies that guide the user's interactions within the system (Figure 2).

Within BALOC, the following roles can be distinguished:

- **Visitor:** This role refers to non-registered users. Visitors can only access general information about the system (Public Web Site). They have the ability to register in the system by filling in a registration form.
- **Member:** Members are users that have been registered in the system. These users can be informed of the available courses, though they cannot access them, as well as to complete and edit, at any time, their profile. They are also able to exchange private messages with other system members.

- **Learner:** This role corresponds to members that have requested the learner's role and filled in a form concerning their educational and professional background. A learner is able to access a course in two modes: browse or study. In browse mode, the learner is delivered with the content of a course in a non-systematic way. He/She is able to jump from topic to topic without his/her interactions being monitored. In study mode, the system "monitors" the learner's interactions within the course.

  A learner is able to choose a mentor that will support him/her in a certain course, and with whom he/she can communicate online though private messages and/or e-mail. He/she can also view information about his/her activities within a course he/she has accessed in study mode. A learner is also able to search and retrieve content of his/her preference.

- **Mentor:** The role of a mentor is assigned to members that wish to upgrade their role in the system, and who have the appropriate educational and professional background (subject experts) to support learners. Users with that role can be mentors for more than one course. A mentor can define the maximum number of learners he/she will support by (a) answering questions or (b) accessing information about the learners' educational and professional background and their interactions with the content of the course, and advising them appropriately.

Figure 2. Role model

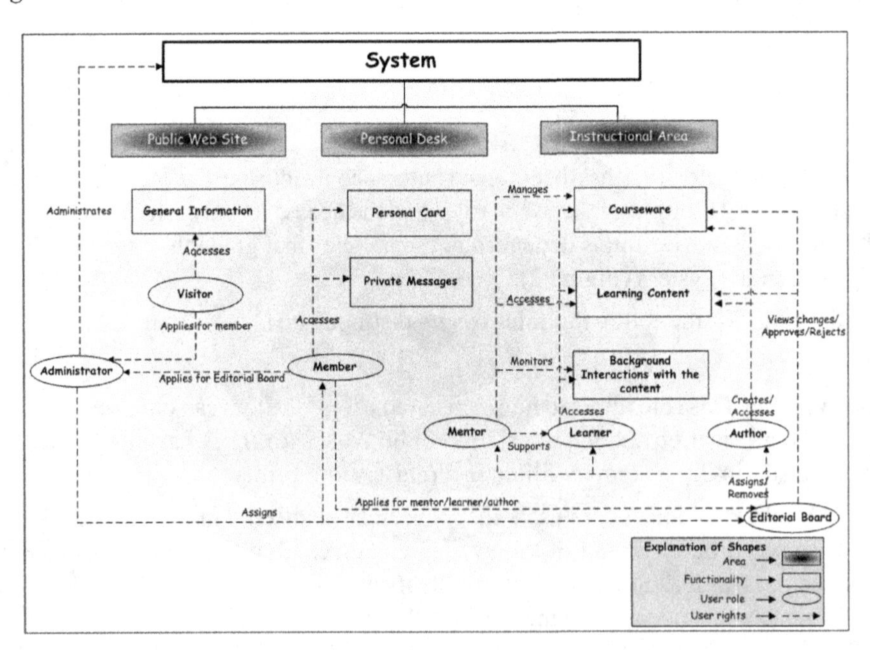

- **Author:** Users that have undertaken this role have, as main responsibility, the learning content provision. They can access a course but, as opposite to a learner, their interactions with the content will not be monitored. In order to be monitored, an author should also take on the learner's role.
- **Editorial Board:** The Editorial Board is a special group that (a) decides on the assignment/withdrawal of the learner's, mentor's, author's role to a system member, (b) can remove a system member from the Instructional Component by taking away the member's additional roles, and (c) controls, qualitatively, any change in the learning content, and approves or rejects it accordingly.
- **Administrator:** This represents a group of users with a technical role having, as main responsibility, to (a) assign/withdraw the role of the Editorial Board to a system member, (b) insert/delete other system administrators to/from the system, (c) insert/delete a member to/from the system, (d) activate new functionality, (e) control the data consistency, and (f) fix possible bugs.

Figure 2 depicts the role model adopted for the purposes of our system.

In conclusion, BALOC adopts a role model that allows any user to upgrade his/her role in the system, by becoming a learner, mentor, author, or a member of the Editorial Board, or to withdraw it. This distribution of the access rights allows for the users' active participation in the learning process.

System Architecture and Implementation Issues

The step that followed the system functional specification was the definition of the computer system that could support all the functional characteristics and services BALOC was envisioned to support to meet its end-users' needs. This system technical specification formed our guide throughout the development process.

Figure 3. System architecture overview

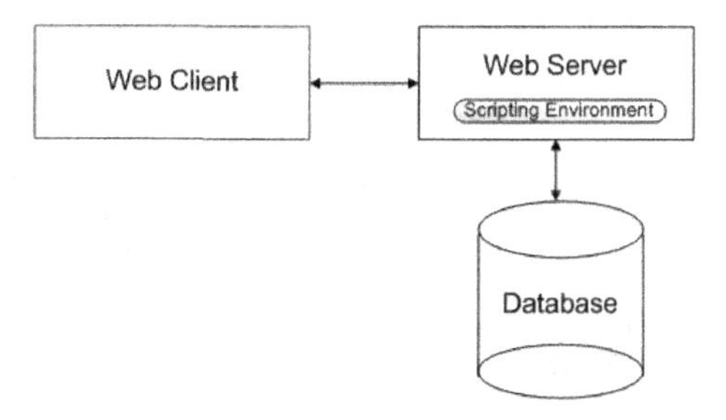

As BALOC was intended to be an easily accessible Web-based learning system, bandwidth and client-side system constraints would be taken into account. The main prerequisites for the system architecture have been (a) Minimization of the client-side system requirements, which means that the end users would be able to access BALOC using a typical computer without excessive H/W or S/W requirements; (b) Cost minimization of the client-side system set-up, which implies that the client-side software would be free of charge with minimal H/W requirements; (c) Cost minimization of the server-side set-up, which means that it would be better to utilize open source technologies, which do not demand excessive H/W requirements; (d) The system would run on a variety of platforms, and (e) as an e-learning system, it would be based on one or more learning technology specifications.

According to these criteria, the BALOC architecture was founded on certain principles: the system would be platform-independent and based on well-known Web and learning technology standards. The main modules of the BALOC architecture are the client, the Web server together with the scripting environment, and the database (Figure 3).

- The client is the end-user's computer, with an Internet connection and a Web browser. The user utilizes the Web browser to enter the system and exploit the offered functionality.
- The Web server is responsible for storing the learning content, as well as for storing and executing the scripts of the scripting environment. It interacts with the Web browser, through the HTTP protocol and with the database, by means of the scripting environment.

In actual fact, the scripting environment is one of the basic components of the system architecture. It constitutes the link through which the other system components can communicate with each other, and contributes to the smooth and effective delivery of the appropriate content and values. It supports interaction with the database, system administration, user authentication, manipulation and extraction of the user's role and access rights in the system, but it also supports the Personal Desk and the Instructional Component.

- The database constitutes the core of the whole system, where the majority of the available information is stored and organized. Both the Personal Desk and the Instructional Component need a database in order to operate efficiently. As far as the Personal Desk component is concerned, the database is responsible for the management of information regarding the users, the messages exchanged, the content that corresponds to each functional module, and all the events taking place in this area. In the Instructional Component, the database is in charge of storing, among others, information about the available learning resources and the interrelationships, as well as about the learners' activities.

In order to have a common understanding regarding the pieces of content that are used within BALOC, we need to present, at this point, the content model we have adopted. We distinguish three types of learning-content-model components: "assets," "learning objects," (including assessments) and "courses." These are defined as follows (Bouras et al., 2003b):

- **Assets:** Assets comprise the basic constitutive element of the courseware. They refer to raw media files that can be viewed by a Web browser, such as slides, flash objects, and 3-D simulations.
- **Learning objects/assessments:** A learning object refers to the learning content launched by the learning-management element and delivered to the BALOC end user during a courseware learning experience. It can be either a collection of one or more assets or an assessment object. Assessments may contain a question of at least four types, namely multiple-choice (true-false and multiple answer are also included), matching, fill-in-the-blanks, and open short-answer questions (including short-paragraph questions).
- **Courses:** A course refers to an aggregation of learning objects and/or courses that forms a cohesive unit of instruction. Using a course as part of another course, authors can develop courses nested in any depth and thus, apply learning taxonomy hierarchy.

In order to meet the requirements for content accessibility and reusability, all the three content model components would be described using metadata. We have exploited the SCORM's potential towards this need, as it seems to be the leading specification on the learning technology field (Bouraset et al., 2003a; Bouraset al., 2003b). SCORM specification maps the metadata elements to its own content model components, "assets," "SCOs," and "content aggregations." These are defined as follows:

- **Assets:** They concern learning content in the most basic form that can be delivered in a Web client. Web pages, images, and text are a few examples of assets.
- **SCOs:** A sharable content object (SCO) is a collection of one or more assets that can be launched by an LMS. However, as opposite to an asset, a SCO can communicate with the LMS, thus allowing the LMS to track down the learner's interactions with the content.

Table 1. Interrelations between SCORM and BALOC supported content model components

SCORM content model component	BALOC supported content model component
Asset	Asset
SCO	Learning Object
Content Aggregation	Course

- **Content aggregations:** A content aggregation concerns a content structure that can be used to aggregate Web-based learning resources into cohesive instructional units (e.g., chapters and courses), define the structure of this unit, and associate learning taxonomies. The content structure defines the sequence according to which the learning content will be presented to the user.

As mentioned, a SCORM-conformant LMS can track the learner's interactions with the content by exchanging information with SCOs. These interactions include the majority, but not all the interactions that need to be tracked down in our system (e.g., open short-answer questions). Of course, SCORM supports many more interactions that, however, are considered out of the system scope. Using the SCORM run-time environment for exchanging all the necessary information between the delivered learning content and the learning management element presupposes the extension of the data model proposed by ADL initiative, the implementation of the appropriate (scripting) functions, to be incorporated in a latter stage into the content, as well as the extension of the API to implement the new functionality. Instead, and in an attempt to create an auspicious but still simple Web-based system, we appose our solution to simplify the whole process. The proposed solution takes advantage of both the course structure and the functionality provided by the scripting environment. Above and beyond, in our system, learners are able to select the mode of learning and thus, chose whether their interactions with the content will be monitored. This option is not supported by SCORM.

In order to apply SCORM-conformant metadata to the content model components supported by BALOC, we assume the interrelations presented in Table 1. For each one of the components, SCORM defines which metadata elements are mandatory, optional, or reserved by the system. Our system supports the entire mandatory and some of the optional metadata elements defined in SCORM. Furthermore, BALOC makes use of two additional elements to identify whether the respective learning resource has been reviewed and approved by the Editorial Board, and whether a metadata record stores a different version of the metadata elements of a particular learning resource.

The way in which authors can aggregate learning resources to create a course has been inspired, but is not identical to that described by IMS content packaging and SCORM specifications, due to simplicity reasons. The structure of a course, and any other information on the relationships among the various learning resources, are stored in the courseware database. This database is also used to store and organize metadata annotations and information on the learners' actions within a course.

As far as the technological solutions for supporting all of the BALOC components are concerned, these have been adopted on the basis of the prerequisites for the system architecture, as well as the results of a technology and standardization survey we have conducted. We have opted for open source technologies not only due to practical reasons (cost minimization), but also due to characteristics certain Web servers, database servers, and scripting languages present, according to our survey, such as high reliability, performance, security, scalability, and configurability. More to the point, open source technologies are well documented, and the code is in use by a community of people around the world that gather around and discuss specific functionality, design, and coding issues. Using open source, we do not need to commit to a certain proprietary software vendor who might decide not to upgrade some software for some old platform (in such a case, we would be forced either to use the old version or switch to another product).

BALOC exploits the potential of the Apache HTTP Server,[1] which is currently the most popular Web server, with over three times the market share of its next-ranked (proprietary) competitor (Wheeler, 2005). Apache is reliable, secure, with good performance; it runs on almost every platform and supports a variety of scripting languages.

For the scripting environment, we have mainly exploited the PHP[2], the most popular server-side Web scripting technology on the Internet today, in combination with the client-side scripting language JavaScript[3]. PHP is cross-platform and extensible. It has excellent connectivity and high performance. JavaScript is also an open scripting language that is supported by all major Web browsers. In order to support the Personal Desk component, the scripting environment has adopted the principles and the clear structure of the PHP-nuke[4], an open source and widely adopted content management and portal solution. To facilitate the creation of the learning objects, which are HTML pages that are ultimately delivered to the learners, the scripting environment is used to provide a WYSIWYG ("what-you-see-is-what-you-get") HTML editor. To that end, we have exploited the HTMLArea[5] WYSIWYG editor, which has been developed entirely in HTML and JavaScript. Such an editor allows authors to easily and rapidly develop learning objects, without requiring programming skills.

For the database, we have exploited the MySQL[6], which is one of the most popular open source databases. MySQL is supported by PHP and many other Web-scripting languages; it can be integrated with the majority of the Web servers (including the

Apache), and runs on almost every platform. MySQL is also supported by PHP-Nuke.

BALOC Functionality

This section is dedicated to the presentation of key characteristics and services BALOC provides to its end users, depending on their role. We put emphasis on functionality provided to authors, members of the Editorial Board, mentors, and learners, as these users are actually involved in the learning process.

Functionality for All System Members

All registered users can access the system through the Public Web Site (http://ouranos.ceid.upatras.gr:8080/baloc/index.php), where they are prompted to provide their username and password. As soon as they are authorized to enter the system, they are granted (or denied) access to certain functional modules exposed by BALOC in the form of a menu (main menu).

System members are granted access to the "Change Role," "Members," and "My Settings" functional modules. The first one allows users to be informed about the roles they can take over (or withdraw), as well as the pending for approval assignments (or withdrawals) they have applied for. The second functional module enables system members to communicate with each other through private messages, whereas the last one allows users to change their personal settings in the system.

Functionality for Authors

Learning content authors are, additionally, granted access to the "Courseware" module. This module presents, in a list, all the main online courses a learner can attend within BALOC. These are courses approved by the Editorial Board that, however, are not part of any other course. Authors, though, are able to view all the approved courses, including those used to form a larger instructional unit, by selecting the "View all courses" option (Figure 4).

Authors, in addition to learners, mentors, and the Editorial board, are also able to search and retrieve learning resources (assets, learning objects, or courses) of their preference by supplying indicative keywords or phrases. These keywords/phrases are searched in the metadata elements. The advanced search functionality allows for a more complex inquiry.

Figure 4. Courseware access for authors

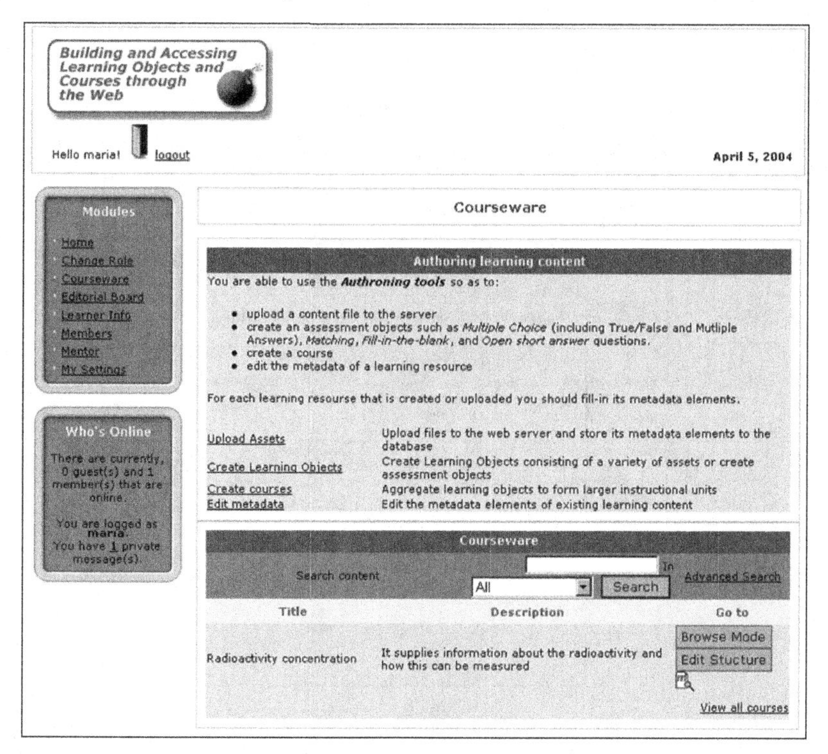

An author can import an asset into the system by locating a file in the local disk of his/her computer and filling in a form with its metadata (at least the mandatory).

He is also authorized to develop learning objects. To create a learning object as an asset collection, authors are provided with an LO Editor (that is actually an extended WYSIWYG editor, as depicted in Figure 5). The editor allows not only for text processing functionality, but also for selecting and importing an asset into the learning object. When the author selects to insert an asset, a list of all the available and approved assets appear in a new pop-up browser window. Authors can insert one asset at a time to the learning object. To create a learning object that is intended to be an assessment, authors are prompted to choose a question type from a drop-down list. The author is provided with a different form for different question types. The assessment can also incorporate an asset (images or graph) for illustrative purposes. Whether an asset collection or an assessment, the authoring process terminates by filling in a form with the appropriate metadata elements (at least the mandatory). Asset collections are stored as HTML pages into the Web server, whereas questions are stored into the Courseware database.

Figure 5. Editor for creating learning objects as asset collections – LO Editor

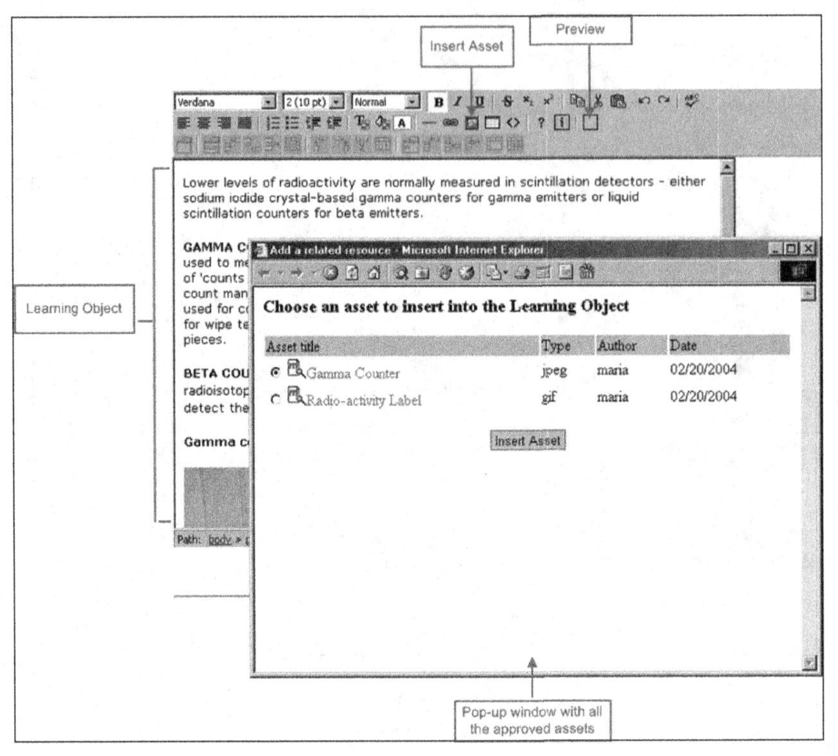

The Courseware module also enables authors to create courses. When an author selects to create a course, a new browser window appears on the user's computer screen (Figure 6). The new Web page presents the structure of "on the stocks" course, a list of all the approved learning objects (assessments and asset collections), and a list of all the approved courses. Authors can select, piece by piece, the learning resources that will be inserted in the course, and define the order in which they will be presented to the learners. When the course is finalized, authors need to describe the new learning resource by means of metadata. The structure of the course is stored in the Courseware database.

The structure of a course that has been approved by the Editorial Board can be edited at any time by authors. In particular, as soon as an author accesses the Courseware's main page, an "Edit Structure" button appears next to the title of each course (see Figure 4). By clicking on it, a new browser window opens, as in the case of the course creation. In this case, however, the left part of the window presents the title and the current structure of the course.

Figure 6. Create course

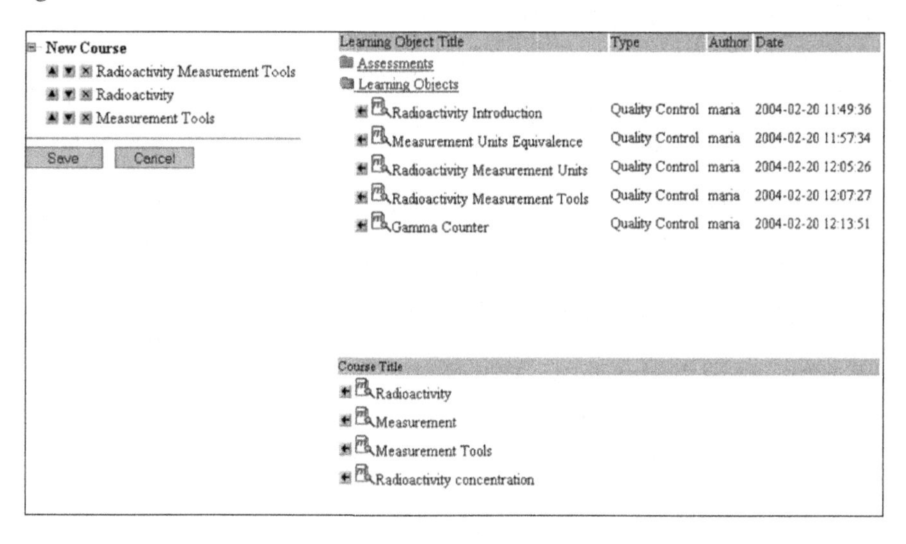

Figure 7. List of the members that have requested the assignment of the author's role

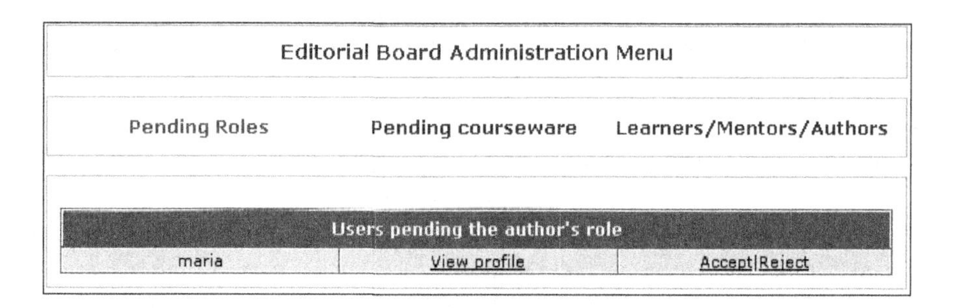

Authors are also able to view and edit the metadata of any learning recourse approved by the Editorial Board. These changes need TO be approved by the Editorial Board before made available to the rest of the users.

Functionality for the Editorial Board

The members of the Editorial Board are the only users granted access TO the "Editorial Board" functional module. This module informs the authorized users about the pending for approval roles, the pending for approval changes in the learning content, as well as about the members assigned the role of a learner, mentor, or author.

Let us consider the case that there are pending requests for the assignment of the author's role to certain users. Any member of the Editorial Board can be informed about the appliers, access their profile (Figure 7), and reject or approve their request, accordingly.

The members of the Editorial Board can also be aware of any change in the courseware material. In the case, for example, that a member of the Editorial Board selects to view the recently imported assets, he/she can view and review their actual content and metadata elements, and then decide on their approval. Approved assets are readily available to authors, mentors, and learners, whereas rejected assets are deleted from the Web server, and their metadata is deleted from the Courseware database.

A member of the Editorial Board is, additionally, able to access information about all the system members assigned to learner, mentor, or author role. He/She can also expel a user from the Instructional Component.

Functionality for Learners

Learners, in addition to "Change Role," "Members," and "My Settings" functional modules, are also granted access to the "Courseware" and "Learner Info" functional modules. To become a learner, a system member needs firstly apply for the learner's role, and then fill in a form with information about his/her educational and professional background (the form is available at the "Learner Info" area).

Within "Courseware," learners can view a list of all the available courses, which they can access in study or browse mode. Regardless the mode of learning, the learner is delivered with the content of the course (that is presented in a new Web page), as depicted in Figure 8.

The table of contents of the selected course has the form of a hyperlink tree. The color code adopted in the hyperlink tree informs the end user about the learning object he/she is currently viewing, the visited, and the non-visited learning objects. In front of each learning object's title an icon appears to denote whether the particular learning object is an asset collection or an assessment.

Learners can navigate within the course using the "Previous" and "Next" navigations buttons, or by selecting a topic from the table of contents. The option "Contact my mentor" allows a learner either to select a mentor to support him/her in this particular course and/or send his/her mentor a private message.

At the bottom-right part of the page, all the resources related to the learning object that the user is currently viewing are listed. For each one of them, the kind of the relationship is presented. If the related resource is part of the current course, then, by

Figure 8. Course access example

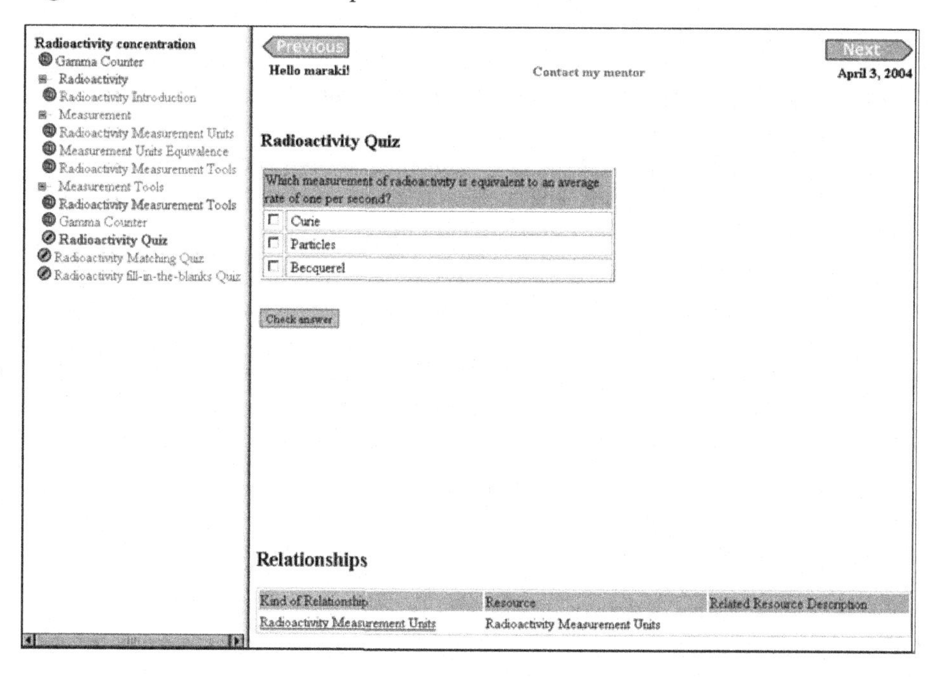

Figure 9. Information on the learning objects the learner has visited

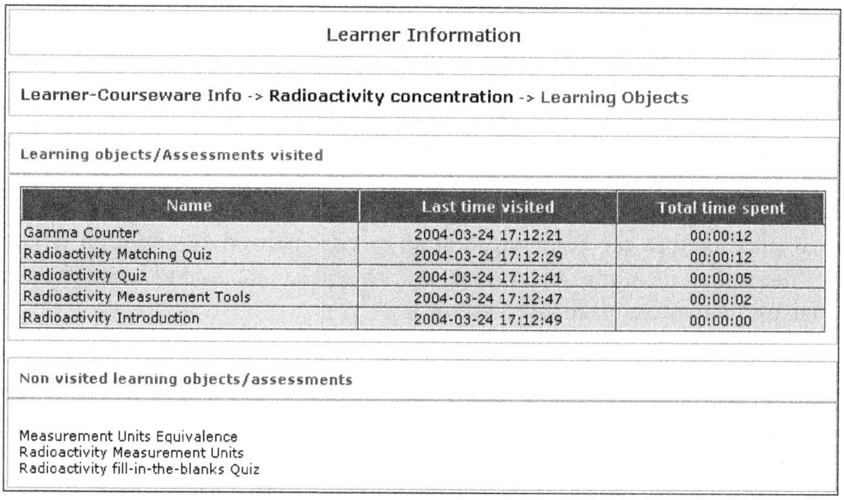

Learner Information

Learner-Courseware Info -> **Radioactivity concentration** -> Learning Objects

Learning objects/Assessments visited

Name	Last time visited	Total time spent
Gamma Counter	2004-03-24 17:12:21	00:00:12
Radioactivity Matching Quiz	2004-03-24 17:12:29	00:00:12
Radioactivity Quiz	2004-03-24 17:12:41	00:00:05
Radioactivity Measurement Tools	2004-03-24 17:12:47	00:00:02
Radioactivity Introduction	2004-03-24 17:12:49	00:00:00

Non visited learning objects/assessments

Measurement Units Equivalence
Radioactivity Measurement Units
Radioactivity fill-in-the-blanks Quiz

clicking on its title, the learner is delivered with its content. Otherwise, the learner is delivered with the content of the course that contains the related resource.

Through the "Learner Info" area, a learner is able to consult, at any time, statistics about his/her interactions with the content of any course he/she has accessed in study mode. Statistics concern the total time the learner has spent on a course, the number of the different learning objects he/she has visited, and the number of the questions he/she has answered. The learner can also be informed of the related resources he/she had moved into from within this course.

Let us consider the case that a learner wants to view more information about the learning objects he/she has visited. He/She is provided with a page, similar to that depicted in Figure 9, where information about the last time visited and total time spent on each learning object is presented. By clicking on a learning object's title, the learner can view its actual content. Additionally, the learner can be informed of the learning objects that fall short to complete the course.

In addition, learners are able to access information about the assessment questions they have answered, such as the question's type, the first provided answer, and a history of all the answers he/she has provided from time to time.

Functionality for Mentors

Mentors are the only users granted access to the "Mentor" functional module, through which they can manage courses and learners per course. Mentors are, obviously, able to access all the available courses, though only in browse mode (this is also the case for authors and members of the Editorial Board). This means that their interactions within a course will not be monitored unless they are taken on the role of a learner. A mentor is able to become a mentor in any available course.

At the "Manage Courses" area (Figure 10), the first block presents to a mentor an overview of all the courses he/she is responsible for. For each certain course, the number of the learners he/she has been assigned to support (the number is, actually, a link to the list of the respective learners), the maximum number of the learners allowed (this number can be changed at any moment), and an option to remove himself/herself as mentor of the course are presented. The second block presents the courses the user can become a mentor for.

The "Manage Learners" area provides a mentor with a list of all the learners he/she has been assigned to support within a certain course. Mentors are able to access, at any time, information about the listed learners' activities within the course (provided that the course has been accessed in study mode), as well as information about the learners' educational and professional background. Based on these, he/she can contact a learner in order to advise him/her.

Figure 10. Course management for mentors

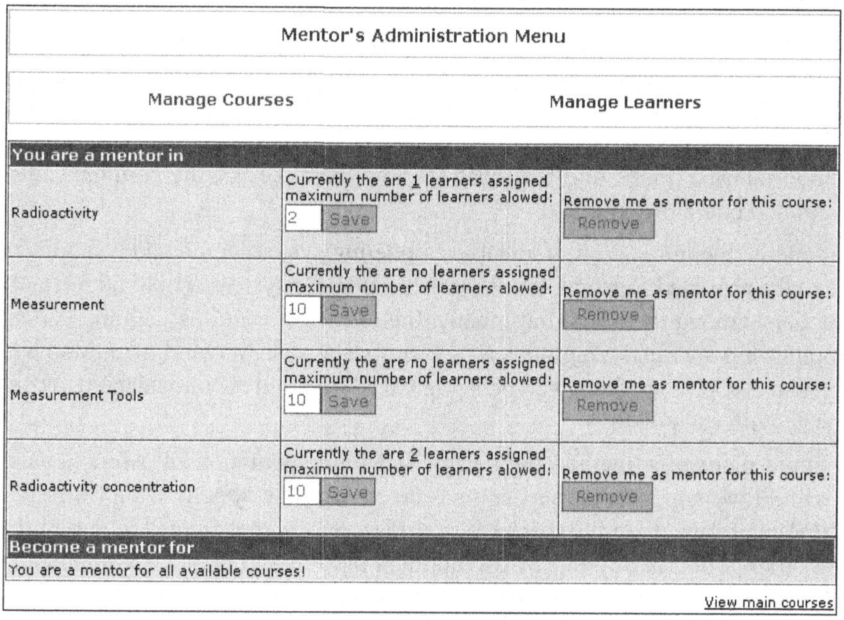

Mentor's Administration Menu

Manage Courses | Manage Learners

You are a mentor in		
Radioactivity	Currently the are 1 learners assigned maximum number of learners alowed: 2 Save	Remove me as mentor for this course: Remove
Measurement	Currently the are no learners assigned maximum number of learners alowed: 10 Save	Remove me as mentor for this course: Remove
Measurement Tools	Currently the are no learners assigned maximum number of learners alowed: 10 Save	Remove me as mentor for this course: Remove
Radioactivity concentration	Currently the are 2 learners assigned maximum number of learners alowed: 10 Save	Remove me as mentor for this course: Remove

Become a mentor for

You are a mentor for all available courses!

View main courses

Future Directions

BALOC, at this moment in time, provides tools and services tailored to the development and delivery of accessible, reusable, and traceable learning objects and online courses through the Web. Despite the fact that it presents a lot of the features all up-to-date e-learning platforms are expected to expose, new functionalities could be added to allow for more flexibility.

It is in our plans, in particular, to extend BALOC to support the replacement of existing assets and the editing of existing learning objects. These, of course, presuppose the implementation of a version control function. All of these services, in combination with the already provided "Edit Course" facility, would allow authors to keep the content constantly update, without having to develop it from scratch.

The authoring capabilities of the proposed system can also be extended to allow the creation of additional types of assessment objects. In this case, though, we should examine how the users' answers could be tracked. The research, design, and implementation of the way in which new user interactions with the content could be monitored are actually in our future plans. Examples of these interactions are a) the time a user spends on an assessment object until he/she provides an answer and b) the alternative content type the user selects to view (e.g., text or video). This information could provide useful information about the learning content usage and efficiency, as well as the user preferences.

Furthermore, in its present form, BALOC allows users to communicate with each other via private messages or e-mail. In a next step, users would explore new ways of communication, asynchronous or synchronous, that could give them the feeling that they are members of a virtual community. Communication can be one-to-one or one-to-many. Forums and text chat are few examples of the communication services that could be exploited.

Additionally, the integration of a learner modeling system could add a significant value to the provided functionality. A learner modeling system should facilitate the interactions among the users, but mainly, the user's interactions with the system. By monitoring and analyzing the user's actions, the system could help them with the system use, provide them with pedagogical advice, and encourage them to communicate with each other.

Our future plans also include the design and implementation of a functionality that will allow authors to export courses created in our system in the form of a SCORM-conformant zip file (package). In this way, content created in our system would be imported in any SCORM-compliant system and thus, be available to a wider audience.

All the new BALOC services will be implemented using open source technologies and tools. This is in line with the arguments outlined earlier, in which we do not want to commit to a certain proprietary software vendor, but instead, use reliable, rich-featured and well-supported free software tools. Above and beyond, it is our intention to distribute BALOC code under a free software license.

After the completion of the aforementioned tasks, assiduous evaluation of the system contribution to the learning process could take place. This presupposes the systematic test of the provided functionality by the potential end users.

Conclusion

The Web-based tool presented in this chapter incorporates many of the design characteristics an up-to-date e-learning platform should expose. In particular, as far as the technological approach is concerned:

- A user can access the system through a standard Web browser without the need to install additional software to his/her system.
- The system can run on a wide variety of platforms.

- The system adopts the metadata elements (all the mandatory and the majority of the optional) that are described in SCORM. The adopted content model is also inspired by SCORM. Its clear structure, in combination with the metadata elements, facilitates the easy reuse of the various learning resources for the creation of larger instructional units. Moreover, metadata facilitates the easy search and retrieval of the learning content.

As far as the pedagogical approach is concerned:

- The system encourages and accepts the user's autonomy and initiative. Learners are able to communicate with their mentors in order to get support, as well as with the other system members. Moreover, all registered users can take part in the learning process though one or more different roles. This distribution of the rights and access levels the role model implies encourages the active participation of all the involved users in the learning process.
- For each action, the system provides the user with continuous feedback. For instance, when a user answers a self-assessment, the system informs him/her immediately about (a) whether his/her answer was right, and (b) which is the indicative answer on this particular question.

In addition, the system offers the following services:

- Services for including and updating user profiles
- Services for creating courses and cataloguing them
- Services for creating tests
- User tracking services
- Services for creating, organizing, and managing learning content
- Asynchronous communication tools, such as the private messages functionality

What is more, learners are able to choose between two modes of learning: browse and study mode. The only difference between these two modes of learning is that only in the latter case, the learner's interactions with the content are monitored. Thus, a learner can go back to the content of a course, at any moment, to review it without his/her actions being tracked.

Within BALOC, every change on the learning material is not readily available to the rest of the users unless approved by the Editorial Board. In this way, it is assured that only learning content of high quality is delivered to the learners.

Last but not least, BALOC is based on open source technologies. Open source technologies are available free of charge, they do not depend on particular companies, they are usually reliable, and they have good quality (due to their qualitative control by many people and the primary evolution of the source code).

References

Álvarez-González, L., Sandoval, A., Ritter, A., & Berger, I. (2005). A virtual high school based in LMS open-source and learning objects. In A. Méndez-Vilas, B. González-Pereira, J. Mesa González & J.A. Mesa González (Eds.), *Recent research developments in learning technologies* (Vol. III, pp. 1355-1360). FORMATEX, Badajoz, Spain.

Banks, B., & McGrath, K. (2003). *E-learning content advisory paper*. Retrieved April 6, 2006, from http://www.fdlearning.com/html/company/papers/e-learnContentPaper.pdf

Bouras, C., & Nani, M. (2004). A Web-based tool for building and accessing learning objects and online courses. In Kinshuk, C.K. Looi, E. Sutinen, D. Sampson, I. Aedo, L. Uden, & E. Kahkonen (Eds.) In *Proceedings of the 4th IEEE International Conference on Advanced Learning Technologies (ICALT)* (pp. 645-647). Los Amamitos, CA: IEEE Computer Society.

Bouras, C., Nani, M., & Tsiatsos, T. (2003a). A SCORM-conformant LMS. In C. McNaught & D. Lassner (Eds.), *Proceedings: ED–MEDIA— World Conference on Educational Multimedia, Hypermedia & Telecommunications* (pp. 10-13). Norfolk, VA: Association for the Advancement of Computing in Education.

Bouras, C., Nani, M., & Tsiatsos, T. (2003b, August 18-20). Building reusable and interactive e-learning content using Web. In W. Zhou, P. Nicholson, B. Corbitt, & J. Fong (Eds.), *Advances in Web-Based Learning (ICWL 2003), Second International Conferences*, Melbourne, Australia (pp. 497-508). Springer.

Colace, F., De Santo, M., & Vento, M. (2002). Models for e-learning environment evaluation: A proposal. Retrieved April 30, 2003, from http://www.ssgrr.it/en/ssgrr2002s/papers/330.pdf

Jesshope, C. R., & Zhang, Z. (2002). A content management system for the TILE managed learning environment. In S. Banks, P. Goodyear, V. Hodgson, & D. McConnell (Eds.), *Proceedings of the Third International Conference on Networked Learning (NLC)* (pp.136-143). Lancaster and Sheffield University.

Kaliakatsos, J., Malamos, A. G., & Damianakis, A. (2002). The implementation of SCORM e-learning standards in a pilot distance learning system in T.E.I. of Crete. In M. Auer & U. Auer (Eds.) In *Proceedings of Interactive Workshop, Interactive Computer aided Learning (ICL 2003), Learning Objects and Reusability of Content.* Kassel University Press.

Langer, E. J. (1997). *The power of mindful learning.* Reading Mass: Perseus Books Group.

Midkiff, S. F., & DaSilva, L. A. (2000). *Leveraging the Web for f versus asynchronous distance learning.* Paper presented in the 2000 International Conference on Engineering Education (ICEE), Tainan, Taiwan.

Papadakis, S., & Hadzilacos, T. (2005). Web cast producer: A simple authoring tool for the automation of the production of video lectures. *Journal of Advanced Technology for Learning, 208*(2), 97-106 .

Wan, L., Zhao, C., Liu, Q., & Sun, J. (2005). Work in progress-An evaluation model for learning content management systems: From a perspective of knowledge management. In *Proceedings, 35th ASEE/IEEE Frontiers in Education* (pp. F3G-15 - F3G-16). Indianaplois, IN: IEEE CS Press.

Wheeler, D. A. (2005, November). *Why open source software/free software (OSS/FS, FLOSS, or FOSS)? Look at the numbers!* Retrieved April 6, 2006, from, http://www.dwheeler.com/oss_fs_why.html

Endnotes

1. Apache HTTP Server Project, http://httpd.apache.org
2. PHP, http://www.php.net
3. The JavaScript Source, http://javascript.internet.com
4. PHP-Nuke - Open Source Professional Portal System, http://phpnuke.org
5. htmlArea - Turn any <textarea> into a WYSIWYG editor, http://www.interactivetools.com/products/htmlarea/
6. MySQL, http://www.mysql.com

Appendix I: Internet Session: Comparing Open Source Course Management Systems Aimed at the Higher Education Market

http://www.e-learningcentre.co.uk

The e-Learning Centre provides e-learning advice and consultancy to businesses and education. In this Web site, you can find a large collection of links to e-learning resources in the Information section, which is accessible to all.

Interaction

Go to the "Products & Services" Web section. There you can find links to e-learning products and services in the following categories:

1. E-learning tools and systems
2. Off-the-shelf e-learning content
3. E-learning service providers

Click on the "Open source educational CMS/VLEs" link that falls into the first category. There you can find links to open source course management systems aimed at the higher education market, together with their short descriptions. After reviewing the information presented in the respective Web sites, prepare a brief presentation comparing these products.

Appendix II: Case Study: An E- Learning Platform for a Geographically Dispread Community of Professionals

You, as an IT expert, have been assigned to provide an e-learning solution targeted at a community of professionals in a highly specialized field and spread all over the world. Those professionals, in an attempt to overcome the problem of isolation and share knowledge with each other, decided to try an e-learning platform. As the majority of them do not have particular computer technology skills, they just want to use an e-learning platform that will enable them to easily create, publish, and access learning material that is as close to on-the-job training as possible. They also want to communicate and collaborate with each other in order to share knowledge, experiences, and best practices.

Questions

1. What do you see as the critical issues to address in establishing a learning platform for those professionals?
2. How would you proceed in creating the e-learning platform?
3. Assuming that you have the resources to design and develop a state-of-the-art e-learning platform to support the real community of professionals, what would be your design and technological choices?

Appendix III: Useful URLs

IEEE Learning Technology Standards Committee (LTSC):

http://ltsc.ieee.org

ARIADNE Foundation for the European Knowledge Pool:

http://www.ariadne-eu.org

CEN/ISSS (European Commission for Standardisation/Infrmation Society Standardisation System) Learning Technologies Workshop (WS/LT):

http://www.cenorm.be/cenorm/businessdomains/businessdomains/informationsocietystandardizationsystem/elearning/learning+technologies+workshop/index.asp

Aviation Industry CBT Comittee:

http://www.aicc.org

IMS Global Learning Consortium, Inc:

http://www.imsproject.org

Advanced Distributed Learning (ADL) Initiative:
http://www.adlnet.org

e-Learning Center:
http://www.e-learningcentre.co.uk

Content-Management Opportunities:
http://www.gii.co.jp/english/cs10068_content_management.html

Learning Object Metadata use survey: sticking the short and wide in the long and thin:
http://www.cetis.ac.uk/content2/20041015015543

eLearning results:
http://www.elearningresults.com

Dept. Computerwetenschappen, Katholieke Universiteit LeuvenResearch unit on hypermedia and databases, Bibliography:
http://ariadne.cs.kuleuven.ac.be/hmdb/jsp/Wiki?Publications

eLearn: In Depth Tutorials, The Basics of E-Learning: An Excerpt from Handbook of Human Factors in Web Design:
http://www.elearnmag.org/subpage.cfm?section=tutorials&article=20-1

Open Source Resources => Project Hosts, Repositories and Directories:
http://opensource.ucc.ie/projects.html

Technology-Enabled Teaching/eLearning Dialogue, Will Open Source Software Unlock the Potential of eLearning?:
http://www.campus-technology.com/news_article.asp?id=10299&typeid=155

Apendix IV: For Further Reading

Campbell, L. M. (2004). *Learning object metadata, updates, issues and developments*. Retrieved from http://www.library.usyd.edu.au/dest/metadata_update_lmc.ppt

Dara-Abrams, B. P. (2002). *Web technologies for multi-intelligent online learning*. PhD dissertation. Retrieved from http://www.brainjolt.com/docs/webtech.pdf

Forth, S., & Childs, E. *White paper on e-learning specifications and standards*. Jointly developed by ITS Inc and Recombo. Retrieved from http://www.itsinc.bc.ca/Samples/Specifications%20and%20Standards%20White%20Paper.pdf

Lytras, M. D., & Pouloudi, A. (2001). E-learning: Just a waste of time. In D. Strong, D. Straub, & J. I. DeGross (Eds.), *Proceedings of the Seventh Americas Conference on Think.*

Naeve, A., Nilsson, M., Palmér, M., & Paulsson, F. (2005). Contributions to a public e-learning platform: Infrastructure, architecture, frameworks, and tools. *International Journal of Learning Technology, 1*(3), 352-281.

OpenUniversiteitNederland. *Barriers to the widespread take-up of standardised e-learning*. Retrieved from http://dspace.learningnetworks.org/handle/1820/282 http://dspace.learningnetworks.org/handle/1820/282

Yue, K.-B., Yang, T. A., Ding, W., & Chen, P. (2004). Open courseware and computer science education. *Journal of Computing Sciences in Colleges, 20*(1).

Possible Titles for Papers/Essays

- The Use of Open Source Technologies to Provide Effective and Efficient Learning
- An Effective E-learning Platform for a Geographically Dispread Community of Professionals
- A Comparison of Open Source E-Learning Platforms

Chapter X

The Development of the OpenACS Community

Neophytos Demetriou, Vienna University of Economics and Business Administration, Austria
Stefan Koch, Vienna University of Economics and Business Administration, Austria
Gustaf Neumann, Vienna University of Economics and Business Administration, Austria

Abstract

OpenACS is a high-level community framework designed for developing collaborative Internet sites. It started from a university project at MIT, got momentum from the ArsDigita Foundation, and split up into a commercial and an open source version. OpenACS has proven its durability and utility by surviving the death of its parent company (ArsDigita) to grow into a vibrant grassroots collection of independent consultants and small companies implementing diverse and complex Web solutions around the globe for NPOs, philanthropy, and profit. A heritage from this history is a still dominant position of contributors with commercial interests that, in its intensity, is above the norm found in open source projects. In this paper, OpenACS, with its community is presented as a case study documenting the forces between commercial interests, securing investments, and technical development in a large open source project with a large proportion of commercial involvement.

Introduction

The free and open source software world has spawned several projects in different application domains, like most notably, the operating system Linux, together with the suite of GNU utilities, the office suites GNOME and KDE, Apache, sendmail, bind, and several programming languages that have achieved huge success in their respective markets.

In the last years, the commercial interest in open source software has increased dramatically (Ousterhout, 1999). This has also lead to changes in many projects, which now include contributors who get paid for their contributions and others who receive no direct payment. This is also reflected in several recent surveys: For example, Lakhani and Wolf (2005) found that 13% of respondents received direct payments and 38% spent work hours on open source development, with their supervisor being aware of the fact (684 respondents from 287 distinct projects). Ghosh (2005) reports a group of 31.4% motivated by monetary or career (mostly for signaling competence) concerns in a sample of 2,280 responses. Hars and Ou (2001) found a share of 16% being directly paid, Hertel et al. (Hertel, Niedner, & Hermann, 2003) report 20% of contributors receiving a salary for this work on a regular basis, with an additional 23% at least sometimes, in a survey of Linux kernel developers. Given these results, many projects currently will be composed of a mixture of paid and volunteer participants, thus distinctly deviating from the "classical" open source development, as described most notably by Raymond (1999). This mixture, and the resulting conflicts of interests, could have severe results on working styles, processes, and also products of open source projects. In this chapter, we will present the case study of OpenACS (n.a., 2006a), a project between commercial interests, securing investments, and technical development. The OpenACS changed its status several times during its lifetime, starting from a university project at MIT, getting momentum from the ArsDigita Foundation, and lastly, splitting up into a commercial and an open source version, where the commercial version failed but the community continues to develop the open source version. While the literature yields discussions and examples on commercial projects going open source or enterprises investing in open source projects (Behlendorf, 1999; Hawkins, 2004; Hecker, 1999), most notably the Mozilla project (Hamerly, Paquin, & Walton, 1999), the history of OpenACS seems unique in its complexity. Nevertheless, we propose that this form of biography will increasingly show up in software development projects, and that the repercussions on processes and products are important to analyze.

The structure of this chapter is as follows: in the following section, we will describe the history of OpenACS. The turbulent past of the project shaped the management framework with its idiosyncrasies. As a next step, we will analyze up to which point the influences of the project management structure and forces of the different stakeholders can be observed from some empirical data obtained from mining the source code management system (Hahsler & Koch, 2005; Robles, Koch, & Gonzalez-Barahona, 2004). The chapter will finish with some conclusions.

History of OpenACS

The Early Days

The roots of OpenACS trace back to Philip Greenspun and his work on the site photo.net starting in 1995, and "Philip and Alex's Guide to Web Publishing" in 1998 (Greenspun, 1999b). The project started out as a rapid prototyping framework for Web applications, based on the experiences of photo.net. The core elements of the framework were a highly scalable Web server (AOLserver (n.a., 2006c)) with a tight integration with relational databases (especially with Oracle and PostgreSQL), and the scripting language Tcl (Ousterhout, 1989).

AOLserver was originally developed by NaviSoft under the name NaviServer, but changed names when AOL bought the company in 1995. AOL uses this server to run its busiest sites, such as digitalcity.com1 and aol.com. It has been reported that as early as mid-1999, multiple AOLserver instances were serving more than 28,000 requests per second for America Online (Greenspun, 1999a). AOLserver is a multithreaded application server with well-abstracted database access and connection pooling mechanisms. Scalability is achieved due to the fact that the most performance-critical functionalities are implemented in C.

AOLserver uses the built-in scripting language Tcl as an extension language (Ousterhout, 1998) to provide a flexible means of composing systems from predefined components. This way, application-specific hot spots can be quickly programmed, and the server can be extended on the fly (without restarting). Based on this combination of scalability and rapid application development, it became possible to develop complex Web applications in short time.

ArsDigita

We want to focus now on the historical development of the framework, which deeply influenced the structure of the project and the active development community. In 1997, Philip Greenspun and a group of students, mostly from MIT, joined forces to produce the world's best toolkit for building scalable community-oriented Web applications. The newly founded company ArsDigita ("Digital Arts") was quickly able to attract high-profile clients, such as Deutsche Bank, WGBH (radio and television

Figure 1. Development of ArsDigita and early OpenACS

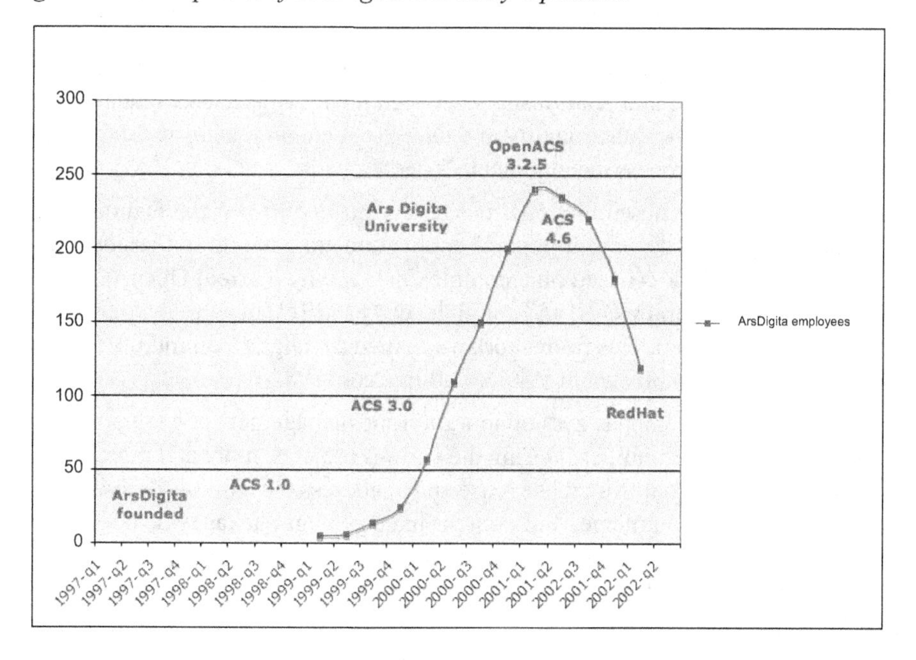

channel), the World Bank, and Siemens. In early 2000, ArsDigita took $35 million from two venture capital firms (Greylock and General Atlantic Partners).

With one of the world's largest corporations on their client list, ArsDigita was already defying the conventional wisdom by actively supporting an open source version of its toolkit. The founders of the ArsDigita Corporation also created a nonprofit organization, the ArsDigita Foundation, which sponsored a yearly programming contest for high school students, and a free brick and mortar school teaching an intensive one-year course in undergraduate computer science (in 2000).

The underlying engineering was supported by millions of dollars of venture capital spent on hiring PhDs in Computer Science from MIT, CalTech, and other major universities across the Atlantic and Europe. At this time, ArsDigita employed more than 240 people (see Figure 1), mostly developers, working on the foundation of what is now called OpenACS (more about this later). However, with the advent of the investors, the interests shifted away from community-supported open source version towards the company's needs. The company decided to redevelop the framework based on Java in order to develop a proprietary enterprise collaboration software. The commercial version was called ACS-Java, while the community-supported Tcl-based version was developed further under the name of OpenACS. The proprietary product was never launched and, in 2002, ArsDigita was acquired by Red Hat.

The ArsDigita Community System (ACS)

In general, most Web applications have the same basic needs: (a) user management (represent people and relationships between them), (b) security management (manage accessibility to functionality and data), (c) content management (content repository), and (d) process management.

Instead of developing these functionalities repetitiously on a per-application basis, ArsDigita decided to develop a general application framework addressing these needs. This framework is based on a complex data model (current OpenACS uses a few hundred tables and views) and a high level API in Tcl (in current OpenACS a few thousand functions). This framework was called ArsDigita Community System (ACS) and was first published in version 1.0 in Dec. 1998.

The code base of ACS emphasizes collaboration and management of geographically distributed online communities. During the various projects, more and more pieces of code were factored out to increase reuse and to address the requests derived from the collaboration, e-commerce, and content management packages developed on top of the core. The system started with a small core of functionality, but only a little more than 1 year after the initial version, ACS 3.0 was released as a rich application framework as open source under the GNU General Public License version 2 (Jan. 2000). Dozens of packages based on the core functionality were created. Ten months later, the next major refactoring led to version 4.0 (release Nov. 2000), where a completely new kernel was developed, based on a highly flexible security management system, subsites, templating, workflow management, and a refactored content repository. Most notably, the package manager was developed that supports creation of packages with version dependencies, data migration scripts, and allowing remote upgrading of packages.

In 2001, the ACS code tree forked inside ArsDigita, with the Tcl code base being maintained and refactored by one group of developers, while the product line was being rewritten in Java EE. By 2002, when Red Hat acquired ArsDigita, the Tcl code base became solely supported by the open source community. At this time a rich set of application packages (such as forums, FAQ, bulk-mail, file-storage, calendar, Web shop, etc.) were already available. This rich set of packages led to the adoption of ACS by programmers and companies worldwide, and fueled the ongoing development of OpenACS without the strong former commercial backing.

OpenACS

Since 2002, the OpenACS project has been run by a group of independent programmers, whose original goal was to add support for the open source PostgreSQL database to ACS (supporting only Oracle). Soon it was clear that building demanding applications needed more than only the free database, so the community started to fix problems in the code inherited by ArsDigita, porting 3.x packages to version 4.0, writing new ones, improving and extending the core platform, and taking ACS in new directions.

The first important enhancements were two new abstractions, namely the XQL Query Dispatcher for database independence, and the Service Contracts API to facilitate greater code reuse, application integration, and package extensibility within OpenACS. ACS 3.x and earlier contained pages with embedded SQL. ACS 4.0 provided named queries and provided APIs onto them. The new XQL Query Dispatcher evolved this idea even further by abstracting these APIs from the application code. The approach involved extracting queries out of the code, and then eliminating the application's need to know about specific implementations of the SQL standard. This proved to be very useful during the porting phase, as new RDBMS support could be added on a per-package basis without editing existing code.

ACS 4.0 was based on a thin object system implemented in the relational structure in the database, but allowing a veneer of object oriented-ness by providing globally unique object IDs, object metadata, and bundling of data and methods as an object. While this permitted a level of reuse on an object or package basis, it required hard-coding the unit of reuse. Inspired by WSDL, the interface specification for Web services, the Service Contracts API allowed these objects and packages to also create contracts that define their functional level of reuse and customization, as well as register their implementation of interfaces, in this way, bringing the level of reuse at the contract level.

The current version is OpenACS 5.2, where numerous user interface improvements, external authentication, automated testing, improved development environment, and so forth, were introduced over the years, and, many application packages were added.

.LRN

As the most general requirements were quite well supported, more specific needs became addressed by the community. Two important subprojects started to emerge, namely .LRN (n.a., 2006d) and ProjectOpen (n.a., 2006b) (an ERP system based on OpenACS, with currently 4,500 installations (Bergmann, 2006)). We address in this chapter only the case of .LRN.

In 2002, MIT's Sloan School of Management contracted the company OpenForce to develop .LRN to replace their aging Course Management solution (SloanSpace, built on ACS 3.x (Gilroy, 2001; Meeks & Mangel, 2000)). The primary goal was to address MIT Sloan's specific needs, but the project had a broader vision than internal deployment.

This investment from MIT provided a strong impulse for the community after such a tumultuous period for the OpenACS project. On the one hand, .LRN became a full-featured course management system with rich community support, providing a substantial promotion of OpenACS as a platform. On the other hand, there was a big part of the OpenACS community comprised of volunteers and developers working on projects, large and small, that had nothing to do with educational technology. These developers preferred OpenACS like it was, basing development decisions on general technical needs, and not on the requirements of the founding project. At the same time, MIT Sloan School wanted to secure their investments, such that no complete split-off from OpenACS is needed, and that general future versions keep functional with future versions of OpenACS, so that .LRN can benefit from future enhancements of OpenACS.

When .LRN 1.0 was released in 2002, some learning management system (LMS) vendors had already started to disappear from the market. Learning institutions feared that a relationship with one vendor would not prove to be of a long-term nature because of the vendors' inability to stay in the market. Different universities had already started to develop learning management based on OpenACS (e.g., Vienna University of Economics and Business Administration (Alberer, Alberer, Enzi, Ernst, Mayrhofer, Neumann, Rieer, & Simon, 2003) or UNED in Spain). The perspective of developing a common community-supported learning-management system based on OpenACS was very appealing.

However, the conflicting goals led to an inevitable governance plan discussion, with lead institutions seeking formalized management structures to secure the investments of the funding organizations. The .LRN Consortium was founded, which is a nonprofit organization with a clearly defined governance and membership structure. The consortium is guided by a board of directors, and sees its mission in "creating and supporting a freely available suite of Web based educational applications to support learning communities." This can be seen as a form of "guarding the commons" (O'Mahony, 2003). Furthermore, OpenACS and .LRN became more attractive to new people, mainly consultants and organizations. But still, some feel that it changed the community, as these new people are not interacting with the community the same way the old grassroot hackers did.

Today, .LRN 2.x is the world's most widely adopted enterprise-class open source software for supporting e-learning and digital communities (n.a., 2006d), and it is installed at prestigious universities like Sloan School of Management at MIT, the JFK School of Government at Harvard University, or the Universities of Mannheim and Heidelberg in Germany, the Vienna University of Economics and Business Administration in Vienna, or the University of Valencia and the Open University of Spain (UNED, Universidad de EducaciÃ³n a la Distancia with about 200,000 students).

The OpenACS Project Management Framework

When OpenACS started as a group on SourceForge to create the ACS port to PostgreSQL, the lead developer gave written permission to anyone who showed enough competence to help out. The group soon grew to more than 20 people, with about 5 active developers. Organization, collaboration, and feedback helped produce a quality product but, in recent years, maintaining a stable, releasable, progressive codebase has become quite a difficult task. We will address these reasons in the following paragraphs.

Designing and evolving these structures has been an important aspect of open source software development for some time. While preconceptions might think of such projects as completely anarchic, this is most often not the case in reality. An important point to consider is the balance between anarchy and control, as Holck and Jorgensen (2004) describe in their account of the organization and process models in the FreeBSD and Mozilla project. They describe the technological infrastructure, but more importantly, the work organization, which includes top-level management, module owners, reviewers and committers, and the process models for releases (the FreeBSD release process is also described in more detail in Jorgensen, 2001) and contributions. In all aspects, there is an approach to strive for a balance between openness towards new participants and contributions, and the need for control, with the acknowledgment that this balance might shift over time. This point is also emphasized by the paper of Ye et al. (Ye, Nakakoji, Yamamoto, & Kishida, 2004), which stresses the co-evolution between the system and the underlying community. Using a set of case studies, they define three types of projects (exploration-oriented, utility-oriented, and service-oriented) and evolution patterns between those types. Also Erenkrantz (2003), in his account of different release management structures in open source projects, stresses the point of decentralization and controlling authority as important factors, as does Gallivan (2001), under the aspects of trust and control.

Source Code Management

OpenACS development is maintained in a central source code repository based on the Concurrent Versions System (CVS2) (Berliner, 1990; Fogel, 1999; Per Cederqvist et al., 2002). Only developers with write privileges, so called commiters, are allowed to make changes to the repository. A developer without these privileges will have to go through a commiter in order to get contributions added to the repository in the form of a patch:

To contribute a small fix, if you do not have a developer account, submit a patch.

The code is divided into packages and for each package, one person is designated as the package owner or maintainer. In the past, the package owner was the only one who had the authority to check in changes or elect other programmers to do so. Low responsibility for some packages led the OpenACS team to revise the CVS guidelines:

If you are making many changes, or would like to become a direct contributor, send mail to the Core Team asking for commit rights. You can then commit code directly to the repository.

Technically, everyone with CVS commit rights can commit changes to the code base. This is sometimes required, since OpenACS has now more than 200 packages, and not all package owners are always available, but at the same time, this lowers the perceived responsibility of a package owner. According to the CVS guidelines, another way to contribute code to the OpenACS is to add a new package:

Contact the Core Team to get approval and to get a module alias.

The analysis of the public CVS repository shows that over a hundred different people had CVS commit rights since the establishment of the repository in Spring 2001. Rather than requiring developers to coordinate with each other to synchronize efforts, CVS enables developers to update repository files continually and in parallel. Today, OpenACS is a complex system, despite the seeming simplicity of its components. A system based on uncontrolled changes to the source code repository is no longer appropriate for a system of this complexity, as it greatly inhibits integration, release, and regression testing.

The current OpenACS development team is more diverse than the original team; they live in different time zones, speak different languages, have different needs and requirements, and different coding styles. A purely CVS-based codebase does not serve the product well in this environment.

Technical Improvement Proposals (TIPs)

On openacs.org, nearly 10,000 users are currently registered. The Web site currently lists more than 120 community sites based on OpenACS (including Greenpeace Planet, United Nations Industrial Development Organization (UNIDO), Creative

Commons, or AISEC (the world largest student organization)), and lists 58 companies providing commercial support for OpenACS. The largest sites have up to 2 million users (Recco, 2005). Since many of the OpenACS contributors are consultants, often in charge of running sometimes dozens of sites, code changes that introduce incompatibilities are very expensive.

Therefore, the community adopted a guideline (Aufrecht, 2004) about dealing with changes in the CVS. This guideline requires a so called technical improvement proposal when an update involves any changes to the core data model, or will change the behavior of any core package in a way that affects existing code (typically, by changing public API), or is a non-backwards compatible change to any core or standard package. The first version of the Core Team governance document was released in May 2003, and serves since then as an instrument to guard against changes in the core product. Since 2003, there were between 18 and 25 TIPs accepted per year; about 25% of the TIPs are rejected.[3] While the TIPs provide an instrument to secure investments, they effectively require a sideways development based on coexistence: while changing existing APIs require a TIP, the development of new functionality does not. Currently, it appears that the only way to make complex architectural changes is to build a coexisting subframework, which certainly has disadvantages from the software engineering point of view. In any large software system, evolution tends to create increasing complexity (Belady & Lehman, 1976), a fact also acknowledged in studies on open source systems (Samoladas, Stamelos, Angelis, & Oikonomou, 2004), necessitating architectural repair actions, as described by Tran et al. (Tran, Godfrey, Lee, & Holt, 2000) in the context of the Linux kernel and the VIM text editor.

Bug Tracking and Fixes

A common project risk is to remain unaware of the existence of a major problem beyond the stage at which it can be contained and corrected. OpenACS addresses this problem by the bug-tracker, a software tool for tracking bugs and feature requests. The bug-tracking tool was developed using OpenACS, and incorporates ideas from BugZilla, Bughost.com, and FogBUGZ.

Figure 2 shows the underlying workflow of the bug management in OpenACS. A bug can be in the state Open, Resolved, or Closed, and is assigned priority and severity. In a true open source fashion ("given enough eyeballs, all bugs are shallow" (Raymond, 1999)), everyone can report bugs and everyone is encouraged to do this. Also Villa (2003) describes a bug tracking system, based on Bugzilla, in a large open source project, GNOME, and highlights the importance of being open while applying the necessary triage to control a possibly massive amount of bug reports.

The OpenACS bug-tracker assigns a bug, per default, to the package owner. At this state, the bug tracker supports an open discussion of the problem in a Web log

Figure 2. OpenACS bug tracker workflow

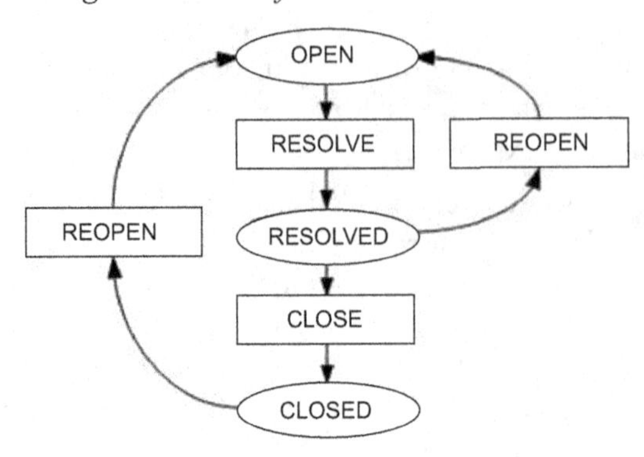

style. Any user can submit candidate patches for this bug. The package maintainer can resolve the bug, maybe by choosing one of the provided patches. The original submitter of a bug is the person who has to close it.

Note that the only quality assurance step is actually the last step, where the bug submitter closes the issue. In practice, it turns out that there is a high number of packages available, where for some of these packages the responsibility seems low, since many reported problems remain open. Also Villa (2003) stresses the importance of closing old bugs. The bug tracker contains, currently, 2,896 entries, of which 1,589 are closed, 422 are marked as resolved, and 886 are open. It seems as if the bug submitters care more about bug fixes than about closing the bugs they have opened.

Code Contributions

At the time of this writing, the CVS repository of OpenACS contains more than 2.5 million lines of code (mostly Tcl, SQL, HTML-templates, and documentation, see Figure 3). In terms of logical units, the OpenACS repository contains more than 200 packages.

In the following, we present an analysis of the contents of the CVS repository to provide empirical evidence about the development. The CVS repository contains OpenACS 4.x and 5.x. For these versions, 107 distinct committers have contributed to the CVS repository. Fifty-one (48%) contributors can be classified as volunteers (non-profit contributors), and 54 (50%) have, as well, a commercial motivation (for-profit contributors, regularly, or at least on several occasions receiving payment for contributions of code to the OpenACS project, or working for a company offering OpenACS support), and therefore we classify these as commercial. Two committers remained unclassified. The contributions of the classified contributors account for

Figure 3. Timeline of the development of the code base

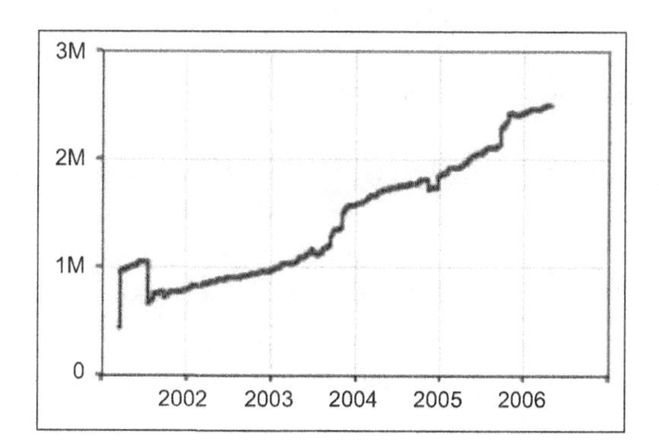

Figure 4. Total number of contributions

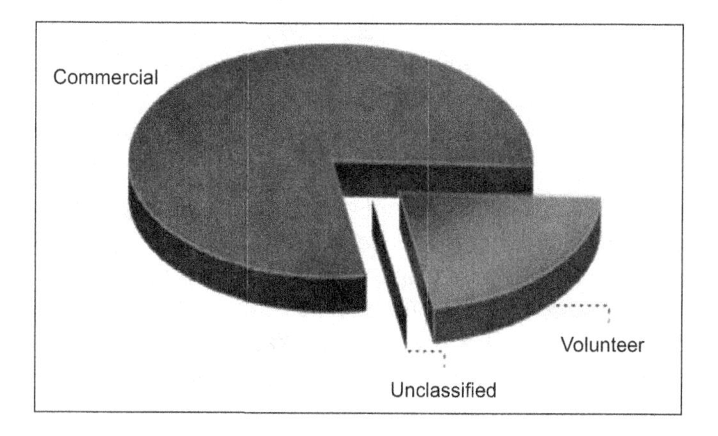

99.97% of the total amount of contributions (see Figure 4). Since the unclassified contributors have little significance, we left these out for the further analysis.

Certainly, the distinction is not easy to draw, not at least since the status of a contributor might shift.[4] People receiving salaries for maintaining sites based on OpenACS, but not for participating in developing OpenACS, have been classified as volunteers. In comparison to the results of several surveys, as described previously (Ghosh, 2005; Hars & Ou, 2001; Hertel et al., 2003; Lakhani & Wolf, 2005), the amount of commercial background within the OpenACS team is above the mean.

The top 15 OpenACS developers have contributed 72% of the total changes, 80% of these developers are rated as commercial. This highly skewed distribution is in line with findings from other studies of open source projects: A case study of the

Apache project showed that 88% of the code was developed by the top 15 programmers (Mockus, Fielding, & Herbsleb, 2002), where in the GNOME project, the top 15 programmers were responsible for "only" 48% of the code (Koch & Schneider, 2002). A similar distribution for the lines-of-code contributed to the project was found in a community of Linux kernel developers (Hertel et al., 2003). Also, the results of the Orbiten Free Software survey (Ghosh & Prakash, 2000) are similar, the first decile of programmers was responsible for 72%, the second for 9% of the total code. In a set of 8,621 SourceForge.net projects, the top decile was found to be responsible for 79% of the contributions (Koch, 2004).

We measure the contributions of the community members by the number of acts where the community members have committed content to the code base (checking in a file). About 104,000 contributions have been performed over the lifetime of the repository. A code contribution can be either a checkin (providing initial code), or a modification or a removal of a file. Using the policy-governed text in changelog messages[5], an additional classification of different contributions has been performed: This resulted in about 1,100 contributions pertaining to a TIP (1.1% of the total), 8,400 being bug fixes (8% of the total) and 1,700 patches (1.6% of the total), defined as being code committed for someone else without commit privilege. As this number of patches is relatively small, and the background of the original programmer is unknown, these would not have a significant effect on the relation between volunteers and commercial contributors, and this effect is therefore neglected.

When we compare the nonprofit committers with the commercial ones, we see that the number of contributions of a commercial commiter is more than three-times higher than the contributions of a volunteer. This reflects well the structure of the OpenACS, where the initial development was performed by the company ArsDigita. Also, after the end of ArsDigita, packages are frequently developed by companies for profit. Also, professional full-time developers can spend often more time on developing a system than volunteers. Using a rank-based Mann Whitney U-test ascertains (at $p<0.05$) that the commercial group leads in lines-of-codes, more TIP-related contributions, more bug fixes, more patches, and more different packages worked on.

By distinguishing the contributions between code, documentation, and others, while the commercial group is responsible for 78% of contributions of source code, this difference is even more pronounced in their efforts in code documentation, with 82%.

Table 1. Comparison of commercial contributors to volunteer contributors

	Contributions	Number	Ratio
Commercial	81,828	54	1,515
Volunteer	22,691	51	445

They also dominate in the group of TIP-related contributions, where commercial committers are responsible for 89%, compared to 78% for non-TIP-related, and for patches, where they are responsible for 87%. This effect is not visible for bug fixes, where the percentage is mostly even (78% for non-bug fixes compared to 76%).

Analysis by Types of Packages

Next, the contributions for different types of packages are analyzed. OpenACS provides a division between kernel packages providing the general infrastructure and application packages, where .LRN is an important subgroup. For all three categories, we distinguish further between optional and non-optional packages. The results are summarized in Figure 5, showing the contributions of the two contributor groups by package type.

It is interesting to see that the non-profit developers account for only 11% of the changes in the kernel, whereas in the code of the application packages or for the .LRN components, the contributions are much stronger (e.g., 57% in .LRN-extra). This can be explained by the strong usage of .LRN on universities worldwide, contributing code developed to satisfy their needs.

Furthermore, we observed that kernel packages score significantly higher in almost all dimensions (Mann Whitney U-test, $p<0.01$) than application packages: They have more committers (both commercial and volunteer), more contributions ($p<0.05$), more bug –fixes, and also TIP-related contributions and patches. Interestingly, the

Figure 5. Contributions per package type

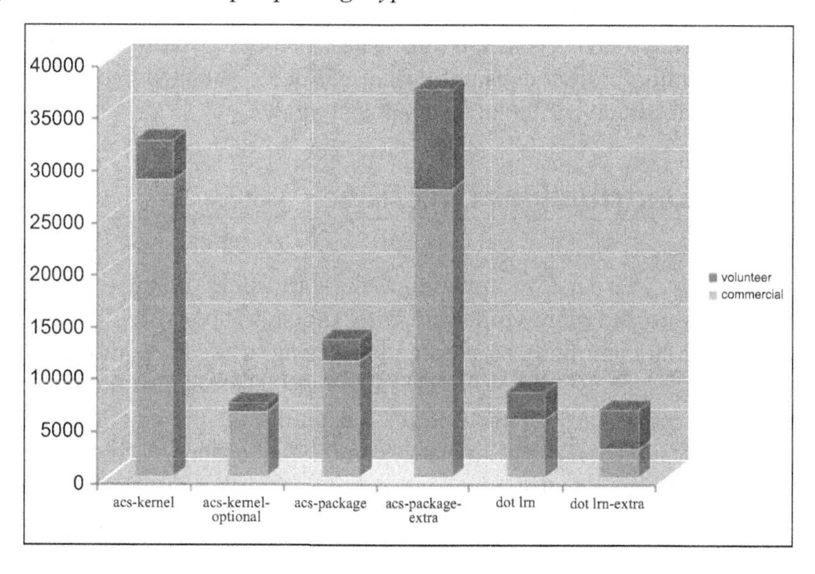

difference in contributions, TIP-related contributions, and bug fixes by volunteers is not significant. Also, the percentage of commercial committers within the packages is not different between kernel and application packages, as is the amount of activity, measured in contributions per day of lifetime, that is, since the initial checkin, although the lifetime itself, and the number of months there was work on the packages, do differ significantly, and are larger for kernel packages.

Another point to explore is whether a dominance of commercial committers has any effect on other attributes of packages. We find that the higher the percentage of commercial background is, measured either by the percentage of committers or contributions, the lower the activity is (Spearman correlation, $p<0.01$). This might be an indication of a form of development in which new packages are created by commercial committers, checked in and seldomly changed later on. This is also underlined by a significant negative correlation (-0.375, $p<0.01$) between the percentage of commercial background and the number of months in which contributions to a package were performed. As there is also a significant correlation to overall lifetime, we computed a stepwise linear regression with numbers of active months as dependent variable. Lifetime of a package alone reaches an R^2-adjusted of 0.338, including the percentage of commercial background leads to significant increase to an R^2-adjusted of 0.471, and has a negative coefficient, supporting the hypothesis. Also, the standard deviation of programmers active within a month with any activity decreases with the amount of commercial background within a package (-0.577, $p<0.01$).

Concluding, we see that a large proportion of commercial background in a package leads to a low number of total and volunteer developers in this package (-0.473 resp. -0.739, $p<0.01$), low activity, and small variations in number of active developers between the periods of activity. It seems that commercial developers tend to contribute these packages, maintain them mostly on their own and only seldomly, maybe depending on receiving respective mandates. Therefore, this form of sideways development seemingly often does not progress in the postulated "open source" way, but might constitute a different development mode.

Changes of Contributions Over Time

The analysis of the CVS data over time shows the shift from primarily commercial contributors to more and more volunteer contributors. As shown in Figure 6, the number of non-profit contributors is constantly growing, while the number of commercial contributors reached its peak at the end of 2003. It is also interesting to see that although more than 100 contributors account for the project, there was no quarter year where more than 38 people have contributed to OpenACS so far. When we look at the number of contributions instead of the number of contributors, we see the number of contributions of the volunteers growing and big changes in the

Figure 6. Distinct contributors

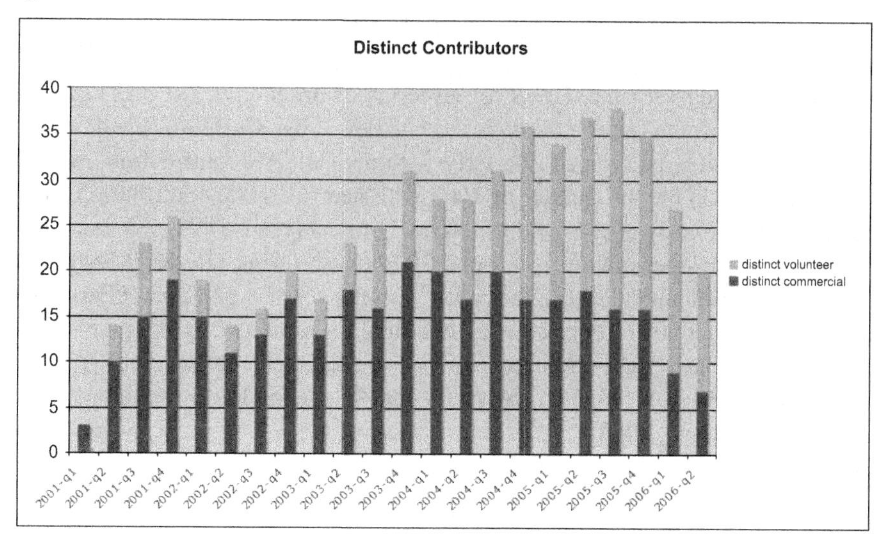

Figure 7. Number of contributions over time by type of contributor

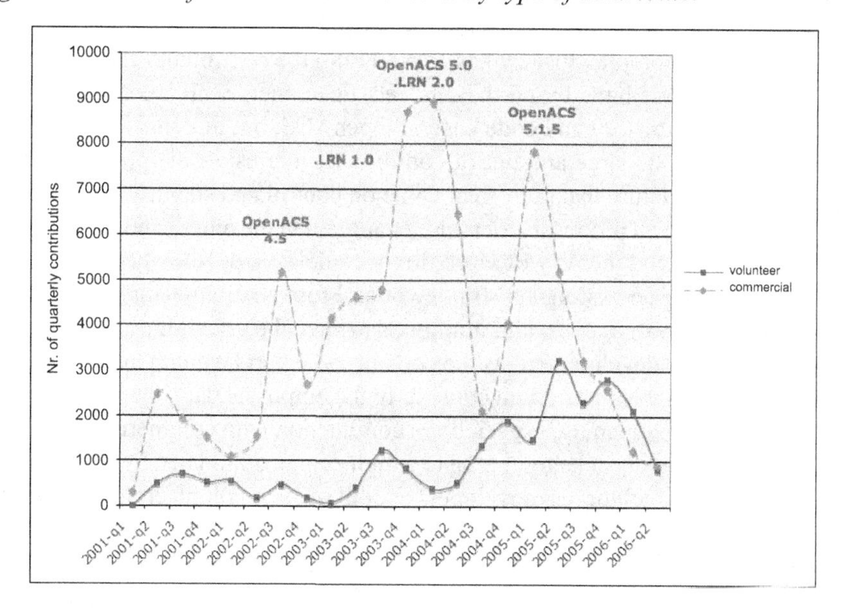

contributions of the commercial group (see Figure 7). The peaks in this diagram reflect the contributions to the major releases of OpenACS and .LRN.

Both of these diagrams hint at the fact that this dominant position of the commercial group might erode over time. However, in terms of productivity, it takes several volunteer developers to replace one commercial developer. Currently, the development of OpenACS is performed quarterly with about 1,700 contributions, where the peak rate was in the 4th quarter of 2003 with nearly 10,000 contributions. For comparison, in the early phases of the GNOME project (1997-1999), a mean number of contributions per quarter of around 30,000, with peak rate of 38,000, was found (Koch & Schneider, 2002), the mean within a set of 8,621 SourceForge.net projects was around 600 (Koch, 2004). Regarding the number of participants, 354 distinct contributors were found in an analysis of the CVS repository of FreeBSD (Dinh-Trong & Bieman, 2005), nearly 400 for Apache and 486 for the Mozilla project (Mockus et al., 2002).

Conclusion

In this chapter, we have detailed OpenACS and its community as a case study of a project between commercial interests, securing investments, and technical development. The complex history has shaped both the community itself, and the practices adopted. We have found that, indeed, developers with a commercial interest dominate the history and code base of OpenACS, but that this fact might be slowly changing. This large amount of commercial interest in the project has led to a governance structure that puts great value on control and stability by requiring technical improvement proposals for major changes. On the other hand, this rigidity seems to have affected the way of work, in that sideways developments might be established creating coexisting sub-frameworks. From an architectural viewpoint, this would be disadvantageous, and it might also have the effect of preventing true "open source" style development, as the code in these parts would tend to be more specific and only usable in a certain context. In the empirical data, there seem to be indications for this happening, especially in conjunction with commercial developers: We have found that packages, being to a high degree dominated by commercial background, tend to include less developers overall and less volunteers, and also tend to be changed less often and by the same group of people. If this trend continued and increased, a series of mostly isolated "islands" could result.

In this respect, OpenACS, with its early and heavy involvement from commercial interests might prove a test-bed for developments possibly taking place in several open source projects. It will be an important issue in the future, how the different interests of volunteer and commercial contributors in such projects can be aligned, and how the community is able to cope with demanding changes such as market forces of Web2. Through the strong investments of companies like ArsDigita and the highly flexible framework approach, OpenACS has started with an advantage over competing projects. Over the last years, both the interest in collaborative Web environments, but as well the competition in this area increased. Without any doubt, the community, the structures and processes, and the product itself will, and must continue, to evolve and to adapt to new and changing requirements and situations. However, the project has come too long a way to die out, and its existence and continuation is ensured by a remarkable conglomeration of interests among companies, NPOs, and volunteers.

References

Alberer, G., Alberer, P., Enzi, T., Ernst, G., Mayrhofer, K., Neumann, G., Rieder, R., & Simon, B. (2003). The Learn@WU learning environment. In *Proceedings of Wirtschaftsinformatik 2003, 6th International Conference on Business Informatics*, Dresden, Germany.

Aufrecht, J. (2004). TIP #61: Guidelines for cvs committers. *OpenACS Improvement Proposals*. Retrieved November 17, 2006, from http://openacs.org/ forums/ message-view?message_id=185506

Behlendorf, B. (1999). Open source as a business strategy. In C. DiBona, S. Ockman, & M. Stone (Eds.), *Open sources: Voices from the open source revolution*. Cambridge, MA: O'Reilly and Associates.

Belady, L., & Lehman, M. (1976). A model of large program development. *IBM Systems Journal, 15*(3), 225–252.

Bergmann, F. (2006). Who is using OpenACS. *OpenACS Q&A*. Retrieved November 17, 2006, from http://openacs.org/forums/message-view? message_id=352641

Berliner, B. (1990). CVS II: Parallelizing software development. In *Proceedings of the 1990 Winter USENIX Conference* (pp. 341–352). Washington, DC.

Dinh-Trong, T. T., & Bieman, J. M. (2005). The freeBSD project: A replication case study of open source development. *IEEE Transactions on Software Engineering, 31*(6), 481–494.

Erenkrantz, J. (2003). Release management within open source projects. In *Proceedings of the 3rd Workshop on Open Source Software Engineering, 25th International Conference on Software Engineering* (pp. 51–55), Portland, OR.

Fogel, K. (1999). *Open source development with CVS*. Scottsdale, AZ: CoriolisOpen Press.

Gallivan, M. J. (2001). Striking a balance between trust and control in a virtual organization: A content analysis of Open Source software case studies. I*nformation Systems Journal*, *11*(4), 277–304.

Ghosh, R. A. (2005). Understanding free software developers: Findings from the floss study. In J. Feller, B. Fitzgerald, S. A. Hissam, & K. R. Lakhani (Eds.), *Perspectives on free and open source software* (pp. 23–46). Cambridge, MA: MIT Press.

Ghosh, R. A., & Prakash, V. V. (2000). The Orbiten free software survey. *First Monday*, *5*(7). Retrieved November 17, 2006, from http://www.firstmonday.org/issues5_7/ghosh/index.html

Gilroy, K. (2001). Collaborative e-learning: The right approach. *ArsDigita Systems Journal*. Retrieved November 30, 2006, from http://www.eveandersson.com/arsdigita/asj/elearning/

Greenspun, P. (1999a). Introduction to AOLserver. *LinuxWorld*. Retrieved November 30, 2006, from http://www.eveandersson.com/arsdigital/asj/aolserver/introduction-1

Greenspun, P. (1999b). *Philip and Alex's guide to Web publishing*. San Francisco, CA: Morgan Kaufmann Publishers Inc.

Hahsler, M., & Koch, S. (2005). Discussion of a large-scale open source data collection methodology. In *Proceedings of the Hawaii International Conference on System Sciences (HICSS-38)*, Big Island, Hawaii.

Hamerly, J., Paquin, T., & Walton, S. (1999). Freeing the source: The story of Mozilla. In C. DiBona, S. Ockman, & M. Stone (Eds.), *Open sources: Voices from the open source revolution*. Cambridge, MA: O'Reilly and Associates.

Hars, A., & Ou, S. (2001). Working for free?—Motivations for participating in Open Source projects. In *Proceedings of the 34th Hawaii International Conference on System Sciences*, Hawaii.

Hawkins, R. E. (2004). The economics of open source software for a competitive firm—Why give it away for free? *NETNOMICS: Economic Research and Electronic Networking*, *6*(2), 103-117.

Hecker, F. (1999). Setting up shop: The business of open-source software. *IEEE Software*, *16*(1), 45–51.

Hertel, G., Niedner, S., & Hermann, S. (2003). Motivation of software developers in open source projects: An internet-based survey of contributors to the Linux kernel. *Research Policy*, *32*(7), 1159–1177.

Holck, J., & Jorgensen, N. (2004). Do not check in on red: Control meets anarchy in two open source projects. In S. Koch (Ed.), *Free/open source software development* (pp. 1–26). Hershey, PA: Idea Group Publishing.

Jorgensen, N. (2001). Putting it all in the trunk: Incremental software engineering in the FreeBSD Open Source project. *Information Systems Journal, 11*(4), 321–336.

Koch, S. (2004). Profiling an open source project ecology and its programmers. *Electronic Markets, 14*(2), 77–88.

Koch, S., & Schneider, G. (2002). Effort, cooperation and coordination in an open source software project: Gnome. *Information Systems Journal, 12*(1), 27–42.

Lakhani, K. R., & Wolf, R. G. (2005). Why hackers do what they do: Understanding motivation and effort in free/open source software projects. In J. Feller, B. Fitzgerald, S. A. Hissam, & K. R. Lakhani (Eds.), *Perspectives on free and open source software,* (pp. 3–22). Cambridge, MA: MIT Press.

Meeks, C., & Mangel, R. (2000). The arsdigita community system education solution. *ArsDigita Systems Journal.*

Mockus, A., Fielding, R. T., & Herbsleb, J. D. (2002). Two case studies of Open Source software development: Apache and Mozilla. *ACM Transactions on Software Engineering and Methodology, 11*(3), 309–346.

n.a. (2006a). *Homepage of OpenACS.* Retrieved from http://www.openacs.org/

n.a. (2006b). *Homepage of ProjectOpen.* Retrieved from http://www.project-open.com/

n.a. (2006c). *Homepage of the AOLserver project.* Retrieved from http://www.aolserver.com/

n.a. (2006d). *Homepage of the .LRN project.* Retrieved from http://www.dotlrn.org

O'Mahony, S. (2003). Guarding the commons: How community managed software projects protect their work. *Research Policy, 32*(7), 1179–1198.

Ousterhout, J. (1999). Free software needs profit. *Communications of the ACM, 42*(4), 44–45.

Ousterhout, J. K. (1989). *Tcl: An embeddable command language.* (technical Report UCB/CSD-89-541), EECS Department, University of California, Berkeley.

Ousterhout, J. K. (1998). Scripting: Higher-level programming for the 21st century. *Computer, 31*(3), 23–30.

Per Cederqvist et al. (2002). *Version Management with CVS.* Bristol: Network Theory Ltd.

Raymond, E. S. (1999). *The cathedral and the bazaar.* Sebastopol, CA: O'Reilly & Associates, Inc.

Recco, G (2005). Who is using OpenACS. *OpenACS Q&A.* Retrieved from http://openacs.org/forums/message-view?message_id= 352641

Robles, G., Koch, S., & Gonzalez-Barahona, J. M. (2004). Remote analysis and measurement of libre software systems by means of the CVSanalY tool. In ICSE 2004—*Proceedings of the Second International Workshop on Remote Analysis and Measurement of Software Systems (RAMSS '04)* (pp. 51–55), Edinburgh, Scotland.

Samoladas, I., Stamelos, I., Angelis, L., & Oikonomou, A. (2004). Open source software development should strive for even greater code maintainability. *Communications of the ACM, 47*(10), 83–87.

Tran, J. B., Godfrey, M. W., Lee, E. H., & Holt, R. C. (2000). Architectural repair of Open Source software. In *Proceedings of the 2000 International Workshop on Program Comprehension (IWPC'00)*, Limerick, Ireland.

Villa, L. (2003). Large free software projects and bugzilla. In *Proceedings of the Linux Symposium (pp. 471–480)*, Ottawa, Canada.

Ye, Y., Nakakoji, K., Yamamoto, Y., & Kishida, K. (2004). The coevolution of systems and communities in free and open source software development. In S. Koch (Ed.), *Free/open source software development* (pp. 1–26). Hershey, PA: Idea Group Publishing.

Endnotes

[1] Now, cityguide.aol.com

[2] The repository is reachable via the Internet via **http://cvs.openacs.org/** and **http://eye.openacs.org/**

[3] The number of TIPs per year are decreasing. As we show later the number of contributions peaked in early 2004, and is decreasing since then. However, it cannot be deduced from this data that the TIPs are responsible for that.

[4] The classification was performed by the authors who are OpenACS contributers, based on project knowledge and Internet recherche.

[5] Quoting: *CVS commit messages and code comments should refer to bug, TIP, or patch number if appropriate, in the format "resolves bug 11", "resolves bugs 11, resolves bug 22", "implements TIP 42", "implements TIP 42, implements TIP 50", "applies patch 456 by User Name", "applies patch 456 by User Name, applies patch 523 by ...".*

Chapter XI

The GALILEI Platform: Social Browsing to Build Communities of Interests and Share Relevant Information and Expertise

Pascal Francq, University of Brussels (ULB), Belgium

Abstract

For a few years, social software has appeared on the Internet to challenge the problem of handling the mass of information available. In this chapter, we present the GALILEI platform using social browsing to build communities of interests where relevant information and expertise are shared. The users are described in terms of profiles, with each profile corresponding to one specific area of interest. While browsing, users' profiles are computed on the basis of both the content of the consulted documents and the relevance assessments from the profiles. These profiles are then grouped into communities, which allows documents of interest to be shared among members of a same community and experts to be identified.

Introduction

Today, the amount of information available on the Internet and on companies' intranets has soared, making the search for relevant information a crucial problem. Most people use specific methods (a given query on a search engine, a specific portal, a set of bookmarks, etc.) to find relevant documents. Due to the lack of time and the limited number of such methods, only a small part of the existing relevant information is found. Social software (Macintosh, 1985), such as del.icio.us, has emerged as one of the solutions to tackle the problem of the mass of information. Social software is based on the idea that individuals are part of several networks of human relationships where human knowledge can be shared. The emergence of virtual communities on the Internet (Rheingold, 2000), and of communities of practice (Wenger, 1998) in organizations, has shown that these social networks are powerful tools to share information across organisational and geographical boundaries. Nevertheless, to identify who must collaborate with whom and on which topic is still an essential issue in the development of these social networks.

To solve the problem of identifying the composition of these social networks, the GALILEI platform was developed (Francq, 2003) to implement an approach based on **social browsing**. The main purpose of this approach is to understand the users' interests as precisely as possible, and to group them accordingly. Since users may have multiple interests, the approach associates a **profile** for each particular field of interest of a user. The platform computes a description for each profile based on relevance assessments on documents and content analysis. These profile descriptions are then clustered on the basis of their descriptions: similar profiles are grouped together in order to define a number of **communities of interests**. Once these communities have been defined, relevant information is exchanged among the different

Figure 1. Schema of the approach

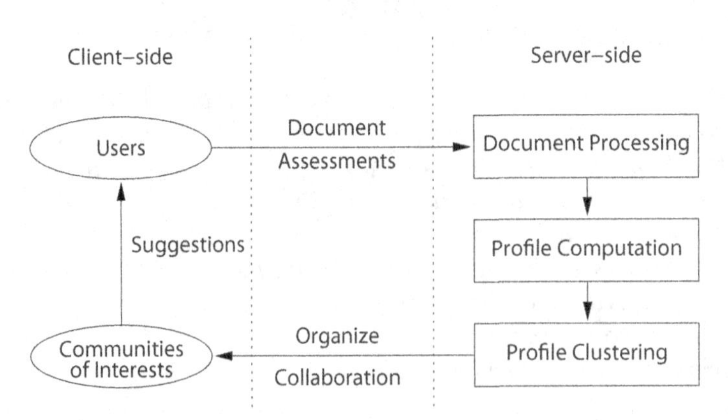

users of the same community, and experts are identified. Figure 1 illustrates the complete flow of the approach. The process is dynamic, as the system is updated regularly, for example, every week.

The proposed approach has several advantages:

- Users must not directly define the description of their interests.
- Users do not need to assess the same documents to be grouped together.
- The communities are not fixed: new communities may appear and others disappear.

Concretely, the second section introduces the main concepts of the approach based on social browsing to build communities of interests. The next sections explain how the proposed approach is implemented on the GALILEI platform:

- The third section explains how the documents' contents can be analysed.
- The fourth and the fifth sections describe, respectively, how the profiles can be computed and grouped.
- The sixth section is a short description of the characteristics of the GALILEI platform.
- Finally, the seventh section proposes some conclusions.

Social Browsing to Build Communities of Interests

The GALILEI platform presented in this chapter implements an approach, based on social browsing, to identify communities of interests. Since people have several distinct interests, the users of the GALILEI platform are made up of profiles, each profile corresponding to a particular field of interest. There are differences between our approach and other existing profiling-based approaches:

1. Some systems ask the users to describe their profiles in terms of keywords or categories, which is not always easy, especially if they do not master the domain of interest. In the GALILEI approach, the profiles descriptions are automatically built and the only users' inputs are relevance assessments on documents, which is something intuitive.
2. In some systems used for information push (for example a list of recommendations of books to buy), users do not need to define several profiles (it is

supposed that they have only one unique "big interest"). But, for communities of interests, it makes no sense to limit the users to one interest.

The goal of the GALILEI platform is to dynamically build **communities of interests**. In fact, these communities are a particular case of **social networks** (Barnes, 1954). It is well known that social networks produce **social capital** (Coleman, 1988), which may have two main forms:

1. The network is used as **information channels** between the actors. This is the reason why deploying communities of interests is a solution to share expertise and knowledge.
2. Actors of a network produce **norms**, which are artefacts that help to interact harmoniously. One of these artefacts is documents, such as specifications or scientific publications.

On the basis of the concept of norms, it can be assumed that online resources on the Internet or in companies' intranets are norms for existing (unknown) social networks. This means that:

- When a user considers a document as relevant, it can be supposed that this document represents a norm according to a specific profile (user's interest).
- If users consider the same kind of documents as relevant, it can be supposed that they share norms and belong to a same social network.

Based on these assumptions, the approach supposes that knowing which documents are relevant for which profiles is sufficient to build communities. Three different assessments are currently proposed in this approach:

- **Relevant:** The document is relevant (for example, the Beatles discography for a "Beatles" profile).
- **Fuzzy relevant:** The document is partially relevant, but does not fall exactly within the scope of the domain (for example, the Wings discography for a "Beatles" profile).
- **Irrelevant:** The document is outside the scope of the domain (for example, the Rolling Stones discography for a "Beatles" profile).

In fact, since it is the documents contents that represent the users' interests, the documents have to be analysed. Based on the analysis of the documents contents and the extraction of the semantic load, it is then possible to compute the profiles (users' interests). Given that different languages are present on the Internet or in intranets (Peeters & Picchi, 1997), it may be necessary to execute some language-dependent processes. In this approach, while describing a profile, the choice was made to compute a separate **profile description** for each language. For example, when a user has assessed, for a given profile, French-language and English-language documents, he or she will have two descriptions for this profile, that is, one in French and one in English.

Communities of interests are then built according to the profiles descriptions. Since the profiles have descriptions in different languages, a specific clustering is made for each language. This makes sense, as a profile is only grouped with profiles speaking the same languages as him or her. For example, when a user has assessed, for a given profile, French-language and English-language documents, he or she will be part of two communities, that is one French-speaking and one English-speaking.

Once the communities of interests are determined, they can be used as information channels. Based on the assessments of the profiles, the GALILEI platform performs analysis:

1. For each profile, all documents assessed as relevant by profiles of the same community form a set of recommendations proposed to each profile.
2. In each community, the authority documents and the experts of this community are identified:
   - The authority documents are the code knowledge of the community and, if available for outside users, provide learning material.
   - The experts are the knowledge holders of the community.

Document Processing

As explained in the previous section, once profiles have assessed documents, the GALILEI platform needs to:

- Analyse the assessed documents (which means that it needs to read the format of these documents).
- Store the results of the analysis (which means that a model representing these results must be adopted).
- Extract content and semantic load from the documents (which means that characteristics of the documents contents must be extracted).

In real environments, documents are of different formats, such as hypertext markup language (HTML), Microsoft Office, OpenOffice.org, Postscript, portable data format (PDF), and so forth. Since the GALILEI platform needs to read these different formats, a specific treatment for each format is needed. On the other hand, the content of a document is independent of a particular format[1]. Therefore, it was decided that, before analysing their content, the GALILEI platform transforms each document into a single format called Document Extensible Markup Language (DocXML), which is used internally to represent documents' contents. DocXML is an Extensible Markup Language (XML) application specifically developed for the GALILEI platform (Francq, 2003)[2]. This approach has the advantage that the documents analysis is independent of their particular formats. To support a new document format, the only thing needed is to develop a "filter" that can transform this format into DocXML.

Next, the DocXML version of each document must be analysed to extract the characteristics representing the content. A popular approach for representing documents in information retrieval systems is the vector space model (Salton, 1968), where documents are described through basic information entities. The documents are represented as vectors in the information entity space. Each document is made up of a set of information entities. A weight is associated with each information entity for each document and represents its importance for the description of the document content. The goal of the analysis of the documents is to choose the information entities that will be used to describe a document, and to compute the corresponding weights. Currently, this analysis is only based on the text extracted from the documents.

Since we decide to do some language-dependent processes, it is necessary to know the language of each document. Unfortunately, this information is not always available, and it is sometimes necessary to determine, automatically, the language of a document. To do so, it is possible to use stop lists. A *stop list* of a given language (Luhn, 1957) is the set of the most common words (*stop words*) having a poor semantic content. For the English language, well-known stop words are "the," "no," "yes," and "or." The language of a document is the one having the highest values for two ratios:

1. The ratio of the number of different stop words present in the document on the total number of different words in the document.
2. The ratio of the number of occurrences of stop words present in the document on the total number of words in the document.

Once the language of a document is determined (automatically or not), the next step is to extract all the **valid words** contained in the documents. A valid word is a sequence of characters respecting some rules, such as to be made up of letters only. The documents are then further processed in order to extract the information entities:

- All the stop words in the language of the document are removed since they usually convey poor semantic content.
- A stemming algorithm is then used to compute their stems (Francq, Rolfo, Wartel, Kumps, & Vandaele, 2004; Paternostre, Francq, Saerens, Lamoral, & Wartel, 2002; Porter, 1980), which are the information entities used to describe a document.

Finally, for each information entity, it is necessary to compute the corresponding weights. A well-known method is to use the *inverse document frequency* (Jones, 1973). It assumes that the information entities best describing a document are defined by their occurrence in this document and as the inverse of their frequency in the collection of documents. This factor quantifies the discriminatory value of an information entity, that is, an information entity appearing in all the documents is not as useful as an information entity appearing in some specific ones only. In fact, this factor supposes that the most discriminating information entities are those appearing often in a small subset of documents.

Users Processing

This section details how the processing of the users is implemented in the GALILEI platform. The computation of the profiles description is detailed in the first subsection. By comparing the documents' assessments, it is possible to compute agreement and disagreement ratios between profiles, as detailed in the second subsection. Finally, the third subsection presents a method that uses links (such as hyperlinks) between documents to refine the profiles descriptions.

Users Profiling

Profiling the interests of a given user to later propose relevant information is an important research topic in the field of information technologies. The *collaborative filtering* methods[3] (Breese, Heckerman, & Kadie, 1998; Shardanand & Maes, 1995) are one category of solutions:

1. The user rates the documents he or she consults.
2. While comparing the assessments of different users on the same documents, the methods compute a similarity factor between users of the system.
3. The methods then compute a predicted rating for all the documents of the system for a given user. This predicted rating is based on a weighted average of each user's rating, scaled by the corresponding similarity factor.
4. With a threshold for the predicted ratings, documents are then presented to the user. If the user follows some recommendations and gives some feedback, the system will "learn" about his or her interests.

The drawback of these methods is related to the second step. Efficient similarity factors require that the users have rated the same set of documents, which can be difficult on large collections like the Internet.

Another category of solutions is based on *user relevance feedback* methods (Gudivada, Raghavan, Grosky, & Kasanagottu, 1997):

1. The user defines his or her profile description, for example as a set of keywords.
2. An initial set of documents is proposed to the user (for example retrieved with a search engine).
3. The user assesses the relevance of the top ranked documents.
4. Based on these assessments and the content of the documents, the methods refine the profile description.
5. A new set of documents is proposed to the user (for example retrieved by a search engine). These methods cycle back to step 3.

In the GALILEI platform, presented in this chapter, a method based on this final category of solutions is used. Nevertheless, there is a main difference due to the fact that we treat languages separately and that, for each users' profile, several descriptions are computed[4].

First, it is necessary to adopt a model to represent the profiles descriptions. As for the document, we choose the vector space model (Salton, 1968). Each profile description is therefore made up of a set of information entities. A weight is associated with each information entity for each profile description and represents its importance related to the corresponding domain of interests.

The method used to compute these weights is based on an intuitive idea: information entities (index terms) that often appear in relevant documents should have high (positive) weights, and information entities that often appear in irrelevant documents should have low (negative) weights. Since the documents are described as vectors in the information entities space, the profiles descriptions can be computed as a linear combination of the documents assessed by the corresponding profile in the different languages (Francq & Delchambre, 2005). In fact, the contribution of each document is weighted by the relevance of this document for the profile computed.

Agreement and Disagreement Ratios

By comparing the assessments of different profiles on the same documents, it is possible to determine if they agree or disagree on relevance. This information can be later used to cluster them into communities. As explained in the previous section, the probability that two profiles assess the same documents in large collections is quite low. On the other hand, when the system evolves and documents are shared within the communities, the number of documents assessed by more than one user will increase.

We therefore define the following simple ratios representing a degree of agreement and a degree of disagreement between two profiles:

- **Agreement ratio:** Ratio between the number of documents assessed as relevant by both profiles on the total number of documents assessed by both profiles. The higher the ratio, the higher the probability that the corresponding profiles have the same domain of interests.
- **Disagreement ratio:** Ratio between the number of documents assessed differently by both profiles on the total number of documents assessed by both profiles. The higher the ratio, the higher the probability that the corresponding profiles have not the same domain of interests.

Of course, these ratios make sense only if there is a minimum number of documents assessed by both profiles, for example, 10 or 20 documents.

Profiles, Documents and Links

In today's documents environments, the number of documents containing links to other documents (hyperlinks, references, etc.) increases, particularly on the Internet. A method has been developed to use these links to enrich the profiles descriptions (Vandaele, Francq, & Delchambre, 2004). The basic idea is that, if two different documents contain links referencing to the same documents, it can be assumed that these referenced documents are linked to the same topic. Moreover, if a profile has assessed the two different documents as relevant, the referenced documents are probably relevant too.

The proposed method is based on the concepts of **hubs** and **authorities**, defined by Kleinberg (1999). Hubs and authorities are documents that are considered as the most relevant documents in a given collection. The main steps of this method are:

1. For each profile, the subset of all documents assessed as relevant is analysed.
2. The hubs and authorities are identified, for example, by using the HITS (hypertext induced topic selection) method (Kleinberg, 1999)[5].
3. These hubs and authorities are then used to refine the profiles descriptions.

In fact, all documents identified as hubs and authorities are not necessarily relevant for the corresponding profile. Therefore, these documents must be considered as less representative of the users' interests by the profiles computing method.

Knowing that the methods of link analysis could emphasize the interesting documents through the profiles, we thus hope to be able to increase the number of documents assessed by more than one profile and the quality of the ratios defined in the previous section. Moreover, this method can also be used to propose new relevant documents to the profiles.

Communities Processing

After analysing documents and computing profiles, the GALILEI platform builds communities of interests. As already explained, the different languages are treated separately, and each profile has a description for each language. Since the profiles descriptions are used to group the corresponding profiles, it is therefore necessary to do a separate clustering for each language (first subsection). The second subsection explains how a description can be computed for these communities. The third subsection provides a basic overview of how users may collaborate within communities. The fourth subsection describes an approach for automatic personal tracking of information based on profiles and communities descriptions. Finally, the last subsection shows how experts and authorities documents can be identified within these communities.

Profiles Clustering

With the clustering of profiles descriptions, we are dealing with an *approximate multi-criteria problem* (Francq, 2003). An approximate multi-criteria problem is a problem where the aim cannot be accurately characterized in any way. A set of criteria is defined to approximate the characteristics of the target without guaranteeing an exact match between the criteria and the characteristics. In fact, for the profiles clustering, it is not possible to find a function or a set of functions that reflect exactly the quality of a solution, because the concept of "two profiles that have sufficiently similar descriptions to be grouped together" is difficult to evaluate (Kleinberg & Lawrence, 2001). Moreover, each user has different expectations concerning the result of the grouping. Some of them prefer to be grouped together with a maximum of other users and accept a certain latitude in quality, while others want to be grouped with highly similar users, even if the corresponding community of interests only contains a few profiles.

In the building of communities of interests, a set of several types of criteria can be used (Francq & Delchambre, 2005):

- **Similarity criterion:** This criterion tries to express the fact that profiles being grouped into the same community of interests should have descriptions that are as similar as possible. Several measures could be used to express this sort of criterion. One measure computes the ratio between the maximum similarity separating two communities and the compactness of each community (Ray & Turi, 1999). To compute the similarity between two profiles descriptions, a popular method is to use the cosines between their corresponding vectors (Salton & McGill, 1983).
- **Behavioral criteria:** These criteria are based on the agreement and disagreement ratios:
  - If two profiles have a high agreement ratio, they should probably be grouped in the same community.
  - If two profiles have a high disagreement ratio, they should probably not be grouped in the same community.
- **Social criterion:** This criterion expresses that some profiles prefer to be grouped with less similar profiles than to remain alone.

Many clustering methods have been developed to solve grouping problems (Jain, Murty, & Flynn 1999), but for *NP-hard problems*[6] (Garey & Johnson, 1979) such as the profiles clustering problem, it is necessary to use *meta-heuristics* such as *genetic algorithms*. A specific genetic algorithm (Francq, 2003) was developed for the GALILEI platform with several characteristics:

1. The number of communities (clusters) must not be specified, but are "discovered" by the algorithm.
2. The algorithm integrates the multi-criteria decision aid system PROMETHEE (Brans & Mareschal, 1994) to evaluate the solutions.
3. The algorithm is incremental:
   - When some profiles are modified, it determines if the corresponding communities are modified too.
   - When new profiles appear, it determines if they must be grouped in existing communities or if new ones must be created.

Communities Descriptions

Once the communities have been computed, it is possible to describe them. In the GALILEI platform, we choose to adopt the same model to represent the communities as for the documents and the profiles descriptions, that is, the vector space model. This choice has several advantages:

- Documents, profiles, and communities descriptions are represented in a consistent way.
- It is possible to "compare" documents, profiles, and communities by computing some similarity measures such as the cosines between their vectors (Salton & McGill, 1983).

Since communities are language-oriented and made of profiles, it is natural to use the profiles descriptions to describe them. Moreover, knowing that these profiles descriptions are represented as vectors, an intuitive computing method will describe a community as the centre of gravity of these vectors in the information entity space (Francq, 2003).

Collaboration within Communities

Once the profiles are grouped in communities, it is possible to make them collaborate. If users share some personal information such as e-mail or instant messaging account, it is possible for users to directly establish communication with people from the same communities of interests. A more sophisticated approach consists in using the community's composition to specify to *collaboration software* (such as the Lotus Notes application), which users must collaborate together. These platforms then provide, for each computed community, a collaborative space such as a document repository, a mailing list, and so forth.

Since communities regroup users sharing the same domain of interests, the assumption can be made that, when a document is assessed as relevant by one profile, it is also relevant for all the other profiles within the same community. It is therefore possible to propose for each profile a list of potentially relevant documents, that is, all the documents assessed as relevant by at least one of the profiles of the same community, and not yet consulted by this profile. Moreover, these documents can be ranked, for example, by using a concept of similarity with the profile, such as the cosines between their vectors (Francq, 2003; Salton & McGill, 1983).

Query Generation for Personalized Tracking of Information

Today, users recurrently need new information related to their domains of interests (profiles):

- Researchers must stay updated to the state-of-the-art in their research field.
- It is vital for organisations to develop a *competitive intelligence* practice.

One of the aspects is to keep up-to-date on new documents related to their domains of interests. In practice, users will spend, daily, a great deal of time and effort to search for new documents through the different sources available (Internet, information systems, databases, ...). Moreover, most users rarely master complex queries formulation (Christensen & Skovgaard, 2002), which makes this search activity inefficient. To help users in this continual information search, monitoring tools appear to partially automatise this activity. Most of these monitoring tools are *intelligent agents* based on documents filtering methods. *Query Tracker* (Somlo & Howe, 2004) is an example of an intelligent agent that assists users in satisfying their long-term information needs. Query Tracker learns a much more complete picture of the user's needs through relevance feedback, and uses a "profile" learned to generate a query.

The GALILEI platform presented then merges the list of documents received and eliminates in this chapter includes such a monitoring approach. The main steps are:

1. On a regular basis, the GALILEI platform generates queries automatically for each profile and broadcasts them to different search engines.
2. Each search engine returns a ranked list of documents.

3. The GALILEI platform then merges lists of documents received and eliminates documents yet examined by the profile.
4. The remaining documents are compared to the original profile to determine a relevance, and are then recommended to the corresponding user.

To build these queries, the proposed approach is based on the assumption that using both community and profile descriptions terms will be interesting (Abbaci, Francq, & Delchambre, 2005). Indeed, it makes sense to use both descriptions:

- Community description terms identify the concepts representing the community interest, which is the profile interest in a global way.
- Profile description terms identify the concepts representing more specific aspects of the profile interest.

Moreover, tests have shown that including logical operators in the query can be useful to decrease the noise retrieved by search engines. Concerning the number of terms, a balance must be found:

- A long and more restrictive query will probably retrieve only relevant documents, but certainly not all the relevant documents of the collection.
- A short and less restrictive query will probably retrieve all relevant documents of the collection, but certainly also a large amount of irrelevant documents.

To avoid these problems, the GALILEI platform builds several long queries for each profile by combining different terms found in the profile and community descriptions (Francq, 2003). Each specialized query will retrieve only a small number of relevant documents (perhaps none), but the entire set of queries can retrieve almost every relevant document. Finally, only a given number of the top-ranked documents are recommended to the profile.

Expert and Authority Documents

After the profiles clustering, each community is composed of several users sharing the same interests and a set of relevant documents (the documents assessed as relevant by at least one member). As a community grows, it can be composed of many users who have assessed a large number of documents. Of course, within a community, the members have not the same degree of expertise, and all the documents have not the same importance. It is therefore useful to identify in each community the **authority**

documents (the documents considered as the most important by the community) and the **experts** (the members providing the most relevant information). In fact, there is a mutually reinforcing relationship between experts and authority documents: for a member to be considered as an expert, he or she must provide (through assessments) a lot of authority documents, while a document is considered as such only if a number of experts assess it as relevant. Currently, one simple method is used within the GALILEI platform to compute the authority documents and the experts. It consists in a two-step process:

1. The authority documents are identified as those being most often assessed as relevant.
2. The experts are identified as those who assessed, firstly most often, authority documents.

This method has several disadvantages:

- Authority documents are directly linked to the number of relevant assessments, whoever made these assessments.
- Experts do not influence the status of authority for a given document.
- the status of expert for a given user is directly linked to the number of documents he or she assesses first, but being the first one to assess a document is actually not a characteristic of an expert.
- The status of expert for a given user is not influenced by the number of documents assessed as relevant by this user and as irrelevant by the other members of the community.

To overcome this problem, new approaches should compute experts and authority documents in parallel. Research in the field of social network analysis proposes to identify the experts by analysing the graph where the different users are the nodes and their communication exchanges (in particular e-mails) are the vertices (Wasserman & Faust, 1997). Once experts are identified, the authority documents are those that were assessed as relevant by most experts within a community. But, while this approach seems realistic inside an organisation, building such a graph at the level of the Internet is difficult and requires large hardware resources. Moreover, another problem with this approach is that additional information (such as communication exchanges) is needed.

Readers have probably noticed the parallel with the concepts of authorities and hubs proposed by Kleinberg (1999), previously discussed. In fact, there are similarities between the problems:

- The authorities (authority documents) represent the same concept in both problems.
- The experts correspond to the concept of hubs of Kleinberg (1999).
- The links between experts and hubs (hyperlinks in the original work) are the assessment of profiles on documents.

The HITS (hypertext induced topic selection) algorithm (Kleinberg, 1999) can be transformed to an AIRS (assessments induced relevance selection) algorithm adapted to the problem of experts and authority documents. As for Kleinberg (1999), the AIRS method computes, within a given community, for each document, an **authority rating**, and for each profile, an **expert rating**. Then, the best documents and profiles (for example, those whose rating is greater than a threshold) are considered respectively as the authority documents and the experts.

Another idea is to track how users react within the community, and to identify those closely following the "hot trends" (new documents relevant for the community). Such a tracking method could be based on several assumptions:

- When a document "arrives" in a community and is assessed by most members as relevant:
  - Members assessing it rapidly as relevant have probably an expertise.
  - Members assessing it rapidly as irrelevant have probably a lack of expertise.
- When a document "arrives" in a community and is assessed by most members as irrelevant:
  - Members assessing it rapidly as irrelevant have probably an expertise.
  - Members assessing it rapidly as relevant have probably a lack of expertise.

Again, as for the AIRS algorithm, a rating is computed for each profile and each document, and the best are chosen as experts and authority documents. The main difference is that the time factor (related to how fast profiles assess documents) will play an important role in the computation of this ranking of documents and experts. Future research will show which of the AIRS of the tracking method gives the best results.

Figure 2. Architecture

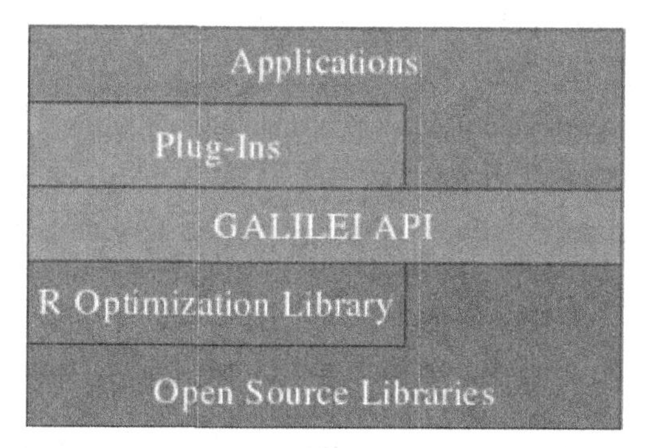

GALILEI: A Research Platform

If the GALILEI platform can be used in industrial applications (see the case study), it was also designed as an open source research platform. In the previous sections, the methods, algorithms, and measures currently implemented were briefly described. In fact, as mentioned here and there, several other choices could have been made and new methods could be developed in the future.

The development of the GALILEI platform was therefore driven by the concept of software modularity to allow new elements to be easily integrated. As Figure 2 shows, the GALILEI platform is a plug-ins-oriented architecture based on five layers:

1. The first layer includes several open source libraries used by the platform.
2. The second layer is dedicated to the *R optimization library*. This C++ library was developed at the Université Libre de Bruxelles and includes some generic portable classes (such as strings, containers, and genetic algorithms).
3. The third layer implements the *GALILEI API*. It is a set of C++ classes implementing the main concepts (information entity, document, profile, community, etc.) and the workflow of activities (for example, to analyse a document, it must first be transformed into DocXML with the right filter, and then analysed with a specific method).
4. The fourth layer is composed of different plug-ins, each plug-in implementing a particular computing method, algorithm, or measure (such as a similarity measure). The different elements presented in this chapter are implemented as open source plug-ins.

5. The final layer is dedicated to the applications based on the GALILEI platform. These applications can be servers, Web services, or debugging tools.

This plug-ins oriented architecture has two main advantages:

1. It provides a high modularity level in the platform. Researchers can concentrate on one specific aspect, for example, the profiles clustering, and test it without taking into account the implementation details of all other elements.
2. For each category of elements, such as the profiles clustering methods, several plug-ins can be written, and one of them chosen as the current method. It is therefore easy to compare different methods to find the most efficient one.

Finally, the GALILEI platform includes a very basic scripting language. This language enables researchers to organise tests plans:

- Based on a collection of categorised documents, it is possible to simulate real users.
- The different steps of the workflow of a particular test procedure can be chosen.
- It is always possible to choose a particular method and/or a specific configuration thereof.
- At each step, statistics can be run (such as quality measures).

The different computing methods, algorithms, and measures described in this chapter were tested using this scripting language (Francq, 2003).

Conclusion

In this chapter, an approach was presented to help users to handle large amounts of information in a collaborative way. The approach is based on social browsing. Indeed, while they browse on documents collections (such as the Internet), users assess their relevance with regards to a particular domain of interests (profile). Based on these assessments, the profiles are described and grouped into communities of interests. Finally, the information is shared within each community and recommendations are made for the different users.

The GALILEI platform is a framework that implements this approach. The models used for computation and all the necessary computing methods and algorithms were described. All these methods and algorithms were tested with different documents collections, and in different simulation situations (Francq, 2003). Finally, the architecture of the GALILEI platform was briefly described and its research goal underlined.

References

Abbaci, F., Francq, P. & Delchambre, A. (2005). Query generation for personalized tracking of information. In Hamid R. Arabnia, & Rose Joshua (Eds.), *Proceedings of the 2005 International Conference on Internet Computing*, Las Vegas (pp. 348-343). CSREA Press.

Barnes, J. A. (1954). Class and committees in a Norwegian island parish. *Human Relations*, *7*, 39-58.

Brans, J.-P., & Mareschal, B. (1994). The PROMCALC & GAIA decision support system for multicriteria decision aid. *Decision Support Systems*, *12*, 297-310.

Breese, J., Heckerman, D., & Kadie, C, (1998). Empirical analysis of predictive algorithms for collaborative filtering. In *Proceedings of Fourteeth Annual Conference on Uncertainty in Artificial Intelligence*, Madison, WI (pp. 43-52).

Christensen, S., & Skovgaard, H. J. (2002). *Web site usability metrics: Search behavior—search trends*. White paper. Mondosoft.

Coleman, J. S. (1988). Social capital in the creation of human capital. *The American Journal of Sociology*, *94*, 95-120.

Francq, P. (2003). *Structured and collaborative search: An integrated approach for sharing documents among users*. PhD thesis, Université Libre de Bruxelles. http://stic.ulb.ac.be/research/information-systems/galilei/galilei6.pdf

Francq, P., Rolfo, S., Wartel, D. Kumps, N., & Vandaele, V. (2004). *GALILEI—Sixième Rapport Semestriel*. Technical report. Université Libre de Bruxelles. http://stic.ulb.ac.be/research/information-systems/galilei/galilei6.pdf

Francq, P., & Delchambre, A. (2005). Using document assessment to build communities of interests. In Wojciech Cellary & Hiroshi Esaki (Eds.),*Proceedings of the 2005 International Symposium on Applications and the Internet*, Trento, Italy (pp. 327-333). IEEE Press.

Garey, M., & Johnson, D. (1979). *Computers and intractabilbity—A guide to the theory of incompleteness*. New York: W. H. Freeman Co.

Gudivada, V., Raghavan, V., Grosky, W., & Kasanagottu, R. (1997). Information retrieval on the World Wide Web. *IEEE Internet Computing*, *1*(5), 56-68.

Jain, A. K., Murty, M. N., & Flynn, P. J. (1999). Data clustering: A review. *ACM Computer Surveys*, *31*(3), 264-323.

Jones, K. S. (1973). A statistical interpretation of term specificity and its application to retrieval. *Information Storage and Retrieval*, 9, 619-633.

Kleinberg, J. (1999). Authoritative sources in a hyperlinked environment. *Journal of the ACM*, *46*(5), 604-632.

Kleinberg, J., & Lawrence, S. (2001). The structure of the web. *Science*, *294*, 1849-1850.

Luhn, H. P. (1957). A statistical approach to mechanized encoding and searching of literary information. *IBM Journal of Research and Development*, *1*(4), 309-317.

Macintosh, N. (1985). *Social software of accounting and information systems*. Wiley & Sons., New York.

Paternostre, M., Francq, P., Saerens, M., Lamoral, J., & Wartel, D. (2002). *Carry, un algorithme de désuffixation pour le français*. White paper, Université Libre de Bruxelles. Retrieved from http://www.stic.ulb.ac.be/research/information-systems/galilei/carry

Peeters, C., & Picchi, E. (1997). Across languages, across cultures: Issues in multilinguality and digital librairies, *D-Lib Magazine*. Retrieved from http://www.dlib.org/dlib/may97/peters/05peters.html

Porter, M. F. (1980). An algorithm for suffix stripping. *Program*, *14*(3), 130-137.

Ray, S., & Turi, R. H. (1999). Determination of number of clusters in k-means clustering and application in colour image segmentation. In *ICAPRDT'99*.

Rheingold, H. (2000). *The virtual community: Homesteading on the electronic frontier*. London: MIT Press.

Salton, G. (1968). *Automatic information organization and retrieval*. New York: McGraw-Hill.

Salton, G., & McGill, M. (1983). *Modern information retrieval*. McGraw-Hill.

Shardanand, U., & Maes, P. (1995). Social information filtering: Algorithms for automating "word of mouth." In *CHI'95 — Human Factors in Computing Systems*, Denver, CO.

Somlo, G., & Howe, A. E. (2004). Querytracker: An agent for tracking persistent information needs. In *AAMAS'04 Autonomous Agents and Multi Agent Systems*, New York.

Vandaele, V., Francq, P., & Delchambre, A. (2004). Analyse d'hyperliens en vue d'une meilleure descriptions des profils. In *Proceedings of les septièmes Journées Internationales d'Analyse statisque des Données Texteulles*, Louvain-La-Neuve, Belgium (pp. 1117-1127).

Wasserman, S., & Faust, K. (1997). *Social network analysis—Methods and applications*. New York: Cambridge University Press.

Wenger, E. (1998). *Communities of practice: Learning, meaning, and identity*. New York: Cambridge University Press.

Endnotes

1 Transforming an OpenOffice.org document into a PDF document does not change the content of this document.

2 The choice to adopt XML as the internal format was driven by the fact that XML is more and more often used as documents format, and that transforming an XML document into another XML document is very easy.

3 These methods are implemented on online shopping Web sites such as Amazon.

4 To compute a profile description in a given language, the user must assess at least one document in this language for the corresponding profile.

5 In fact, the method computes a *hub rating* and an *authority rating* for each document, and only the documents having a rating higher than a given threshold are considered respectively as hubs and authorities.

6 A problem is considered to be NP-hard if the best-known algorithm finding an exact solution computes it in polynomial time compared to the size of the problem (the number of profiles descriptions to group).

Appendix I: Case Study: Dynamic Internet Communities

As already explained, the approach described in this chapter can be run in two contexts:

- **Private:** The GALILEI platform is developed within organisations where the documents handled have some degree of confidentiality.

- **Public:** The GALILEI platform is developed on the Internet with public online documents.

E-parkos, a spin-off of the Université Libre de Bruxelles providing consultancy services around the GALILEI platform, launched the e-GALILEI product in March 2006. It is an implementation of the GALILEI platform for the Internet for the net surfers (public context). The goal of the e-GALILEI product is to dynamically build Internet communities grouping net surfers sharing the same kind of interests. The documents assessed are supposed to be public online documents* that net surfers have consulted with their Web browser.

To use the e-GALILEI product, net surfers have just to download a toolbar for their browser and to create an account on the E-parkos Web site (*http://www.e-parkos.com/sol_toolbars.php)*. Once the toolbar is configured with the account information, they can directly start to use the product.

Net surfers can interact with the e-GALILEI product through the downloaded toolbar:

- they can choose their active profile (current domain of interests);
- assess documents through a set of three buttons;
- consult the members of their communities;
- consult a history of all assessments made;
- consult the recommendations.

The whole e-GALILEI product is updated once a week, which means that users receive recommendations once per week.

* *Since the product needs to access the content of the documents to analyze them, it is necessary that these documents be public and online.*

Appendix II: Useful URLs

del.icio.us—share of favorites:

http://del.icio.us/

Digg—technology news Web site combining social bookmarking:

http://www.digg.com/

Etienne Wenger home page (communities of practice):
http://www.ewenger.com/

Findory—personal news aggregators:
http://www.findory.com/

Flickr—share of photos:
http://www.flickr.com/

GALILEI Platform:
http://galilei.ulb.ac.be/

Howard Reingold home page (virtual communities):
http://www.rheingold.com/

socialsoftwares.com—a blog on cooperation technologies:
http://www.socialsoftware.com/

YouTube—digital video repository on the Internet:
http://www.youtube.com/

Wikipedia's social software page:
http://en.wikipedia.org/wiki/Social_software/

Wink social search engine—share of collections about any topic:
http://www.wink.com/

Appendix III: Further Reading

Baeza-Yates, R., & Ribeiro-Neto, B. (1999). *Modern information retrieval.* Addison-Wesley.

Dasgupta, S. (Ed.). (2005). *Encyclopedia of virtual communities and technologies.* Idea Group Publishing.

Hildreth, P. (2003). *Going virtual: Distributed communities of practice*. Idea Group Publishing.

Huysman, M., & Wulf, V. (2005). The role of information technology in building and sustaining the relational base of communities. *The Information Society, 21*, 81-89.

Renninger, K., & Wesley Shumar, R. (Eds). (2002). *Building virtual communities: Learning and change in cyberspace*. Cambridge University Press.

Wenger, E., McDermott, R., & Snyder, W. (2002). *Cultivating communities of practice*. Harvard Business School Press.

Possible Titles for Papers/Essays

- Identify Experts and Authority Documents in Online Communities
- How to measure the Social Activity in Online Communities
- Communities of Interests: Approaches and Methods
- Communities of Practice and Virtual Communities: Common Rounds and Differences

Chapter XII

Making Government Policies for Education Possible by Means of Open Source Technology: A Successful Case

Marcos A. Castilho, Federal University of Paraná, Brazil
Marcos S. Sunye, Federal University of Paraná, Brazil
Daniel Weingaerter, Federal University of Paraná, Brazil
Luis Carlos Erpen de Bona, Federal University of Paraná, Brazil
Fabiano Silva, Federal University of Paraná, Brazil
Alexandre Direne, Federal University of Paraná, Brazil
Laura Sánchez García, Federal University of Paraná, Brazil
Andre Guedes, Federal University of Paraná, Brazil
Carlos Carvalho, Federal University of Paraná, Brazil

Abstract

In this chapter, we describe the products and services offered by the Department of Computer Science of the Federal University of Paraná within the scope of the Paraná Digital project. The department has designed laboratories with Internet access for 2,100 public schools of the state, with innovative technology through an environment entirely based upon free software tools, centralized management as well as continuous maintenance, and betterment of the services offered. We place special emphasis on our strategies, aiming at contributing to the adoption of such strategies in contexts relatively similar to ours, with which a parallel may be drawn concerning the hypothesis situation of the present project.

Introduction

The structure of this chapter is presented in Box 1.

Paraná Digital (PRD) project is a governmental initiative funded by the state of Paraná (Brazil), aimed at the large-scale expansion of hardware and software to support public school education. It offers a standard base of computational resources that are suitable to a wide range of primary and secondary school environments. Additionally, teachers and students are allowed to access such resources through centrally managed, individual profiles, permitting long-term tracking of student records, as well as courseware production and delivery by teachers.

In the past, only 953 state schools (out of 2,057) had computer laboratories. Out of 18,500 machines, a fair amount was obsolete, according to current market demands of commercial proprietary software. As a result, the main motivations for the PRD project were the following context:

- A 14-year experience of the Department of Computer Science (Dinf) at the Federal University of Paraná (UFPR) in managing computer laboratories and networks for educational purposes
- A 12-year experience of Dinf/UFPR in dealing with free software
- The existence of a vast optical fiber network, owned by the state, connecting various central and remote locations, that could be used both for setting up and for maintaining the PRD project
- The expertise of Dinf/UFPR in producing high-end technologies aiming at lowering the costs of software licenses, as well as machine administration and maintenance

The general aims of the PRD project are:

- To allow easy-to-use access to the main server, "Portal Dia-a-dia-Educacao" (http://www.diaadiaeducacao.pr.gov.br), a software environment for sharing information and experiences, as well as for broadcasting courseware that covers the official curriculum of primary and secondary schools

Box 1. Chapter structure

- To provide the general public, students, teachers, and technicians with utility, free software (text editors, spreadsheets, etc.)
- To recommend appropriate educational software that has been tested and thus can be useful for teachers and students
- To enforce availability and longevity of school laboratories

The project lasted for 24 months under the responsibility of the Paraná State Secretary of Education (SEED), and was carried out by means of a partnership among SEED, CELEPAR (Paraná State Computing Services), COPEL (Paraná State Energy Company).

The model adopted in the PRD project was fully based on the architecture of the computer laboratories of the Department of Computer Science at UFPR. Such architecture, which has been perfected through the past six years, consists of turning users' workstations into graphical X-window terminals, all connected (ideally) to a single processing server. This is achieved through the use of the GNU/Linux operating system, combined with an innovative philosophy of laboratory management that permits consistent lowering of hardware and software costs as well as of network managing. Furthermore, such a model also allows a substantial increase in the quality of laboratory services (Carmo et al., 2001; Castilho et al., 2001).

The PRD project network only differs from the one in the Department of Computer Science at UFPR in the number of processing servers. There are some 2,053 servers spread among the Paraná State schools, each one connecting the terminals of a laboratory that is, in turn, similar to the main one set up originally at UFPR. Since each internal school laboratory network is planned to typically connect twenty graphical terminals, there will be, as soon as July 2006, a total of 41,000 desktop service points available for educational purposes. So far, the main challenge has been to find an original solution for such a large-scale integration of local laboratories, ensuring availability.

The present chapter describes the PRD project phases, its main tasks, the models adopted, and the problems encountered along the years of research and development. The solution strategies are also described, including theoretical and practical results that lead to future work, oriented towards the pedagogical view of laboratory resources.

Background

The concern for management and maintenance of computer laboratory systems has been the greatest differential of the PRD project when compared with other similar initiatives. In Brazil, during the last decades, there have been a substantial number of governmental programs and funding agencies that failed to foster research and development in the field. This failure history indicates that the critical point lies in the territory of dynamic variables that determine which parameters should be managed and maintained more carefully. In other words, most of the previous initiatives carried out under town- state-, or federal-office responsibility were limited to buying and delivering hardware and software without a proper planning of the physical, logical, and human resources that are necessary for running the continuous procedures after the whole apparatus is installed. This already critical panorama of public institutions was worsened by the poverty scenario in which countryside schools evolved and are managed, having access to limited resources of all sorts (human, financial, health, etc.).

Among the theoretical and practical concepts and products developed in the scope of the PRD project, the main ones are: (a) management and maintenance concepts; (b) tools for managing free software; (c) single-processing multi-terminal hardware and software kit, or simply, multi-terminal.

Project Description

Project Formulation

Assembling and managing a large-scale laboratory network, such as the one of the PRD project, requires great cooperation and effort among the partners. The initial phase consisted of periodical meetings to write the contract terms and to determine the exact terms of the official open bid in which private companies made their offer to sell hardware and services. The open bid is mandatory according to the Brazilian law, and may require many months to be run completely, during which refutation of the winner's offer conditions input by the counterparts is a real possibility.

The outcome of this very first phase also included a first selection of the model for laboratory management and maintenance, whose two main components are (a) the general philosophy of how to manage the large network of state school laboratories; (b) the ways of dealing with the peculiarities of the local structure of each school. Still in this first phase, the concept of multiterminal was understood as a key factor of cost balance. The following subsections are dedicated to both, separately.

The Management Philosophy of the State Network

The model for network management of state school laboratories, considered "centralized, with minimal intervention," proposes an innovative approach in that all the managing procedures of each laboratory are carried out by one large kernel, located at CELEPAR. This means that all managing interventions in local laboratories have to be done remotely, that is, staff members are not required to take trips to each school. This is a key factor, since the state of Paraná is rather large, and there are very few Linux-specialized technicians in the countryside.

This means that each of the 44,000 machines may be partially or fully configured by the staff through the kernel at any time, ensuring safety and system standardization. In addition, from the initial installation of the machines on, each machine may communicate with the kernel and reconfigure itself when necessary.

In order to do so, a high-performance and high-availability network is simply essential, which, in our case, is an optical fiber private network. For safety reasons, the network contract should allow schools to be connected to two logical networks, being one for students and the other one for the schools' management system. On the other hand, the service should also be safe enough to deny access of unauthorized members to the management network. Therefore, each school has a firewall for its internal network.

The complete network is made up of approximately 40,000 computers, and it will be managed in a centralized way, by a sole kernel, whose number of managers must also be reduced. The objectives were, then, to lower the network management costs, maintain the homogeneity of the network, ensure safety and continuous availability, and finally, carry out audits and monitoring of the use of the laboratories.

The kernel was also protected by a modern security system, which should perform the tracking of possible flaws, audits, package control, as well as any other safety measures that may be necessary.

Being an exclusive competence of the kernel, the management of the labs could not be done locally in the school, unless otherwise determined by the kernel coordinators. The processes should be automated as often as possible, and should ensure integrity, safety, and the complete functioning of the system.

For this reason, we have chosen the Debian distribution of GNU/Linux, which has an advanced installation system and software package configuration, in addition to the fact that it had already been in use in Dinf/UFPR for over 8 years.

The Model of Each School

Each school has received a laboratory containing approximately 20 terminals, which will simply be called "terminals" or "workstations" from now on. The terminals are machines through which users may access the laboratory resources by means of a high-quality graphical interface based upon Windows, enabling the access to programs through menus and icons, as it usually is nowadays. These terminals have been connected to a processing server through a high-performance network.

The processing server (or school's server) is also a hard disk server (where users will store their data). Because it is a single machine, it is easier to manage the network, and it is possible both to guarantee periodical copies and to lower network managements costs. The processing servers have the following basic functions:

- To store all students, teachers, and school technicians' accounts
- To store the operating system of the schools' terminals

- To allow remote access through the server kernel for maintenance and remote management of the laboratory
- To make the necessary applications available to the schools' users in the terminals
- To tackle flaws and to recover automatically

From a functional point of view, every laboratory presents a certain unity. The terminals are mere vehicles to the access of resources offered by the processing server, which means that they do not carry out local processing except for controlling network resources and graphical elements on the screen.

As a result, users feel as if they were processing in each terminal when, in fact, all the processing demand is taken up by the server, which must obviously be an adequate machine for the processing load of approximately 20 simultaneous users.

One of the main advantages of such model is that it is possible, with a low budget, to better the performance of the processing server leading to the improvement of the global performance of the computer environment installed in the school. This makes the job of local sponsors (such as the associations of parents and teachers, for instance) easier, since they may simply add more memory to the processing server, or even purchase an entirely new machine to replace the server.

Another advantage is the terminals' low maintenance demand. Normally, only if there is a hardware problem will they stop working, which any poorly specialised computer technician may be able to solve. The computer component with the highest flaw probability is the HD. The terminals do not have an HD, only floppies booting remotely in the processing server, which in turn possesses a very modern hardware, connected to a security device against electrical flaws, and is installed in an isolated room, protected against users and heat, which increases its durability.

The Multi-Terminal

These days, computers possess a processing capacity significantly higher than the demand load of many users. This is especially true in the model we adopted, in which the processing is carried out by the server, which makes each terminal responsible for the Windows system management only.

Taking this fact into account, the PRD staff has developed a system in which two to six sets (monitor, keyboard, mouse, and sound interface) are connected to one processing unit (CPU). These sets function independently, which means that the same CPU may be shared by two to six users. Therefore, this system has been named "multi-terminal," and the reduction to a maximum of four users, which was adopted in due course, refers exclusively to physical restrictions, that is, the size of tables and length of cables.

The multi-terminal system is entirely based upon free software, which allows it to be installed in practically any distribution of the GNU/Linux system. The distribution used for carrying out the experiment was Debian, which will turn out to be the standard distribution of the project.

The hardware requirements for the multi-terminal do not differ much from those of the terminals specified in the first phase of the bid, considering that the terminals became multi-terminals by simply adding new monitors, keyboards, mice, and sound interface.

The development of a multi-terminal may be divided into two areas: software and hardware. For the software area, an operating system kernel has been built, in order to fulfil both the requirements of the multi-terminal (to support several keyboards and mice), and the needs to support the remote charge of the operating system and the connection to the processing server. Furthermore, configuration files, necessary to initializing the terminals, have been created.

As for the hardware area, several devices (especially motherboards and video boards) were tested, in order to determine a list of components compatible with the system. These tests were carried out in the development laboratory of Dinf/UFPR. Two tetraterminals were purchased for such experiment: one operating with the most stable version of the system and being used by the project interns for their daily tasks, and the other being used for carrying out hardware tests as well as tests of the new software versions. For a more detailed architecture, please access http://www.c3sl.ufpr.br/multiterminal. Figure 2(a) shows a four-headed interface of a real multi-terminal, while Figure 2(b) shows an overview of hardware configuration for the same machines.

However careful, the development of the multi-terminal encountered some challenges (already sorted out), among which we may mention the incompatibility of various models of video boards, the overheating of the video boards due to their proximity, and the difficulty in configuring the necessary software for its functioning.

The main advantage of a multi-terminal system is the cost reduction it provides, including:

- **Equipment purchase costs:** For four users it is 45% of the cost of four individual workstations.
- **Implementation costs:** The multiterminal requires five times as few network cables and switch points when compared to a corresponding traditional laboratory.
- **Management costs:** By cutting down the number of CPUs to one fourth, the flaw probability of the electrical sources and cooling systems is automatically reduced.

Figure 2. (a) Four-headed interface of a multi-terminal; (b) overview of hardware configuration

(a)

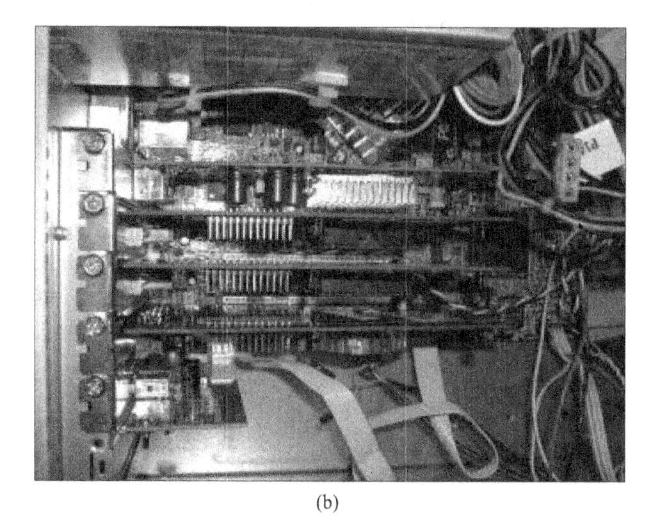

(b)

- **Total cost:** The cost of one workstation, after the bid by PNUD, was US$430,00, including the cost of the processing server, the terminals, the video boards, the mice and keyboards, the USB hubs, switches and logic, and electric cable sets.

Main Activities of the Project

Once the partnership contract among several institutions involved in the project was signed, the main activities carried out to fulfill the project were staff selection and installation, development laboratory installation, and pilot laboratories installation.

Staff Selection and Installation

After the analysis of the problem, which culminated in the results previously described, eight internal coordinations have been established, in order to fulfill the following tasks:

- Pilot laboratories management
- Development laboratory management
- Security model definition
- Final users' environment project
- Pedagogic applications selection
- Multi-terminals project
- Training and documentation

Each coordination developed its tasks with the support of approximately two interns, which leads to a total of 17 computer science students working on the project. During the development of the project, some interns were rearranged within the groups according to their specific demands.

The need for more effort in the creation of an initial image led to a new staff selection, which required that the laboratory be adapted in order to work as development laboratory.

Development Laboratory Installation

The development laboratory was structured in such a way as to enable the development of the various tasks of each work group, and consisted of two sets of computers: one for subprojects, which did not require special equipment (only Internet access and programming tools), and another one for development tests, comprising configured computers with CD-ROM burners and special configurations for experiments.

The first set of computers was conceived as a stable environment for the staff to work tranquilly, whereas the second one was fully equipped so that hardware or software components could be specifically tested, or even complete reinstallations of computers could be carried out, if it were the case. This first environment comprised two computer servers, one firewall, one laptop and six graphical terminals, one of which was under the multi-terminal system. The testing environment, on the other hand, comprised six computers with hard disk, CD burners, sound boards, as well as other devices that were being tested, such as USB hubs and network equipment for assessing the performance of low-performance networks, that is, modems, for instance. The assessment of such networks was necessary in case of the implementation of the chosen model in schools where there is no connection by optical fibers.

The installation of the development project was undertaken since the very beginning in such a way as to ensure total network security. In addition, a subnetwork with its own firewall was configured, demanding subnetwork reconfiguration in Dinf. The computer servers were planned in order to have a restricted, safe access system, and a redundancy system was designed for computers and data. The electrical system was adapted, and a special room for the main servers was prepared.

Pilot Laboratories Installation

It was absolutely imperative for the fulfillment of the project that the development staff be aware of the possible problems that may occur with both the computer server and the remote terminals. Furthermore, in order to install a network in about 2,100 schools, it is essential to validate the model in a similar environment first. Those are the reasons why the staff has installed two pilot laboratories.

The motivation for keeping two pilot laboratories is to carry out experiments at different levels. The first one was a stable environment, with the same group of users (who were attended to after the network installation), located in a public school of the state of Paraná. The second, located in Dinf, was not necessarily stable, but physically close enough to the staff, to make testing and experiments easy and to avoid disturbing the school's people.

The school we chose for our pilot laboratory was the "Instituto de Educação do Paraná Professor Erasmo Piloto" (IEPPEP), both for its relative closeness to the project staff, which allowed them to get there quickly in case of emergencies, and for the fact that the school's computer installations had been done by Dinf in May, 2003.

In February 2004, the 2003 installation was fully replaced to be adapted to the model of the project. Two interns were responsible for monitoring this laboratory, getting information from users as well as helping tackle problems.

However, the laboratory installed in IEPPEP was not enough to validate the model. Despite the feeling that both students and teachers were pleased with the GNU/Linux operating system, the laboratory contained one processing server only, which is insufficient to validate the set of programs that will enable communication among 2,100 schools.

Therefore, we started installing the second pilot laboratory, which was located in Dinf, and received the name "Multi-terminal Laboratory." This laboratory was designed to simulate 15 processing servers (or 15 schools), working as a test and experiment base for the remote management tools. Taking advantage of its structure, it also served to validate the multi-terminal project. The project comprises 60 workstations, and is destined to students of courses other then computer science, so as to get the impressions of users not acquainted with the GNU/Linux system. It is in this laboratory that classes of dozens of courses offered at UFPR (including the schools of mathematical sciences, biology, humanities, arts, technology) have been taking place.

Pilot Laboratory Validation in IEPPEP

In May 2003, the first pilot laboratory was installed in IEPPEP, including 20 computers that the school already had, plus 2 servers supplied by CELEPAR. The terminals were prepared to carry out remote charge in the server, for which 20 EPROMs were recorded in the network boards.

The server was installed with general use software, such as the Openoffice package, Galleon, and Mozilla. Various educational programs and games were also available. Moreover, the server was configured in order to establish Internet access to other IEPPEP laboratories as well.

The IEPPEP laboratory has been managed by the Dinf staff since then. Many experiments have been carried out in this laboratory, especially aiming at establishing the minimum capacity of the server for the teaching laboratories. Through such experiments, we have learned that one machine with one server would not be adequate for the teaching laboratory environment.

In February 2004, we installed a server more similar to those that would be used in the project. This server was completely reinstalled, including more recent versions of the applications as well as some new tools, especially concerning sound use. The use of sound in the terminals was rather difficult, since the applications were executed in the central sever, and the audio needed to be redirected to the terminal in use by the student.

One of the problems detected by the school's computer science coordinator was the lack of laboratory use by teachers due to poor training. Once the problem was identified, we started a negotiation process in order to provide public school teachers with a proper training through SEED/CETEPAR.

Dinf has been assisting in the training of the SEED trainers by offering courses through a partnership with CELEPAR. Such courses aim at preparing trainers so that they become fully equipped for training the public school teachers. This is absolutely essential for the project to be welcomed in the schools and for the teachers to take advantage of the pedagogical possibilities that it offers. Three basic tasks have been accomplished by Dinf: the preparation of technical-pedagogic material, the preparation of trainers, and the loan of laboratories for the training sessions.

The material developed consisted of a user's manual for the final users in the schools; a local manager's manual for the school employee who will be in charge of managing the laboratory; an installation guide for assisting in the CD installation in the processing servers and multiterminals; as well as the corresponding software package documentation.

The preparation of trainers enabled the development of the necessary workforce to disseminate the free software culture in the public schools of the state of Paraná. The loan of laboratories for training, in addition to avoiding the common sub-utilization problem, guaranteed the necessary feedback to the continuous software update.

Main Problems

The Dinf staff pointed out the main problems that may occur and that must be dealt with to ensure the success of the suggested model. Such problems were classified as follows: implementation, users' management, management of each server, terminal management, and network kernel management. Each problem category will be discussed, and their possible solutions will be indicated in the section titled "Solutions and Recommendations."

Implementation

Due to the great number of machines (44,000), the installation process may be overly time-consuming if not properly planned. Therefore, it is imperative that the bid winner deliver the machines with the system already installed. Such measure may be superfluous for mainstream operating systems, but surely not for GNU/Linux systems, especially for a system that must be managed remotely from a kernel. The installation of the laboratories must be "ready-to-use," and once installed, it should no longer require local intervention, except in the case of complete system loss, which is a possibility that should be avoided.

The installation process must also take the proper reutilization of the equipment installed into account, so as to ensure, even in the case of new machines, the quality of the equipment, its compatibility to the GNU/Linux system, as well as the homogeneity of the system, which facilitates its management. For this reason, elaborating the opening bid and previewing the installation process of the computer environment were quite challenging tasks. It was essential that we guarantee equipment quality, compatibility with the GNU/Linux operating system, and maximize the quantity of machines purchased, all at once.

User Management in Each Server

The fact that the system will be accessed by approximately 1,500,000 users requires that some aspects be well-planned so as to make the job of the very few managers easy.

In addition to that, it is also mandatory that we properly define the processes that allow the automatic creation of 300,000 new accounts annually (of those users that may be admitted into the schools), and that, in turn, allow the elimination of the same number of users who may no longer be part of the system.

Other examples of problems that have already been spotted by the Dinf staff include the large number of users that lose their passwords (estimated over 500 a day) or overpass the established disk limits, blocking their access to the system (estimated over 1,500 a day).

These problems are usually solved by local interventions of the system managers, which implies the use of the privileged access password, potentially compromising the safety of the entire network. Therefore, since the model adopted by the PRD project is centralized, we must consider automation, otherwise the kernel staff will dedicate all their time to solving this sort of problem.

Management of Each Server

The Dinf staff has identified a series of minor problems shared by multi-user environments, comprising, for instance: possible freezing of some processes that in fact should be suspended, since they take up a great amount of memory and processing, usually when the user is not even connected to the system; possible screen freezing due to hardware flaws or power failure, which normally leads to hardware breakdown or system charge failure, which in turn may require local intervention of the network manager. These are well-known, easily solvable problems, as long as they are dealt with traditionally, that is, by manual interventions of local operators. As we have already mentioned, in the PRD project the management is centralized, which makes this sort of problem solving a great challenge. Therefore, it is absolutely imperative that we develop automatic programs to tackle these kinds of problems. In order to do so, an in-depth study of the programs executed in the computer server must be carried out, which implies the installation of pilot laboratories for such studies to be performed. For this purpose, the Dinf staff currently maintains two pilot laboratories.

The staff has also identified another series of problems, this time not as simple, that must also be solved automatically, since they involve security aspects of the entire network. These problems include the control of which terminals are authorized to access the network (in order to avoid the connection of machines that do not belong to the school), the control of disk and printing limits to which each user has the right, the monitoring of which Web pages can be accessed by students (avoiding Web sites whose content is inadequate), and the control of which students should be granted e-mail accounts (since this may cause serious network problems due to viruses or spam).

However, the foremost problem tackled by the Dinf staff is the great vulnerability of the network security system of the server of each school, and there is a simple explanation for it. The server is where users will be operating the system, which means that these servers must be equipped with automatic software updating mechanisms, which must be carried out under the absolute control of the network kernel. Great care must be taken in order to ensure that users shall not have privileged access to the system, or else the PRD network will be susceptible to becoming a source of Internet attack. However, it is well known that malicious users may possibly get privileged access to the system, despite all security measures adopted. For this reason, it is important that the server of each school exchange information with the network kernel periodically. It is through these exchanges that the network kernel should be able to update the security systems of the school servers (indirectly updating even the internal terminals), carrying out even global system updates. It should also be able to exchange information that enables safe system auditing to take place, allowing the investigation of suspicious behavior of certain users.

It is important to bear in mind that in such a model where all terminals are connected to a computer server, it cannot fail, otherwise the entire school would be off the network, including the management staff. This threat leads to measures, such as the use of a redundancy system strategy in which, ideally, there is a processing alternative in case of possible main server failure. It is equally essential that there be restricted access to the server, that the server be placed in a protected area, preferably cooled, and that it be equipped with electric security devices.

Terminal Management

In spite of the fact that terminals are pieces of equipment susceptible to failure, this tendency is minimized in the PRD project. Since the terminal image is unique and is kept in the server, the behavior of the terminals should be rigorously the same for the entire laboratory. In this model, the software failure possibility in the workstations is practically eliminated completely. Inasmuch as the terminals do not have hard disks, which are the components most susceptible to failure, the HD failure possibility is thus reduced as well. The most common failures, then, will be associated to power breakdowns due to flaws in the electrical installations of the schools (because of vandalism, theft, carelessness handling laboratory substances). In this case, compatibility lists for the substitution of terminal components or even of the entire computer must be elaborated, paying attention to the hardware homogeneity in order to simplify the system management. The Dinf staff has put a guide together concerning such cases where problems may be solved locally, without kernel intervention. Such material also contains the description of the most common problems, as well as how they should be dealt with. When kernel intervention is required, the local operator must be able to describe the problem, especially in the very rare cases of software failure. This may be the case when a network board is substituted by a new one, for instance, unless the kernel is told about it, the terminal will not charge the system.

In this model, the terminals are indeed a good potential source for solving problems concerning the overcharge of the servers. Technically, it is possible to turn a remote graphical terminal into a full processing machine. If the server were overcharged, for instance, a possible solution would be to have the terminals carry out local processing of programs, which would only demand a simple kernel intervention. Another alternative that cannot be overlooked is using the set of network terminals for assembling a computer grid, allowing the 44,000 computers to be employed to carry out parallel and distributed processing. This kind of environment is a powerful tool for weather forecast, simulations, and other scientific purposes of public interest. It is part of the project's scope to provide the state with a great supercomputer by means of all these terminals. At the moment, this is only a technically possible alternative, though.

Network Kernel Management

The network kernel management is, undoubtedly, one of the most important components of the model. Its purpose is to manage all laboratories, requiring minimum intervention of the local managers. One of our main concerns is to provide for its adequate protection. The fact that the network grants Internet access and comprises a large number of users makes this task even more difficult. If 0.01% of users is dangerous, we will have 150 potential invaders, and a kernel invasion would imply a safety compromise of 40,000 terminals. These terminals could be regarded, thus, as sources of powerful attacks to computers connected to the Internet.

Solutions and Recommendations

In this section, we will describe the work carried out by the Dinf staff regarding the final model of network management. At first we had several meetings with the inter-teams (SEED, CELEPAR, COPEL, Dinf, as well as BID and PNUD representatives).

We shall also describe a set of tasks that aim at refining problem identification and pointing out the suggested solutions, including the ones that have been discarded, the ones that have been adopted, and those that still await validation.

The PRD project is a challenge that may be fulfilled only by the joint efforts of all people involved, not only because of its natural complexity, but also due to conflicts and correct work division. All teams must know one another, understand one another's problems, classify them, and carefully determine the scope of each team, clearly defining the role of each group and identifying the intersection points.

The present and the subsequent sections will be dedicated to the discussion of the problems pointed out in the previous sections.

Opening Bid

The opening bid was put together by SEED, CELEPAR, and Dinf/UFPR, with the advice of BID and PNUD. During this process, countless computer enterprises presented their offers, which were carefully analyzed. It was Dinf who validated the software and hardware choices.

The project coordinators in SEED decided to separate the acquisition of the 44,000 computers into three bids, the first of which with a deadline in May 2004, so that the network installation could start taking place from July 2004 on.

Due to the characteristics of the model to be implemented, the great number of computers to be purchased, and the large amount of money involved, one of the greatest challenges faced by the project was the acquisition and installation of computers in the schools. Basically, there are three great difficulties: to ensure that the computers purchased were compatible with the GNU/Linux operating system, to ensure that the machines were correctly installed in the schools, and to maximize the number of computers installed. The opening bid was conceived to attend to the needs of the model adopted. The configurations of the following items were specified: of the processing server (capable of running up to 20 remote terminals), of the terminals, and of the network structure (including switches, racks and nobreaks).

During this process, starting in June 2003, the Dinf staff tested different processing server architectures. The features that varied were the processor manufacturer, the assembler, the disk quality, the amount of memory, and the tower quality, including the internal cooling. We have decided for an architecture with two processors,

SATA in RAIDI disks (mirroring redundancy) and a 1GB RAM memory for each 10 terminals installed in the laboratory, because this was the most cost-effective architecture. In addition, we tested different terminal architectures, varying the processor manufacturer, the assembler, and especially the compatibility of the components to the GNU/Linux operating system, particularly the video and network boards, which were assessed according to their capacity to fulfill the current standards of system remote charge.

Still concerning terminal configuration, the staff has tested various PC-like models of computers (or "thin clients"), as well as closed options based upon RISC architecture. The team comprising the staffs of CELEPAR, SEED, and Dinf opted for a desktop PC architecture for two reasons, mainly to maximize the amount of suppliers capable of fulfilling the opening bid, and to prepare the second and third phases of the bid for the purchase of multiterminal-like workstations. This option cut down the opening bid cost to about 50%.

Definition of the Management Model

By the beginning of the project, there were not enough tools available for managing such a great network. Therefore, the Dinf staff developed a series of tasks concerning users' authentication, backup systems, intruder monitoring and detection, firewalls, monitoring systems, use follow-up systems, and systems for automatic installation of processing servers.

The basic features of such a set of programs and tools should be to carry out all tasks automatically; make everyday tasks of user management easy; create accounts, end processes, manage printers; carry out automatic procedures such as backup, auditing, installation, recovery and maintenance; search for security flaws; verify the integrity of the machine.

One of the fundamental steps was to define a management philosophy, also defining a set of measures that allows the staff to perceive the actual state of the network, particularly detecting possible invasion or package alteration attempts and, eventually, carrying out a safe and fast system recovery in case of breakdowns.

Network Kernel Management

In the model adopted in the project, the network kernel is located in CELEPAR, Curitiba. The kernel is responsible for providing server management and centralized network services, including Internet access. The definition of such a kernel is among the tasks we developed.

One of the most relevant and ambitious aspects of this project is the need to manage the school laboratories remotely. In order to do so, a fundamental system is what shall ensure updating, integrity, and homogeneity of the server software.

We have also designed a server monitoring system, which consists of periodic information exchanges between servers and kernels regarding their state, as well as the statistics concerning the use of laboratories and the server charges.

Another major concern was the kernel safety. Since kernel vulnerabilities may allow someone to have access and to make use of all network servers (for attacking other national or international servers, for example), it must be heavily protected. The kernel safety policy to be employed was elaborated within this project, too. There is a firewall that blocks the exit of packages belonging to the PRD network, unless via proxy. The entire network uses invalid IPs and a private VPN (virtual private network).

The system that received the greatest priority was the one of remote and automatic machine updating. The reason for such a measure is that the system must be ready for distribution in the schools together with the servers, thus ensuring remote updating and management in schools from the very beginning.

Sever Updating

Ensuring software updating is one of the tasks of a system manager. This task is important, especially when the updating involves security failure. Such failures must be promptly corrected in order to avoid that malicious users take advantage of the system vulnerability.

When there is a reduced number of machines, the manager may carry out updating tasks individually, in each machine. However, in the PRD project, it would be impossible to manually update 2,000 servers, which requires an automatic updating system.

This automatic updating model presents some difficulties in performing some tasks, such as:

- Ensuring that the updating was successfully performed in all machines.
- Blocking the managers' intervention requests during the installation.
- Allowing the selection of which updating should and should not be installed, since the official Debian distributions may suggest unwanted updating.
- Allowing the return to an older software version (downgrade) when necessary.

- Allowing the updating of machines that for some reason had been off the network, and therefore missed some of the updating stages.
- Preview the existence of three versions of the servers' software sets (development, experimental, stable).

Taking these requirements into consideration, experiments were carried out, and programs were developed to perform server updating. In the suggested model, the machines will be updated by means of mirrors based upon the Debian GNU/Linux distribution. We have developed, thus, the necessary programs for controlling the three versions of such mirror (development, experimental, and stable).

Furthermore, we have worked on the possibility of machine updating automation through the mirrors installed in the kernel. We have created procedures that permit the automatic installation of packages through a question-absent process.

Another challenge faced by the project consists of updating all packages in such a way as to keep the configuration of the packages homogenous, the only configuration difference being the local parameters, such as the servers' network addresses.

All solutions were integrated, and an automatic updating experiment was carried out in the IEPPEP server. Fifteen machines that simulated the schools' servers were updated successfully, allowing us to validate and refine the model.

Generation of the Servers' Image

The image generation containing the servers' operating system shall be sent to the bid winner. It will be stored in a self-installable CD-ROM that will automatically partition the HDs and perform the basic necessary configurations to get the server ready for implementation. Due to the centralized model adopted, the large number of schools, and also the geographic distribution of the schools in the state, the network implementation process was extremely complex, and had to be carefully planned. The equipment must be easily installed in the schools, ensuring network safety from the beginning. Such a measure required a minimum intervention of the school technician.

The model determines that each server be configured with a network address previously settled for each school according to the region distributions within the state, thus allowing the management of the entire network via kernel. Preliminary tests in the development laboratory, as well as exhaustive tests in the Dinf pilot laboratory, were carried out. We have gathered information concerning the regions, kernels, and schools belonging to each kernel. These data worked as a basis for automating the process of logical structuring of the network. All servers were delivered containing the same basic configuration, and once connected to the network, they needed to be configured.

In the server installation process, after connecting and turning the server on, a local technician will have to select the name of the school by means of a graphic interface. The list of schools presented on the implementation interface was supplied by SEED, and the project staff had previously attributed the network addresses to each school. The network address format was also examined by the CELEPAR and COPEL staffs.

The moment the school is selected on the interface, its network address will be validated in the project kernel, and it will automatically start network operation. Next, all the local technician has to do is turn on the terminals and they too will be automatically validated in the server, beginning operation as well. An installation guide has been prepared by the Dinf staff, describing the possible problems the local technician may have to solve, the basic server use and maintenance, and the instructions on how to contact the kernel support.

The initial installation should comprise the main packages as well as the fundamental packages for the remote management of the servers. The selection of such packages was the outcome of an in-depth study of the schools' demand, and a server prototype has been in operation in the IEPPEP laboratory since May 2003.

Server Recovery CDs

A drawback of the centralized model proposed for the PRD network is how to decide what to do in case of server breakdown in the schools. Normally, this is solved by manual interventions of the local network manager. This should be minimized in this project, in order reduce the number of trips around the state.

Basically, there are two kinds of problems that may occur: severe hardware failure or minor configuration problems derived from temporary power flaws, for instance. In the first case, the equipment must be replaced, and a maintenance team must be taken to the laboratory. In order to avoid useless trips, the local technician must be certain of the severity of the problem. The Dinf staff has prepared a manual containing the ways in which such problems may be detected. Once through with the hardware replacement, the local technician must insert the self-installation CD, and the kernel synchronism process will automatically restart.

As for the temporary flaws, they normally derive from minor breakdowns caused by hard disk temporary flaws. In this case, the team has decided to adopt a reinstallation CD, as described. The team has assessed some mainstream packages available in free software, and opted to develop a mixed solution by using many experiences reported in the Internet. The solution consists of an auto-recovery CD that evaluates machine integrity and automatically charges a server recovery scheme. In this process, two alternatives have been identified, the first of which being those cases where the partition containing user data has not been affected. In these cases, the system will automatically format the remaining partitions, as well as perform a reinstallation preserving the users' area. The second alternative must be used in extreme situations in which data have been completely lost (if the HD has been damaged, for instance). In such cases, the server will be reinstalled and validated in the kernel once again. This process requires that some network resources become available for that laboratory, as well as the list of users. The auto-recovery scheme is an efficient alternative for the maintenance of this model in situations of severe flaw, avoiding thus that specialized staff travel to the school. It also allows the technician himself to replace the damaged hardware without compromising laboratory use. This is possible because the auto-recovery CD contains the very same image supplied on the first installation. We shall also develop a system of auto-recovery CD generation with new versions of the image, making the CD distribution easier, since they would no longer have to be mailed to the schools but simply created in the laboratories. In order to do so, the specification of the servers must contain a CD-RW or DVD-RW unit.

Generation of the Clients' Eprom Image

This item used to be part of the first version of the opening bid, when the project was being written down to be sent to the Paraná Technology Fund, but was no longer required in the final version, elaborated in May and sent right after to PNUD. This happened because we substituted, in the opening bid, the requirement to have an external network board for an internal one that accepts the new system remote charge protocol recently launched by the hardware industry, entitled PXE (Pre-boot execution environment). The Dinf staff carried out a series of tests with several different motherboards that supported such protocol, and helped write the new version of the opening bid to guarantee that the protocol version was correct, so that the machines could effectively charge the network.

User Management in the Schools

Amongst the tools developed within the scope of the project, it is important to mention the local intervention interface, which is a graphic application that allows the school laboratory responsible to carry out some small everyday tasks, such as the exchange of lost passwords, removal of blocked printing tasks, backup of the local data in CD-ROM, and adjustment of the users' disk limits. Such a local intervention graphic interface will also enable the safe and easy execution of management tasks by common users, which normally demand the intervention of an experienced UNIX manager, thus reducing the amount of tasks of the system kernel.

Project Wrap-Up

The greatness and complexity of the problems and solutions involved demanded, in the last month of the project, joint efforts of all groups in order to eliminate remaining software flaws and to adjust any possible discrepancies within the system, so as to ensure consistency among the environments offered to final users and to local managers (in the schools), as well as the consistency of the assistance documentation to each user profile.

Future Trends

The Paraná Digital project was completed and all objectives were fulfilled. Thanks to its success, a new partnership contract has been signed in order to guarantee the presence and support of UFPR in the school laboratory implementation phase, involving the final use of the system and its follow-up, aiming at perfecting it by eliminating flaws pointed out by the users. Dinf will accompany all kernel interventions in the schools, as well as the functioning of the model in the schools, always aiming at spotting possible problems and correcting them promptly, so as to guarantee the correct, permanent, and autonomous operation of the suggested model.

Conclusion

The Paraná Digital project is innovative because it is the first of its kind to attend to such a large number of schools and to guarantee the operation of its systems by remote management. The effectiveness of the suggested model clearly demonstrated the pertinence of the adoption of certain strategies of the project, among which are the laboratory remote management, the local access infrastructure and the multi-terminal model.

In addition, the project is strategic because not only has it accomplished the initial goals, being successfully available to the public to whom it was destined (Portal dia-a-dia-Educação), it also assures the Paraná State Education Secretary and the local public computer company of the technological autonomy necessary to the feasibility of continuous services and products developed.

This project grants the State of Paraná the status of major technological pole in free software and international reference in technological management in primary and secondary schooling.

The fulfillment of the project involved the partnership among several entities, each of which played a specific role within the context. The main activities of the project were discussions among the partner institutions, at first, followed by the acquisition of equipment, the development of software, the validation of hardware and software, the assessment of alternative models, the specification of bids, the maintenance of pilot laboratories, the selection and training of interns, the preparation of trainers and the elaboration of technical and didactic documentation for the different user profiles.

References

Carmo, R., Castilho, M., & Hexsel, R. (2001). Aparafusando Parafusos: Um modelo de Laboratório de Computação com Qualidade e Otimização de Recursos. In *Anais do Workshop em Ensino de Informática, Fortaleza/CE*, 2001. Sociedade Brasileira de Computação.

Castilho, M., Carmo, R., & Hexsel, R. (2001). Um Modelo de Gestão Eficiente de Recursos Computacionais. In *Anais do II Workshop Sobre Software Livre, Porto Alegre/RS*, 2001. Projeto Software Livre-RS.

Acknowledgments

This research and development project is sponsored by a grant from the UGF/SETI/PR (Estate Secretariat for Science and Technology in Paraná). We would like to thank Professor Aldair Rizzi for the ideological support, who acted jointly with the Secretary of Education in Paraná, Maurício Requião. Especial thanks also go to Mr. Jefferson Schreiber, who ventured, along with us, to lead the Paraná Digital project in order to make it feasible.

We also thank the invaluable work of the student's team that developed the libraries and scripts that compose the solutions described in this paper. They are: Alan Fischer e Silva, Ander Conselvan de Oliveira, Bruno César Ribas, Diogo Kollross, Edson Vinicius Schmidt, Egon Hilgenstieger, Jorge Augusto Meira, João Gustavo Gazolla Borges, Juliana Bueno, Juliano Picussa, Márcio Roberto de Miranda, Tiago Vignatti.

Appendix I: Case Study

A scenario of your interest: Imagine a context involving many user groups geographically apart whose common motivations are educational, governmental, religious, or any socially relevant aspect.

Questions

1. Identify the institutions (and their respective roles) which you would need to bring together by means of a partnership to make a project similar to the one described in the present chapter feasible.
2. Gather the necessary information and discuss the pertinence of using this model, taking into consideration the human and technological resources of the chosen area and institutions involved.
3. Gather the necessary information and discuss the pertinence of adopting the multiterminal model, taking into account the currentness of the equipment available in the institutions.
4. Outline the strategies to connect the project to the institutions you have envisaged as partners.

Appendix II: Useful URLs

From the moment of its Internet divulgation, the Paraná Digital project, and particularly the multiterminal system, has been attracting the attention of the international community. The multiterminal Web page has had, since July 2004, X visitors, and the team has been receiving electronic messages daily from many public and private institutions, asking for information on how to install the system.

http://www.c3sl.ufpr.br/fourhead/index.php?lang=pt-br (site do Projeto)

http://developers.slashdot.org/developers/04/07/03/1923255.shtml?tid=1067TID=137&TID=1857tid=189

http://brlinux.linuxsecurity.com.br/noticias/002799.html

Possible Titles for Papers/Essays

- The Multiterminal Model Applied to Other Gnu/linux Distributions
- Software Configuration for Multiterminals

Chapter XIII

A Social Constructionist Approach to Learning Communities: Moodle

Marc Alier Forment, Universitat Politècnica de Catalunya, Spain

Abstract

This chapter will discuss the influence of the main learning paradigms: conductism and constructivism. We will also talk about the need to apply the OSS development model and licences to the creation of open contents, to be also collaboratively created in communities. The social reality of OSS communities that become learning communities is described by the principles of social constructionism; this paradigm has been applied in the creation of Moodle.org, a true learning community built around the OSS learning management system: Moodle.

Introduction

Conductism and Constructivism

There are two main pedagogical theories used to approach any education process (including the e-learning focused): **conductism** and **constructivism**. We can find antecedents of these theories on Classic Greece, in **Plato's Academia**. The rhetorical masters based their teaching in the recitation of a discourse previously written in a special book of contents. On the other hand, **Plato**, founder and director for more than twenty years of the Academia, did defend and practiced a way of teaching consisting in stimulating the student's individual investigation, complemented by related debates inside and outside the classroom (**Aristotle** named his own school after the teacher student debates during *peripatetic* (wandering) walking). **Plato** applied active learning methods that enabled the students to work and study by themselves, in order for them to discover the difficulty and find out how to overcome it. Plato's method also stimulated criticism among his students. And you never know where this process will lead, you cannot control what the student is going to learn.

Conductism proposes a detailed instructional design based on:

- A concrete definition of the learning objectives
- The use of well-designed and normalized contents
- The fragmentation of the information in small units, to be studied separately and following a defined sequence
- Continuous evaluation of the students progress, evaluate (and pass) one unit before coming into the next
- Reinforcement of desired student responses
- Control over the student learning pace

On the other hand, the constructivist approach relies more on:

- Creating proper opportunities to allow the students to face situations that create intellectual conflict with their past experiences, forcing them to think
- Suggesting activities that help students to build and restructure their knowledge
- Suggesting problem-solving activities, with real case studies (whenever possible)
- Proposing activities that require interaction and collaboration (with other students and the teacher himself)

The **conductist** approach focuses on the use of contents; these must be structured to deliver exactly the knowledge we want the student to learn. This leads to two issues:

- We know for a fact that the student will not learn 100% of the contents. Meaning that if students only learn from their lesson, they will never achieve the same knowledge as the author's. This model may be valid to deliver knowledge, but never to create a new one.
- The second issue makes me uncomfortable. Who designs, elaborates, and controls what will and what will not the students learn? Who has got that kind of power?

If we think about a teacher writing his lectures for a 30-student classroom, there is no problem in that. But this is not the scenario. We talk about a whole industry creating expensive advanced multimedia learning contents.

The Cost of E-Contents

Think about an online 20-hour course based on SCORM and Learning Objects[1], discussed in previous chapters[2]. These contents are attractive, interactive, cool, and multimedia; they capture the attention of the target[3]. It is the dream of the conductist paradigm come true. But, oh yes, they are expensive to produce. Guerra (2004) designed a 1 to 10 scale to measure the increase of the cost of production of e-learning contents based on his experience:

- **Levels GS-1→GS-3:** PDF files, Web-based *page turners*, *hypertext* contents
- **Levels GS-4→GS-6:** quiz with feedback, motion, and multimedia
- **Levels GS-7→GS-9:** user input workbook, knowledge repository, simulation
- **Level GS-10**→coaching, virtual reality, and so forth

Our own research in UPC (Alier, 2004) confirmed Tim Guerra's proposition that production cost increases exponentially as you go up in the Guerra Scale.

Figure 1. Relative cost of development of online contents (Source: Own elaboration from experience and original paper, Guerra, 2004)

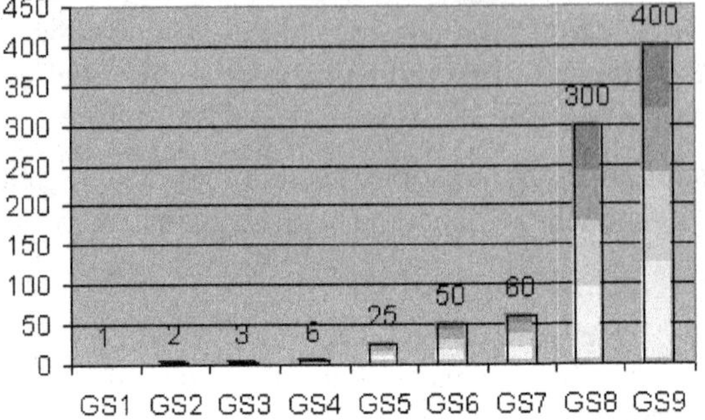

The Dangers of Having Only One Version of the Reality

We can build and deliver our e-contents with open source software (OSS) and benefit from the OSS model that has been exposed through this book. But will the e-contents benefit from OSS paradigm? With that costs structure so high, GS degree contents must be widely used by a large number of students to guarantee the return of investment (ROI) in its development. To ensure the ROI, they should be distributed under strong copyright restrictions, and even copy protections. The revision, update, and maintenance is also expensive and is the responsibility of the owner of the copyrights. The OSS development paradigm resolves the software development complexity, and we just removed all these problems in the content development process.

If education is based on this kind of content, only a few versions of each theme will be available for students and teachers. I am afraid this model leads to a scenario where each area of expertise has only a few high-quality[4] contents with only a few visions of it. And who decides what students must learn? An example of an extreme case: in Spain, some people still remember a time when conductist learning was widely used in our schools to effectively spread the dictatorial regime ideology.

To prevent this from happening, we need to foster an **open contents development** model.

Open Contents

From Open Source to Open Contents

There is a common agreement (and has been exposed in many chapters of this book) that the OSS development model improves the quality of software; that within OSS communities thrives the learning processes and the creation of knowledge that, in the end, leads to the building of better software. But e-contents need also to benefit from open source strategy, not only for learning purposes, but also for the development of the *Information Society* itself, compulsive consumer and generator of information (Castells, 1997).

A key tool for the creation of open contents is the Creative Commons initiative. The Creative Commons Licences have enabled the creation of open content repositories, places where internauts collaboratively create, share, contribute, use, and modify the contents:

Creative Commons' first project, in December 2002, was the release of a set of copyright licenses free for public use. Taking inspiration in part from the Free Software Foundation's GNU General Public License (GNU GPL), Creative Commons has developed a Web application that helps people dedicate their creative works to the public domain—or retain their copyright while licensing them as free for certain uses, on certain conditions. Unlike the GNU GPL, Creative Commons licenses are not designed for software, but rather for other kinds of creative works: Websites, scholarship, music, film, photography, literature, courseware, etc.(taken from http://creativecommons.org)

Open Contents Communities

Lots of communities dedicated to the elaboration and sharing of these contents have appeared in the last few years. The best example would be Wikipedia[5] (more than one million articles only in English should be proof enough), the most successful open content community, and its associate open source community, Mediawiki. But as you may suspect, Wikipedia is not about learning objects and acrobatic multimedia, but about the success of collaborative software. Other open content communities are emerging worldwide; the Creative Commons Web site keeps track of some of them.

Some GNU and Creative Commons Licences allow the creation of derivative work. In OSS communities, this has allowed some projects to survive the decision of the copyright owners to go private and abandon GPL. The community can take over the development, under another name or brand, creating a *fork* from the last GNU-licensed stable code. This happened with SourceForge, Mambo, PHP Nuke, and other OSS projects. This principle applied to open contents can be an asset to ensure diversity of contents, the diffusion of knowledge worldwide, and the creation of translations. A story can be told in many ways, and most of them may be right. But the society (the *Information Society*) needs the very existence of all the versions and approaches. Then students can develop their criticism by comparing different versions and forming their own opinion.

The OSS Learning Model?

Revision of the Learning Models

The conductist model has its own advantages that would not be wise to give loose in certain domains of knowledge. Among others we want to mention:

- It is the optimal approach when facing highly structured areas of expertise.
- It facilitates the memorization of contents and instructions.
- It allows the definition of sequenced learning itineraries.

The constructivist model is superior in:

- Comprehension of complex information and processes
- Problem solving
- To acquire abilities

So, it seems reasonable that a good pedagogic approach to any educational initiative should arise from any point between conductism and constructivism (for my taste closer to the second part). What we should consider when adopting e-learning standards is that the standard approach to learning may not be neutral, that behind each standard underlies a way of thinking about learning, and a business model. We should also remember that the really fresh learning approaches do not care much about standards and more about people learning. We should be talking about Web 2.0 and e-learning 2.0, but this would be another story.

It is obvious that the learning model related to open source communities and open content communities is definitively not conductism and maybe, it is something beyond constructivism. That is because constructivism does not consider the social issues and their implication in the learning process.

Social Constructionism

Social constructionism is a sociological theory of knowledge developed by L. Berger and Thomas Luckmann (1966). Applied to education, it implies that learning is particularly effective when the subject builds (*constructs*) something for others to experience. And when this task of development takes place within a social group that is constructing things for one another (the society, maybe the group itself), the whole group is **collaboratively creating** a small culture of shared artifacts with shared meanings. When one is immersed within a culture like this, one is learning all the time about how to be a part of that culture, on many levels, and creating knowledge. **Maybe that is what this book is really about**.

Within this paradigm, contents are not in the center of the education. Contents are just another tool and do not deserve more importance than that. What really matters is the interaction teacher-student (or expert-apprentice), and the interaction of students.

Social constructionism stands for an activity-based learning, and not a content-based learning. LMS software like Moodle allows this kind of learning approach, and yet keeps a place to enable the use of learning objects, SCORM, and other standards.

Moodle

About Moodle?

Moodle is a learning management system distributed freely under GPL license. Moodle has two particular distinctive elements:

- Moodle is designed using the pedagogical principles of social constructionism. This is what differentiates Moodle from other LMS software. That is one of the keys for its success.
- The leadership of the founder and owner Martin Dougiamas. Martin has achieved building a true learning community of more than 120,000 members around the world that collaborate and learn together every day.

Figure 2. Moodle registered sites (Source: http://moodle.org/stats)

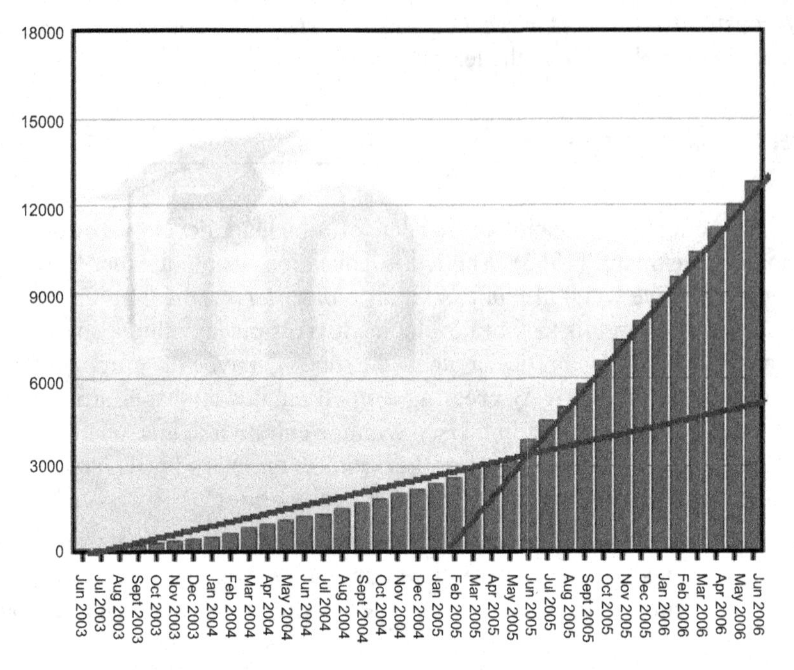

Figure 3. Moodle community growth (Source: http://moodle.org/stats)

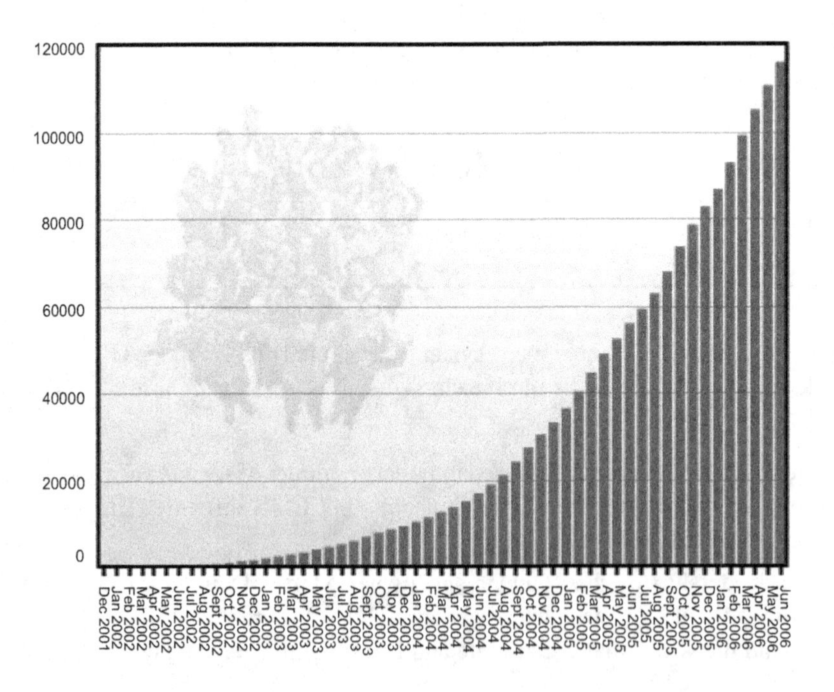

Moodle's design is really flexible and easy to learn for teachers and students. Based on LAMP[6], Moodle can be installed on almost any desktop computer with any operating system. Using one of the distributions, the XAMPP[7]-based distribution can be installed by a non-expert user to be used as single teacher or departmental server, and also can be scaled to a 50,000-student university virtual campus.

There are 151 registered Moodle sites that are larger than 5,000 users. The site with the most users is moodle.org, with 40 courses and 122,719 users. The site with the most courses is Online Campus, with 8,282 courses and 54,955 users.[8]

The growth of the pool of Moodle installations has been sustained since 2002, and increased dramatically on May 2005, in coincidence with the shipment of the 1.5 version. The software-spreading rate can only be compared with the growth of the Moodle community that, from the very first day, grows exponentially.

The Moodle Community

All in moodle is about learning. More than a piece of software, Moodle is a community that builds software for e-learning and by doing so, the community members (social constructively) learn more about education, online education, building software, and being part of an online community. The members of the Moodle community are not only developers, but also teachers that use moodle, content authors, designers, computer security experts, and students that collaborate while doing their research and development projects.

Moodle is a true learning community, but this is not casual. I will let Martin Dougiamas explain himself in an abusive, but necessary quote (Dougiamas, 2003):

Over several years I have noticed certain features of the projects that seem to attract and maintain such learning communities, and applied this experience in setting up the environment for the Moodle community. Some of the necessary features are:

- *A clear, obvious Web site design (and Web address, like moodle.org)*
- *Demonstrations of the software that are easy to get into*
- *Simple but extensive documentation for developers and users*
- *Structured, easy-to-use forums and mail lists for different purposes (support, discussion, suggestions)*
- *A central transparent place to safely store all source code (a CVS server)*
- *2A tracker to keep track of issues (e.g., bugs, new features) and their status*

I try to model professional behaviour that is consistently constructive and connected. My guidelines are grounded in the experiences from our Constructivism courses, as well as ongoing study of the behaviours that seem to be successfully helping the Moodle community grow and develop:

- *I release software "early and often" (Raymond, 1999), so that even non-developer users can feel more a par of the development process and new bugs can be caught more quickly.*
- *I respond to e-mail and forum posts as quickly as I can. Not only does it help encourage people to communicate, it gives more life to the site as it's always changing with new content.*
- *I try to be as friendly and helpful as possible at all times, even when it's tempting to flame someone. Negative posts become a permanent part of the site and can dampen further interaction between people.*
- *I try to be particularly supportive to contributors. With encouragement, some people can really blossom. If their interest is stimulated, some people feel more able to make larger contributions.*
- *I continually evaluate the learning environment and make changes as necessary, evolving in a way that brings the user along on an adventure*
- *I look for links and publish them (e.g., between discussions, or finding people who could help each other, or to Web sites/resources). As the site and community grows, this reduces the distances people have to travel to connect with the information they are looking for.*

Putting this sort of energy into moodle.org is one factor that "keeps the pot bubbling."

A large advantage of focussing on moodle.org as a learning community is that participants are able to experience Moodle from a student's perspective, and learn about online learning from their fellow participants. Again in the words of Martin:

If the behaviour I am modelling at moodle.org (with it's theoretical background of social constructionism, connected knowing and transformative learning) is effective, it can potentially transform participants and so affect the teaching behaviour within their own Moodle installations.

And it certainly does.

The Moodle community has transcended the online existence with the **Moodle-Moots**. MoodleMoot is the name of a Moodle-centred conference. The word Moot comes from the world of J.R.R. Tolkien's *Lord of the Rings,* and is used to describe the gathering of the Ents, ancient wise creatures, to discuss their plans. And in this context, it fits perfectly with what Moodle Moots have become: A gathering of **Moodlers** (Moodle users and developers) who come together to discuss ideas and share strategies. According to Ridden (2006) it is an event for social networking for new and old Moodle users alike. Currently, there are nine MoodleMoot events around the world that take place once a year.

The Learning Community as an Opportunity for the Researcher and Developer

Moodle's modular design allows developers to contribute with their own activity modules, themes, blocks, course styles, and patches. Moodle leaders allow a space in the CVS repository for third-party contributions, and publish a directory for interested users (http://moodle.org/mod/data/view.php?id=6009). All contributions are welcome, and some even come into the main Moodle distribution (but it can be a hard job).

Every time I go to a conference, I attend presentations where brilliant researchers and developers expose their innovations. And those, unfortunately, will not go beyond the scope of their lab, or experimental classrooms. I decided 3 years ago to frame my research within the Moodle community, rather than starting a project on my own. It was one of the best decisions I could take. I lost the opportunity to create a project from scratch and the freedom of decision that comes with it, but in return, I gained lots of advantages:

- The knowledge latent inside the Moodle design and code that is embedded with the philosophical principles of social constructionism; know how of online learning and how to build software
- The help and cooperation of the Moodle community
- An invaluable base test ground. From the first day I started exposing my ideas, the community responded with feedback, guidance, and constructive criticism. When we released early versions of our code, lots of users from around the world started testing and giving us feedback: reporting bugs, asking for improvements, and helping us with the translation to languages that we did not even know existed.

By starting my research and development inside the Moodle Community, I had to follow every step detailed in chapter 2 referring to the KDE community. After some time of Moodling, I built a team of developers among my students of last year in computer science in the Universitat Politècnica de Catalunya (UPC, http://www.upc.edu). After 2 years of work, we feel that our research and development has become something real; real solutions for real needs that really use our innovations (Alier, 2006).

But that is not all. As a reward, the learning experience collaborating with Moodle exceeds our expectations. In 2 years of work, six students of my team have earned a scholarship to collaborate in customizing Moodle for our University, and even giving support to teachers. Actually, now two of them work for the UPC in the successful, huge project of setting up a Moodle-based virtual campus site for more than 30,000 students, and integrating the Moodle software with the university's management software, PRISMA. But that is another story according, to Ribot and Erenchun (2005).

Conclusion

Contents should not be allowed to be the center of the learning design, especially when we deal with online learning. The role of the teacher/expert, and the activities that the learners' collective must face should be the focus of learning. Moodle is an example of how this can be accomplished. The Moodle software carries within it the very essence of social constructionism (while keeping the possibility of using fancy e-contents), and the Moodle community is the perfect example of how a learning community works, and how the open source model for learning within a community is not restricted only to developers.

References

Alier, M. (2006), Lions tigers and Wikis ... Oh my! *Moodle Newsletter, 2*. Retrieved from http://moodlezine.org

Alier, M., & Barceló, M. (2004, June 7-9). *E-learning and engineering education: Some examples*. Second Conference for Innovation, Good Practice and Research in Engineering Education, University of Wolverhampton, Wolverhampton, UK.

Berger, P. L., & Luckmann, T. (1966). *The social construction of reality: A treatise in the sociology of knowledge.* Garden City, NY: Anchor Books.

Castells, M. (1997). La era de la información: Economía, sociedad y cultura. *La sociedad red, 1.*

Dougiamas, M. (1998). *A journey into constructivism.* Retrieved from http://dougiamas.com/writing/constructivism.html

Dougiamas, M., & Taylor, P. C. (2003). *Moodle: Using learning communities to create an open source course management system.* Proceedings of the ED-MEDIA 2003 Conference, Honolulu, Hawaii.

Guerra, T., & Heffernan D. (2004). *The Guerra Scale: Learning circuits.* Retrieved from http://www.learningcircuits.org/2004/mar2004/guerra.htm

Ribot, E., & Erenchun, N. (2005). *Implantación de Moodle en la UPC: Proyecto institucional.* MoodleMoot Spain '05.

Ridden, J. (2006). What in the blazes is a Moot? *Moodle Newsletter, 2.* Retrieved from http://moodlezine.org

Endnotes

1 Which in most cases will be just an old interactive CD-ROM adapted for the Web.

2 I am sure the reader has identified that conductism has a strong influence in SCORM and learning objects

3 I would rather call him target or information consumer than student, because from my point of view, student implies an intellectually active role, not just to follow the breadcrumbs.

4 Quality in sense of technically and professional design, not necessarily under educational parameters

5 http://www.wikipedia.org

6 LAMP: Linux Apache MySQL and PHP. Moodle also runs under PotsgreSQL

7 http://www.apachefriends.org/en/xampp.html

8 From Moodle Statistics page http://moodle.org/stats (July 2006).

About the Authors

Miltiadis Lytras holds a PhD from the Department of Management Science and Technology of the Athens University of Economics and Business (AUEB), Greece. His first degree was in informatics (AUEB, Greece) while his further studies include an MBA from AUEB as well as a postgraduate diploma in adult learning (Selete Patras). His research focuses on e-learning, knowledge management and the Semantic Web, with more than 35 publications in these areas. He is guest co-editing a special issue of the *International Journal of Distance Education Technologies* with the special theme "Knowledge Management Technologies for E-Learning" as well as one in the *IEEE Educational Technology and Society Journal* with the theme "Ontologies and the Semantic Web for E-Learning" (with Gerd Wagner, Paloma Diaz, Demetrios Sampson, Lisa Neal). In Greece, he has published the book *Knowledge Management and E-Learning*, while he co-edits with Professor Ambjorn Naeve the book *Intelligent Learning Infrastructures for Knowledge Intensive Organizations: A Semantic Web Perspective*. In early 2005, he published the authored book *Knowledge Management Strategies: Applied Technologies Handbook* with Idea Group Inc. He is the founder of the Semantic Web and Information Systems Special Interest Group in Association for Information Systems and serves on the SIG Board (www.sigsemis.org). He has been a program committee member in eight international conferences and serves on the editorial board of two international journals. His teaching experience, especially in adults seminars, exceeds 3,500 hours in themes including e-business, information systems, knowledge management, e-learning, IT skills and management. He has participated in 15 Greek and European funded projects.

Ambjörn Naeve (www.nada.kth.se/~amb) has a background in mathematics and computer science and earned his PhD in computer science from KTH in 1993. He is presently the coordinator of research on interactive learning environments and the Semantic Web at the School of Computer Science and Communication (Nada) at the Royal Institute of Technology (KTH) in Stockholm, Sweden, where he heads the Knowledge Management Research group (KMR: http://kmr.nada.kth.se). He has been involved with research and development of interactive learning environments since he initiated the Garden of Knowledge project at Nada in 1996. He has also taught mathematics at KTH since 1967 and in the last two decades he has headed the development of several tools for ICT-enhanced mathematics education (http://kmr.nada.kth.se/math). Ambjörn Naeve is also a well-known industry consultant with extensive experience in various forms of modeling for software engineering and business applications. He has invented the concept browser Conzilla (www.conzilla.org) and has developed a modeling technique called Unified Language Modeling (http://kmr.nada.kth.se/cm), based on UML, which has been designed to "draw how we talk about things," (i.e., to depict conceptual relationships in a linguistically coherent way). Over the last decade the KMR group has developed an information architecture (the Knowledge Manifold), an infrastructure (Edutella), two frameworks (SCAM and SHAME) and a number of tools (Formulator, Meditor, VWE, Confolio and Conzilla). These items should be considered as contributions towards a publicly accessible Knowledge and Learning Management Environment, based on open source and open international ICT standards as well as on Semantic Web technology. The KMR group is active within several international networks for technology-enhanced learning and Semantic Web, notably WGLN, Prolearn, SIGSEMIS, and Sakai.

* * *

Marc Alier Forment received an engineering degree in computer science. He then worked in software development and e-learning industry. He has participated in the development of several LMS and authoring tools, and has been an online teacher. Since 2001, he has taught project management and computing ethics at the Universitat Politecnica de Catalunya (http://www.upc.edu), in computer science studies. He is director of a master's program in software for organization management, and a post-degree course on software development for PDAs and smart phones. He is the technical advisor and teacher in the Sciences of Education Institute, UPC (http://www.ice.upc.edu) in the implantation of Moodle. Since early 2004, he has been a member of http://moodle.org, where he developed the spell check integration and the modules *Internalmail* (http://appserv.lsi.upc.es/palangana/moodle/course/view.php?id=18), *DFWiki* (http://appserv.lsi.upc.es/palangana/moodle/course/view.php?id=15), and the future new Wiki module. He hopes to finish his PhD before 2007.

Christos Bouras obtained his diploma and PhD from the Computer Science and Engineering Department of Patras University (Greece). He is currently an associate professor in that department. Also, he is a scientific advisor of Research Unit 6 in Research Academic Computer Technology Institute (CTI), Patras, Greece. His research interests include analysis of performance of networking and computer systems, computer networks and protocols, telematics and new services, QoS and pricing for networks and services, e-learning, networked virtual environments, and WWW issues. He has extended professional experience in design and analysis of networks, protocols, telematics, and new services. He has published 200 papers in various well-known refereed conferences and journals. He is a co-author of seven books in Greek. He has been a PC member and referee in various international journals and conferences. He has participated in R&D projects such as RACE, ESPRIT, TELEMATICS, EDUCATIONAL MULTIMEDIA, ISPO, EMPLOYMENT, ADAPT, STRIDE, EUROFORM, IST, GROWTH, and others. Also, he is a member of experts in the Greek Research and Technology Network (GRNET), advisory committee member to the World Wide Web Consortium (W3C), IEEE Learning Technology Task Force, IEEE Technical Community for Services Computing WG 3.3 Research on Education Applications of Information Technologies and W 6.4 Internet Applications Engineering of IFIP, Task Force for Broadband Access in Greece, ACM, IEEE, EDEN, AACE, and New York Academy of Sciences.

Tom Butler is senior lecturer in business information systems at University College Cork, Ireland. Before joining academia, Butler had an extensive career in the telecommunications industry. While his previous research was primarily qualitative, interpretive, and case based in nature, being centred on IT capabilities and the development and implementation of information systems in organizations, since 2003 he has been focusing on action research on, and applied R&D in, knowledge management and IT-enabled knowledge management systems (KMS). He has published his research in international journals such as *Information Systems Journal, Journal of Strategic Information Systems,* and the *Journal of Information Technology,* and in the proceedings of major international conferences such as ICIS, ECIS, and IFIP 8.2 and 8.6.

Carlos Carvalho, (PhD in Physics, 1990). He is a Senior Lecturer of the Physics Department at the Federal University of Paraná, Brazil. His main research interest is in Free Software and in the design and administration of clusters for High Performance Scientific Computing. He currently leads one of the largest computing clusters in Brazil, located at the Federal University of Paraná.

Marcos A. Castilho, (PhD in Computer Science, 1998). He is a senior lecturer of the Informatics Department at the Federal University of Paraná, Brazil. His main research interests and publications are in free software as well as in artificial intelligence techniques for planning. He has served as program committee member and reviewer of many conferences. He is currently the head of the Informatics Department.

Ernesto Damiani is a professor with the Department of Information Technology of the University of Milan. He has held visiting positions at George Mason University, VA (USA), La Trobe University, Melbourne, Australia, and the University of Technology, Sydney, Australia. His research interests include knowledge extraction and processing, secure mobile architecures, software process engineering, and soft computing. On these topics, he has filed international patents, and published more than 80 refereed papers in international journals and conferences. He is the vice-chair of the IFIP WG on Web Semantics (WG 2.12), and a co-author of the book *Human-Centered E-Business* (Kluwer, 2003).

Luis Carlos Erpen de Bona, (PhD in Electrical Engineering and Industrial Informatics, 2006). He is a lecturer of the Informatics Department at the Federal University of Paraná, Brazil. His main research interests and publications are in free software and distributed systems. He has been a reviewer in many conferences and journals.

Neophytos Demetriou is a graduate of the University of Cyprus and works as a research scientist in the iCAMP project at the Institute of Information Systems and New Media at the University of Economics and Business Administration in Vienna. Demetriou has spent many years as an active contributor to the OpenACS project, and has developed the software for phigia.net, the first and largest Internet community in Cyprus.

Alexandre Direne (PhD in Computer Science, 1993) is a senior lecturer of the Informatics Department at the Federal University of Paraná, Brazil. He is a former chair of the Special Interest Group on Computers in Education of the Brazilian Computing Society. His main research interest lies in the application of artificial intelligence techniques to education. He has served as chairman, program committee member and reviewer of many conferences. He is on the editorial board of the *Brazilian Journal of Computers in Education*. He is currently the head of postgraduate studies in computer science.

Björn Decker earned his diploma in computer science from the University of Kaiserslautern in 1999. Since that time, he has worked as a scientist and project manager on different internal, public, and industrial projects in the domain of knowledge management, software product lines, and process modeling at the Fraunhofer Institute for Experimental Software Engineering. He has gathered further experience in Web services, Wikis (semantic Wikis, practical application), and agile requirements engineering. His PhD topic focuses on the collaborative maintenance and evolution of software engineering repositories. He organized the first workshop on intelligent office appliances at the Conference for Professional Knowledge Management (WM2005), and is PC member of different workshops.

Joseph Feller is a senior lecturer in business information systems at University College Cork, Ireland. His work on open source software includes co-authorship of two books (*Perspectives on Free and Open Source Software*, The MIT Press, 2005; *Understanding Open Source Software Development*, Addison-Wesley, 2002) as well as international conference and journal papers. Feller was the lead organiser of the IEE/ACM workshop series on open source software engineering (2001-2005), and has been a speaker/panelist on the topic at academic conferences, industry workshops, and European Commission briefings and roundtables. Feller is a member of the EU FP6 Co-ordination Action project CALIBRE, co-leading the dissemination and awareness work package and conducting research on open source software business models.

Pascal Francq earned his master's degree in applied science from the University of Brussels (ULB) in 1996. After a 2-year experience in a private company, he came back to the University of Brussels (ULB), where he earned his PhD in 2003. Since 2004, he has been a professor and currently holds the digital information chair. His main research topic is Internet as a media for knowledge sharing between people. He studies social aspects as well as technologies that may be useful in the sharing process. Since 1997, he has been working on automatic communities' detection, and is the main contributor of the open source platform, GALILEI. He is currently involved in research on social networks analysis, search technologies, genetic algorithms, and software design. His current researches try to create a mathematical framework for computing an authority rating for documents and an expert rating for social softwares' contributors.

Laura Sánchez García, (PhD in Computer Science, 1995). She is a Senior Lecturer of the Informatics Department at the Federal University of Paraná, Brazil. She has been working with computer-human interaction (CHI) since 1985. She has served as a consultant in many Science and Technology Ministry programmes, like the "National Research Network," the "Information Society" and the "Brazilian System of Digital Television," always in subjects directly related to her main research area. She is currently the head of undergraduate studies in computer science.

John Gøtze is an independent consultant and a nontenured associate professor at Copenhagen Business School and at the Danish IT University, where he lectures and supervises projects in enterprise architecture. As chief consultant in the Danish National IT and Telecom Agency from 2001 to 2005, Gøtze was developing the Danish national policy for a government-wide enterprise architecture. In the EU IDA programme, he has been involved with developing the European Interoperability Framework. He has co-authored several Danish and Swedish official policy documents. Gøtze is a member of the Open ePolicy Group and a co-author of its *Roadmap for Open ICT Ecosystems* (Harvard, 2005, http://www.openization.org). He holds an MSc in engineering and a PhD in participatory design, both from the Technical University of Denmark.

Andre Guedes (PhD, computer science, 2001) is a senior lecturer of the Informatics Department at the Federal University of Paraná, Brazil. His main research interest is free software and graph theory. He has served as program committee member and reviewer of many journals and conferences. He is a former head of undergraduate studies in computer science.

Andrea Hemetsberger is an assistant professor in the Department of Strategic Management, Marketing and Tourism, University of Innsbruck School of Management, Austria. After 3 years of pedagogical studies, she engaged in business administration studies and finished in 1989. After a few years of project work for the Austrian Chamber of Commerce, and the management of an entrepreneurs club, she decided to start an academic career. She finished her PhD in marketing in 1997. From 2000 to 2001, she was a Marie Curie research fellow at the Center of Economic Research at Tilburg University, The Netherlands. Her main areas of interest are consumer and user behaviour related, and revolve around branding and advertising research, e-loyalty, knowledge creation, customer integration in innovation processes, and consumer resistance. She has been researching the free and open source movement since 1999, and published several articles in that particular area. Her contributions range from insights into developer motivation and self-realization, social exchange processes within the community, knowledge creation processes, to socio-cultural investigations of the ideological foundations of the movement.

Kristoffer Herning holds a degree in political science from the University of Copenhagen and public administration from the University of Roskilde. He has worked in the Danish Ministry of Employment, the Danish Ministry of Culture, and for various public institutions before joining Unisys as a business consultant in 2004. Herning is active in the public debate on the public sector's use of IT, open source, and digitalisation, and has written several articles on "the digital service society." Besides interest in using it as a platform for a more service-oriented and cost-efficient society, Herning co-authored the report "Safety and Security in Denmark," analyzing some of the threats emerging from the intensified digitalization and reliance on critical IT-infrastructures.

Christian Höcht graduated in educational sciences, psychology, and sociology at the University of Bamberg, Germany, and is a scientist with the Department of Educational Sciences and Professional Development at the Technical University of Kaiserslautern, Germany. He leads a regional group of usability professionals within the German chapter of the Usability Professionals' Association. He is also an active member of the national technical committee, NI-Erg/UA5, within the German Institute for Standardization (DIN), and thus involved in the international standardization process related to ergonomics for interactive systems. In his research, he focuses on ways of professional support for software engineers that have to comply with user requirements. His aim is to establish methods and techniques to assist developers in that way.

Eirini Kalliamvakou is a research officer at the Athens University of Economics and Business in ELTRUN (the e-Business Center). She was also accepted as a PhD candidate in November 2004 in the Department of Management Science and Technology at the Athens University of Economics and Business (AUEB). Kalliamvakou holds a Bachelor in Economics from the University of Athens and an MSc in decision sciences (specialization in e-business) from the Athens University of Economics and Business. Her research interests concern the evolution of open source software development communities, the dynamic influence of social networks between developers, and the investigation of these networks' topology

Stefan Koch is an assistant professor of information business at the Vienna University of Economics and Business Administration. He received an MBA in management information systems from Vienna University and Vienna Technical University, and a PhD from Vienna University of Economics and Business Administration. Currently, he is involved in the undergraduate and graduate teaching program, especially in software project management and ERP packages. His research interests include cost estimation for software projects, the open source development model, software process improvement, the evaluation of benefits from information systems, and ERP systems.

Paul G. Mezey (PhD in Chemistry; DSc in Mathematics) is the Canada research chair in scientific modelling and simulation, Department of Chemistry and Department of Physics, Memorial University of Newfoundland, St. John's, Canada. Mezey is a member of the European Academy of Sciences, Arts, and Humanities, Paris, France and also of the Hungarian Academy of Sciences. Mezey is editor-in-chief of the *Journal of Mathematical Chemistry* and three book series. Mezey is involved with the external faculty of the Institute for Advanced Study, Collegium Budapest, Hungary, has served as vice president of the World Association of Theoretical Chemists (WATOC), as well as secretary general of CODATA, (UNESCO/ICSU) and foreign member of the Institute for Fundamental Chemistry, Kyoto, Japan. He is the author of 370 refereed publications and two books: *Potential Energy Hypersurfaces* (Elsevier, 1987) and *Shape in Chemistry: An Introduction to Molecular Shape and Topology* (VCH, 1993).

Ciaran Murphy is Bank of Ireland professor of BIS at UCC, head of the BIS Group, and director of the Executive Systems Research Centre. He has over 20 years of research and commercial experience, and has acted as a consultant to a wide variety of organizations in Ireland and internationally. Murphy was the organizing and programme committee chair of the 1997 European Conference on Information Systems. As co-author of *A Manager's Guide to Current Issues in Information Systems*, he has published widely, including articles in *Decision Support Systems*, the *Journal of Decision Systems*, the *Journal of Information Technology*, and in the proceedings of ICIS and ECIS conferences.

Maria Nani obtained her diploma and master's degree in computer science and technology from the Department of Computer Engineering and Informatics of Patras University. Currently, she is working as a computer engineer at Systema Technologies S.A. She has published research articles in well-referred conferences and journals on educational multimedia, advanced learning technologies, and VR learning environments. Her research interest is particularly concentrated in the following areas: telematics, multimedia, hypermedia, e-learning, and virtual reality.

Gustaf Neumann is chair of the Institute of Information Systems and New Media at the University of Economics and Business Administration (WU) in Vienna, Austria. Earlier career points were chair of the Department of Information Systems and Software Techniques at the University of Essen, Germany, and a visiting scientist at IBM's T. J. Watson Research Center in Yorktown Heights, NY. Professor Neumann has published books and papers in the areas of program transformation, data modeling, and information systems technology, with a focus on e-learning applications. He is actively developing open source software, and is a main author of the scripting language Extended Object Tcl (XOTcl). Professor Neumann is a member of the board of directors of the .LRN Consortium, and was recently elected into the OpenACS core Team (OCT), which is leading the technical development of OpenACS.

Andrew Pope (BSc) is a manager of the Business Information Systems Innovation Centre at University College Cork. Since joining the Centre, he has authored several white papers on innovative software solutions for business, and is currently completing an MSc in KM systems at UCC. Pope played a significant role in research and development on the portable knowledge asset development system (pKADS) for the UNFPA. He is currently a member of eGovernment Knowledge Platform (eGovKP) project team, which is developing a knowledge management system for the Irish government.

Paolo M. Pumilia graduated in physics in 1986 from the Milan State University, and had advanced courses on physics and computational techniques (NATO/ASI, NATO/MIDIT and CNRS) during his career as researcher. He has long-lasting professional experience in setting up and analysing results of large atomic systems numerical simulations matching experimental measurements of nuclear magnetic resonance signals, infrared absorption and raman spectroscopy, x-ray diffraction patterns.

Eric Ras earned his diploma in computer science from the University of Kaiserslautern in 2000. Since that time, he has worked as a scientist on different public and industrial projects in the domain of knowledge management, e-learning, and document engineering at the Fraunhofer Institute for Experimental Software Engineering. He has gathered experience in reuse-based learning material production, work-process oriented vocational training methods, and has worked intensively with current e-learning standards and tools. His PhD topic focuses on context-ware delivery of e-learning content to software engineers in order to enhance experience-based learning. He is organizing the workshop on Learning-oriented Knowledge Management and KM-oriented E-Learning 2005 (LOKMOL), and is PC member of different workshops and conferences.

Jörg Rech is a scientist and project manager of the Fraunhofer IESE. He earned a BS (Vordiplom) and an MS (Diplom) in computer science, with a minor in electrical science from the University of Kaiserslautern, Germany. He was a research assistant at the software engineering research group (AGSE) by Prof. Dieter Rombach at the University of Kaiserslautern. His research mainly concerns knowledge discovery in software repositories, defect discovery, code mining, code retrieval, software analysis, software visualization, software quality assurance, and knowledge management. He published a number of papers, mainly on software engineering and knowledge management, and is a member of the German Computer Society (Gesellschaft für Informatik, GI).

Christian Reinhardt is driven by the strong belief that information and communication technology is capable to beneficially support human social collectives that engage in collaborative value creation. Currently, he explores free and open-source software development projects as best-practice examples for collaborative work, learning and knowledge creation within online communities of practice. He initially started the research on the KDE project as part of his master's thesis to achieve a degree in business administration at the University of Innsbruck (Austria). After his graduation, he is continuing, revising, and extending this research as PhD project, and publishing the findings together with his guiding professor Andrea Hemetsberger, Department of Strategic Management, Marketing and Tourism, University of Innsbruck School of Management.

Karl Sarnow works for the European Science Education Portal Xplora as project manager. Xplora is directed towards teachers, helping them to attract more students into a scientific/technical career. Sarnow's main responsibilities are creating content, together with a group of teachers from all over Europe, and to make sure of the usability of the portal's resources for teachers in daily school life. Sarnow previously worked as a teacher of mathematics, physics, and computer science in Germany, he studied physics at the University of Hannover. He was the coordinator in Germany of the European school project ESP, and was involved in a number of projects to promote the teaching of science through the use of ICT.

Patrice-Emmanuel Schmitz (Master of Law and 20 years of practical IT experience as an enterprise lawyer, consultant, and certified information architect) is director at Unisys Belgium, where he manages studies delivered to the European Institutions. He engaged Unisys in evaluating the strategic opportunities of free/open source software, and was awarded in 2000 with the European Commission's "study into the use of Open Source Software in Public Sector." In 2002, Schmitz proposed innovative ways in his report "Pooling Open Source Software" (POSS), which was the most downloaded document ever produced in the framework of the IDA European programme. In 2004, his consultant team was awarded with the "Open Source Observatory" (http://www.europa.eu.int/idabc/oso).

Fabiano Silva, (PhD in Electrical Engineering and Industrial Informatics, 2005). He is a lecturer of the Informatics Department at the Federal University of Paraná, Brazil. His main research interests and publications are in free software and artificial intelligence techniques for planning. He has been a reviewer in many conferences and journals. Currently, he leads two major free software projects funded by Estate and Federal government funds.

Marcos S. Sunye (PhD in Computer Science, 1993) is a senior lecturer of the Informatics Department at the Federal University of Paraná, Brazil. His main research interests and publications are in free software as well as in database systems. He is a former head of the Informatics Department and is currently on sabbatical research cooperation, funded mainly by the Brazilian government, at the Université Pierre et Marie Curie (Paris VI), France.

Anna Maria Tammaro is teaching at the University of Parma for the undergraduate course on electronic publishing, and postgraduate course on digital library, the postgraduate and International Master in Library and Information Studies by distance, a joint master's with the University of Northumbria (UK), of which she is course Italian coordinator. Her actual research interests are quality assurance, e-learning and learning resources, and digital library. Before joining the University of Parma, she has had different duties: she was the director of Firenze University Press and the Unversity Librarian of the Florence University Libraries System (1995-2000), libraries coordinator of the Bologna University Center Interfaculties (1992-1994), and head of reader services at the European University Institute Library (1989-1990). She is author of numerous publications and reports in information science, automation of library systems, and internationalisation of higher education in LIS.

Christian Wernberg-Tougaard (Degree in Theoretical Macroeconomics), has been working both for government and private organisations—among them, the Danish Ministry of Science and CSC. For the last one and a half years, he has been working for Unisys Nordic, and he has been appointed as director for marketing and communication for Continental Europe's Global Public Sector practice and Marketing Executive for the EU account. He is widely used in IT-industry organisations, and is currently member of the Danish IT-security panel, which is appointed by the Danish Government. Wernberg-Tougaard has also been appointed by the Danish Board of Technology to act as a member of the impact groups on RFID technology as well as IT-security. Within EU, he is serving as vice chair of the ENISA (European Network and Information Security Agency) Working Group on "Awareness Raising." He was part of the government team creating the IT-University of Copenhagen.

Riina Vuorikari has worked in European Schoolnet (EUN) since March 2000 as a research analyst. She deals with a wide variety of issues ranging from e-learning interoperability and content exchange to the issues related with open standards. Currently, she holds a part-time position in EUN as a research analyst and editor for http://insight.eun.org. In her editorial role, and her role of a researcher, she has studied and reported on issues related to the use of open source and open standards in education. Since 2005, Vuorikari pursues her PhD in KULeuven in the area of Social Information Retrieval for learning resources.

Daniel Weingaerter (MSc, electrical engineering, 2003) is a PhD student in the Medical Informatics School at the Federal University of Paraná, Brazil. His research interests and publications are in free software and digital image processing. He is involved in many key free software projects at the Federal University of Paraná as a research assistant.

Index

B

C

D

J

K

L

M

N

O

R

S